Dictionary *of* Bible Knowledge

Mark D. Taylor

Dictionary of Bible Knowledge

Published by Rose Publishing
An imprint of Tyndale House Ministries
Carol Stream, Illinois
rose-publishing.com

ISBN: 979-8-4005-0266-8

Adapted from *The Complete Book of Bible Basics*, copyright 1992, 2005 by Mark D. Taylor (previously published as *The Complete Book of Bible Literacy* in 1992 and *The Complete Book of Bible Knowledge* in 1998)

The Library of Congress has cataloged the previous edition as follows:

Taylor, Mark D.
[Complete book of Bible literacy]
The complete book of Bible basics / Mark D. Taylor
p. cm. — (Complete book)
Originally published: The complete book of Bible literacy. Wheaton, Ill. : Tyndale, c1992.
Includes index.
ISBN-10: 1-4143-0169-3 (sc)
ISBN-13: 978-1-4143-0169-3 (sc)
1. Bible—Handbooks, manuals, etc. 2. Church history—Handbooks, manuals, etc. 3. Theology—Handbooks, manuals, etc. 4. Arts and religion—Handbooks, manuals, etc. I. Title. II. Complete book (Wheaton, Ill.)
BS417.T39 2005
220.6'1—dc22

2005002915

Printed in the United States of America
December 2024, 1st printing

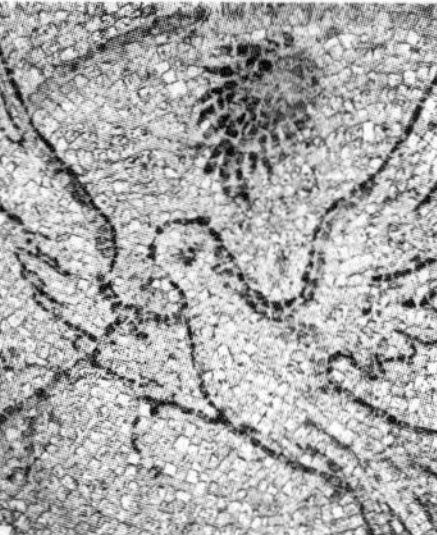

Contents

Introduction

The Bible has been a bestseller for centuries. In fact, according to Guinness World Records, it is the most printed book of all time, with an estimated five to seven billion copies produced since the invention of the printing press in the mid-1400s.

Yet, despite all those Bibles printed and distributed, many people never open a Bible! And whether due to intimidation, distraction, or a false sense of familiarity, many Christians know very little about the most important book of their faith. *Dictionary of Bible Knowledge* aims to help change that.

How to Use This Book

- Most definitions contain other key words or phrases that are also defined in the book. The index includes every key entry, and it is generously cross-referenced. For instance, *Babylonian Captivity* references the entry for *Exile*.

- Some entries include a note explaining how the term is used in today's culture. Each note is preceded by a pin icon (📌).

- Self-grading quizzes are included at the end of each chapter, and a comprehensive quiz in the appendix covers all subject areas. Answers appear immediately after each quiz.

- There are differing opinions among scholars about who wrote certain books; this book reflects the traditional views of authorship.

Enjoy browsing this resource to gain a solid knowledge of the Bible and the many important ways it has impacted history, culture, and Christian theology.

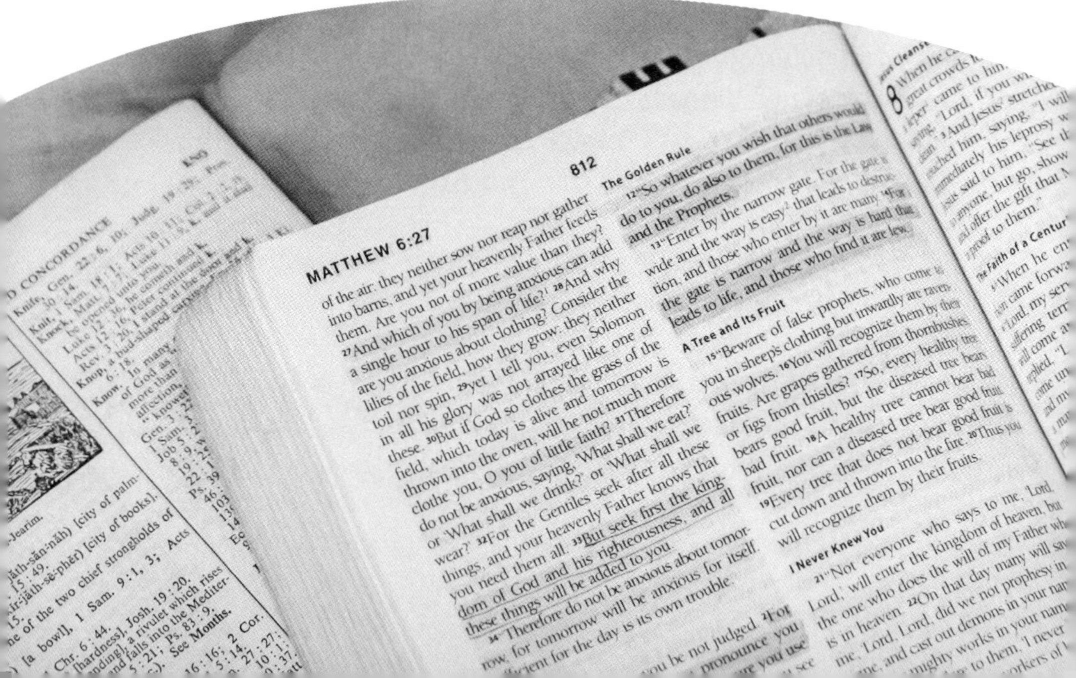

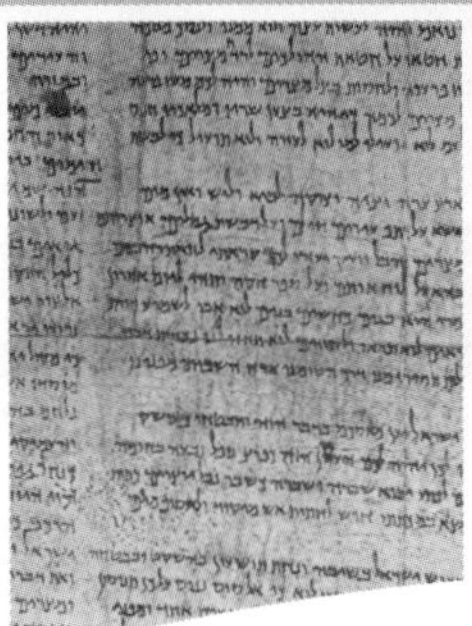

Bible Overview

While this entire book touches on biblical themes, this first chapter is about the Bible itself. It includes an entry for every book of the Bible, with a brief statement about the theme of the book. Each book is also identified as part of the Old Testament (OT) or the New Testament (NT).

This chapter also includes a list of the best-known English translations of the Bible, such as the King James Version, the New International Version, and the New Living Translation. Also included are descriptions of Bible study tools, such as Bible dictionaries and commentaries. You will also find terms that relate to how the Bible was first written and then handed down through the centuries.

ACTS, or **ACTS OF THE APOSTLES** (NT) The book of Acts follows the four Gospels (Matthew, Mark, Luke, and John) and tells of the founding and growth of the Christian church in the first century AD. It was written by Luke and continues where the narrative of the Gospel of Luke ends. In the second chapter, just ten days after Jesus's ascension into heaven, we see the coming of the Holy Spirit at Pentecost. The main character in the first twelve chapters is Peter, who became one of the leaders in the emerging church in Jerusalem. The remaining chapters then follow the apostle Paul on his various missionary journeys. The time period covered by the book of Acts is approximately AD 30–65.

The coming of the Holy Spirit is often represented by a dove.

AMOS (OT) One of the Minor Prophets, this book contains the messages of the prophet Amos. Amos was a shepherd who pronounced God's judgment upon the people of the Northern Kingdom of Israel shortly before Israel was taken into exile by the Assyrians in 722 BC.

APOCALYPSE Another name for the New Testament book of Revelation. The word *apocalypse* means "disclosure" or "revelation."

APOCRYPHA Seven books in the Old Testament (plus additions to the books of Esther and Daniel) that are included in Roman Catholic Bibles but not in the Jewish Bible and most Protestant Bibles. These books, often called "Apocrypha" by Protestants, are called "Deuterocanonical books" by Catholics. When the Old Testament canon was being consolidated several centuries before the birth of Christ, the apocryphal books were considered to be of lesser authority than the books that were accepted into the canon. For a list of books in the Apocrypha, see "Books of the Old Testament" after the entry *Old Testament*. Although the word *Apocrypha* comes from a Greek word meaning "hidden," the word *apocryphal* has generally come to mean spurious, or something that is probably not true.

ARAMAIC An ancient language closely related to Hebrew. Several portions of the Old Testament were originally written in Aramaic. The Jews of Jesus's day spoke Aramaic, so presumably Jesus's own teachings were originally spoken in Aramaic, then later recorded in Greek.

BIBLE The holy book of the Christian faith, containing the Old Testament and New Testament. It is often called the Holy Bible. Most Christians believe the Bible to be the inspired Word of God. The books of the Bible were written by dozens of writers over a period of about 1,500 years. For a complete list of the books of the Bible, see *Old Testament* and *New Testament*. The books that Christians call the Old Testament constitute the entirety of the Jewish Bible. The Old Testament tells of the creation, the fall of man, God's covenant with Abraham, and the history of Abraham's descendants, the Jews, until about 430 BC. It also contains the Mosaic law, Hebrew poetry (including the Psalms and Proverbs), and the messages of the prophets. The New Testament contains the four Gospels, which tell the stories of the life and ministry of Jesus, culminating in his suffering, crucifixion, and resurrection. Next comes the book of Acts, which tells of the early church in the first century, and then the Epistles, which are letters to the Christians of the first century. 📌 The Bible defines many concepts that are foundational to Western culture—concepts such as justice and mercy, fair play (see *Do to others what you would have them do to you* in the chapter "Famous Sayings from the Bible"), marriage, and family relationships. 📌 The Bible, particularly the King James Version, has had more impact on the literature of the English language than any other single source.

Amphitheater at ancient Ephesus, where a crowd rioted against Paul (Acts 19:23–41)

MOST POPULAR ENGLISH TRANSLATIONS OF THE BIBLE

CHRISTIAN STANDARD BIBLE (CSB) A translation sponsored by the Southern Baptist Convention, first published in 2016. Its predecessor was the Holman Christian Standard Bible, and its publishers refer to it as an "optimal equivalence" translation.

ENGLISH STANDARD VERSION (ESV) A revision of the Revised Standard Version, first published in 2001 and updated in 2016. Its publishers refer to it as an "essentially literal" translation.

KING JAMES VERSION (KJV) Until the 1980s, the King James Version was the most widely used English translation of the Bible. It was first published in 1611 under the authorization of King James I of England. In Britain it is called the Authorized Version (AV). Its stately language has had a great influence on spoken English and on English literature over four centuries. Many biblical phrases and quotations that are popularly known are from the King James Version or the New King James Version (see the chapter "Famous Sayings from the Bible"). See also *James I, King* in the chapter "Church History."

LIVING BIBLE, THE (TLB) A popular paraphrase by Kenneth N. Taylor that has been widely used since its initial publication in 1971. In the early 1970s it was the best-selling book in the United States.

MESSAGE, THE (MSG) A popular translation by Eugene Peterson that uses contemporary and sometimes edgy language to convey the meaning of the biblical text. It was first published in 1993 (NT) and 2002 (complete Bible).

NEW AMERICAN BIBLE (NAB) A translation sponsored by the Roman Catholic Church. Sometimes called the Confraternity Bible, it was first published in 1970 and updated in 2010. It is the translation now most widely used by Catholics.

NEW AMERICAN STANDARD BIBLE (NASB) A translation first published in 1971, it gained popularity among evangelical Christians as an accurate word-for-word style of translation. It was updated in 2020.

NEW INTERNATIONAL VERSION (NIV) A popular translation that has been widely accepted by evangelicals since its publication in 1978. It soon surpassed the King James Version as the most widely used English translation of the Bible. A revised edition was published in 2011. The New International Readers Version (NIRV) is a children's edition based on the NIV.

NEW KING JAMES VERSION (NKJV) A revision of the King James Version, first published in 1982. Many difficult and archaic words (for example, *thee* and *thou*) have been replaced with contemporary terms.

NEW LIVING TRANSLATION (NLT) A dynamic-equivalence, or thought-for-thought, translation first published in 1996 and updated in 2004 and 2015. It was created by a team of ninety scholars, and it combines the accuracy of the best translations with the readability of *The Living Bible*.

NEW REVISED STANDARD VERSION (NRSV) A revision of the Revised Standard Version, first published in 1989 and updated in 2021. It is widely used in academic circles.

REVISED STANDARD VERSION (RSV) A translation sponsored by the National Council of the Churches of Christ in the USA, first published in 1952.

BIBLE COMMENTARY A book that provides information and interpretation to help readers understand the biblical text. Some commentaries cover the entire text of the Bible in one volume. Other commentary series devote an entire volume to each of the books of the Bible.

BIBLE CONCORDANCE A listing of key words in the Bible, along with references to where they are found. Many Bibles include abridged (shortened) concordances at the back. Complete concordances list every occurrence of every word in the Bible, usually with a phrase to show the context for the word.

BIBLE DICTIONARY A dictionary that defines all the terms and names found in the Bible.

BIBLICAL CRITICISM The process of applying scientific methods in studying the text of the Bible. Biblical criticism is often divided into lower and higher criticism. Lower (or textual) criticism focuses exclusively on the text itself. Its objective is to determine as nearly as possible the exact wording of the original text. Higher criticism addresses issues such as date of writing, authorship, and the oral traditions assumed to lie behind the written text. Higher critics have often been accused of starting with presuppositions that deny the supernatural or that assume that prophetic passages could not have been written before the occurrence of the events they foretell. Many higher critics doubt the historical accuracy of many parts of the Bible. Other scholars, who prefer to take the text at face value, feel that higher criticism is not a valid way of approaching the text.

BOOKS OF MOSES The first five books of the Old Testament are called the Books of Moses, reflecting the traditional view that they were written by Moses (see *Genesis*; *Exodus*; *Leviticus*; *Numbers*; *Deuteronomy*). They are also called the Pentateuch (Greek for "five books") and Torah. The Books of Moses contain the stories of the creation, the fall of man, God's covenant with Abraham, the Exodus of the Israelites from Egypt, the Ten Commandments and the rest of the Mosaic law, and the experiences of the Israelites as they wandered in the wilderness for forty years.

BOOKS OF THE BIBLE The word *Bible* comes from the Greek word for "book." The Bible is made up of sixty-six individual books (seventy-three books when the Apocrypha is included). Each book is divided into chapters and verses. Titles of books that start with a number (for example, 1 Samuel, 2 Samuel) are usually pronounced *First Samuel* (rather than *One Samuel*) and *Second Samuel* (rather than *Two Samuel*). The longest book in the Bible is Psalms, with 150 chapters. Five books have only one chapter. The books of the Bible were written by many different authors over a long period—possibly as long as 1,500 years (1400 BC–AD 95). For a complete list of the books of the Bible, see *Old Testament* and *New Testament*.

CANON The official list of books that are included in the Old and New Testaments. Since the books of the Old Testament were written over a period of 800 or more years, the development of the Old Testament canon was a gradual process. The earliest Old Testament writings were accepted as having unique significance early in the history of the nation of Israel. For instance, the Lord was speaking of the Mosaic law when he said to Joshua, "Keep this Book of the Law always on your lips; meditate on it day and night, so that you may be careful to do everything written in it. Then you will be prosperous and successful" (Joshua 1:8 NIV). According to tradition, Ezra played a role in compiling the canon of Jewish Scripture in the fifth century BC. The Jewish canon contains the same books that comprise the Old Testament for Protestants. The New Testament canon was recognized by the church fathers as early as AD 200 and was largely undisputed by the fourth century AD. It is accepted by all Christian churches (see *New Testament canon established* in the chapter "Church History").

CANTICLES See *Song of Solomon*.

CHAPTER AND VERSE Each book of the Bible is divided into chapters, and each chapter is divided into verses. Passages in the Bible are identified by their chapter and verse. The longest and shortest chapters are both in the Psalms. Psalm 119 has 176 verses; Psalm 117 has only two verses. The original manuscripts were not divided into chapters and verses. In fact, the New Testament was first divided into verses in the sixteenth century. (For a comment about other features that have been added to the

Bible text, see *red-letter editions*.) ✎ More broadly, to quote "chapter and verse" is to give the specific source of any quotation.

1 CHRONICLES (OT) The books of 1 & 2 Chronicles tell the story of the history of Israel during the period from King David to the fall of the Kingdom of Judah. They emphasize the role of the priests and the establishment of the pattern of worship in the temple. The book of 1 Chronicles begins with a genealogy of Israel and then tells the story of the reign of King David. It covers much of the same time period that is covered in the book of 2 Samuel.

2 CHRONICLES (OT) The book of 2 Chronicles begins where 1 Chronicles ends. It covers the period from the reign of King Solomon to the fall of Judah and the Exile to Babylon. It covers much of the same period that is covered in the books of 1 & 2 Kings.

COLOSSIANS (NT) The apostle Paul's letter to the church in Colosse (an ancient city in present-day Turkey; see map near *2 Corinthians*). This letter was written about AD 60, while Paul was in prison in Rome. (The letters to the Ephesians and the Philippians may also have been written about the same time.) The purpose of this letter was to combat theological errors that had crept into the Colossian church. The primary theme is that the fullness of divinity and of the divine purpose is embodied in Christ, and that Christ is the head of the church. The letter then draws numerous conclusions as to how Christians should live.

COMMENTARY See *Bible commentary*.

CONCORDANCE See *Bible concordance*.

1 CORINTHIANS (NT) One of the apostle Paul's letters to the church in Corinth (in present-day Greece; see map near the entry for *2 Corinthians*). This letter was written about AD 55, while Paul was on his third missionary journey. The primary purpose of the letter was to offer solutions to problems in the Corinthian church. The thirteenth chapter is often called "the love chapter." It begins, "If I could speak all the languages of earth and of angels, but didn't love others, I would only be a noisy gong or a clanging cymbal" (verse 1 NLT).

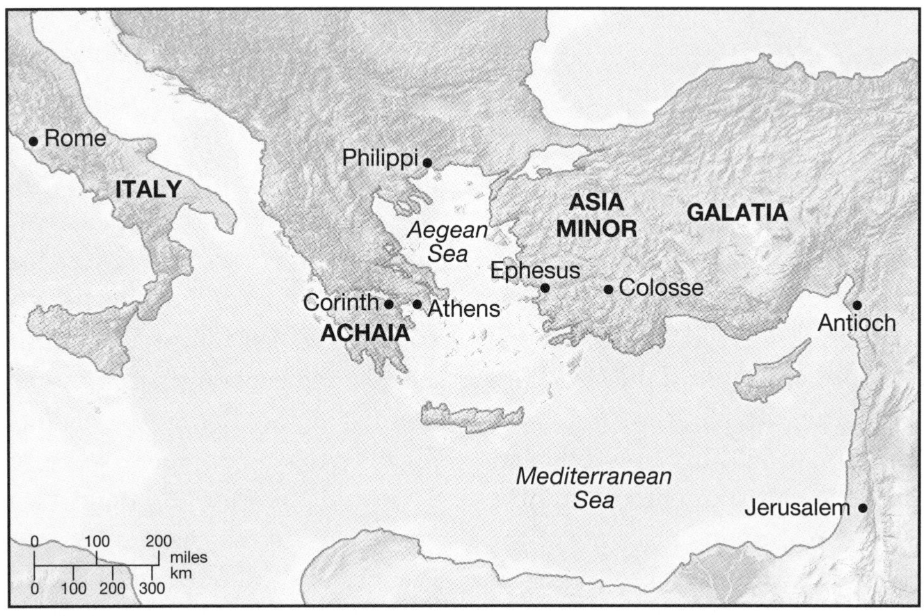

Churches Established Paul founded the churches in Corinth and Ephesus during his missionary journeys. The books we call 1 & 2 Corinthians and Ephesians are letters to those churches. The book of Colossians is a letter to the church in Colosse, a group Paul had never visited.

2 CORINTHIANS (NT) Another of Paul's letters to the church in Corinth (in Greece). This letter was written about AD 55–57, while Paul was on his third missionary journey. The primary purpose of the letter was to affirm Paul's own authority as an apostle so he could continue refuting the false teachers in Corinth. This is an intensely personal letter.

CROSS-REFERENCES Notations in the margin or center column of a Bible to indicate other verses where a similar subject is found.

DANIEL (OT) Daniel and his friends Shadrach, Meshach, and Abednego were among the group of Israelites who were exiled to Babylon in 605 BC, nineteen years before the fall of Jerusalem. The first half of the book of Daniel contains familiar stories about Daniel—interpreting Nebuchadnezzar's dream about the statue with the feet of clay, the fiery furnace, the handwriting on the wall, and Daniel in the lions' den. We also see the Babylonians defeated by King Darius, which marks the start of the Persian Empire. The second half of the book contains prophetic visions about the future.

DEAD SEA SCROLLS A collection of scrolls, manuscripts, and manuscript fragments dating from the third century BC to the first century AD. Most of them were found in 1947–1952 in caves along the northern shore of the Dead Sea. They include Hebrew, Aramaic, and Greek manuscripts of parts of the Old Testament and are the oldest existing manuscripts of the Bible. The Dead Sea Scrolls include an entire text of the book of Isaiah. Most of the scrolls are made of leather (some are papyrus) and are believed to have been part of the library of a religious community of Essenes (an ascetic and communal sect within Judaism) at Qumran. They were stored (or perhaps hidden) in pottery jars, where they remained hidden for 2,000 years.

DEUTERONOMY (OT) The fifth and last of the Books of Moses. After wandering in the wilderness for forty years, the generation of Israelites that left Egypt in the Exodus had died, and their children were ready to enter the Promised Land. Deuteronomy contains Moses's messages to this new, young generation, reminding them of all that the Lord had done for his chosen people. Moses also reviewed the Law for them (see *Mosaic law* in the chapter "People, Places, and Events in the Old Testament") and challenged them to commit themselves to the Lord.

ECCLESIASTES (OT) This book shows the futility of life apart from God. The author, traditionally said to be Solomon, tells of his own search for meaning through wisdom, pleasure, work, success, and wealth. He says at various points

Cave of the Dead Sea Scrolls at Qumran

along the way that everything is meaningless, "a chasing after the wind" (1:14 NIV). In the end he concludes, "Fear God, and keep his commandments: for this is the whole duty of man" (12:13 KJV) (see *What is the chief end of man?* in the chapter "Church History"). The book of Ecclesiastes (the name comes from the Greek word for "preacher") is the source of such well-known phrases as "Vanity of vanities; all is vanity"; "There is nothing new under the sun"; "Eat, drink, and be merry"; and "To everything there is a season."

EPHESIANS (NT) Paul's letter to the church in Ephesus (see map near *2 Corinthians*). Like Philippians and Colossians, the letter to the Ephesians was written about AD 60 while Paul was in prison in Rome. Its primary purpose was to strengthen and encourage the Ephesian Christians, whom Paul knew very well. This letter contains such well-known phrases as "Children, obey your parents" and "Put on the whole armor of God."

EPISTLES An epistle is a letter, and the New Testament Epistles are letters written by the apostles Paul, Peter, and John, as well as James and Jude, brothers of Jesus. This section of the Bible outlines various aspects of Christian doctrine and contains practical instructions for Christian living. See also the list "Books of the New Testament" at the entry for *New Testament*.

ESTHER (OT) This book tells the story of Esther, a beautiful young Jewish woman who had been selected to become a member of the harem of King Ahasuerus (Xerxes) of Persia. He later made her the queen. When Esther's cousin and foster father, Mordecai, heard that the prime minister, Haman, had launched a plan to kill all the Jews in the kingdom, he urged Esther to ask the king to revoke the plan. Although she was the queen, she was not permitted, on pain of death, to approach the king without being summoned by him. So Esther devised a plan to gain the attention and favor of the king. She succeeded, and the plan to exterminate the Jews was reversed. The story of Esther takes place about 474 BC, sixty years after the first group of Jews had returned to Jerusalem from the Exile in Babylon and Persia. Esther was part of the Jewish community that had stayed in Persia. The Jewish holiday of Purim commemorates this rescue of the Jews.

EXODUS (OT) The second of the Books of Moses. It contains the account of Moses, the first Passover, and the Exodus from Egypt. God had promised to rescue the Israelites from their enslavement in Egypt, so the Lord sent Moses to tell Pharaoh (the king), "Let my people go" (Exodus 5:1 NLT). When Pharaoh refused, the Lord sent ten plagues to convince him to heed the word of the Lord. The last plague was the death of the firstborn son and the firstborn of the livestock in every Egyptian home and barn. The Lord instructed the Israelites to put blood on their doorposts; he would then pass over their houses as he killed the sons of Egypt. After this dramatic and painful display of God's power, Pharaoh allowed the Israelites to leave Egypt, and God miraculously spared their lives in the parting of the Red Sea. Yet even after God's miraculous provision, the Israelites did not trust God to lead them safely into the land he had promised them. In his anger, God told Moses the people would have to wander in the wilderness for forty years. The remainder of the book tells of God's covenant with the people in giving them the Law, including the Ten Commandments. There are also long sections detailing the manner in which the tabernacle was to be constructed. See also *Moses; Moses in the bulrushes*; *burning bush; plagues of Egypt*; and *Mosaic law* in the chapter "People, Places, and Events in the Old Testament."

EZEKIEL (OT) One of the Major Prophets, this book contains the messages of the prophet Ezekiel. Along with thousands of other Jews, he was captured by the Babylonians in 597 BC, eleven years before the fall of Jerusalem. His prophetic ministry took place in Babylon among his fellow captives, telling them that the Exile was because of their sins. The prophecies at the end of the book are from the period after the fall of Jerusalem, when Ezekiel gives a message of hope to his people.

EZRA (OT) Like Nehemiah and Esther, this is one of the historical books from the period during and after the Exile in Babylon and Persia. King Cyrus of Persia conquered Babylon in 539 BC and issued a decree that permitted the captive Jews to return to their homeland. In 538 BC, the first group of about 42,000 Jews returned under Zerubbabel and began rebuilding the temple. Eighty years later, in 458 BC, Ezra, a priest and prophet, traveled to Jerusalem with another group of about 1,800 Jews. When Ezra arrived, he found the Jews in Jerusalem living in a state of religious indifference because of their intermarriage with the heathen nations around them. Though the prophets Zechariah and Haggai had urged the people to repent, it was not until Ezra's arrival that the people returned to God. The third and final contingent of Jews to return from Babylonia was led by Nehemiah in 445 BC. Their story is recounted in the book bearing his name. See also *canon*.

GALATIANS (NT) Paul's letter to the churches in Galatia (an ancient region in present-day Turkey). The primary purpose of the letter (which may have been written about AD 49) was to refute the arguments of those who said gentile Christians (see *gentile* in the chapter "People, Places, and Events in the Old Testament") had to obey the Mosaic law in order to be saved. This issue was officially resolved in about AD 50 at the Council at Jerusalem. The letter to the Galatians stresses the Christian's freedom in Christ.

GENESIS (OT) The first book in the Bible and the first of the Books of Moses. The word *genesis* means beginning, or origin—a fitting title for a book that tells of the origin of all creation. It contains the accounts of the creation, Noah and the ark, the Tower of Babel, and the patriarchs of Israel—Abraham, Isaac, Jacob, and Joseph and his brothers. The book begins with the creation ("In the beginning God created the heavens and the earth," Genesis 1:1) and ends with the death of Joseph in Egypt. Genesis is interesting to read since it contains so many familiar Bible stories.

GOSPELS The first four books of the New Testament: Matthew, Mark, Luke, and John. Each of the Gospels (the word *gospel* means "good news"; see *gospel* in the chapter "Church Life and Theology") tells the story of the life, death, and resurrection of Jesus. There is much overlap of content between the four accounts, but each Gospel also has unique material not found in any of the others.

GREEK The language of ancient Greece, in which the books of the New Testament were first written. The New Testament was not written in classical Greek, but in *Koiné* Greek, the form of the language that was spread throughout the Near

East by the conquests of Alexander the Great. It was the language of the marketplace at the time of the early church. Since Greek was spoken as a trade language throughout much of the Roman Empire, Christianity was able to spread without a language barrier.

2 Corinthians 11:33–12:9, from Papyrus 46

HABAKKUK (OT) One of the Minor Prophets, this book contains the messages of the prophet Habakkuk to the people of the Kingdom of Judah. Like Jeremiah, Habakkuk prophesied during the final years before the fall of Jerusalem to the Babylonians.

HAGGAI (OT) One of the Minor Prophets from the period after the Exile. This book contains the messages of the prophet Haggai to the Israelites who had returned to Jerusalem. It is a challenge to finish rebuilding the temple, which had been started twenty years earlier by Zerubbabel but never completed. The messages of Haggai fall between the two events recorded in the book of Ezra—the return of Zerubbabel and the return of Ezra. See also *Zechariah*; *Nehemiah*.

HEBREW The language of the ancient Israelites. Most of the Old Testament was written in Hebrew. Modern Hebrew, used in the modern state of Israel, is based on ancient Hebrew, but thousands of words have been added to the vocabulary to allow for communication in our present complex world. Hebrew is written and read from right to left.

HEBREWS (NT) A New Testament epistle that was written to Jewish Christians during the first century AD. The author is not identified. The primary theme of the letter is the superiority of Christ, including his superiority over the prophet Moses and the Old Testament priesthood. Many quotations from the Old Testament are woven throughout the book of Hebrews.

Scroll of the book of Esther in Hebrew

HOLY BIBLE See *Bible.*

HOSEA (OT) One of the Minor Prophets, this book contains the messages of the prophet Hosea to the people of the Kingdom of Israel shortly before that nation fell to the Assyrians in 722 BC. At God's command, Hosea married a woman named Gomer, a prostitute. She and her children served as object lessons as Hosea preached about Israel's faithlessness and God's willingness to forgive them.

ISAIAH (OT) The book that contains the messages of the prophet Isaiah. It is one of the Major Prophets. Isaiah's ministry was to the people of the Kingdom of Judah at the time the Kingdom of Israel fell to the Assyrians (722 BC). The book of Isaiah contains many prophecies regarding the coming of the Messiah, some of which were set to music in Handel's *Messiah.* A familiar passage is this prophecy concerning the future Messiah: "Behold, a virgin shall conceive, and bear a son, and shall call his name Immanuel" (Isaiah 7:14 KJV).

JAMES (NT) This epistle was written by James (brother of Jesus) to Jewish Christians living outside Judea. (For a comment about varying interpretations of who "Jesus's brothers" were, see *James (brother of Jesus)* in the chapter "People, Places, and Events in the New Testament.") James is a practical letter that shows the importance of living out one's faith in day-to-day life. 📌 Since the book of James emphasizes the importance of works in proving one's salvation, the Reformer Martin Luther did not believe it should be part of the canon.

JEREMIAH (OT) This book, one of the Major Prophets, contains the messages of the prophet Jeremiah. His ministry was to the Kingdom of Judah in the years just before it was conquered by Babylon. He urged the people to repent of their sins and turn back to God.

JOB (OT) The story of Job (pronounced *Jōb*), the man who bore great suffering with great patience, is not placed at any particular time or place in history. The author of this book is unknown, but the purpose is to answer the perennial question, Why do good people suffer? See *Job* in the chapter "People, Places, and Events in the Old Testament" for more details about Job and his trials.

JOEL (OT) One of the Minor Prophets, containing the messages of the prophet Joel to the Kingdom of Judah. The people had become prosperous and had turned away from God. Joel called them to repentance and predicted that a great plague of locusts would destroy their crops.

JOHN, GOSPEL OF (NT) This Gospel was written by John, the disciple of Jesus. It opens with the familiar verse, "In the beginning was the Word, and the Word was with God, and the Word was God" (John 1:1). John tells the stories of the life and ministry of Jesus, but he includes more of Jesus's discourses than are found in the other Gospels. One of the most familiar verses in the Bible is John 3:16: "For God so loved the world, that he gave his only begotten Son, that whosoever believeth in him should not perish, but have everlasting life" (KJV).

1 JOHN, EPISTLE OF (NT) There are three epistles in the New Testament written by John the Elder. There are various scholarly views as to the identity of John the Elder, but the traditional view is that John the disciple of Jesus wrote these epistles late in his life. The first epistle of John was written to all the gentile churches. Its primary purpose was to reassure the believers about their faith. John was perhaps the last survivor of Jesus's twelve disciples by this time, so he wrote to the younger generations of believers as an eyewitness of Jesus's ministry.

2 JOHN, EPISTLE OF (NT) This is the second of three epistles written by the apostle John late in his life. It is the shortest book in the Bible (just one chapter, comprising thirteen verses). The letter is written to "the elect lady and her children" (verse 1), which may be a reference to a specific person or to a church that is not otherwise identified. John warns the recipient to guard against the false teachers who were prevalent in the early church.

3 JOHN, EPISTLE OF (NT) This is the third of the three epistles of John. It is a personal letter to a man named Gaius, encouraging and affirming him in his practice of hospitality, especially to visiting teachers and missionaries.

JONAH (OT) This book, one of the Minor Prophets, contains the familiar story of Jonah and the great fish. Jonah tried to run away when God sent him to preach to Nineveh, the capital of Assyria and a hot spot of wickedness. He was swallowed by a great fish and stayed in its belly for three days and three nights. After Jonah finally obeyed God and preached in Nineveh, the people of Nineveh repented and turned to God. God chose not to destroy the city when the people repented, but this made Jonah angry. He had been preaching that the city would be destroyed because of the people's sinfulness, and he may have resented God's compassion for the Assyrians. Jesus referred to Jonah's experience in the belly of the fish as a picture of his own death and subsequent resurrection (Matthew 12:40).

JOSHUA (OT) The book of Joshua begins where Deuteronomy leaves off. Moses has died, and the people of Israel are just about to enter the Promised Land after wandering in the wilderness for forty years. The book of Joshua tells of the Israelites' conquest of the land of Canaan under the leadership of Joshua, who had been Moses's assistant. The Lord shows his care for the people by holding back the waters of the Jordan River so the entire nation can cross on dry ground. Then comes the story of Rahab and the Battle of Jericho, when the walls of the city come tumbling down. After the land is conquered, the tribes of Israel receive their allotted territories.

JUDE (NT) This short epistle was written by Jude, one of Jesus's brothers who became a leader in the early church. (For a comment about varying interpretations of who "Jesus's brothers" were, see *James (brother of Jesus)* in the chapter "People, Places, and Events in the New Testament.") Jude's letter was written to all the churches, and it reminds believers to stay away from false teachings.

JUDGES (OT) After the Exodus, the Israelites returned to the

Promised Land and conquered the land under Joshua's leadership. Then came a period of 200 or more years (some scholars believe it was as long as 325 years) during which Israel had no king. Instead, the people were led by "judges." The book of Judges tells the history of this period and includes the stories of Deborah, Gideon, and Samson, among others. See also *judges, period of the* in the chapter "People, Places, and Events in the Old Testament."

1 KINGS (OT) This book contains the history of the reign of Solomon and the first eighty years of the Divided Kingdom (Judah and Israel). It includes stories of the great prophet Elijah, including his contest with the prophets of Baal, when Elijah called down fire from heaven. The books of 1 and 2 Kings were originally one book. The book of 2 Chronicles covers the same time period from a different perspective.

2 KINGS (OT) This book begins where 1 Kings ends. It contains the rest of the history of the Kingdoms of Judah and Israel, until the fall of Israel to the Assyrians in 722 BC and the fall of Judah to the Babylonians in 586 BC. It includes stories about the prophet Elisha. The books of 1 and 2 Kings were originally one book, and the book of 2 Chronicles covers the same time period from a different perspective.

KOINÉ The New Testament was written in *Koiné* Greek, the language spoken throughout most of the Roman Empire at the time of the early church. Since *Koiné* (Greek for "common") was the common language of nearly the entire Mediterranean world, the gospel (the message of salvation through Christ) was able to travel quickly without language barriers.

LAMENTATIONS (OT) This book was written by the prophet Jeremiah (known as "the weeping prophet") after Jerusalem fell to the Babylonians. It is a funeral dirge for the fallen city and its people.

LAW, BOOKS OF The first five books of the Old Testament are called the Books of Moses, the Books of Law, the Torah, or the Pentateuch. In addition to the early history of the Hebrew people, they contain the Ten Commandments and the rest of the Mosaic law.

LEVITICUS (OT) This book contains a substantial portion of the Mosaic law—detailed instructions for the Israelite priests as well as specific regulations for the people of Israel. Leviticus is the third of the five Books of Moses.

LUKE, GOSPEL OF (NT) This Gospel was written by Luke, a gentile physician who was a companion of the apostle Paul's. Like the other Gospels, it contains an account of the life and ministry of Jesus, culminating in his suffering, crucifixion, and resurrection. The most familiar account of the birth of Jesus is taken from the second chapter of Luke's Gospel (see *Nativity* in the chapter "People, Places, and Events in the New Testament").

MACCABEES The books of 1 and 2 Maccabees are included in the Apocrypha. They tell of the history of Israel during the second century BC, which is in the 400-year period between the Old Testament and the New Testament. One of the Jewish leaders of that period was Judas Maccabaeus, who led a revolt against the tyranny of Antiochus, the Syrian king. 📌 Hanukkah is the Jewish holiday that commemorates the cleansing of the temple during the days of the Maccabees.

MAJOR PROPHETS The Old Testament books of Isaiah, Jeremiah, Lamentations, Ezekiel, and Daniel. They are called the Major Prophets because of their length. See also *Minor Prophets*; *Prophecy, Books of*.

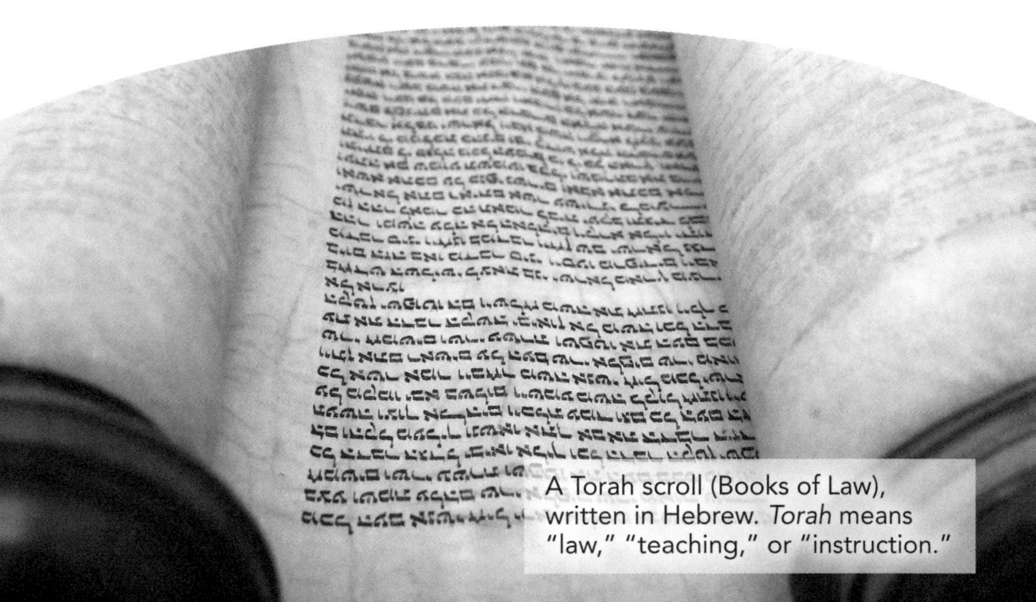

A Torah scroll (Books of Law), written in Hebrew. *Torah* means "law," "teaching," or "instruction."

MALACHI (OT) The last book in the Old Testament, it contains the messages of the prophet Malachi. After the Exile, many Jews returned to Jerusalem. The temple had now been rebuilt (see *Ezra*), and the wall of the city had been rebuilt (see *Nehemiah*), but the people again neglected the Lord. Malachi called them to repentance and held out the promise of God's forgiveness and grace.

A portion of the Dead Sea Scrolls

MANUSCRIPTS, BIBLICAL The word *manuscript* literally means "written by hand." Originally, each of the books of the Bible was written by hand, and for many centuries all copies were also written by hand. There are no original manuscripts of the Bible still in existence, but thousands of handwritten Hebrew and Greek manuscript copies or fragments of copies have been found (for example, the Dead Sea Scrolls). For the most part, the oldest manuscripts are deemed to be closest to the exact wording of the original manuscripts. There are minor variations in wording among the various manuscripts—due primarily to scribal errors when the manuscripts were being copied—but overall the manuscripts show an amazing degree of accuracy and faithfulness.

MARK, GOSPEL OF (NT) This is the shortest of the Gospels, and the action is fast. Like the other Gospels, it contains an account of the life and ministry of Jesus, culminating in his suffering, crucifixion, and resurrection. It was written by Mark; he was not one of the twelve disciples, but he was an eyewitness of Jesus's ministry. Mark's Gospel was written for a gentile audience. Many scholars believe it was the first of the Gospels to be written.

MATTHEW, GOSPEL OF (NT) This Gospel was written by Matthew, one of Jesus's disciples. It was written primarily for a Jewish audience, so it emphasizes the ways in which Jesus fulfilled Old Testament prophecies. It begins with a genealogy that shows that Jesus was a descendant of Abraham and of King David.

MICAH (OT) One of the Minor Prophets, this book contains the messages of the prophet Micah to the people of both Israel and Judah. He describes God's hatred of the sins of his chosen people. The Northern Kingdom fell to the Assyrians during Micah's ministry. This book includes the prophecy that the insignificant village of Bethlehem would be the birthplace of a future king. Hundreds of years later, this prophecy led the wise men to Bethlehem.

MINOR PROPHETS The twelve short books of prophecy found at the end of the Old Testament. They are called Minor Prophets because they are short books. The prophets whose messages are recorded in these books lived and prophesied over a period of about 400 years. Some preached in the Northern Kingdom of Israel, and some preached in the Southern Kingdom of Judah. See also *Major Prophets*; *Prophecy, Books of*.

MOSES, BOOKS OF See *Books of Moses*.

NAHUM (OT) One of the Minor Prophets, this book contains the messages of the prophet Nahum. His ministry was to the people of the Southern Kingdom of Judah, but this book contains a pronouncement of God's judgment on Nineveh, the capital city of Assyria, the world power that had already defeated the Northern Kingdom of Israel. (Jonah had preached to the people of Nineveh more than 120 years earlier.) Assyria was indeed defeated—by the Babylonians—before many years passed.

NEHEMIAH (OT) The events in this historical book took place long after the Jews had begun returning to Jerusalem from the Exile in Babylon (see *Ezra*). Nehemiah was a cupbearer to King Artaxerxes of Persia, but he went to Jerusalem in 445 BC to lead the people there in rebuilding their city wall. After the wall had been built, Nehemiah and Ezra led the people into a renewed relationship with God.

NEW TESTAMENT The portion of the Christian Bible that contains the record of the life and ministry of Jesus, the spread of the gospel, and the establishment of the church. The Greek word that is translated "testament" is also commonly translated "covenant," so the New Testament tells of the new covenant between God and humankind, made possible by the life, death, and resurrection of Jesus Christ. The New Testament contains twenty-seven books—four Gospels, the Acts of the Apostles, twenty-one letters (or epistles), and Revelation. The books were written over a period of about fifty years, from AD 40–90, by nine or ten different authors. Although none of the original manuscripts has survived, thousands of subsequent manuscripts and fragments have been found, one dating from about 125. The New Testament canon in its present form was largely in place by about 200, but the first list of the books we now know as the New Testament is found in a letter written by the early church leader Athanasius in 367. Thirty years later the same canon was listed by a church council, at which time it seemed to be undisputed (see *New Testament canon established* in the chapter "Church History").

BOOKS OF THE NEW TESTAMENT

4 Gospels

1. Matthew
2. Mark
3. Luke
4. John

Acts, *or* Acts of the Apostles

21 Epistles

1. Romans
2. 1 Corinthians
3. 2 Corinthians
4. Galatians
5. Ephesians
6. Philippians
7. Colossians
8. 1 Thessalonians
9. 2 Thessalonians
10. 1 Timothy
11. 2 Timothy
12. Titus
13. Philemon
14. Hebrews
15. James
16. 1 Peter
17. 2 Peter
18. 1 John
19. 2 John
20. 3 John
21. Jude

Revelation, *or* the Apocalypse

NUMBERS (OT) The fourth of the five Books of Moses. It contains the stories of the people of Israel during their forty years in the wilderness—after the Exodus and before they entered the Promised Land of Canaan. The first portion contains data about a census of the nation (hence the name of the book). On their first approach to the land of Canaan, the people had grown rebellious when they heard the reports of the spies whom Moses had sent into the land (Joshua and Caleb were the only spies who came back expressing confidence that God would help them defeat the Canaanites). As a result, the Lord had told Moses that the people would not enter the Promised Land until that entire generation of adults (except for Joshua and Caleb) had died in the wilderness.

OBADIAH (OT) One of the Minor Prophets, this is the shortest book in the Old Testament (just one chapter, with twenty-one verses). It contains a prophetic vision of the destruction of Edom, a country southeast of Israel. The Edomites were descendants of Abraham and Isaac through Isaac's son Esau.

OLD TESTAMENT The Greek word that is translated "testament" is also translated "covenant." The Old Testament contains the same books that are in the Jewish (Hebrew) Scriptures, although they are arranged in a different order. These books are a record of God's covenants with the Israelites—his chosen people—and the history of the Israelite people. The Old Testament contains thirty-nine books—five Books of Moses (the Pentateuch, or Torah), twelve books of history, five poetic books, and seventeen Books of Prophecy (see the list on the following page). The various books were written over a period of hundreds of years by numerous authors. All of them were written before the birth of Jesus. Although none of the original manuscripts has survived, hundreds of Old Testament manuscripts and fragments have been found, some dating from slightly earlier than 200 BC (see *Dead Sea Scrolls*). For Jesus and his Jewish contemporaries, as well as for the early church, what is now called the Old Testament was the entire Scripture. ➧ Today Roman Catholics and some Protestants include the Deuterocanonical books (see *Apocrypha*) in the Old Testament, in which case there are forty-six Old Testament books.

BOOKS OF THE OLD TESTAMENT

Pentateuch/Books of Law/ Books of Moses/Torah

1. Genesis
2. Exodus
3. Leviticus
4. Numbers
5. Deuteronomy

12 Historical Books

1. Joshua
2. Judges
3. Ruth
4. 1 Samuel
5. 2 Samuel
6. 1 Kings
7. 2 Kings
8. 1 Chronicles
9. 2 Chronicles
10. Ezra
11. Nehemiah

Tobit
Judith

12. Esther

1 Maccabees
2 Maccabees

5 Poetic Books

1. Job
2. Psalms
3. Proverbs
4. Ecclesiastes
5. Song of Solomon (*or* Song of Songs *or* Canticles

Wisdom (of Solomon)
Sirach (or Ecclesiasticus)

17 Books of Prophecy

5 Major Prophets

1. Isaiah
2. Jeremiah
3. Lamentations

Baruch

4. Ezekiel
5. Daniel

12 Minor Prophets

1. Hosea
2. Joel
3. Amos
4. Obadiah
5. Jonah
6. Micah
7. Nahum
8. Habakkuk
9. Zephaniah
10. Haggai
11. Zechariah
12. Malachi

Note: Deuterocanonical books (the apocryphal books) are listed in italic.

PENTATEUCH The first five books of the Old Testament (see *Genesis*; *Exodus*; *Leviticus*; *Numbers*; *Deuteronomy*). They are also called the Books of Moses or Books of Law. The word *Pentateuch* comes from two Greek words meaning "five books." For Jews, the Pentateuch is called the Torah.

1 PETER (NT) The first of two epistles written by the apostle Peter. This letter was written to Jewish Christians scattered across Asia Minor (present-day Turkey). Its purpose was to encourage these Christians, who were facing increasing persecution under the heavy hand of the Roman Empire.

2 PETER (NT) The second of two epistles written by Peter. This letter was written to the church at large. Its purpose was to warn Christians about false teachers and to encourage them in their faith.

PHILEMON (NT) A short and tender letter from the apostle Paul to Philemon. It was hand carried to Philemon by Onesimus, a slave who had run away from Philemon but was now a believer and was returning to his master. Paul appeals to Philemon to treat Onesimus as a brother.

PHILIPPIANS (NT) A letter from Paul and Timothy to the church in Philippi (in Greece; see map near *2 Corinthians*). Paul had started the church there on his second missionary journey. He was now in prison in Rome, and the Philippians had sent a gift to him there. In this letter, he thanks them for their gift and reminds them that true joy comes only from Jesus Christ.

POETRY, BOOKS OF The Books of Poetry (*or* Books of Wisdom) in the Old Testament include Job, Psalms, Proverbs, Ecclesiastes, and Song of Solomon.

PROPHECY, BOOKS OF These Old Testament books include the five Major Prophets and the twelve Minor Prophets. In the Hebrew (Jewish) Bible, the grouping of books called "The Prophets" includes some of the historical books as well as the Major and Minor Prophets. After Jesus identified the two greatest commandments, he said, "On these two commandments hang all the Law and the Prophets" (Matthew 22:40) (see *You shall love the Lord your God ...* and *Love your neighbor as yourself* in the chapter "Famous Sayings from the Bible"). By "all the Law" he meant the Books of

Law, and "the Prophets" meant the Books of Prophecy and the historical books.

PROVERBS (OT) An Old Testament book of poetry that contains a collection of wise and often pithy sayings. The first several chapters contain advice to young men about the importance of wisdom and pure living. Many of the Proverbs were written by King Solomon.

PSALMS (OT) A collection of 150 Hebrew poems and songs that express a full range of human emotion in relation to God. Many of the psalms were written by King David. The book of Psalms contains a treasury of well-loved passages.

RED-LETTER EDITIONS Bibles in which all the words spoken by Jesus are printed in red. Red-letter editions are a twentieth-century innovation in Bible publishing. The original manuscripts of the Bible did not highlight the words of Christ in any way. Other features that have been added to the Bible text for ease of readability include

SELECTIONS FROM PROVERBS

(New Living Translation)

- *Trust in the LORD with all your heart; do not depend on your own understanding. Seek his will in all you do, and he will show you which path to take.* (Proverbs 3:5–6)
- *A gentle answer deflects anger, but harsh words make tempers flare.* (Proverbs 15:1)
- *Direct your children onto the right path, and when they are older, they will not leave it.* (Proverbs 22:6)
- *Who can find a virtuous and capable wife? She is more precious than rubies.... Charm is deceptive, and beauty does not last; but a woman who fears the LORD will be greatly praised. Reward her for all she has done. Let her deeds publicly declare her praise.* (Proverbs 31:10, 30–31)

SELECTIONS FROM THE PSALMS
(New King James Version)

- † *The* LORD *is my light and my salvation; whom shall I fear? The* LORD *is the strength of my life; of whom shall I be afraid?* (Psalm 27:1)
- † *Your word is a lamp to my feet and a light to my path.* (Psalm 119:105)
- † *Unless the* LORD *builds the house, they labor in vain who build it.* (Psalm 127:1)
- † *Search me, O God, and know my heart; try me, and know my anxieties; and see if there is any wicked way in me, and lead me in the way everlasting.* (Psalm 139:23–24)

paragraphs, quotation marks, parentheses, and the division of the text into chapters and verses.

REVELATION (NT) Also called the Apocalypse, it is the last book in the Bible. It is presumed to have been written by John (Jesus's disciple). It is his description of a vision in which he saw future events: the persecution of the church; the coming of the Antichrist; the triumph of God over evil at a great battle (Armageddon); the Millennium, when Satan is bound for 1,000 years; the final judgment (Judgment Day); and the New Jerusalem. The vision ends with the promise that Jesus is coming again soon (the Second Coming). Many popular descriptions of heaven come from Revelation: angels singing, white robes, pearly gates, streets of gold. John's vision also includes the four horsemen of the Apocalypse, representing judgment to come upon the earth because of people's wickedness. Note that Revelation should not be pronounced *Revelations*, a common error.

ROMANS (NT) An epistle in which the apostle Paul sets forth an extensive theology of the Christian faith. It emphasizes justification by grace, through faith. Martin Luther's study of Romans led him to the conclusion that the prevalent teachings of the sixteenth-century church were not consistent with Scripture.

RUTH (OT) The book that tells the story of Ruth, Naomi, and Boaz. Ruth was a poor widow from the land of Moab (east of the Dead Sea), whose husband had been an Israelite. When her widowed mother-in-law, Naomi, returned to Israel, she encouraged Ruth to stay with her own people in Moab. But Ruth responded, "Wherever you go, I will go; wherever you live, I will live. Your people will be my people, and your God will be my God" (Ruth 1:16 NLT). When they arrived in Naomi's hometown, Ruth gathered food in the fields of Boaz, a wealthy relative of her deceased husband. Boaz noticed Ruth because of her generosity to her mother-in-law, and he soon married her. Their great-grandson was David, the great king of Israel.

1 SAMUEL (OT) The book that tells the stories of Samuel, the great prophet, and Saul, the first king of Israel. First Samuel also contains stories about David before he succeeded Saul as king. This book includes the story of the friendship of David and Jonathan, the story of David and Goliath, and accounts of Saul's jealousy of David.

2 SAMUEL (OT) This book continues the history of Israel where 1 Samuel ends—with the death of King Saul and David's rise to the throne of Israel. It recounts the history of David's many conquests in battle as well as his personal struggles, including his adultery with Bathsheba. Much of the latter part of the book revolves around the rivalry between David's sons and the problem of succession to the throne. The time period covered is presented from a different perspective in the book of 1 Chronicles.

SCRIPTURE The term *Scripture* (from the Latin word for "writings") is often used to mean the Bible, or a passage from the Bible. There are frequent references to "the Scriptures" in the New Testament, and in that context the writers meant the Hebrew (Jewish) Scriptures, which Christians now call the Old Testament.

SCROLL A long strip of paper or leather rolled up on two sticks. The text of the Scripture was written on scrolls. Even today, ornamental Torahs (the Books of Moses written in Hebrew) are scrolls.

SEPTUAGINT A Greek translation of the Old Testament, parts of which date from the third century BC. At the time of Christ and in the early church, the Scriptures (the Old Testament) were known both in the original Hebrew and in this Greek translation. The word *Septuagint* comes from the Latin word for "seventy," because seventy scholars are said to have worked on the translation. It is often abbreviated LXX, the Roman numeral for seventy.

SONG OF SOLOMON (OT) This book of poetry celebrates romantic love and the sexual relationship between a husband and wife. On another level, it is also an allegory of God's love for Israel and the church. Traditionally said to have been written by King Solomon, this book is also called Canticles or Song of Songs.

SONG OF SONGS See *Song of Solomon.*

STUDY BIBLE A Bible with notes that help readers understand the text. The notes of some study Bibles are largely technical in nature, dealing with the original Hebrew or Greek text. Other study Bibles help the reader apply the truth of Scripture to contemporary life. Readers of study Bibles must take care to distinguish between the text of Scripture, which is the Word of God, and the text of the study notes. The notes, however wise, are still only the words of man.

SYNOPTIC GOSPELS The Gospels of Matthew, Mark, and Luke. *Synoptic* means seeing things from the same point of view, and the first three Gospels are similar in their approach to the life of Jesus. The Gospel of John also tells of the life and ministry of Jesus, but it gives fewer details and presents longer passages of Jesus's discourses.

TEXTUS RECEPTUS A Greek text of the New Testament that was compiled in 1550. It was based on Greek manuscripts that were known in the sixteenth century but are now considered less accurate than older manuscripts discovered in the last 150 years. The King James Version of 1611 was translated from the Textus Receptus (Latin for "received text").

THEE* AND *THOU Many contemporary readers are frustrated by the archaic English of the King James Version of the Bible, which includes frequent use of *thee* and *thou* and the verb suffix *-est* ("The eyes of all wait upon thee; and thou givest them their meat in due season," Psalm 145:15). There used to be a distinction in English between singular pronouns (*thou, thee*) and plural pronouns (*ye, you*). In the King James Version, the singular pronouns in Hebrew and Greek were translated "thou"(nominative) and "thee"(objective), and the plural pronouns were translated "ye" (nominative) and "you" (objective). Most modern translations simply use "you" for all four cases. Since God was always addressed as *thou* (singular) in the King James Version, the terms *thee, thou,* and *thy* took on a special sense of dignity and reverence. Many people still use those terms when they pray.

1 THESSALONIANS (NT) The first of the apostle Paul's letters to the church in Thessalonica, Greece—and one of Paul's earliest letters. It was written to encourage the Christians in Thessalonica and to assure them of Christ's return (the Second Coming). It also answers their questions about the state of believers who had already died.

2 THESSALONIANS (NT) Paul's second letter to the church in Thessalonica, Greece. It was written shortly after 1 Thessalonians and again contains information about the Second Coming of Christ.

1 TIMOTHY (NT) The first of the apostle Paul's letters to his friend Timothy, who was a young pastor. It is a very practical letter, addressing such issues as qualifications for church leaders and the care of different groups of people within the church.

2 TIMOTHY (NT) The second of the apostle Paul's letters to Timothy. Written shortly before Paul's death, it includes instructions and encouragement to the younger pastor. It includes the familiar statement about the authenticity and value of Scripture: "All Scripture is inspired by God and is useful to teach us what is true and to make us realize what is wrong in our lives. It corrects us when we are wrong and teaches us to do what is right" (2 Timothy 3:16 NLT).

TITUS (NT) A letter from the apostle Paul to Titus, who was supervising the churches on the Mediterranean island of Crete. It is a very practical letter about various aspects of church leadership and how Christians ought to live.

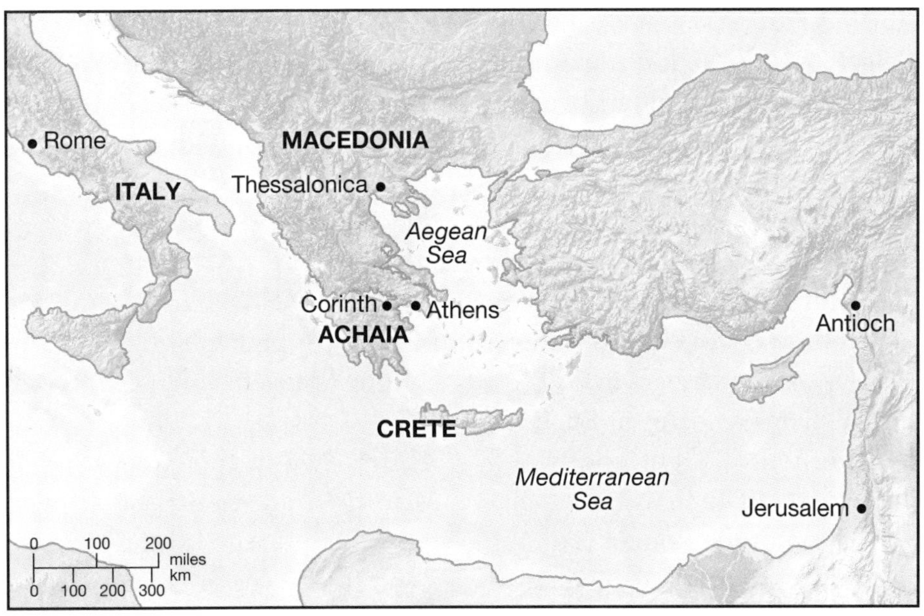

Letters to Thessalonica When Paul and Silas visited Thessalonica, many people became believers as a result of Paul's preaching. The books called 1 & 2 Thessalonians were letters to the churches there. The book of Titus was a letter written to Titus, a church leader on the island of Crete.

TORAH A scroll containing the Hebrew text of the Pentateuch. The text of the books, whether or not on a scroll, is also called the Torah. More broadly, the Hebrew Scripture in its entirety (the Old Testament) is sometimes called Torah.

TRANSLATION The Bible was originally written in Hebrew and Aramaic (Old Testament) and Greek (New Testament). Accordingly, all English Bibles are translations from the original languages. The Bible has been translated into thousands of languages by missionaries and organizations such as Wycliffe Bible Translators and the United Bible Societies. There are various methods of translation, from a strict word-for-word style to a thought-for-thought style. Word-for-word translations are helpful for understanding the syntax of the original language, but thought-for-thought translations are easier to read and understand.

VERSE See *chapter and verse.*

VULGATE A Latin translation of the Bible prepared by Jerome in the fourth century AD. It was called the Vulgate (from the Latin word for "common" or "popular") because it was written in the "vulgar," or common, language. It was the predominant translation used by the church for the next 1,100 years. As the Reformers began to stress the value of these types of translations (such as Martin Luther's in German and William Tyndale's in English), the Council of Trent confirmed the Vulgate in 1546 as the official translation of the Roman Catholic Church, a position it held until the twentieth century. The Douay-Rheims Bible is an English text translated for the most part from the Vulgate.

WISDOM, BOOKS OF See *Poetry, Books of.*

WORD OF GOD Another name for the Bible. It is called the Word of God because of the belief by most Christians that the Bible is God's written revelation to mankind. In John 1:1, Jesus is called "the Word." See *Scripture, inspiration of* in the chapter "Church Life and Theology."

ZECHARIAH (OT) One of the Minor Prophets, this book contains the messages of the prophet Zechariah (not to be confused with Zechariah, the father of John the Baptist). Zechariah's ministry was to the people of Israel while the temple was being rebuilt after the Exile (the details of which are included in the first half of Ezra). The book of Zechariah contains many prophecies regarding the coming Messiah.

ZEPHANIAH (OT) One of the Minor Prophets, this book contains the messages of the prophet Zephaniah. He preached to the Kingdom of Judah during the reign of King Josiah, a good king who led the people away from idol worship and back to the Lord. The last years of Zephaniah's ministry coincided with the early years of the prophet Jeremiah's ministry.

HOW BIBLE TRANSLATIONS DIFFER

The following translations of 1 Corinthians 13:4–7 show the difference in style of translation between the New Living Translation, the New International Version, and the King James Version.

> *Love is patient and kind. Love is not jealous or boastful or proud or rude. It does not demand its own way. It is not irritable, and it keeps no record of being wronged. It does not rejoice about injustice but rejoices whenever the truth wins out. Love never gives up, never loses faith, is always hopeful, and endures through every circumstance.* (NLT)

> *Love is patient, love is kind. It does not envy, it does not boast, it is not proud. It does not dishonor others, it is not self-seeking, it is not easily angered, it keeps no record of wrongs. Love does not delight in evil but rejoices with the truth. It always protects, always trusts, always hopes, always perseveres.* (NIV)

> *Charity suffereth long, and is kind; charity envieth not; charity vaunteth not itself, is not puffed up, doth not behave itself unseemly, seeketh not her own, is not easily provoked, thinketh no evil; rejoiceth not in iniquity, but rejoiceth in the truth; beareth all things, believeth all things, hopeth all things, endureth all things.* (KJV)

Bible 101

A Quiz on Bible Basics

Select one answer for each question.
Answers appear immediately after the quiz.

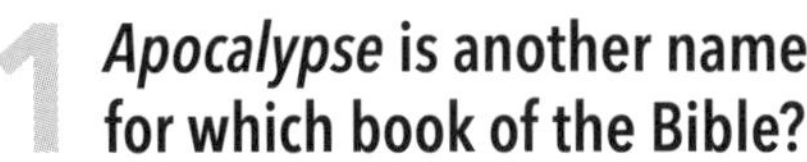

1 *Apocalypse* is another name for which book of the Bible?

a. Genesis

b. Malachi

c. Matthew

d. Revelation

2 Different parts of the Bible were originally written in several different languages. Which one of these languages is not one of the original languages?

a. Greek

b. Latin

c. Hebrew

d. Aramaic

3 Which term is used to refer to the first five books of the Old Testament?

a. Books of Moses

b. Pentateuch

c. Torah

d. All of the above

4 Who is generally considered to have written the book of Acts?

a. Matthew

b. Mark

c. Luke

d. None of the above

5 The books in the following lists contain portions of the history of the people of Israel. Which list is in the proper chronological sequence?

a. Genesis, Daniel, 1 Samuel, Nehemiah

b. Numbers, Joshua, 2 Kings, Ruth

c. Exodus, 2 Samuel, 1 Kings, Ezra

d. 1 Chronicles, 2 Chronicles, Judges, Esther

6 **Which of the following books is one of the Minor Prophets?**

a. Isaiah

b. Ezekiel

c. Daniel

d. Amos

7 **In which book do we read about the statue with the feet of clay, the fiery furnace, and the handwriting on the wall?**

a. Daniel

b. Exodus

c. Matthew

d. Revelation

8 **The book of Deuteronomy consists primarily of a long speech to the people of Israel. Who gave the speech?**

a. Abraham

b. Moses

c. David

d. Paul

9 **Which of the following books did Jeremiah write?**

a. Genesis

b. Lamentations

c. Proverbs

d. Romans

10 **Which book contains the story of Moses leading the people of Israel out of Egypt?**

a. Exodus

b. Joshua

c. Judges

d. 1 Kings

11 **Which translation of the Bible is sometimes called the Authorized Version?**

a. Vulgate

b. King James Version

c. Revised Standard Version

d. New International Version

12 **Which is the first book in the Bible?**

a. Matthew

b. John

c. Genesis

d. Psalms

13 **Which book of the Bible begins with the phrase "In the beginning was the Word"?**

a. Genesis

b. Psalms

c. Matthew

d. John

14 **Which of the following statements is true of the original manuscripts of the Old Testament?**

a. They are now in a museum in Jerusalem.

b. They are no longer in existence.

c. They are called the Dead Sea Scrolls.

d. None of the above

15 **The book of Judges contains the stories of:**

a. Abraham, Isaac, and Jacob

b. Moses, Aaron, and Miriam

c. Deborah, Gideon, and Samson

d. Peter, James, John

16 **The books of 1 and 2 Kings contain, for the most part, which genre?**

a. Poetry

b. Prophecy

c. Theology

d. History

17 **Matthew, Mark, Luke, and John are:**

a. Gospels

b. Epistles

c. Books of poetry

d. Part of the Pentateuch

18 **Which three books are generally considered to have been written by Paul?**

a. Acts, Romans, 1 Corinthians

b. Galatians, Ephesians, Philippians

c. Hebrews, James, 1 Peter

d. 3 John, Jude, Revelation

19 **Who was the original recipient of the letter we now know as the book of Philemon?**

a. Philemon

b. Onesimus

c. Paul

d. James

20 **Romans, a letter that sets forth a theology of the Christian faith, was written by:**

a. Jesus

b. Peter

c. David

d. Paul

Answers

1. d
2. b
3. d
4. c
5. c
6. d
7. a
8. b
9. b
10. a
11. b
12. c
13. d
14. b
15. c
16. d
17. a
18. b
19. a
20. d

People, Places, and Events in the Old Testament

The Old Testament is the account of God's dealings with his chosen people, the Israelites. Many Old Testament names are familiar in our culture, such as Adam and Eve, Noah, Abraham, Moses, and David.

Since the Old Testament was the entirety of "the Scriptures" for Jesus and his contemporaries, knowing the people, places, and events of the Old Testament is essential to fully understanding the teachings of the New Testament. For instance, the eleventh chapter of Hebrews lists by name nineteen people from the Old Testament, sixteen of whom are included in this chapter.

The Old Testament begins with the words "In the beginning God created the heavens and the earth" (Genesis 1:1). The account of the creation is followed by the fall of man, then the story of Noah and the ark.

Next come the stories of Abraham and Sarah, Isaac and Rebekah, Jacob and Esau, and Joseph and his coat of many colors. The descendants of Jacob are in Egypt for 430 years, and then comes the story of Moses and the Exodus, followed by the forty years in which the Israelites wandered in the wilderness.

After that, Joshua leads the people in conquering the Promised Land. Next comes the period of the judges, and then the United Kingdom and the Divided Kingdom (the Northern Kingdom of Israel and the Southern Kingdom of Judah). God's people are taken into exile when Assyria conquers Israel and Babylon conquers Judah. The Old Testament ends with the return of the people of Judah from the Exile.

We get a little bit of insight into the 400 years between the Old Testament and the New Testament by reading the Apocrypha. Otherwise, the Bible is silent about that time period.

There are many terms that are equally important in understanding the Old and New Testaments, including *Jordan River*, *Jerusalem*, *circumcision*, *Passover*, *the Law*, and *temple*. For the sake of consistency, terms that could have been listed either in this chapter or in "People, Places, and Events in the New Testament" are listed here.

AARON Moses's older brother. Aaron plays a key role in the events relayed in the books of Exodus and Numbers. When God told Moses to lead the enslaved Israelites out of Egypt into the freedom of the Promised Land, Moses protested that he was not an eloquent speaker. God responded by saying that Aaron could be Moses's spokesman. Moses and Aaron delivered God's message to Pharaoh, king of Egypt: "Let my people go" (Exodus 5:1 NLT). After the Exodus from Egypt, while the Israelites were wandering in the wilderness, Moses met with God on Mount Sinai. In Moses's absence, Aaron gave in to the demands of the people and made a golden calf for them to worship. In spite of this sin, Aaron later became the first high priest of Israel. All subsequent priests were descendants of Aaron.

ABEL See *Cain and Abel.*

ABRAHAM (ABRAM) He was the first of the patriarchs of Israel (Genesis 12–25). According to Acts 7:2–4, the Lord spoke to him in Ur of the Chaldeans (in present-day Iraq) and told him to move to Canaan (present-day Israel). Genesis 15:6 says that Abraham's faith in God was counted to him

The Dome of the Rock on Jerusalem's Temple Mount is built over the bedrock of Mount Moriah, the traditional site where Abraham prepared to sacrifice Isaac.

as righteousness. The Lord made a covenant with Abraham: Although Abraham and his wife, Sarah, were both too old to have a child, the Lord promised they would have a son and that their descendants would be as numerous as "the sand which is on the seashore" (Genesis 22:17). When Sarah did not conceive, she gave her servant Hagar to Abraham to be his concubine and to bear him a son. Hagar did have a son, Ishmael. Modern-day Arabs commonly regard themselves as descendants of Ishmael and consider Abraham the father of their race. Finally, at age ninety, Sarah miraculously gave birth to a son and named him Isaac. When Isaac was still a boy, the Lord tested

Abraham's faith by asking him to sacrifice Isaac. Abraham was getting ready to do so when the Lord saw his faith and told him to stop. Through the descendants of Isaac, Abraham is also the father of the Jewish people. Prior to receiving God's promise that he would be a father of many nations (Genesis 17:4), his name was Abram. Abram means "exalted father"; Abraham means "father of many." See also *covenant* in the chapter "Church Life and Theology."

ABSALOM One of King David's sons who led a rebellion against his father (2 Samuel 15–18). When Absalom's donkey ran under a low-hanging branch, his long hair became tangled in the tree. He was left hanging there, and Joab, David's general, killed him. When David heard about Absalom's death, he mourned, "O my son Absalom, my son, my son Absalom!" (2 Samuel 18:33 KJV).

ADAM The first person created by God. He was created "in the image of God" (Genesis 1:27). Adam tended the Garden and named all the animals God had created. According to the Genesis account of the creation, God created Adam's wife, Eve, from one of Adam's ribs. Adam and Eve lived in the Garden of Eden, in a state of perfect communion with God. The serpent, identified in Revelation 20:2 as Satan, tempted Eve to eat fruit from the tree of the knowledge of good and evil, which is the only tree God had forbidden them to eat from. She ate the fruit and gave some to Adam to eat. This event is called "the fall of man." As a result of their disobedience, they were expelled from the Garden of Eden (see *Expulsion*). God cursed the ground so it would produce thorns and thistles, and God told Adam he would now have to toil to produce food by the sweat of his brow. God told Eve she would have pain in childbirth. God also told Adam, "Dust you are, and to dust you shall return" (Genesis 3:19). Adam and Eve's sons included Cain and Abel.

ADULTERY Any act of sexual intercourse between a married person and someone other than his or her spouse. In the Old Testament, adultery was punishable by death (Leviticus 20:10). One of the Ten Commandments is "You shall not commit adultery" (Exodus 20:14). Jesus expanded on this commandment by saying in the Sermon on the Mount, "Anyone who even looks at a woman with lust has already committed adultery with her in his heart" (Matthew 5:28 NLT).

AHAB One of the most wicked of the kings of Israel (1 Kings 16–22). He and his wife, Jezebel, promoted the worship of the Canaanite god Baal. It was during their reign that the prophet Elijah had his famous contest with the priests of Baal and called down fire from heaven.

ALLELUIA See *hallelujah.*

Replica of the tabernacle altar

ALTAR A stone, wood, or earthen structure on which sacrifices are offered in worship. When the Mosaic law was instituted, God instructed Moses to construct an altar at the tabernacle for the Israelites to use in offering their sacrifices. The Canaanites also had altars to their gods, and the Israelites were ordered to destroy those heathen altars as they took possession of the Promised Land. The Israelites never fully obeyed that command, and they were continually drawn into worship of foreign gods. 📌 In churches today, the table at the front of the sanctuary where the Eucharist (Holy Communion) is blessed is often called an altar.

ARARAT The mountain range where Noah's ark came to rest after the Flood. Ararat is believed to be in present-day Turkey. See also *Noah.*

ARK See *ark of the covenant* and *Noah.*

ARK OF THE COVENANT A gold-plated box that was first kept in the tabernacle and then in the temple, in a partition called the Holy of Holies. Above the ark were two cherubs (a type of angel) carved from gold. The ark is described in Exodus 25. The ark (not to be confused with Noah's ark) was the most sacred article in Israel. Only the high priest could approach the ark, and only once a year. It symbolized God's presence among the people of Israel. The ark contained the stone tablets on which God had inscribed the Ten Commandments, a jar of manna, and the rod Aaron used to perform miracles at the time of the Exodus. At one point the ark was captured by the Philistines, but it brought a curse to them, so they returned it to Israel. 📌 Notwithstanding the story in the film *Raiders of the Lost Ark*, it is safe to assume that the ark was destroyed during the destruction of Jerusalem by the Babylonians in 586 BC. There was no ark in the second temple (built by Zerubbabel) or the third temple (built by Herod the Great).

Replica of the ark of the covenant

ASSYRIA, ASSYRIANS Assyria was an ancient empire in what is now northern Iraq and western Turkey. The Assyrians attained prominence in the Near East during the ninth century BC. The prophet Jonah went to Nineveh, the capital of Assyria, to call the people to repentance (see *Jonah and the great fish*). The Assyrians laid siege to Samaria, the capital of Israel (the Northern Kingdom), for three years. Samaria finally fell in 722 BC, and many of the Israelites were taken as captives to Assyria (2 Kings 17). This marked the end of the Northern Kingdom of Israel. We know from secular history that Assyria later fell to Babylon (in 612 BC), the world power that also destroyed Jerusalem in 586 BC.

BAAL The most important of the many gods of the Canaanites. Baal represented fertility and a good harvest, and worship of Baal often included prostitution. The people of Israel were repeatedly warned not to worship Baal, but they repeatedly fell into such worship. During the reign of King Ahab and Queen Jezebel, the prophet Elijah challenged the priests of Baal to a contest to show whether the God of Israel was stronger than Baal. The priests of Baal were unable to send fire from heaven, but God sent fire that burned up the altar itself in addition to the sacrifice.

BABEL, TOWER OF A great tower built by the descendants of Noah. In their pride, they intended to build the tower all the way to heaven. It was located in the area that later became the city of Babylon. To keep them from completing the tower,

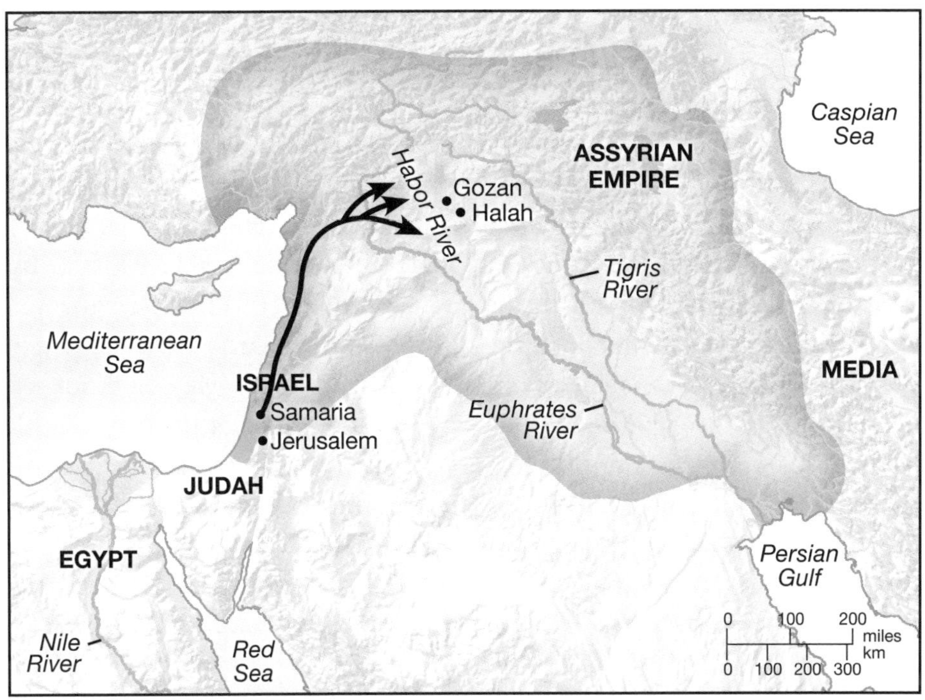

Assyria Takes Israel Captive Samaria, the capital of the Northern Kingdom of Israel, was destroyed by the Assyrians. The people of Israel were led into captivity, swallowed up by the mighty, evil Assyrian Empire. This marked the end of the Northern Kingdom, as the Israelites never returned.

God confused their language so that they no longer understood one another. According to Genesis 11, this is the beginning of the multiplicity of languages in the world. Today a "babel" is any scene of confusion, especially a confusion of multiple languages.

BABYLON, BABYLONIANS

Babylon was the capital of the Babylonian Empire, which flourished in the region of present-day Iraq during the sixth century BC. Secular history tells us that the Babylonians defeated the Assyrians (the empire that had earlier defeated the Northern Kingdom of Israel) in 612 BC. Twenty-six years later, in 586 BC, the Babylonians destroyed Jerusalem (2 Kings 25). Many of the inhabitants were taken as captives to Babylon (see *Exile*). About fifty years later, the Babylonians were defeated by the Persians (Daniel 5). The stories in the book of Daniel take place in Babylon during the time of the Jews' captivity there. Babylon is frequently mentioned in the Bible as a place of sin. It was the location of the Tower of Babel, and in Revelation 14:8 Babylon is symbolic of ultimate evil. During the 1980s, Saddam Hussein, the president of Iraq who fancied himself to be a latter-day Nebuchadnezzar, began rebuilding the ancient city of Babylon. The word *Babylon* can be used to represent any place of sin and corruption.

BABYLONIAN CAPTIVITY, THE See *Exile.*

BALAAM Before the conquest of the Promised Land by Joshua, Balaam was hired by Balak, an enemy of Israel, to curse Israel and its army (Numbers 22). While Balaam was on his way to curse Israel, an angel blocked his path. He could not see the angel, but his donkey could, and the donkey spoke to Balaam. The angel then instructed Balaam to bless Israel instead of cursing it.

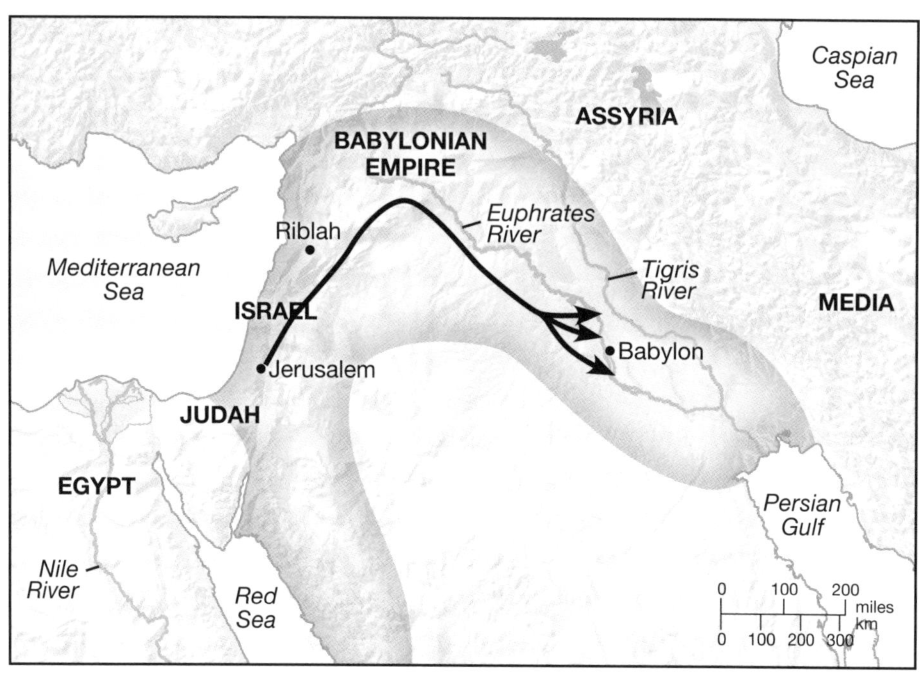

Babylon Takes Judah Captive Evil permeated the Kingdom of Judah, and God's anger flared against his rebellious people. Babylon conquered Assyria and became the new world power. The Babylonian army marched into Jerusalem, burned down the temple, tore down the city's massive walls, and carried the people into captivity.

BATHSHEBA The wife of Uriah, a soldier in King David's army. David committed adultery with Bathsheba while her husband was away at war, and she became pregnant (2 Samuel 11). David wanted to marry Bathsheba, but there was an obstacle—her husband, Uriah. So David arranged for Uriah to be killed in battle. David then married Bathsheba. David repented of his sin, but their first child died. Bathsheba later became the mother of Solomon, who succeeded David as king of Israel. Bathsheba is included in the Gospel of Matthew's genealogy of Jesus, where she is referred to as the wife of Uriah.

BEHEMOTH The book of Job (chapter 40) contains a lengthy description of the behemoth, a large and very strong creature, perhaps an elephant or hippopotamus. God was showing Job his great power in creating such an awesome animal. 📌 The word *behemoth* has come to mean any person or animal that is huge. See also *leviathan.*

BENJAMIN The youngest son of Jacob and Rachel, and Joseph's full brother. When Joseph was prime minister of Egypt, all of his brothers except Benjamin went to Egypt to buy grain (Genesis 42). The brothers did not recognize Joseph, and he accused them of being spies. Then, to test their sincerity, he insisted they bring Benjamin to Egypt, and he kept Simeon as a hostage. Jacob did not want to let Benjamin go, but the brothers knew they could not return to Egypt for more food without Benjamin. When they did return to Egypt, Joseph finally revealed his identity to them.

BENJAMIN, TRIBE OF The descendants of Benjamin, Jacob's youngest son, became the tribe of Benjamin. King Saul and the apostle Paul were from the tribe of Benjamin. During the period of the Divided Kingdom, the tribes of Benjamin and Judah constituted the Kingdom of Judah.

BLESSINGS AND CURSES When the Lord made a covenant with a person or nation in the Old Testament, the covenant included both obligations and consequences. The consequences were blessings for those who obeyed the Lord and were faithful to the covenant, but curses for those who disobeyed the Lord. Although the people of Israel disobeyed more than they obeyed, the Lord offered blessings far greater than the curses.

When the Lord gave Moses the Ten Commandments, he said, "I, the LORD your God, am a jealous God, punishing the children for the sin of the parents to the third and fourth generation of those who hate me, but showing love to a thousand generations of those who love me and keep my commandments" (Exodus 20:5-6 NIV). An important part of Hebrew culture was the blessing that a father bestowed on his children. The oldest son, in particular, received a special blessing. Jacob tricked his aged father, Isaac, into blessing him with the blessing that would normally have gone to Jacob's older brother, Esau.

BOAZ A wealthy farmer who befriended and then married Ruth. Their great-grandson was David. The beautiful story of Ruth and Boaz is told in the book of Ruth.

BURNING BUSH When Moses was a shepherd, he saw in the wilderness a bush that "was burning with fire, but the bush was not consumed" (Exodus 3:2). Moses went to investigate, and the Lord spoke to him from the fire. The Lord told him to return to Egypt and to tell Pharaoh, king of Egypt, to release the Israelites from slavery. Moses was then to lead the Israelites to the Promised Land. Moses asked the Lord what his name was, and the Lord replied, "I AM WHO I AM" (Exodus 3:14). Moses did return to Egypt, and he and his brother, Aaron, led the Israelites out of Egypt (see *Exodus, the*). 📌 Today a "burning bush" experience is an experience with God that significantly changes the course of a person's life.

CAIN AND ABEL Cain was the eldest son of Adam and Eve, and Abel was their younger son (Genesis 4). Abel was a shepherd and brought portions of a firstborn lamb to the Lord as a sacrifice. Cain was a farmer and brought some of his crops as a sacrifice to the Lord. The Lord accepted Abel's sacrifice, but he did not accept Cain's sacrifice. This made Cain angry, and he murdered Abel. When the Lord asked Cain where Abel was, Cain responded, "Am I my brother's keeper?" (Genesis 4:9). Cain was then banished from the Lord's presence, to become a wanderer upon the earth. He told the Lord that he was fearful he himself would be murdered because of his crime, so the Lord put a mark upon him as a warning to others not to harm him. Cain settled in the land of Nod, east of Eden. 📌 Today the expression "to raise Cain" means to make a disturbance or generally cause trouble. John Steinbeck's novel *East of Eden* contains many allusions to the story of Cain.

CALEB With Joshua, Caleb was one of the twelve Israelite spies sent into the Promised Land of Canaan after the Exodus from Egypt (Numbers 13). Caleb and Joshua were the only two who reported that with God's help the Israelites could overcome the Canaanites. Because the people did not believe the Lord would help them conquer the land, they were condemned to stay in the wilderness for forty years—until that generation of adults had died. Joshua and Caleb were the only ones of their generation who did eventually enter the Promised Land.

CAMEL The camel was an important means of transportation during Bible times and was often a measure of personal wealth. The description of Job as a wealthy man includes the fact that he owned 3,000 camels.

CANAAN The land at the eastern edge of the Mediterranean Sea, encompassing present-day Israel and parts of Lebanon, Syria, and Jordan. When Abraham left his home in Ur of the Chaldeans (what is now Iraq), God guided him to Canaan. God promised Abraham that his descendants would receive the entire land of Canaan as an inheritance. Several generations later, when Jacob and his family moved to Egypt, their descendants never forgot that God had promised

Blessings and Curses: Mount Gerizim (*l*), where the blessings of the Law were spoken; Mount Ebal (*r*), where the curses were spoken (Deuteronomy 27:11–13)

Canaan to their ancestor Abraham. Accordingly, when Moses led the people of Israel out of Egypt 430 years later (see *Exodus, the*), they saw Canaan as the Promised Land—a land "flowing with milk and honey" (Exodus 3:8).

CANAANITES The inhabitants of Canaan. When the Israelites were about to enter Canaan, God instructed the Israelites (through Moses) to destroy the Canaanites and their false gods (Deuteronomy 7:1–6). This seemingly bloodthirsty command was given both to punish the Canaanites for their wickedness (Leviticus 18) and to keep the Israelites from being influenced by the evil of the Canaanites. During the conquest of Canaan under Joshua, many Canaanite cities were destroyed, but Israel never fully obeyed God's command to destroy the Canaanites. As a result, they had problems with their Canaanite neighbors for centuries.

CAPTIVITY, THE See *Exile*.

CHARIOT A two-wheeled vehicle pulled by one or more horses. Chariots were important in warfare both in Old and New Testament times. In the story of Deborah, the Canaanites were formidable foes because they had 900 iron chariots. The prophet Isaiah warned the people of Judah not to trust in chariots, but to seek their help from the Lord (Isaiah 31:1).

Ancient Egyptian chariot

CHARIOT OF FIRE At the end of the prophet Elijah's life, he was taken up into heaven in a chariot that was made of fire and drawn by horses of fire (2 Kings 2:11). The title of the movie *Chariots of Fire* comes from a phrase in a poem by William Blake, which in turn is an allusion to Elijah's chariot of fire.

CHERUBIM AND SERAPHIM Types of angels. When the Lord drove Adam and Eve out of the Garden of Eden, cherubim with flaming swords guarded the way to the tree of life (Genesis 3). When the Lord commanded the Israelites to construct the ark of the covenant for the tabernacle, the

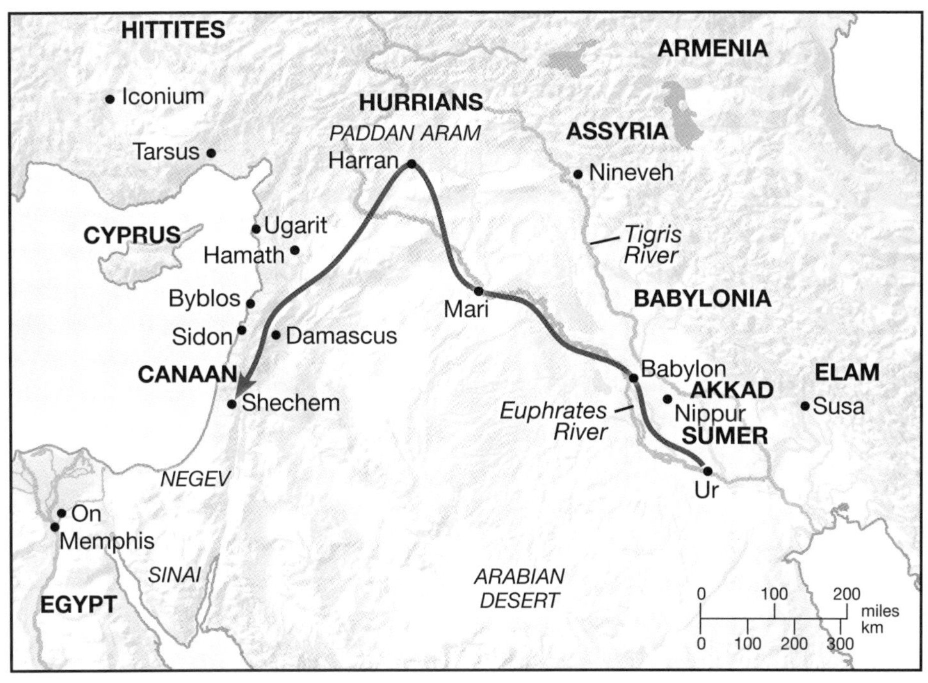

Abraham's Journey to Canaan God told Abraham to leave Ur of the Chaldeans and travel to the land of Canaan.

design included two gold-plated, carved cherubim, whose wings were spread above the ark of the covenant. In Solomon's temple, two larger gold-plated cherubim spread their wings above the ark of the covenant, stretching from wall to wall within the partition called the Holy of Holies. When the prophet Isaiah saw the Lord in a vision, he also saw seraphim worshiping the Lord (Isaiah 6). They were human in form, but with six wings.

CHILDREN OF ISRAEL Another name for the Hebrew people, or Israelites—the descendants of Abraham through Isaac and Jacob.

CHOSEN PEOPLE The descendants of Abraham, through Isaac and Jacob, were God's "chosen people." He chose them to receive his covenant. They are also called Hebrews, Israelites, and the children of Israel. During and after the Babylonian Exile, the term *Jews* is used in referring to members of the tribes of Judah and Benjamin.

COAT OF MANY COLORS A special coat that Jacob gave to

his favorite son, Joseph. Joseph flaunted his position of privilege, and his brothers took revenge by selling him into slavery. Then they spilled a goat's blood on the coat and brought it back to their father, saying that Joseph had been killed by a wild animal (Genesis 37).

CONCUBINE A woman who was not a free wife but was a legitimate sexual partner of a man, who was responsible for her support. The most famous concubine in the Bible is Hagar, the servant girl whom Sarah gave to her husband, Abraham. She bore Abraham a son, Ishmael. King Solomon had 700 wives and 300 concubines.

CREATION, THE The creation of the universe and of mankind by God, as described in the first two chapters of the book of Genesis. The first chapter of Genesis begins, "In the beginning God created the heavens and the earth." The account goes on to describe God's creation of light; sky and water; sea and earth; sun, moon, and stars; fish and birds; land animals; and man and woman (Adam and Eve) during a six-day period. On the seventh day, God rested from his labors (see *Sabbath*). In the nineteenth century, Charles Darwin devised the theory of evolution, which explains the diversity of species (including mankind) through mutation, natural selection, and the survival of the fittest. In the twentieth century, physicists and astronomers explained the existence of the sun, earth, stars, and all celestial matter (the entire universe) as having originated from a single explosion—a big bang. The big bang theory and the theory of evolution have come to be accepted by most scientists as logical explanations for the present existence of the universe and the diversity of species. Most scientists who accept these theories do not accept the biblical explanation that the creation was the act of an all-powerful, pre-existent God. There is much debate today in America over the appropriate teaching in public schools of the origin of the universe and the origin of life on earth. Some Christians argue that evolution should be presented as a theory rather than as fact, and that biblical creation should also be presented as a theory. For the most part, however, the biblical account of creation is not presented at all in the public schools. See also *Scopes trial* and *separation of church and state* in the chapter "Church History."

CROSSING OF THE RED SEA See *Red Sea, parting of the.*

DANIEL A Jewish man who was taken to Babylon as a captive in 605 BC, nineteen years before Babylon destroyed Jerusalem. Various stories are told in the book of Daniel about Daniel's faithfulness to God in a heathen culture: His friends Shadrach, Meshach, and Abednego were thrown into a fiery furnace when they refused to worship a golden statue, but an angel kept them safe. Some of Daniel's enemies, knowing he prayed to his God three times a day, tried to have him destroyed by convincing King Darius to pass a law requiring everyone to pray only to the king. Daniel was thrown into a den of lions when he insisted on praying to God rather than to the king, but an angel kept him from harm (see *Daniel in the lions' den*). Daniel's prophecies include the interpretation of King Nebuchadnezzar's dream about the statue with the feet of clay, and the interpretation of the handwriting on the wall. He also had visions about future events, including events at the end of time.

DANIEL IN THE LIONS' DEN Daniel was a Jew, but he was a powerful official in the government of Darius, the king who took over when the Persians defeated the Babylonians. Some of Daniel's adversaries wanted to get rid of him, and they saw their chance

Daniel in the Lions' Den

when they found that he prayed to the Lord three times a day. They convinced the king to pass an edict that his subjects could pray only to the king for a period of thirty days—or be thrown to the lions. When Daniel continued to pray to the Lord, his enemies triumphantly brought him to the king and accused him of breaking the law. The king was sorrowful, but he had to comply with his own law. Before Daniel was thrown to the lions, Darius said he hoped Daniel's God would be able to rescue him. Darius then spent a sleepless night, worrying about Daniel. Early the next morning, Darius went to the lions' den to see what had happened to Daniel. He was overjoyed to find that Daniel was safe—an angel had kept the lions from harming him. Darius ordered Daniel pulled out of the lions' den, and he had Daniel's enemies thrown to the lions, who hungrily devoured them. Darius then issued an edict throughout the land that the people were to fear Daniel's God. This story is found in Daniel 6. Today, if you are "in the lions' den," you are in a situation where you are surrounded by adversaries.

Possible ruins of David's palace have been uncovered in the village of Silwan in Jerusalem.

DAVID The second and greatest king of Israel, whom God called "a man after my own heart" (Acts 13:22 NLT). His story is told in 1 Samuel 16–31 and in 2 Samuel. When David was a young shepherd living in Bethlehem, the prophet Samuel anointed him as King Saul's successor. While still a lad, David visited the army of Israel, which was engaged in warfare with the Philistines. The Philistine giant, Goliath, had been terrorizing the Israelites. David asked Saul's permission to fight the giant, but he turned down Saul's offer of armor. Instead, David prayed and used a stone and a sling, with which he killed Goliath. This enabled the Israelite army to defeat the Philistines. Saul's son Jonathan became David's closest friend. Saul was jealous because of David's great popularity with the people, and he tried to kill David on several occasions. David had several opportunities to kill Saul, but he refused to harm the one who had been anointed by God. After Saul and Jonathan were killed by the Philistines, David was crowned king—first of the tribe of Judah, then of the entire nation of Israel. He was a great warrior, a musician, and a poet. He wrote many of the Psalms. David had numerous wives, including Saul's daughter, Michal, and Bathsheba (for the story of David and Bathsheba, see *Bathsheba*.) David's sons included Absalom and Solomon. David was king of Israel for forty years, and his descendants ruled Israel for another 373 years. Jesus was a descendant of David and was called the Son of David. Bethlehem, where Jesus was born, was known at that time as the "city of David."

DAY OF ATONEMENT The word *atonement* refers to the reconciliation between God and sinful humanity. Under the Mosaic law of the Old Testament, the high priest made a special sacrifice once a year as an atonement for the sins of the entire nation of Israel (Leviticus 16). Known as the Day of Atonement, the sins of the people were placed symbolically on the head of a goat, who became the scapegoat that carried the people's sins away into the desert. It was only on the Day of Atonement that the high priest could enter the partition of the temple called the Holy of Holies. The Day of Atonement was a reminder that the sacrifices made on a daily, weekly, and monthly basis were able to atone for sins only temporarily. 📌 Jews still observe the Day of Atonement (Yom Kippur) as their holiest day of the year. For Christians under the new covenant, the death of Jesus, the perfect Lamb of God, replaces all sacrifices as the perfect atonement for sins.

Shore of the Dead Sea

DEAD SEA A very salty body of water at the southeastern corner of the land of Israel. The Jordan River flows into the Dead Sea, but the Dead Sea has no outlet. It is called the Dead Sea because fish cannot survive in water with such a high salt content. The Dead Sea is not very large and is shrinking in size—it is now about 230 square miles, or about one-fourth the size of Utah's Great Salt Lake. The surface of the Dead Sea lies about 1,400 feet below sea level in the geological rift that includes the Great Rift Valley in East Africa. Its surface is the lowest elevation on the surface of the earth. Sodom and Gomorrah may have been located in an area now covered by the Dead Sea. The Qumran community that created most of the Dead Sea Scrolls was located on the northwestern shore of the Dead Sea.

DEBORAH A judge over Israel during the period of the judges. She instructed a man named Barak to take 10,000 soldiers to do battle with Sisera, a Canaanite army general. Barak said he would go only if Deborah went with him. She agreed to go, but she told Barak he would not receive the honor, for Sisera would be killed by a woman. The Israelite army defeated Sisera's army, even though the Canaanites had 900 chariots. Sisera escaped, however, and hid in the tent of a woman named Jael. He asked her to keep a lookout while he slept. Instead, she killed him by hammering a tent peg through his temples as he slept. After Israel's victory, Deborah sang the "Song of Deborah," which is found in Judges 5.

Mount Tabor, site of Deborah and Barak's battle with Sisera (Judges 4:14)

DELILAH One of Samson's Philistine lovers (Judges 16). She tricked Samson into divulging that his great strength would disappear if his hair was cut. She then arranged for his hair to be cut while he slept so that his Philistine enemies could capture him. Today a "Delilah" is a woman who cunningly entices a man and then deceives or betrays him.

DIVIDED KINGDOM (ISRAEL AND JUDAH) The 200-year period (930–722 BC) from the death of King Solomon till the fall of the Northern Kingdom of Israel. Solomon's son Rehoboam

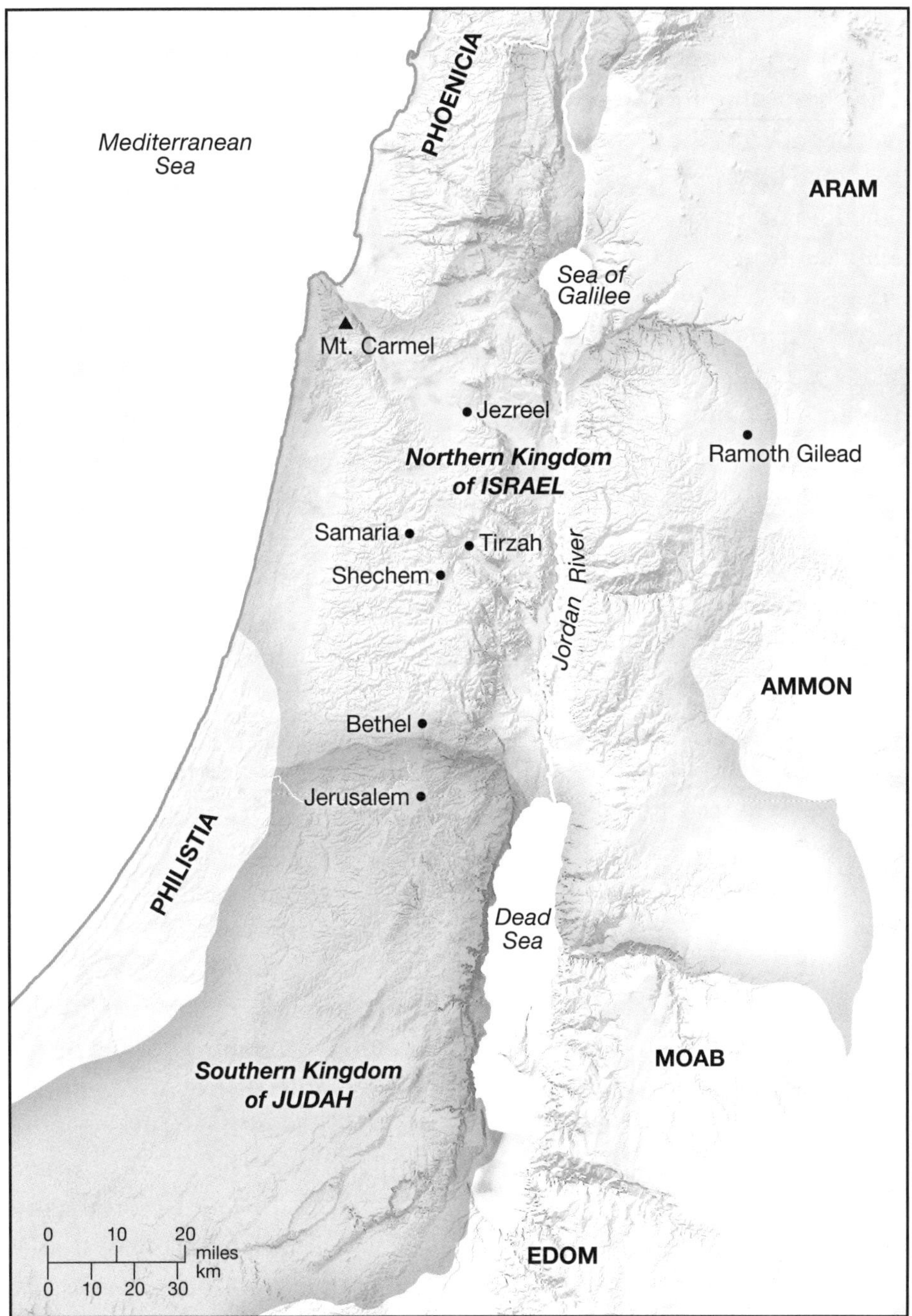

The Divided Kingdom After King Solomon's death, the United Kingdom of Israel was divided into the Northern Kingdom of Israel and the Southern Kingdom of Judah. See 1 Kings 11–12.

succeeded him as king of Israel. The ten northern tribes of Israel refused to submit to his authority, however, and they established their own kingdom (still called the Kingdom of Israel) with Jeroboam as king (1 Kings 12). One of the key cities (and the capital during part of this period) was Samaria. The two southern tribes, Judah and Benjamin, made up the Southern Kingdom of Judah, whose capital was Jerusalem. The Kingdoms of Judah and Israel coexisted until the Northern Kingdom of Israel fell to the Assyrians in 722 BC. The Southern Kingdom of Judah fell to the Babylonians in 586 BC.

EDEN, GARDEN OF The Garden where God placed Adam and Eve after the creation. It was a perfect environment where Adam and Eve lived in harmony with one another and with God. God told Adam he could eat of the fruit of any tree in the Garden except the fruit of the tree of the knowledge of good and evil in the center of the Garden. After Adam and Eve disobeyed this command, God expelled them from the Garden, lest they also eat the fruit of the tree of life and live forever. Cherubim with flaming swords were placed at the entrance to the Garden to ensure that Adam and Eve would not return. See also *forbidden fruit*; *fall of man*; *Expulsion*. 📌 Figuratively, today "Eden" is any perfect or idyllic spot.

Egyptian pyramids

EGYPT A country in northeastern Africa, at the mouth of the Nile River. Egypt plays a major role in biblical history, from the time of Abraham until the time of Jesus (see *flight to Egypt* in the chapter "People, Places, and Events in the New Testament"). Abraham and Sarah journeyed to Egypt to escape a famine in Canaan. Joseph, Jacob's favorite son, was sold by his brothers into slavery in Egypt. He later became prime minister of the land and oversaw a food storage program that saved the land from seven years of famine (Genesis 41). At that time, Jacob and his sons and their families all moved to Egypt. Their descendants lived there for 430 years and became a mighty nation. With the passage of time, Joseph's role in saving Egypt from famine was forgotten. Exodus 1:8 says the Israelites were eventually enslaved by a pharaoh (king) "who did not know Joseph," and the Israelites were allowed to leave (see *Exodus, the*) only after God sent plagues on Egypt. At various times in biblical history, Egypt was either an ally or an enemy of the Israelites.

Excavations at ancient Shiloh, where Eli ministered at the tabernacle

ELI A judge over Israel and one of Israel's high priests when the tabernacle was located at Shiloh (1 Samuel 1–4). When Samuel was a child, his mother took him to Shiloh to work and live with Eli. Eli's sons were wicked, and Eli died when he heard that the ark of the covenant had been captured by the Philistines and that his sons had been killed in the battle. Samuel then succeeded Eli as a prophet and the last judge during the period of the judges.

ELIJAH One of the great prophets of the Old Testament (1 Kings 17–22; 2 Kings 1–2). During the reign of wicked King Ahab and Queen Jezebel of the Northern Kingdom of Israel, Elijah prophesied that there would be no rain in Israel for three years. Elijah went into the wilderness to hide from Ahab, and the Lord sent ravens to bring him food. At the end of that time, Elijah challenged the prophets of the false god Baal to a contest on Mount Carmel. He built an altar on the mountain and told the prophets of Baal to call upon their god to send fire to light the sacrifice. When they failed, Elijah called upon the Lord, who sent fire from heaven that consumed the sacrifice and even the stones of the altar. At the end of his life, Elijah left his mantle (a cloak representing his prophetic power) to Elisha and was taken up to heaven in a chariot of fire. Moses and Elijah were the two prophets who appeared with Jesus on the Mount of Transfiguration. 📌 Figuratively speaking, today a leader "passes the mantle" by formally handing over leadership to his or her successor.

ELISHA One of the great prophets of the Old Testament (2 Kings 2–13). He was a disciple of, and then the successor of, Elijah. Before Elijah was taken to heaven in a chariot of fire, he gave his mantle to Elisha, symbolizing the transfer of his leadership and authority. Elisha performed many miracles, including parting the Jordan River and raising back to life a boy who had died.

ESAU One of the sons of Rebekah and Isaac, and the twin brother of Jacob (Genesis 25–33). Esau was the older of the twins and was characterized by a ruddy appearance, with hair all over his body. One day when he returned from hunting, Esau was famished and sold his birthright to Jacob for some stew Jacob had made. Later, when Isaac was old and blind, Jacob tricked Isaac into blessing him (see *blessings and curses*) rather than Esau by wearing goatskins on his arms and neck so Isaac would think he was the hairy Esau. Esau's descendants, the Edomites, were enemies of the people of Israel. By extension, to "sell one's birthright" is to give up something of great value for a paltry price, especially if it is done as an act of desperation.

Queen Esther

ESTHER A Jewish woman who was part of the exiled community of Israel in Persia (see *Exile*). Because of her beauty, Esther was selected to become a member of the harem of King Ahasuerus (Xerxes) of Persia. She later became queen. When Esther's older cousin and foster father, Mordecai, heard that Haman, the prime minister, had launched a plan to kill all the Jews in the kingdom, he urged Esther to ask the king to stop the plan. Mordecai sent her a message that said, "Who knows but that you have come to your royal position for such a time as this?" (Esther 4:14 NIV). Although she was the queen, she could have been put to death for speaking to the king without being summoned. Before going in to see the king she said, "If I perish, I perish!" (Esther 4:16). The king granted her an audience, and the plan to exterminate the Jews was reversed. The story of Esther is told in the book of Esther. The Jewish holiday of Purim commemorates Esther's rescue of the Jews.

Euphrates River in Syria

EUPHRATES RIVER A river that flows from present-day Turkey through Iraq to the Persian Gulf. It is the largest river in western Asia. The basins of the Euphrates River and Tigris River formed part of the Fertile Crescent of the ancient world. The region of the Tigris and the Euphrates was called Mesopotamia in the Bible (the name comes from the Greek for "between the two rivers"). The city of Babylon was located on the banks of the Euphrates.

EVE The first woman, and Adam's wife (Genesis 2–4). According to the Genesis account of the creation, God created Eve from one of Adam's ribs. Adam and Eve lived in sinless harmony in the Garden of Eden until the serpent (identified in Revelation 20:2 as Satan) came to tempt Eve to eat fruit from the tree of the knowledge of good and evil, which God had forbidden. Eve ate the fruit and gave some to Adam, who also ate it. This event is called "the fall of man." God told Eve that she would bear children in great pain and suffering as a result of her sin. Adam and Eve were expelled from the Garden (see *Expulsion*) lest they also eat the fruit of the tree of life and live forever. Adam and Eve's first sons were Cain and Abel.

EXILE, THE Two exiles are described in the Old Testament. When the Northern Kingdom of Israel was defeated by Assyria in 722 BC, many of the people of those ten tribes of Israel were deported, or exiled, to Assyria. They never returned to Israel, and for the most part they were assimilated into other cultures (2 Kings 17). These are the lost tribes of Israel. Those who were not exiled intermarried with the nations around them, and their descendants became the

Samaritans of the New Testament period. More than 100 years after the fall of the Northern Kingdom, King Nebuchadnezzar of Babylon took some captives (including Daniel) from the Southern Kingdom of Judah (Daniel 1). This first invasion took place in 605 BC, and the Kingdom of Judah was finally defeated in 586 BC, when Jerusalem and the temple were destroyed by the Babylonians (2 Kings 25). Many of the surviving residents of Jerusalem were taken to Babylon as captives. This is called the Exile, the Captivity, or the Babylonian Captivity. Psalm 137 begins, "Beside the rivers of Babylon, we sat and wept as we thought of Jerusalem" (NLT). The stories in the book of Daniel take place in Babylon during the Exile. Persia overthrew Babylon in 539 BC. Zerubbabel then led a group of Israelites back to Jerusalem in 538 BC (Ezra 1–6). They reconstructed the temple, though not to the same grandeur as Solomon's temple had been. This return to Jerusalem marked the end of the Exile, but some Jews remained in Persia. Ezra returned

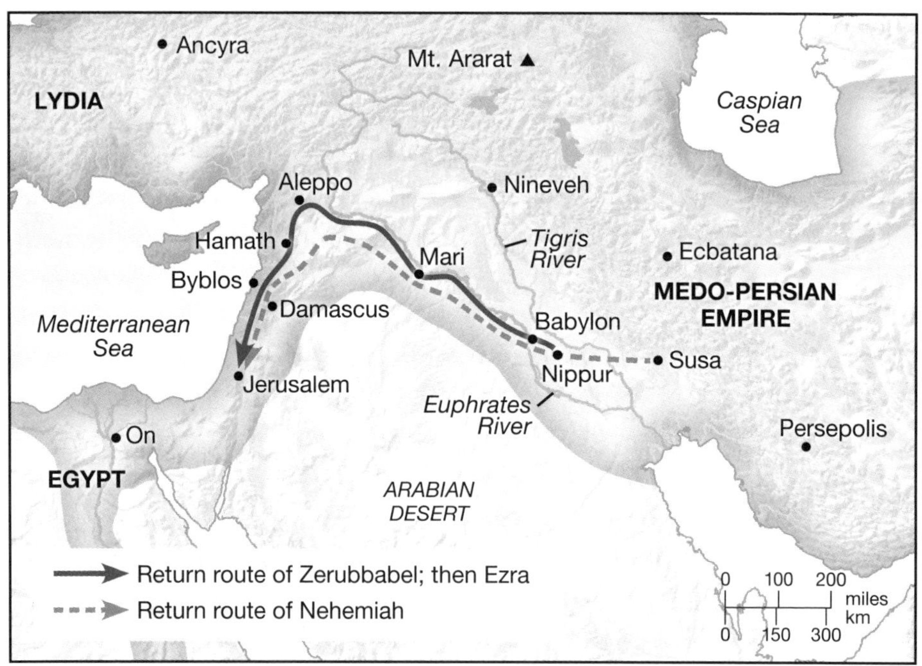

Return from Exile Zerubbabel, Ezra, and Nehemiah returned from exile to help rebuild and unify Jerusalem.

to Jerusalem about eighty years later (Ezra 7–10) in 458 BC, and Nehemiah rebuilt the walls of Jerusalem in 445 BC. Esther was part of the post-Exilic Jewish community still in Persia.

EXODUS, THE The Exodus is the mass departure of the Israelites from Egypt, as related in the book of Exodus (see a map of possible routes on the next page). The Israelites had been in Egypt for 430 years, ever since Jacob and his sons moved there to be with Joseph (Exodus 12:40). As the years went by, the Israelites grew to be a large nation, and they were enslaved by Pharaoh, the king of Egypt. After they had been slaves for many years, the Lord appeared to Moses in a burning bush and told him to lead his people out of Egypt and back to Canaan—the Promised Land. Moses and his brother, Aaron, told Pharaoh, "Let my people go" (Exodus 5:1 NLT), but Pharaoh refused. The Lord then sent plagues upon the land of Egypt to convince Pharaoh to cooperate. The final plague was the death of the firstborn son in each family of Egypt. The Israelites, however, followed the Lord's instructions to put the blood of a lamb or a goat on the doorposts of their houses so the Lord would pass over their houses. This last plague convinced Pharaoh that the Israelites should be allowed to leave. As soon as they left, however, Pharaoh changed his mind. His army pursued the Israelites, but the Egyptian army was drowned in the Red Sea. See also *Passover*; *Red Sea, parting of the*.

EXPULSION, THE When Adam and Eve sinned in the Garden of Eden by eating the forbidden fruit from the tree of the knowledge of good and evil (see *fall of man*), God sent them out of the Garden lest they also eat the fruit of the tree of life and live forever (Genesis 3). This is often called the Expulsion. Cherubim with flaming swords kept Adam and Eve from returning to the Garden.

EZEKIEL A prophet to the Jews during the Exile in Babylon. His prophecies, recorded in the book of Ezekiel, include a vision of a valley filled with dry bones that come back to life again. It was a prophecy that the captives would one day "come back to life again" by returning to their homeland.

EZRA A priest and scribe who led a group of Jews back to Jerusalem from the Exile in Babylon while

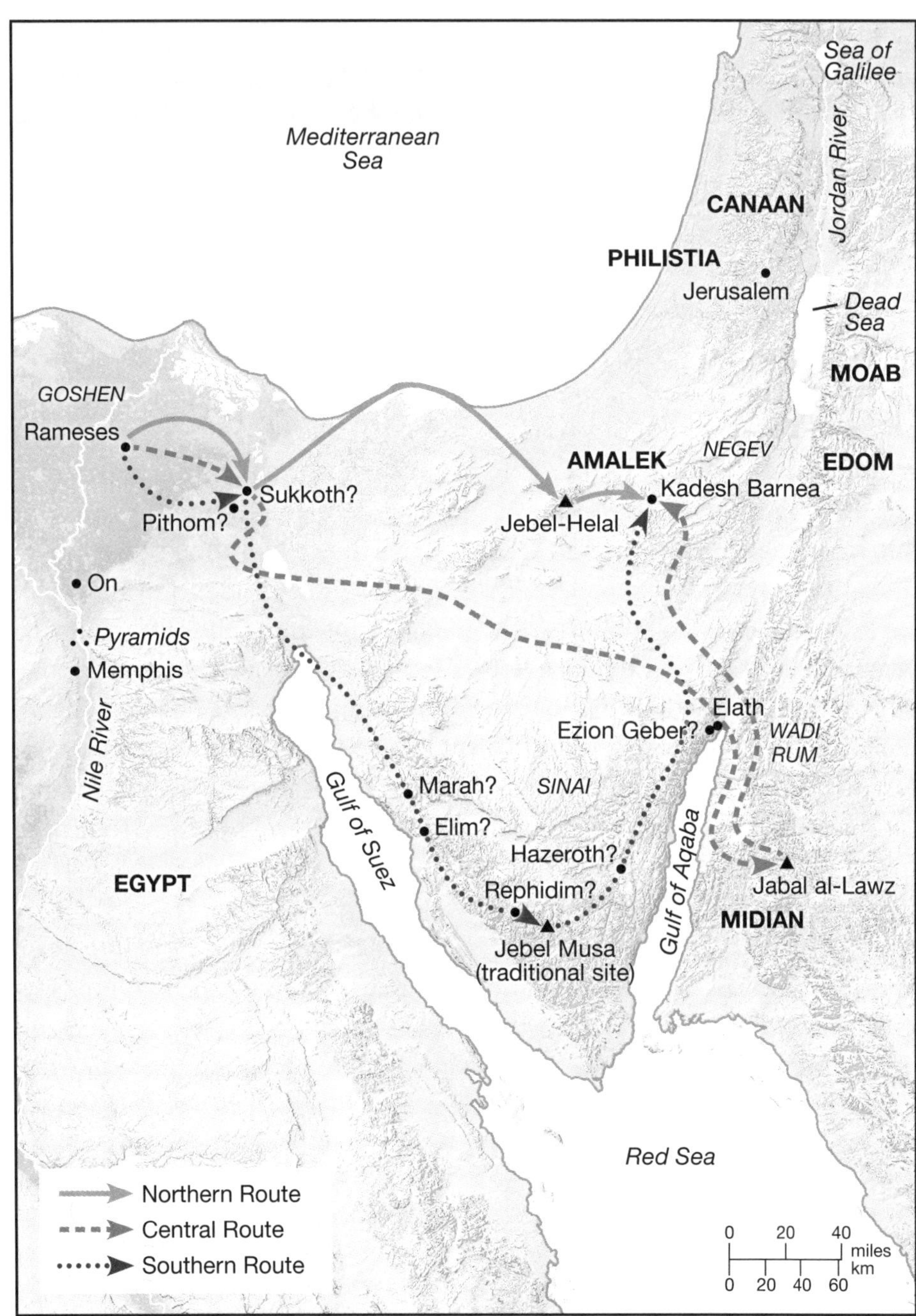

Route of the Exodus When the Israelites left Egypt in the Exodus, they traveled through the Sinai Peninsula. The Lord gave Moses the Ten Commandments at Mount Sinai. The exact location is uncertain; speculative routes and locations are shown here, with Jebel Musa being the traditional site.

Nehemiah was governor in Jerusalem. His messages to the people of Jerusalem are contained in the book of Ezra.

FALL OF MAN (THE FALL) God created Adam and Eve as sinless beings, holy and happy. When the serpent tempted Eve and she and Adam disobeyed God by eating the forbidden fruit, they became sinful and miserable (Genesis 3). This is called the fall of man, or simply the Fall. As a result of the Fall, all humans are born in a state of sin and misery, inheriting from Adam what is called original sin. 📌 John Milton's epic poem, *Paradise Lost*, is about the fall of man.

FEET OF CLAY In Daniel 2, King Nebuchadnezzar of Babylon has a dream about a large statue of a man. Its head is of gold, its chest and arms are of silver, its belly and thighs are of brass, its legs are of iron, and its feet are made of a mixture of iron and clay. A rock hurtles down the mountainside and hits the feet of the statue, crushing them and causing the entire statue to collapse. Daniel interprets the dream for the king, telling him the different parts of the statue represent successive world powers, beginning with Nebuchadnezzar himself (the head of gold). The feet of mixed iron and clay represent a split kingdom, some parts of which would be strong and some weak. Some biblical scholars interpret the last stage (the mixture of iron and clay) to be the breakup of the Roman Empire, when its territory became a mixture of strong and weak nations. Others see it as interethnic marriage after Alexander the Great's conquest of the region. 📌 Today, "feet of clay" is used to describe the weak point in an otherwise strong person.

FIERY FURNACE When the Israelite captives Shadrach, Meshach, and Abednego refused to bow down and worship King Nebuchadnezzar's huge statue, they were thrown into a fiery furnace (Daniel 3). Before they were sent to the furnace, however, they assured the king that their God was capable of keeping them safe. The king ordered that the furnace be heated seven times hotter than usual, and the three men were bound and thrown in. But when Nebuchadnezzar looked in, he saw four men walking around in the fire, unbound and unharmed. Nebuchadnezzar said that the fourth man looked "like a son of the gods" (Daniel 3:25 NIV).

The king then called Shadrach, Meshach, and Abednego out of the furnace and declared that no one in the kingdom was to speak against their powerful God.

FIRE AND BRIMSTONE When Sodom and Gomorrah were destroyed, the King James Version says "brimstone and fire from the LORD" fell from the sky (Genesis 19:24). The New International Version calls it "burning sulfur." Brimstone is another word for sulfur, a flammable element that occurs naturally in the vicinity of the Dead Sea, where Sodom and Gomorrah were located. This burning sulfur may have been a natural volcanic phenomenon, or it may simply have been a miraculous act of God. Today the phrase "fire and brimstone" describes a brand of preaching characterized by dire warnings about hell.

FIRE FROM HEAVEN When the prophet Elijah challenged the prophets of Baal on Mount Carmel (1 Kings 18), he told them to ask their god to send fire from heaven to light a sacrifice that had been prepared. When Baal failed to respond, Elijah prayed to the Lord, who sent fire from heaven that consumed not only the sacrifice, but also the stones of the altar and the water that Elijah had poured over the sacrifice. Elijah then killed all the prophets of Baal. On another occasion, Elijah called down fire from heaven on two different

Mount Carmel—the traditional site of Elijah's confrontation with the prophets of Baal

contingents of fifty soldiers each (2 Kings 1). Today the expression "fire from heaven" can be used to describe any instance in which God responds supernaturally to a believer's prayer.

FLOOD, THE See *Noah.*

FORBIDDEN FRUIT When Adam and Eve were in the Garden of Eden, God told them they could eat the fruit of any tree in the Garden—except fruit from the tree of the knowledge of good and evil. When the serpent came, he tempted Eve to eat this forbidden fruit. He told her, "Your eyes will be opened, and you will be like God, knowing good and evil" (Genesis 3:5). Eve went ahead and ate the forbidden fruit and also gave some to Adam. This is called "the fall of man." "Forbidden fruit" has come to mean anything that is attractive but is not allowed.

GARDEN OF EDEN See *Eden, Garden of.*

GENTILE Any person who is not a Jew. In the Old Testament, the Israelites were commanded to treat foreigners (gentiles) in their midst with kindness, but God also strictly forbade the worship of the gods of the nations around them. Partly to protect the Israelites from worshiping other gods, the Lord also gave strict instructions that his people were not to intermarry with the gentiles around them. In the New Testament, there was a dispute among the early Christians as to whether gentiles had to become Jews first in order to become Christians. This dispute was resolved at the Council at Jerusalem (see *Jerusalem, Council at* in the chapter "People, Places, and Events in the New Testament"), where the conclusion was that gentile believers did not need to convert to Judaism.

GIDEON A judge and military leader in Israel during the period of the judges. When God told him to fight the Midianites (Judges 6–7), he wanted to confirm that he had really received a message from God. He put out a fleece (a sheepskin) overnight and prayed that the fleece would be wet with dew but that the ground around it would be dry. After this happened, he wanted further confirmation and prayed the next night that the fleece would be dry but the ground around it would be wet. When this also happened, he was convinced that God had spoken to him. He wanted to take an army of thousands, but God told him to take only 300 so he would know that the Midianites were defeated by the power of God rather than by Israel's own military might. ➧ Today a person who "puts out a fleece" is looking for a sign from God to confirm his plans.

GOATS Important domestic animals both in Old and New Testament times. They were used to provide food and milk, skins for tents and bottles (for example, wineskins), and wool for clothing. They were frequently used as sacrifices (see *scapegoat*). Because of the goat's independent nature, biblical writers sometimes used goats to symbolize the waywardness of God's people. Jesus described Judgment Day as a time when God will separate the sheep from the goats (Matthew 25). The sheep, representing people who showed God's love to others, will receive an eternal reward. The goats, representing those who did not show God's love to others, will receive eternal punishment.

GOD, GODS A supernatural deity that is considered by its adherents to be powerful in some or all spheres of human life. In ancient Near Eastern cultures, each nation or people had its own god or gods, and they were typically depicted by man-made idols. In the Old Testament, the Lord repeatedly told the Israelite people not to accept or worship the gods of the neighboring nations. And the Israelites were strictly forbidden to make an image of their God, Yahweh, who is seen by Jews and Christians as the one true God (see *Ten Commandments*).

GOLD Just like today, gold was a precious metal and a sign of wealth in both Old and New Testament times. The instruments in the tabernacle and the temple were made of gold to symbolize their purity. Gold was one of the gifts the wise men brought to the infant Jesus.

GOLDEN CALF After the Exodus from Egypt, the people of Israel went to Mount Sinai, where the

Lord met with Moses and gave him the covenant Law. Moses was on the mountain for forty days, so the people thought he had died. They asked Aaron to make a god for them, so he made a golden calf. The people said, "This is your god, O Israel, that brought you out of the land of Egypt!" (Exodus 32:4), and then they worshiped the golden calf. When Moses came down from the mountain, he was so angry that he threw down and broke the stone tablets on which God had inscribed the Law. Moses then ground up the golden calf and made the people drink it. He instructed the Levites to go among the people and kill many of them because of their sin.

GOLIATH A Philistine giant who was over nine feet tall (1 Samuel 17). Goliath had been taunting the army of Israel for forty days, challenging their best warrior to fight him one on one. None of the Israelites was willing to take the challenge. When young David heard about it, he declared that God would give him the power to defeat Goliath. David picked up five smooth stones and killed Goliath with his sling. Then, using Goliath's own sword, he cut off the giant's head. At this, the Israelite army routed the Philistine army. Today a "David and Goliath" contest is any situation in which the smaller or weaker opponent beats a vastly superior opponent.

GOMER A prostitute who became the wife of Hosea the prophet. She continued to commit adultery, but

Valley of Elah—the traditional location of David vs. Goliath

Hosea kept forgiving her and inviting her to return home. Hosea used this as an object lesson to show God's patience and forgiveness toward the idolatrous Northern Kingdom of Israel. He said they kept going after foreign gods as a prostitute goes after other men. But God kept offering to forgive the people of Israel and welcome them back to himself.

HAGAR When Sarah was unable to conceive a child, she gave her servant Hagar to Abraham as his concubine (Genesis 16). Hagar then had a son named Ishmael. Fifteen years later, in fulfillment of God's promise, Sarah finally had a son and named him Isaac. Sarah became so jealous of Hagar and Ishmael that she forced Abraham to send them away. Ishmael is commonly understood to be the ancestor of the Arabs.

HALLELUJAH A Hebrew word that means "praise Yahweh," or "praise the Lord." It is used frequently in the Old Testament as an expression of praise. Some English translations simply use the word *hallelujah*, while others translate it "praise the Lord." *Alleluia* is an alternate form of the word *hallelujah*. 📌 One of the best-known pieces of sacred music is the "Hallelujah Chorus" from Handel's *Messiah,* which quotes many Old and New Testament passages about the Messiah of Israel, Jesus Christ.

Partially restored ruins of the Babylonian king's palace

HANDWRITING ON THE WALL Several years after King Nebuchadnezzar's death, Belshazzar became king of Babylon. During a huge banquet in the palace, a hand appeared and wrote words on the plaster wall (Daniel 5). Belshazzar was terrified and called for his astrologers, but none of them could read the words or tell him their meaning. Then Daniel was called, and he interpreted the words for the king. The message was that God had numbered the days of the king's reign, that God had weighed the king in the balances and found him wanting, and that his kingdom would be divided and given to the Medes and the Persians. That very night, Belshazzar was killed, and the Persians took control of the kingdom (539 BC). 📌 Today the phrase "handwriting on the wall" is used to mean that the outcome to a situation is obvious, though perhaps not to the person who will be most affected by it.

HANNAH A devout woman who prayed for years that God would give her a son (1 Samuel 1–2). She promised that if she had a son, she would give him back to the Lord. When she finally did have a son, Samuel, she took him to the tabernacle as a young child to be an assistant to Eli, the high priest and a judge of Israel. Samuel became a great prophet and the last of the judges of Israel (see *judges, period of the*).

HEBREWS (THE PEOPLE) The descendants of Abraham through Isaac and Jacob—the Israelites—are sometimes called Hebrews. The Old Testament was written in Hebrew. This ancient language began its revival in the late nineteenth century, and a modern version of Hebrew is spoken today in the state of Israel.

HEZEKIAH The king of Judah at the time the Kingdom of Israel fell to the Assyrians in 722 BC. He was a good king, and he destroyed the pagan idols and altars in Judah and reopened the temple in Jerusalem (2 Kings 18–20). Once when he was deathly ill he prayed that the Lord would spare his life. Through the prophet Isaiah, the Lord promised Hezekiah that he would live another fifteen years.

Vestments of Israel's high priest on display at the Temple Institute in Jerusalem

HIGH PRIEST In the Old Testament, the descendants of Aaron, the older brother of Moses, were the priests in Israel. Aaron was the first high priest, the chief among the priests. This was a position that was passed from father to son. The high priest went into the Holy of Holies on the Day of Atonement to burn incense and sprinkle sacrificial blood to make atonement for the Israelites. In New Testament times, the high priest was the president of the Sanhedrin—the highest office among the priests of Israel. Caiaphas was the high priest during the time of Jesus's ministry. Caiaphas's father-in-law, Annas, is also called the high priest in the Gospel accounts. He had actually been removed from that position by the Romans, but he was honored by the people as though he were still the high priest.

HOLY LAND A name often used today for the land of Israel.

HOLY OF HOLIES Also called the Most Holy Place, this was the innermost room of the tabernacle and of the temple (Exodus 26). It was here that the presence of the Lord dwelt among the people of Israel. The ark of the covenant and the gold cherubim were the only objects in the Holy of Holies. The cover of the ark—called the mercy seat, or atonement cover—had gold-plated cherubim attached at each end. Only the high priest could enter the Holy of Holies, and even he could enter only once a year—on the Day of Atonement.

HOSEA A prophet in the Northern Kingdom of Israel; his prophecies are recorded in the book of Hosea. The Lord told him to marry a prostitute to show that Israel was like an unfaithful wife. Hosea's wife, Gomer, continued to commit adultery, and Hosea continued to forgive her and invite her to return to their home. This became an object lesson of God's patience with the people of Israel.

HYSSOP An aromatic shrub. In preparation for the first Passover at the time of the Exodus from Egypt, the Israelites used hyssop branches to spread blood on the doorposts of their houses. When Jesus was on the cross, a sponge with wine was put on a stalk of hyssop and lifted up to him.

IDOL Any man-made image that is worshiped. The Ten Commandments are very explicit in stating that the Israelites were not to make or worship idols. Nonetheless, starting with Aaron's golden calf, the people of Israel repeatedly turned to idol worship, often borrowing the gods of the nations around them.

ISAAC The son who was promised to Abraham and Sarah and who was born in their old age. When Isaac was just a lad, God tested Abraham's faith by telling him to sacrifice Isaac on an altar (Genesis 22). Abraham sorrowfully prepared to do so. At the last moment, just before Abraham would have killed Isaac, an angel stopped him and showed him a ram caught in a thicket. Abraham sacrificed the ram in place of Isaac. Years later, Isaac and his wife, Rebekah, had twin sons, Esau and Jacob. Isaac was one of the great patriarchs of Israel.

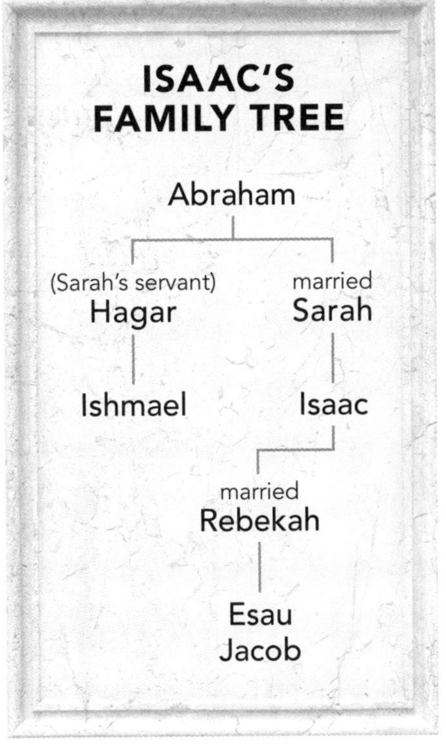

ISAIAH One of the great prophets in the Southern Kingdom of Judah. Isaiah's ministry began when he saw a vision of the Lord in the temple. He records in Isaiah 6:1, "In the year that King Uzziah died, I saw the Lord." The Lord asked, "Whom should I send as a messenger to this people? Who will go for us?" Isaiah responded, "Here I am. Send me" (verse 8 NLT). Isaiah's messages include prophecies of the coming Messiah: "The virgin will conceive a child! She will give birth to a son and will call him Immanuel" (Isaiah 7:14 NLT); "For to us a child is born, to us a son is given, and the government will be on his shoulders. And he will be called Wonderful Counselor, Mighty God, Everlasting Father, Prince of Peace" (Isaiah 9:6 NIV). Another prophecy was, "He is despised and rejected of men; a man of sorrows, and acquainted with grief.... Surely he hath borne our griefs, and carried our sorrows.... He was wounded for our transgressions, he was bruised for our iniquities: the chastisement of our peace was upon him; and with his stripes we are healed. All we like sheep have gone astray; we have turned every one to his own way; and the LORD hath laid on him the iniquity of us all" (Isaiah 53:3–6 KJV).

ISHMAEL The son of Abraham and his concubine, Hagar (Genesis 16). Isaac was born to Abraham and Sarah when Ishmael was about fifteen years old. Sarah had always been jealous of Hagar, but now that she had a son of her own, she couldn't stand to have Hagar and Ishmael around. She forced Abraham to send them away. The Lord cared for Hagar and Ishmael in the wilderness, and Ishmael grew up to be a great hunter. The Arabs, who commonly regard themselves as descendants of Ishmael, are still at enmity with the Jews, the descendants of Isaac.

ISRAEL (THE LAND) Ancient Israel was the region on the southeastern shore of the Mediterranean Sea. It included all of the territory in the modern state of Israel (including the West Bank) and part of what is now Lebanon, Syria, and Jordan. It was bounded by the Mediterranean Sea on the west, Syria on the north, the Arabian Desert on the East, and Egypt on the south. It is a dry and hilly land, though it is described in the Old Testament as a land flowing with milk and honey. See also *Canaan*; *Israel, Israelites (the people)*; *Israel, Kingdom of.*

ISRAEL (THE MAN) When Jacob wrestled with God, God changed Jacob's name to Israel, which means "he struggles with God" (Genesis 32). His sons were the patriarchs of the twelve tribes of Israel. The name Israel was later used for the entire nation, then for the Northern Kingdom. The name Israel is also used in the New Testament to represent believers who have been grafted in to the nation of Israel through belief in Jesus Christ.

ISRAEL, ISRAELITES (THE PEOPLE) The descendants of Abraham through Isaac and Jacob (who was later called Israel) are called the Israelites, or simply Israel. They are also called the children of Israel, the chosen people, or Hebrews. See also *Israel, Kingdom of.*

ISRAEL, KINGDOM OF After the period of the judges, the people of Israel demanded that they have a king, as the nations around them had. The prophet Samuel told them they needed no king but God, but the people insisted. God then told Samuel to anoint Saul as king (1 Samuel 9). Saul ruled over the Kingdom of Israel for forty years, but he had no remorse for disobeying God's instructions, and God told him his descendants would

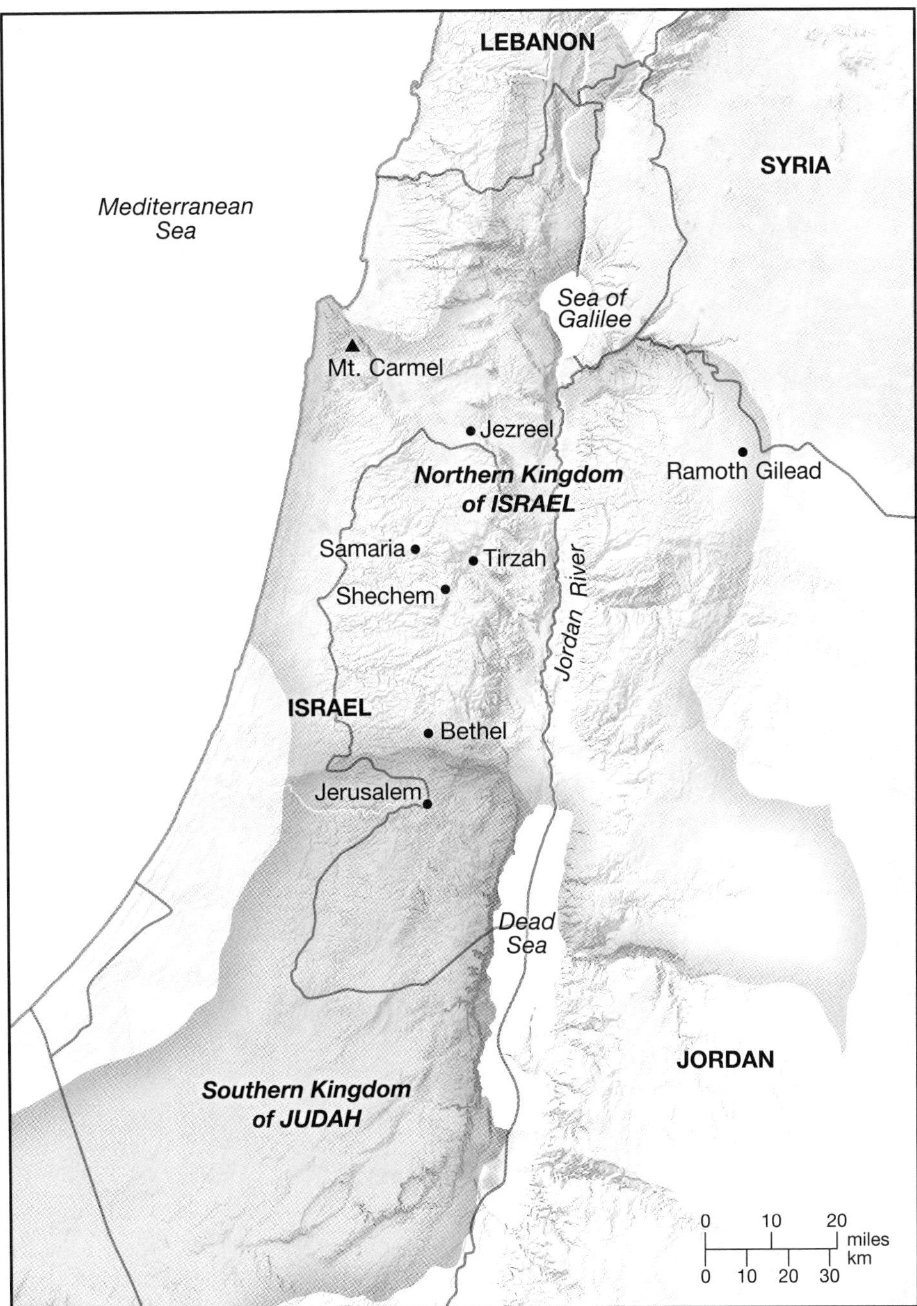

The Land of Israel In Bible times, as today, Israel was at the southeastern edge of the Mediterranean Sea. All of Israel was under one government during the reigns of Saul, David, and Solomon. The kingdom was then divided into the Kingdoms of Israel and Judah (see 1 Kings 11–12).

not succeed him. Instead, God chose David as king, and David's son Solomon after him. These three monarchs reigned for a total of 120 years. This period is often called the United Kingdom, in contrast to the Divided Kingdom that followed. After Solomon's death in 930 BC, his son Rehoboam became king (1 Kings 12). The ten northern tribes of Israel refused to submit to his authority, however, and they established their own kingdom (called the Kingdom of Israel) with Jeroboam as king. The two southern tribes, Judah and Benjamin, became the Kingdom of Judah (the Southern Kingdom) under Rehoboam. The people of the Northern Kingdom of Israel worshiped idols and survived as an independent nation only until 722 BC, when it fell to Assyria as a result of God's judgment.

JACOB Esau and Jacob were the twin sons of Isaac and Rebekah and grandsons of the Israelite patriarch Abraham and his wife, Sarah. Once when Esau, the older of the two, had been out hunting, he became famished and sold his birthright to Jacob for stew that Jacob had just made. When Isaac was old and blind, he was ready to give Esau his blessing. Esau went hunting so he could prepare Isaac's favorite meal, but Jacob tricked his father by wearing goatskins on his arms and neck so Isaac would think

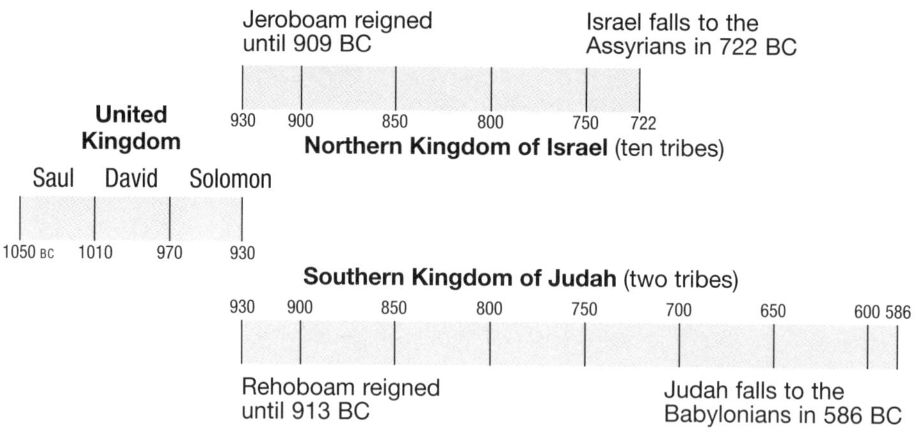

Kingdom of Israel After Solomon's reign, the Kingdom of Israel was divided and became the Northern Kingdom of Israel and the Southern Kingdom of Judah. See 1 Kings 11–12.

he was Esau, who was very hairy. Thus Isaac blessed Jacob with the blessing of the firstborn, instead of Esau. Jacob had four wives, twelve sons, and one daughter. His favorite sons were Joseph and Benjamin, from his favorite wife, Rachel. Jacob gave Joseph a coat of many colors as a sign of his favoritism. Joseph's brothers were offended, so they sold Joseph into slavery and reported to Jacob that Joseph had been killed by a wild animal. Years later, when Joseph was prime minister of Egypt, Jacob and his other sons went to Egypt to live. The stories of Jacob are found in Genesis 25–47. See also *Israel (the man)*.

JACOB'S LADDER After Jacob tricked his father and stole his brother Esau's firstborn blessing, Jacob left home to escape Esau's wrath (Genesis 28). While en route to live with his uncle Laban, he had a dream. He saw a ladder (stairway) stretching from heaven to earth, with angels going up and down. The Lord was at the top of the stairway and promised to bless Jacob and

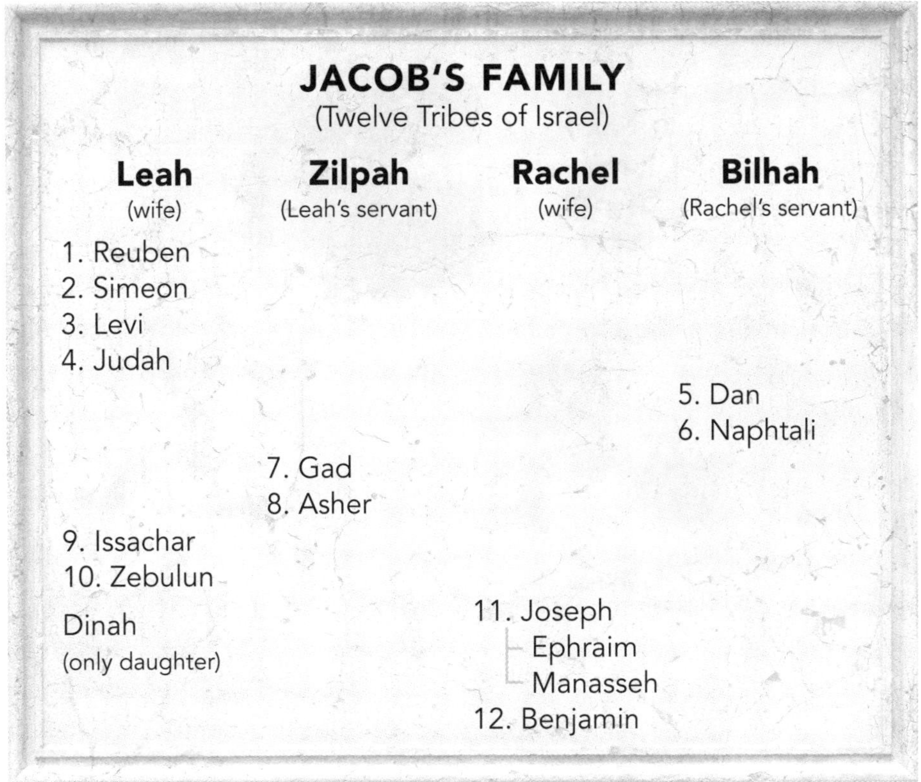

JACOB'S FAMILY
(Twelve Tribes of Israel)

Leah (wife)	**Zilpah** (Leah's servant)	**Rachel** (wife)	**Bilhah** (Rachel's servant)
1. Reuben 2. Simeon 3. Levi 4. Judah			
			5. Dan 6. Naphtali
	7. Gad 8. Asher		
9. Issachar 10. Zebulun			
Dinah (only daughter)		11. Joseph – Ephraim – Manasseh 12. Benjamin	

his descendants—just as he had promised to bless his grandfather Abraham and his father, Isaac. Jacob named the place Bethel, which means "house of God."

JEHU An army commander who became one of the kings of the Northern Kingdom of Israel (2 Kings 9–10). He was responsible for the death of the wicked queen Jezebel. He tricked all the priests of Baal into coming together in the temple of Baal—and he slaughtered them there. Jehu was renowned for driving his chariot fast, so today a "Jehu" is a fast and wild driver.

JEREMIAH One of the great prophets in the Southern Kingdom of Judah. He is known as the "weeping prophet." His prophecies are recorded in the book of Jeremiah, where he predicted the destruction of Jerusalem. Later, looking back, he wrote the book of Lamentations, which is a lament about the destruction of Jerusalem. Because much of the book of Jeremiah is a prophecy of the doom of Jerusalem and the Kingdom of Judah, the word *jeremiad* means a long lamentation or complaint.

JERICHO A walled city east of Jerusalem, near the Jordan River and the Dead Sea. It is one of the oldest cities in the world. When Joshua led the Israelites into the Promised Land, their first conquest was Jericho (see *Jericho, Battle of*). The treacherous road between Jerusalem and Jericho was the setting for Jesus's Parable of the Good Samaritan.

Ancient ruins of Jericho

JERICHO, BATTLE OF When Joshua led the Israelites into the Promised Land, their first conquest was the walled city of Jericho (Joshua 6). Joshua had earlier sent spies into Jericho, who had been assisted by Rahab, a prostitute. Because of her bravery, the spies assured her that she and her family would not be killed when Jericho was attacked. Following instructions from an angel, Joshua told his army to march around the walled city of Jericho each day for six days.

On the seventh day they marched around the city seven times. The Lord then caused the walls of the city to fall down, and the Israelite army went in and destroyed all the inhabitants of the city except Rahab and her family.

JEROBOAM After King Solomon's death, his son Rehoboam succeeded him as king of Israel. The people of the ten northern tribes rebelled against Rehoboam, however, and crowned Jeroboam as their king (1 Kings 12). Only the tribes of Judah and Benjamin remained loyal to Rehoboam. This was the start of the Divided Kingdom, which consisted of the Northern Kingdom of Israel and the Southern Kingdom of Judah. Jeroboam was a wicked king who set up new centers of worship to rival Jerusalem, and he led his people into idol worship.

JERUSALEM The capital city of Israel from the time of King David to the time of the New Testament. It is located on hills between the Mediterranean Sea and the Jordan River. King Solomon built the temple in Jerusalem on the spot where the Israelite patriarch Abraham was thought to have taken his son Isaac to sacrifice him. So Jerusalem, in addition to its political significance, was the central place of worship for the Israelites. Many key events in the Bible took place in and around Jerusalem, including the crucifixion and resurrection of Jesus. In

The Old City of Jerusalem is enclosed by walls dating from the sixteenth century.

AD 70 Jerusalem was destroyed by the Romans. In a theological sense, Jerusalem is frequently used in the Bible as a symbol of God's justice and mercy, just as Babylon is often used as a symbol of wickedness. The New Testament refers to the "new Jerusalem" (Revelation 21), a heavenly and holy city. Today Jerusalem is a holy city for Jews, Christians, and Muslims. The Temple Mount is sacred to Jews, but it has for centuries been the site of a Muslim shrine called the Dome of the Rock. The Western Wall (Wailing Wall), all that remains from Herod's temple, is the most sacred spot for all Jews. Jerusalem contains many spots sacred to Christians, including the garden of Gethsemane, the Church of the Holy Sepulchre (an ancient church on the traditional site of Jesus's crucifixion and resurrection), and the Garden Tomb (an alternate site of the Resurrection). From 1948–1967, Jerusalem was divided: The eastern part (the walled "Old City") was controlled by the Kingdom of Jordan, and the western part (the "new city") was controlled by the state of Israel. Following the Six-Day War of 1967, the two parts of the city were united under the control of Israel. Jerusalem is still a source of great conflict and tension between Israelis and Arabs. Jerusalem is the capital of modern Israel, but for political reasons most other countries do not recognize it as the capital.

JEWS Descendants of the Israelite patriarch Abraham through Isaac and Jacob. For the most part, the Jews descend from the tribes of Judah and Benjamin, which comprised the Southern Kingdom of Judah (the word *Jew* is derived from the name Judah). Jesus and his disciples were Jews, as were the apostle Paul and most of the earliest Christians. Jews today fall into four main groups: Orthodox, Conservative, Reform, and those who characterize themselves as cultural Jews but without religious affiliation. Unfortunately, although the Christian church has its roots in Judaism, Jews have suffered greatly at the hands of Christians since the time of Christ. Jews have been persecuted and killed in the "Christian" nations of Europe for centuries, the most atrocious example of which was the Holocaust during World War II.

JEZEBEL Daughter of a Phoenician king and wife of King Ahab of the Northern Kingdom of Israel. Jezebel ranks as the most wicked woman mentioned in the Bible (1 Kings 16–22). A wicked woman in the New Testament book of Revelation is also called Jezebel—an allusion to the Jezebel of the Old Testament. Jezebel promoted worship of the false god Baal and persecuted the prophets of God. During her reign, Elijah defeated the prophets of Baal by calling down fire from heaven. At Jehu's instigation, Jezebel was thrown out a window and trampled to death by horses (2 Kings 9). Dogs ate her body, as prophesied by Elijah.

JOAB The general of King David's army, he was a brilliant military leader. He murdered Abner, King Saul's general, and later he murdered King David's son Absalom when Absalom led a revolt against David (2 Samuel 18).

JOASH One of the kings of the Kingdom of Judah (2 Kings 11–12). His father died when Joash was an infant, and his wicked grandmother tried to kill all of the royal line. But Joash was saved by a loyal aunt and hidden in the temple for six years. He was crowned king when he was seven years old. He had a long and good reign, during which he renovated the temple, but he allowed the reintroduction of pagan practices. He sent the temple treasures to Syria as a bribe to keep Syria from invading Judah.

JOB (pronounced *Jōb*) A righteous and wealthy man who lost all his possessions, his children, and his own health—but refused to curse God. According to the story in the book of Job, God pointed to Job as a particularly good and God-fearing man. Satan responded that Job would curse God if Job's wealth were taken away. God told Satan he could attack Job's wealth and his family, but he could not kill Job himself. So Satan arranged for Job's wealth to be destroyed and for his ten children to be killed. But Job still said, "Blessed be the name of the LORD" (Job 1:21). After Satan caused Job to break out with boils all over his body, his wife told him to "curse God and die" (Job 2:9), and three of Job's friends (see *Job's comforters*) told him that his misfortunes were the result of sin in his life. When Job stayed true to God through it all, God rewarded him with ten more children, and twice as much wealth as he had before. The expression "patience of Job" is proverbial (it is even mentioned as a proverb in James 5:11) because Job trusted God despite all the tragedy in his life.

JOB'S COMFORTERS The book of Job (pronounced *Jōb*) tells the story of Job, a righteous man who was tormented by Satan. Three of Job's friends came to comfort him in his distress, but they told him that his problems were the result of sin in his life. Today people may be called "Job's comforters" if they claim to give comfort but really bring blame upon the person they are "comforting."

JONAH A prophet to the Northern Kingdom of Israel who was sent to preach to the people of Nineveh, the capital of Assyria. Jonah was afraid to go to Nineveh and tried to run away, but God intercepted him (see *Jonah and the great fish*) and sent him to Nineveh anyway. Jonah's message in Nineveh was that God would destroy the city if the people did not repent from their wicked ways. The people of Nineveh responded to Jonah's

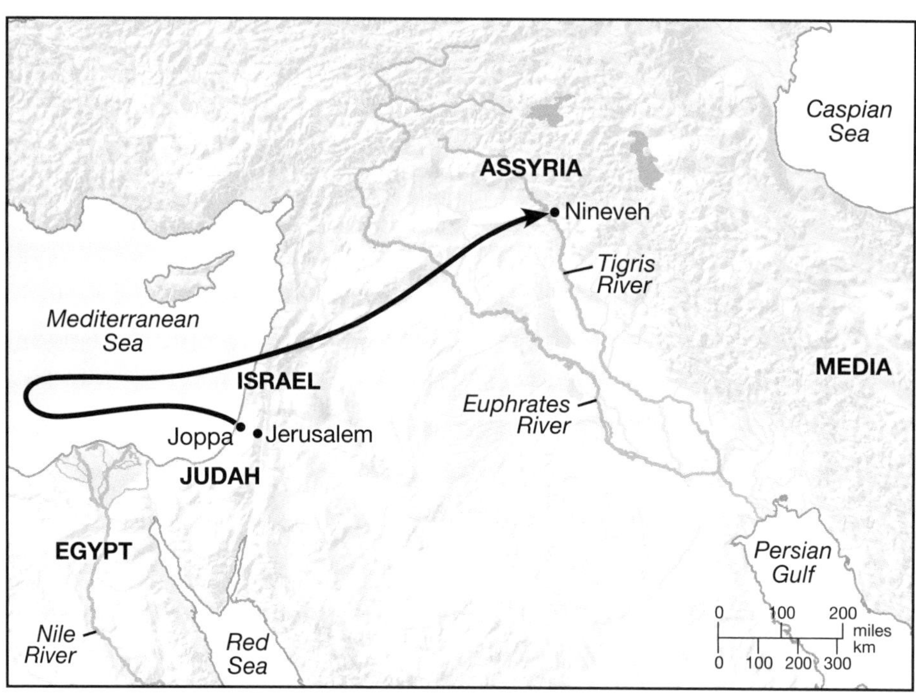

Jonah's Roundabout Journey God told Jonah to go to Nineveh, the capital of the Assyrian Empire. Many of Jonah's countrymen had experienced the atrocities of these fierce people. The last place Jonah wanted to go on a missionary journey was Nineveh. So he went in the opposite direction. In Joppa he boarded a ship that was headed to Tarshish. But Jonah could not run from God.

message and did repent of their sins, so God relented and did not destroy the city. Jonah was angry that God did not destroy Nineveh, but God showed Jonah that he felt compassion for the many inhabitants of Nineveh.

Modern-day port of Jaffa (Joppa), where Jonah began his journey

JONAH AND THE GREAT FISH When Jonah was sent to preach in Nineveh, the capital of Assyria, he rebelled and tried to run away from God. He boarded a ship on the Mediterranean Sea and sailed westward. A great storm arose, and Jonah realized that the storm had been sent by God because of his sin, so he convinced the sailors that the storm would stop only if they threw him overboard. They did so and the storm stopped, and Jonah was swallowed by "a great fish" (Jonah 1:17). He was in the fish's belly for three days, which gave him an opportunity to reflect on his situation and repent. The fish then spit Jonah onto the land, and Jonah went and preached in Nineveh as he had been directed. His story is told in the book of Jonah. Biblical critics have said this story could never have happened because a person could not live to tell about being swallowed by a gigantic fish. In 1891, a story was widely circulated regarding James Bartley, a sailor on a whaling ship, who was swept overboard and swallowed by a sperm whale. The whale was subsequently harpooned and killed. As the whale was being butchered the next day, Bartley's fellow whalers found him in the whale's stomach and rescued him.

JONATHAN The son of King Saul, and David's close friend (1 Samuel 18). Saul was very jealous of David, and on several occasions Jonathan protected David from Saul. Jonathan was a brave soldier, but he and Saul died in a battle with the Philistines. David was then crowned king of Israel.

JORDAN RIVER The primary river that runs through the land of Israel. Its headwaters are on Mount Hermon, from which it flows into the Sea of Galilee, then south to the

Dead Sea, where it ends. Although it is only about seventy miles long, it drops more than 1,500 feet during its brief course. Most of the river is below sea level. The Jordan River plays a significant role in both Old and New Testament history. When Joshua led the Israelites into the Promised Land, they had to cross the Jordan River. The Lord performed a miracle for them by holding back the water of the river so they could cross on dry land. John the Baptist baptized Jesus in the Jordan River. 📌 "Crossing the Jordan River" has frequently been used as a metaphor for dying, as in the spirituals "Gonna Lay Down My Burden" and "Michael, Row the Boat Ashore."

Jordan River

JOSEPH Joseph and Benjamin were the sons of Jacob and Rachel (Genesis 37–50). Jacob gave Joseph a coat of many colors, which made Joseph's brothers jealous. His brothers wanted to kill him, but Judah persuaded the others not to do it. Instead, they sold Joseph as a slave. Joseph was taken to Egypt, where he became chief steward in the household of Potiphar. Potiphar's wife tried to seduce him, then accused him of raping her when he would not yield to her seduction. He was thrown into prison, where he interpreted dreams for several of Pharaoh's staff (Pharaoh was the king of Egypt) who were also in prison. Joseph was released from prison when Pharaoh needed someone to interpret a dream. Joseph told him the dream meant that there would be seven years of plenty followed by seven years of famine. He recommended that Pharaoh institute a plan of food storage during the years of good harvests in preparation for the years of famine. Joseph was put in charge of this program and was second only to Pharaoh in power. The famine affected the land of Canaan also, where Jacob and his family lived, so Jacob sent his ten older sons to Egypt to buy grain. Joseph recognized his brothers, but they did not recognize him. When Joseph found that they were sorry for what they had done to their brother, he identified himself.

Jacob and his sons and their families all moved to Egypt, where their descendants lived for 400 years until the time of the Exodus.

JOSHUA Succeeded Moses as the leader of the Israelites. His story is told in the books of Exodus, Numbers, and Joshua. He was both a military leader and a spiritual leader. When it was time for Joshua to lead the people into the Promised Land, the Lord held back the water of the Jordan River so the entire nation could cross over on dry ground. Joshua's first victory in Canaan was in the Battle of Jericho, and he led the people of Israel in a systematic conquest of the land. When he was an old man, he again challenged the people to follow the Lord, saying, "Choose for yourselves this day whom you will serve.... But as for me and my house, we will serve the LORD" (Joshua 24:15). See also *Caleb*.

JOSIAH Became king of the Southern Kingdom of Judah at the age of eight (2 Kings 21–23). The people of Judah had drifted away from the Lord and no longer remembered the Mosaic law. When a scroll containing the Law was found in the temple, Josiah led the nation into repentance and then back into vibrant worship of the Lord. Because of this, the Lord promised Josiah that Judah would not be destroyed until after Josiah's death. It was twenty-three years after his death that the Babylonians destroyed Jerusalem (586 BC) and took many of its people to Babylon as captives.

JUDAH One of Jacob's twelve sons (Genesis 38) and the patriarch of the tribe of Judah. King David was a descendant of Judah, as was Jesus.

JUDAH, KINGDOM OF After King Solomon's death in 930 BC, his son Rehoboam became king. The ten northern tribes of Israel refused to submit to his authority, however, and they established their own kingdom (called the Kingdom of Israel) with Jeroboam as king. The two southern tribes, Judah and Benjamin, became the Kingdom of Judah (1 Kings 12), with Jerusalem as its capital. The Kingdoms of Judah and Israel coexisted until Israel (the Northern Kingdom) fell to Assyria in 722 BC. Judah (the Southern Kingdom) survived as an independent nation until it fell to the Babylonians in 586 BC (2 Kings 25). See also *Israel, Kingdom of*; *Divided Kingdom*.

JUDAH, TRIBE OF The descendants of Jacob's son Judah became the tribe of Judah. David and his royal descendants were from the tribe of Judah. Judah and Benjamin were the two tribes that remained loyal to King Solomon's son Rehoboam, forming the Southern Kingdom of Judah. Jesus was a descendant of Judah and of David. The English word *Jew* is derived from Judah.

JUDAISM The religion of the Jews, particularly as it developed from the time of the Babylonian Exile. Judaism came to include a complex system of regulations to help the Jews keep the 613 commandments in the Torah (also called the Books of Moses or the Pentateuch). These additional regulations, codified in the Jewish religious text called the Talmud, "make a hedge around the Torah." If the people obeyed all the regulations, they would automatically be obeying the laws in the Torah.

JUDGES, PERIOD OF THE After the death of Moses, Joshua led the Israelites into the Promised Land (Canaan). Joshua was the military and religious leader of the nation during the conquest of Canaan. After his death, there was a period of about 200–325 years (there are varying scholarly opinions) called the period of the judges. There was no central government, and it was a time of anarchy in Israel, for "everyone did what was right in his own eyes" (Judges 21:25). The neighboring nations, particularly the Philistines, raided Israelite cities and generally made life difficult for Israel. Occasional leaders, called judges, arose to lead the people against their enemies. Some of these judges were Deborah, Gideon, and Samson, whose stories are told in the book of Judges. The period of the judges came to an end when the people told the prophet and judge Samuel they wanted a king—just like the nations around them (1 Samuel 8). Samuel knew this was a mistake, but the Lord let the people have their way and instructed Samuel to anoint Saul to be the first king of Israel.

LAND FLOWING WITH MILK AND HONEY This is a description of Canaan, the Promised Land—eventually known as the land of Israel. The expression means that the land was fruitful and pleasant. When Joshua and Caleb and the other spies returned from spying out the land after the Exodus, they reported, "It is indeed a bountiful country—a land flowing with milk and honey" (Numbers 13:27 NLT). ➤ Visitors to Israel today wonder at this description of a lush and fruitful land, because much of the land now is arid and rocky. The land has never had a very moderate climate, but evidently there were substantial areas of forest at the time of the Exodus. The land was deforested after the Roman conquest and during the time of the Ottoman Empire, and tremendous amounts of erosion have washed away much of the topsoil. Over recent decades, however, a significant amount of trees have been replanted, and agriculture is advancing through the use of greenhouses, irrigation, and innovative technologies. As prophesied in the book of Isaiah, "Israel will bud and blossom and fill the whole earth with fruit!" (27:6 NLT).

LAW, THE In the Bible, the term *the Law* refers to the Mosaic law or to the Books of Law in their entirety. (See also *Torah* and *Law, Books of* in the chapter "Bible Overview." For a more complete explanation of the Law, see *Mosaic law* in this chapter.) After Jesus gave the two greatest commandments, he said, "On these two commandments hang all the Law and the Prophets" (Matthew 22:40) (see *You shall love the Lord your God ...* and *Love your neighbor as yourself* in the chapter "Famous Sayings from the Bible"). By "all the Law" he meant the Books of Law, and "the Prophets" meant the books of history and the Books of Prophecy.

LEAH Leah and her sister, Rachel, were both wives of Jacob (Genesis 29–30). Jacob worked for seven years to earn the right to marry Rachel, but her father tricked Jacob and gave him Leah instead. Jacob was then allowed to marry Rachel also after he promised to work another seven years. Leah bore six of Jacob's twelve sons, including Judah and Levi.

LEAVEN Another name for yeast, the agent that causes bread to rise. In the Bible, leaven is often used as a metaphor for evil and its corrupting power (for example, see Matthew 16:5–12). See also *unleavened bread.*

LEPER, LEPROSY An infectious disease that was dreaded in Bible times because there was no cure for it. The disease deadens nerve endings, so a leper (a person with leprosy) could cut or burn himself without even realizing it. Lepers were quarantined outside the camp or village and became social outcasts. Jesus broke the social custom by talking to and even touching lepers as he healed them. 📌 Leprosy is now called Hansen's disease, and it still afflicts approximately 200,000 people in parts of Africa, India, and South America. It is unclear, however, whether this is the same "leprosy" mentioned in the Bible.

Healing of the Leper at Capernaum

LEVI One of Jacob's sons and the patriarch of the tribe of Levi. His descendants were called Levites, and they became priests and temple workers. Moses, Aaron, and Miriam were descendants of Levi.

LEVIATHAN There is a lengthy description of the leviathan, a very fierce sea creature, in Job 41. It may have been a crocodile. God was rebuking Job by showing his great power in creating such an awesome animal. See also *behemoth.*

LEVITES The members of the tribe of Levi (the descendants of Levi, one of the sons of Jacob) were called the Levites. They were given special responsibility for the care of the tabernacle and then the temple. The Levites did not receive any land of their own when the Israelites entered the Promised Land. Instead, the other tribes were to support the Levites through their tithes. The descendants of Aaron constituted one branch of the Levites, and they alone were allowed to serve as priests. In Jesus's Parable of the Good Samaritan, the two men who passed by without helping the man who had been robbed and beaten were a priest and a Levite.

LOST TRIBES OF ISRAEL The ten northern tribes are the lost tribes of Israel. When the Northern Kingdom of Israel was defeated by the Assyrians in 722 BC, many of the people of those ten tribes of Israel were deported to Assyria (see *Exile*). They never returned to their own land (2 Kings 17). They were assimilated into the cultures around them and ceased to exist as a distinct people. Those who were not taken into exile in Assyria also intermarried with the nations around them, and they lost their distinctiveness as Israelites. Their descendants became the Samaritans of the New Testament period. They too eventually lost their distinctiveness and nearly ceased to exist as a separate people. There is a very small community of Samaritans, however, still living in Israel. From the fall of the United Kingdom of Israel onward (including the entire New Testament period), "the Jews" are primarily members of the tribes of Judah or Benjamin, the two tribes that made up the Southern Kingdom of Judah. 📌 There has been much speculation as to what happened to the lost tribes of Israel, including fanciful conclusions that they migrated to the British Isles or to America.

LOT Nephew of the Israelite patriarch Abraham, who traveled with Abraham from Ur to Canaan. When the land became too crowded for both of them and their vast flocks, Abraham allowed Lot to choose which part of the land he wanted for himself, and Abraham took the other portion. Lot moved toward Sodom and Gomorrah, where he barely escaped with his life when the cities were destroyed (Genesis 18–19). Lot's wife turned into a pillar of salt when she looked back as they fled from the fiery destruction of the cities.

LOT'S WIFE Her name is not given in the Bible, but she is well known because of the way she died. When she and her family were fleeing from the destruction of Sodom and Gomorrah, the angel who was leading them told them not to look back. Lot's wife disobeyed, and she was turned into a pillar of salt (Genesis 19).

MANNA When the Israelites were in the wilderness after the Exodus, they soon ran out of food. God miraculously provided for them by sending manna, a white substance that fell on the ground each morning (Exodus 16). The people gathered it and ate it. God provided food for them in this way each day (except on the Sabbath) for forty years. We're not sure exactly what it was, but neither did the Israelites. They called it "manna," which means "what is it?" Manna provided spiritual lessons as well as physical sustenance. When Moses gave his farewell address to the Israelites before he died, he reminded them that God had provided manna to teach them "that man does not live on bread alone but on every word that comes from the mouth of the LORD" (Deuteronomy 8:3 NIV). When Jesus was tempted by Satan in the wilderness, he quoted this passage of Scripture (see *temptation of Jesus* in the chapter "People, Places, and Events in the New Testament").

The Mediterranean coast—
Tel Aviv, Israel

MEDITERRANEAN SEA The great sea between Europe, Africa, and Asia. Most of the events in the Bible take place in the lands immediately surrounding the eastern end of the Mediterranean Sea. The story of Jonah and the great fish takes place in the Mediterranean Sea, and the apostle Paul traveled the Mediterranean on each of his missionary journeys. The land of Israel is at the southeastern end of the Mediterranean Sea.

MELCHIZEDEK He was the king of Salem (probably an early name for the city of Jerusalem) and the priest of "God Most High" (Genesis 14:18) when Abraham moved to Canaan. Abraham gave Melchizedek one-tenth of the spoils he had gotten in a battle. This is all the information the Bible gives us about Melchizedek, but Psalm 110 and the book of Hebrews indicate that he is seen as superior to all subsequent priests of Israel. He is an Old Testament person who points the way to Christ.

METHUSELAH The grandfather of Noah, he is the oldest person listed in the Bible. He lived to the age of 969 years. According to the genealogy in Genesis 5, it appears that Methuselah died in the year of the Flood.

MIRIAM The sister of Moses and Aaron. When the infant Moses was found by the pharaoh's daughter, his big sister, Miriam, offered to find a Hebrew woman (the baby's own mother) to care for him (see *Moses in the bulrushes*). With her brothers, Miriam was a leader of the people through the entire event of the Exodus and the years the Israelites were in the wilderness (as recounted in Exodus and Numbers). After the parting of the Red Sea, Miriam led all the women of Israel in praising the Lord through singing and dancing. Later, Miriam and Aaron were jealous of Moses's unique position of leadership, and God punished Miriam by inflicting her with leprosy for seven days.

MOSAIC LAW After the Israelites left Egypt, the Lord gave Moses the Ten Commandments and numerous other laws (Exodus 19–40). This entire system of laws, called the Mosaic law or simply the Law, provided the framework for the Israelites' relationships with God, with one another, and with the nations around them. It included the laws regarding the sacrifices, by which the people of Israel could worship God and make atonement for their sins. The Mosaic law is a central theme of the Books of Moses, or Torah. After the Exile the Jews developed the Talmud, a complex system of additional laws to "build a hedge around the Torah." A person could be certain of keeping the Torah by strictly observing all these additional regulations. Christian teaching, particularly as developed by the apostle Paul, shows that we can never keep the Law to God's satisfaction. Instead of the sacrifices required under the Mosaic law, Jesus's death serves as the ultimate sacrifice to provide atonement for our sins once and for all. Many people are confused as to why Christians have traditionally kept some but not all of the Old Testament laws or regulations. The distinction is between the ceremonial law, which no longer applies to Christians under the new covenant, and the moral law (for example, the Ten Commandments), which is still God's standard for right living.

MOSES One of the greatest leaders in Israel's history. His story is told in the books of Exodus and Numbers. His parents were slaves in Egypt when he was born, but through unusual circumstances he grew up in the household of Pharaoh, king of Egypt. When he became an adult, he recognized his heritage and killed an Egyptian while trying to help a fellow Israelite. He fled to Midian (in present-day Saudi Arabia), where he was a shepherd for forty years. There he met the Lord at the burning bush. The

Lord told him to tell Pharaoh, "Let my people go" (Exodus 5:1 NLT). Moses and his brother, Aaron, asked Pharaoh to let the Israelites leave Egypt. Pharaoh refused, so the Lord sent a series of plagues upon Egypt. Finally, after the death of the firstborn son in each family of Egypt, Moses was able to lead the people out of Egypt. He led them for forty years as they "wandered" in the wilderness. During that time Moses received the Ten Commandments and the rest of the Law from the Lord at Mount Sinai. He also wrote the Books of Moses, which are the first five books of the Old Testament. He is revered as the great lawgiver for Israel. See also *Moses in the bulrushes*; *Exodus, the*; *Mosaic law.*

MOSES IN THE BULRUSHES
Moses was born in Egypt at a time when the Hebrews (the descendants of Jacob's twelve sons) had become a large nation and were a threat to the Egyptians. To keep the Hebrews from becoming an even greater threat, Pharaoh decreed that all boys born to Hebrew women were to be thrown into the Nile River and drowned (Exodus 1). Moses's parents did not obey this command, but as their infant grew, they were fearful he would be found. They prayed and then trusted God to protect their baby. They made a basket of bulrushes (papyrus reeds) and waterproofed it with tar. Then they put Moses in the basket and set the basket adrift on the river. His older

Pharaoh's Daughter Finding Baby Moses

sister, Miriam, hid in the bulrushes to see what would happen. One of the daughters of Pharaoh came to the river to bathe and saw the basket. When she saw the baby, she decided to keep him and raise him as her own son. Miriam stepped out and offered to find a Hebrew nurse for the baby—then ran home to get her own mother! As a result, Moses spent his first several years with his own parents, then lived in Pharaoh's royal household as a son of the princess.

MOUNT SINAI See *Sinai, Mount.*

NAOMI Ruth's mother-in-law. Naomi was from Israel, but she and her husband and two sons moved to Moab (east of the Dead Sea) to escape a famine in the land of Israel. Her sons both married women from Moab. When Naomi's husband and her sons died, she returned to Israel. She urged her daughters-in-law, Ruth and Orpah, to stay in Moab, but Ruth insisted on staying with Naomi. Ruth said, "Wherever you go, I will go; ... Your people shall be my people, and your God, my God" (Ruth 1:16).

NAZIRITE A person specially dedicated to service to God by means of a vow, usually for a specified period of time. Nazirites could not drink wine or other intoxicating drinks, they could not cut their hair, and they were not allowed to touch dead bodies (Numbers 6). Samson was a Nazirite, and John the Baptist is thought to have been one. *Nazirite* should not be confused with *Nazarene*, which means simply a native of the village of Nazareth. Jesus was a Nazarene (he grew up in Nazareth), but he was not a Nazirite.

NEBUCHADNEZZAR The king of Babylon who defeated the Kingdom of Judah in 586 BC (2 Kings 24–25). He took many captives from Judah to Babylon (see *Exile*), both before and after the final defeat of Judah. Daniel was among an earlier group of captives. When Nebuchadnezzar had a dream about a statue with feet of clay, Daniel interpreted it for him. Nebuchadnezzar later threw Daniel's friends Shadrach, Meshach, and Abednego into a fiery furnace when they refused to bow down before a great statue the king had constructed. Later in life he was insane for seven years and lived "with the beasts of the field" (Daniel 4:32). This was a judgment of God on his pride, but he later regained his throne. 📌 The Hanging Gardens of Babylon, constructed by Nebuchadnezzar, were one of the Seven Wonders of the Ancient World. In the 1980s, Saddam Hussein, president of Iraq (the land that was once Babylon), rebuilt portions of the ancient city of Babylon. He styled himself as a modern-day Nebuchadnezzar.

NEHEMIAH A prophet and political leader in Jerusalem after the Kingdom of Judah returned from exile; his story is told in the book of Nehemiah. He was a cupbearer to King Artaxerxes of Persia, but he went to Jerusalem to lead the people there in rebuilding their city wall. After the wall had been built, Nehemiah and Ezra led the people into a renewed relationship with God.

NILE RIVER One of the longest rivers in the world, it flows north through Egypt and empties into the Mediterranean Sea. In the King James Version of the Bible it is called the River of Egypt. The Nile River played an important part in biblical history. It has always provided water for Egypt, and the annual flooding irrigates the fields. If there was a famine in the land of Canaan, there was usually food available in Egypt (see *Joseph*). In the story of Moses and the bulrushes (Exodus 2), the baby's basket was placed in the Nile River.

Satellite image of the Nile River

NOAH The story of Noah and the ark is one of the best-known stories in the Bible (Genesis 6–9). Noah lived at a time when people had become so wicked that God decided to destroy all mankind with a great flood. The only exception was Noah and his family, for "Noah found grace in the eyes of the LORD" (Genesis 6:8). God told Noah to build a great boat—an ark—450 feet long and 75 feet wide. Then he was to put a male and female of every kind of animal on the ark. When the ark was finished and the animals and Noah and his family were all aboard, the Lord shut the door and the rain started. It rained for forty days and nights, and the floods covered all the land and drowned all the people. Eventually the water began to recede, and the ark came to rest on the mountains of Ararat (possibly in present-day Turkey). God promised never again to destroy all people with a flood, and he gave the rainbow as a sign of his covenant. Noah lived in the time before recorded history. Since he and his family were the only survivors of the Flood, all people on earth are his descendants. ➧ Other ancient civilizations (for example, the Sumerians and Babylonians) had similar flood stories. Some scholars have taken this as evidence that the Genesis story was simply borrowed from another culture. Others see it as evidence that indeed all peoples on earth were descendants of Noah and his sons; as a result, many ancient people groups would have their own oral history of the great flood their ancestors had survived.

NORTHERN KINGDOM (ISRAEL) When the Kingdom of Israel split apart after King Solomon's death (1 Kings 12), the ten northern tribes were still called the Kingdom of Israel. It is sometimes called the Northern Kingdom, in contrast to the Southern Kingdom of Judah. See also *Divided Kingdom.*

Reenacting the first Passover

PASSOVER One of the most important festivals of the year for the people of Israel, both in Old and New Testament times. The first Passover took place at the time of the Exodus, when the people of Israel were finally able to leave Egypt after their long captivity there (Exodus 11–12). Pharaoh, king of Egypt, had refused to let the Israelites go, so the Lord sent nine plagues to afflict the Egyptians. The Lord then told Moses he would send a final plague to convince Pharaoh. The Lord would pass through the land and kill the oldest son in each family of Egypt. The Israelites were to kill lambs and paint blood from the lambs on the doorframes and above the doors of their houses. When the Lord saw the blood, he would "pass over" those houses. That very night, while all Egypt was in mourning,

Pharaoh finally told the Israelites to leave. The Lord commanded the Israelites to celebrate the Passover each year as a reminder of the way the Lord had rescued them. Immediately after Passover came a weeklong celebration called the Feast of Unleavened Bread (because on the night before the Exodus, the people ate unleavened bread since they did not have time to wait for their bread to rise). The Lord gave very specific instructions as to how the Passover and the Feast of Unleavened Bread were to be celebrated. These annual celebrations would remind the people of the Lord's protection and providence for them. Throughout most of the rest of the Bible, the Israelites did observe these great feasts. Jesus and his disciples were celebrating the Passover when they ate the Last Supper together. The next day Jesus was crucified. In 1 Corinthians 5:7, the apostle Paul refers to Jesus as our Passover Lamb. He meant that Jesus was the perfect sacrifice to save us from the wrath of God, just as in Egypt the Passover lambs were sacrificed to save the firstborn sons of the Israelite families from death. Today the Passover is still celebrated by Jews around the world. It occurs in the spring, about the same time as Easter.

PATRIARCHS The patriarchs ("fathers") of the nation of Israel were Abraham, Isaac (son of Abraham), Jacob (son of Isaac), and Jacob's twelve sons, the forefathers of the twelve tribes of Israel.

PERSIA, PERSIANS Persia was an ancient empire that flourished in the region of present-day Iran from the sixth to the fourth centuries BC. The Persians defeated the Babylonians in 539 BC, during the time that the people of the Kingdom of Judah were in exile in Babylon. The events in the first five chapters of the book of Daniel took place during the rule of the Babylonian kings Nebuchadnezzar and Belshazzar. After Daniel interpreted the handwriting on the wall, Belshazzar was killed by the Persians, and the rest of the events in the book of Daniel took place under the reigns of the Persian kings Darius (who had Daniel thrown into the lions' den) and Cyrus (who allowed the Jews to return to Jerusalem to rebuild the temple). Secular history tells us that Persia was eventually defeated by Alexander the Great.

PHARAOH The ancient kings of Egypt were known as pharaohs. Several pharaohs are mentioned in the Old Testament, the most infamous being the pharaoh at the time of the Exodus (Exodus 1–14). The Hebrews were slaves in Egypt, and Moses and Aaron delivered the Lord's message to Pharaoh: "Let my people go" (Exodus 5:1 NLT). Pharaoh refused to consider their request, so the Lord sent ten plagues upon the Egyptians. Pharaoh finally consented to let the Hebrews leave after the last plague, when the Lord killed the firstborn son and firstborn of the livestock in every Egyptian household. But Pharaoh soon retracted his permission and chased after the Hebrews with a great army. The Lord miraculously parted the waters of the Red Sea, and Moses led the people across on dry land. Pharaoh and his army chased them, but the waters engulfed them and they all drowned.

PHILISTINES Constant enemies of the Israelites during the period of the judges and the reigns of Saul and David. The Philistines frequently influenced the Israelites to worship heathen gods. Today the term *philistine* means uncouth, or it describes being more interested in material goods than in intellectual or spiritual pursuits.

Statue of Pharaoh Ramses II

PILLAR OF CLOUD, PILLAR OF FIRE When the Hebrew people (the Israelites) left Egypt (see *Exodus, the*), the Lord caused a great cloud—the text calls it a "pillar of cloud"—to come between them and the Egyptian army that was pursuing them. This afforded them protection before the Lord caused the parting of the Red Sea (Exodus 14). During the forty years that the Israelites were in the wilderness, the Lord led and protected them by means of the cloud (Numbers 9). During the day it rested over the tent of meeting (the sacred tent where Moses met with the Lord). At night the cloud appeared to be of fire. When the pillar of cloud moved, the people also moved. When it stayed, they stayed.

PILLAR OF SALT See *Lot* and *Lot's wife*.

PLAGUES OF EGYPT When Pharaoh refused to release the Israelites from slavery, the Lord sent a series of plagues upon the land of Egypt to convince Pharaoh to grant Moses's request (Exodus 7–11). Pharaoh's magicians were able to duplicate some of the plagues, so Pharaoh wasn't impressed. The tenth and final plague was the death of the oldest son in each family in Egypt. At this, the Israelites were finally able to leave Egypt (see *Passover*).

POTIPHAR'S WIFE When Joseph (one of Jacob's twelve sons) was overseer in the house of Potiphar, Potiphar's wife tried to seduce him (Genesis 39). Joseph continually resisted her advances, saying it would be wrong for him to sleep with her. She was offended by his rebuffs, so one day she framed Joseph. She screamed that she was being raped, and she pulled Joseph's shirt off him as he ran away from

THE TEN PLAGUES OF EGYPT

1. The water of the Nile River turned to blood.
2. Frogs covered the entire land.
3. There were gnats everywhere.
4. There were flies everywhere.
5. All the livestock died of a disease.
6. Boils broke out on all the people and animals.
7. A hailstorm ravaged the land.
8. Clouds of locusts covered the land.
9. Darkness covered the land for three days.
10. The firstborn son and firstborn of the livestock in every household in Egypt were killed.

her. The shirt was used as evidence against him, and Potiphar threw Joseph in prison.

PRIEST In both the Old and New Testaments, the priests of Israel were men who performed religious roles in the community. The priests were descendants of Aaron, from the tribe of Levi. They officiated in the offering of sacrifices. In the New Testament, the priests and chief priests (see *Sanhedrin* in the chapter "People, Places, and Events in the New Testament") were generally antagonistic toward Jesus and the early Christians. See also the entry for *high priest* in this chapter and the entry for *priest* in the chapter "Church Life and Theology."

PROMISED LAND A name for the land of Israel. God promised Abraham that his descendants would inherit the entire land of Canaan (Genesis 13:15). Later, when Moses led the people of Israel out of slavery in Egypt, they looked forward to returning to the land of the patriarchs—the Promised Land, "a land flowing with milk and honey" (Leviticus 20:24).

PROPHECY The term *prophecy* is often used to refer to a prediction of future events. It can also mean any message from God. The role of the Old Testament prophets was to proclaim God's messages to his people. Many of these messages included predictions of the

The Promised Land in modern times produces a wide variety of agricultural crops.

judgment that would fall upon God's people or the surrounding nations because of their sins. The prophets also foretold the coming of a future Messiah who would save his people. Christians see Jesus Christ as the fulfillment of those prophecies.

PROPHET In the Old Testament, the prophets were spokesmen who proclaimed God's messages to the people of Israel. Moses, Samuel, Elijah, Elisha, Isaiah, Jeremiah, and Ezekiel were a few of the important prophets of Israel. The prophets constantly called the people to repentance and reminded them of the blessings they would receive if they obeyed God's commands. But they also reminded the people that God would judge them for their disobedience. The prophets were frequently rejected and ridiculed by the people. There are many references in the New Testament to "the Prophets" and "the Law and the Prophets." "The Prophets" were the Old Testament books of history and prophecy (see *Prophecy, Books of* in the chapter "Bible Overview"). John the Baptist was received as a prophet, and many people also saw Jesus as a prophet, as evidenced by his statement that "a prophet is not without honor except in his own country" (Mark 6:4). 📌 Although Muslims do not accept Jesus as the Son of God, they do see him as an important prophet.

QUEEN OF SHEBA A wealthy queen who visited King Solomon to see if he was as wise as he was reputed to be. When he answered her hardest questions and she saw all his wealth, she said, "In wisdom and wealth you have far exceeded the report I heard" (1 Kings 10:7 NIV). 📌 Scholars believe Sheba was at the southern end of the Arabian peninsula. Ethiopian legend says the Queen of Sheba became one of Solomon's wives and that she bore a son who became the first king of Ethiopia. King Haile Selassie of Ethiopia (1892–1975) claimed to be a direct descendant of Solomon and the Queen of Sheba.

RACHEL Jacob's favorite wife, and the mother of Joseph and Benjamin. (Jacob's ten other sons were from other wives.) When Jacob fled from his brother, Esau, he went to live with Laban, his mother's brother. Laban had two daughters, Leah and Rachel (Genesis 29). Jacob asked if he could marry Rachel, and Laban said he could marry her if he worked for seven years. He faithfully fulfilled his seven years of work, but Laban tricked Jacob and gave him the elder sister, Leah, as a wife. When Jacob objected, Laban said he could also marry Rachel if he promised to work another seven years! Rachel died as she was giving birth to Benjamin.

RAHAB A prostitute who lived in the city of Jericho at the time of Joshua's conquest of the Promised Land (Joshua 2–6). Joshua sent two spies into Jericho, and Rahab hid them under piles of flax on her roof when soldiers came to look for them. Then she told the soldiers the spies had already left. She asked for safety from the Israelite army in exchange for saving the spies, and they assured her she would be safe if she hung a red rope from her window for identification. She then helped the spies escape by letting them down by a rope through a window in the city wall. She and her family were the only residents of Jericho who were allowed to live after the Battle of Jericho. Rahab later married a man of the tribe of Judah, and the genealogy in Matthew 1 lists Rahab as the mother of Boaz and an ancestor of David and of Jesus.

REBEKAH Isaac's wife, and the mother of twin sons, Esau and Jacob. Rebekah was selected as Isaac's wife when Abraham sent his servant to Haran (the city in northwestern Mesopotamia where Abraham had once lived) to find a wife from among Abraham's relatives (Genesis 24). When the servant arrived in the vicinity, he prayed that the Lord would show him the right girl by having her offer to water his camels when he asked for a drink. Rebekah came out to the well and did offer to water his camels, so the servant identified himself and asked her father if he could take her to be Isaac's wife. After her twins were born, Rebekah was more fond of Jacob than of Esau. When it came time for the aged Isaac to bless his eldest son (see *blessings and curses*), Rebekah helped Jacob deceive Isaac, thereby stealing the blessing that should have gone to Esau.

Ancient city gate of Haran, the hometown of Rebekah

RED SEA, PARTING OF THE When Moses led the Israelites out of Egypt, they were pursued by Pharaoh's army. With the Red Sea in front of them and the Egyptian army behind them, the people were trapped. Then the Lord sent a pillar of cloud to come between the Egyptians and the Israelites so the Egyptians could not attack. God told Moses to stretch his rod over the sea. He did so, and God opened a path through the sea so the people could cross on dry land. The Egyptian army pursued them, but as soon as the Israelites were safely through, God caused the water to cascade back into place, drowning Pharaoh's entire army (Exodus 14). This was just one of a series of miracles God performed as the Israelites moved from Egypt back to Canaan, the Promised Land. Some translations and commentaries point out that the Hebrew words traditionally translated "Red Sea" actually mean "Sea of Reeds." The exact location of the crossing—and even which body of water was crossed—is uncertain, but God's miraculous protection for his chosen people is evident.

REHOBOAM Solomon's son who succeeded him as king (1 Kings 12). Rehoboam followed bad advice and was very hard on his people. The people of the tribes of Judah and Benjamin stayed loyal to him, but the other ten tribes rebelled and selected Jeroboam as their king. This was the beginning of the Divided Kingdom. The Southern Kingdom, consisting of only the tribes of Judah and Benjamin, came to be known as the Kingdom of Judah. The Northern Kingdom, representing the other ten tribes, continued to be known as the Kingdom of Israel. Rehoboam was a wicked king, although his grandfather, King David, had been "a man after [God's] own heart" (1 Samuel 13:14).

RUTH The story of Ruth, told in the book of Ruth, is one of the great love stories in the Bible. Ruth was a poor widow from the land of Moab, but her husband had been an Israelite. When her mother-in-law, Naomi, decided to return to Israel, she encouraged Ruth to stay in Moab. But Ruth responded, "Wherever you go, I will go.... Your people shall be my people, and your God, my God" (Ruth 1:16). When they arrived in Naomi's hometown, Ruth went to the fields of Boaz, a wealthy relative of her late husband's. There she collected stalks of grain that the harvesters dropped.

Because of Ruth's generosity to her mother-in-law, Boaz instructed his workers to drop grain on purpose so Ruth could pick up enough. At the end of the story, Boaz marries Ruth. Their great-grandson was David, the great king of Israel.

SABBATH The weekly day of rest. According to the Genesis account of the creation, God created the world in six days and then rested on the seventh day. One of the Ten Commandments is "Remember the Sabbath day, to keep it holy" (Exodus 20:8). The Israelites were to do no work on the Sabbath day, which was the last day of the week. By the time of Jesus, the Pharisees had added hundreds of regulations to the laws of the Old Testament, including laws that defined exactly what one could or could not do on the Sabbath. Jesus pointed out that God had never intended the Sabbath law to be burdensome for his people. Jesus made the Pharisees angry when he said, "The Sabbath was made to meet the needs of people, and not people to meet the requirements of the Sabbath" (Mark 2:27 NLT). Saturday is the Jewish Sabbath, but the early church evidently met on Sunday (Acts 20:7) in commemoration of the Resurrection, which took place on the first day of the week. Most Christians follow this pattern and observe Sunday as their day of rest. Seventh-day Adventists observe Saturday as their day of rest.

SACKCLOTH AND ASHES As a sign of mourning, people in the Old Testament wore clothes made of sackcloth, a coarse and uncomfortable fabric, and put ashes on their heads.

SACRIFICE Under the Mosaic law, the system of sacrifices and offerings was spelled out in great detail (for example, in Leviticus 1–7), including both "thank offerings" and sacrifices for atonement. For atonement, each Israelite was to take a dove or a sheep or a goat to the tabernacle (later to the temple), kill it, and give it to the priest, who would sprinkle the blood on the altar, burn part of the sacrifice, and set the remainder aside for eating. Since the penalty for sin was death, the animal's blood was shed to atone for the sins of the person making the sacrifice. The Jews practiced the system of sacrifices until AD 70, when the temple and the altar were destroyed with the rest of Jerusalem. Jesus, the Lamb of God, was the ultimate sacrifice. He was sinless, so he did not have to die. His death on the cross, therefore, was an acceptable sacrifice on behalf of all who believe in him.

SAMSON One of the judges of Israel (see *judges, period of the*). The Lord gave Samson an unusual measure of strength. Once he killed a lion with his bare hands. Another time he removed the doors of a city wall and carried them to a distant hillside. Yet another time he killed 1,000 Philistines with the jawbone of a donkey. Samson loved Delilah, a Philistine woman. Delilah tricked Samson into telling him the source of his strength. He admitted that if his long hair were cut (he was a Nazirite), he would lose his strength. She arranged for it to be cut while he was sleeping, and the Philistines captured him and gouged out his eyes. While in captivity, Samson prayed that the Lord would give him his strength one last time. Samson then caused a large hall to collapse by pushing out the supporting pillars. In his death he killed more Philistines than he had up to that point in his life (Judges 13–16).

Samson Pushing Down the Pillars

SAMUEL One of the great prophets of Israel (1 Samuel 1–16). When he was a child, his mother, Hannah, took him to the tabernacle at Shiloh, where he became an assistant to Eli, the high priest. There he heard a message from God in the middle of the night. He thought Eli was calling him, but Eli recognized that God was calling the boy. Eli told him to say, "Speak, your servant is listening" (1 Samuel 3:10 NLT). When Samuel was an old man, the Israelites wanted a king. Samuel objected, but the people insisted, so Samuel anointed Saul. When King Saul disobeyed the Lord, Samuel anointed David as the next king.

SARAH (SARAI) Abraham's wife (Genesis 12–23) and the mother of Isaac. The Lord had promised Abraham that his descendants would be as numerous as the stars of the sky, but he and Sarah had no children. Sarah took matters into her own hands and gave her servant Hagar to Abraham so Hagar could bear him a son. Hagar gave birth to Ishmael, but he was not the child of the promise. Finally, when Sarah was ninety, Isaac was born. Prior to Abraham's receiving God's promise that he would be a father of many nations (Genesis 17:4), Sarah was called Sarai.

SAUL The first king of Israel (1 Samuel 9–31). Saul was handsome, and he stood head and shoulders above his countrymen. The Lord selected him when the Israelites demanded a king like the nations around them. Saul did not fully obey the Lord, however, so the Lord said he would give Saul's throne to David rather than to Saul's son Jonathan. Saul was king at the time young David defeated Goliath, and shortly thereafter David married Saul's daughter Michal. David was very popular with the people, and on several occasions Saul tried to kill David, whom he saw as a great threat. David had several opportunities to kill Saul but was careful not to harm the one who had been appointed king over Israel. Saul and his son Jonathan died in a battle with the Philistines, and David took the throne.

Mount Gilboa, where Saul died in a battle with the Philistines (1 Samuel 31)

SCAPEGOAT On the Day of Atonement, the high priest offered a special sacrifice as an atonement for Israel's sins. Then he placed his hands on the head of a goat, confessing the sins of the people and symbolically transferring them to the goat. It was then taken out to a lonely place in the desert. This goat was called the scapegoat (Leviticus 16). The term *scapegoat* has come to mean a person or group that bears blame in place of others.

The Scapegoat

SELAH A notation found primarily in the Psalms. It may have indicated that the musicians or the congregation were to pause and lift up their hands or instruments, or it may have been comparable to the expression "Amen."

SERAPHIM See *cherubim and seraphim.*

SERPENT In the Garden of Eden, Eve was tempted by a serpent to eat the forbidden fruit (Genesis 3). She succumbed to the temptation and also gave some of the fruit to Adam. In this way sin entered the world. The Genesis account of the fall of man does not give us many details about the serpent, but we need not assume that it was just a common garden snake. It may have been a beautiful creature. It is assumed that the serpent was actually Satan, the chief of the forces of evil. In Revelation 12:9, the great dragon who fights against Michael (the archangel) and heaven's armies is identified as "that ancient serpent called the devil, or Satan, who leads the whole world astray" (NIV).

SHADRACH, MESHACH, AND ABEDNEGO These three Israelite men were friends of Daniel's (Daniel 1–3). Like Daniel, they were captives in Babylon, but they were made advisers to King Nebuchadnezzar because of their great wisdom. They stayed true to their faith in God, however, so they refused to obey the king's command that everyone in the kingdom was to bow down and worship a huge golden image constructed by Nebuchadnezzar (Daniel 3). Anyone who defied the king's order was to be thrown into a fiery furnace. Before Shadrach, Meshach, and Abednego were sent to the furnace, however, they assured the king that their God was capable of keeping them safe. The king ordered that the furnace be heated seven times hotter than usual, and then the three men were bound and thrown in. But when Nebuchadnezzar looked in, he saw four men walking around in the fire, unbound and unharmed. Nebuchadnezzar said that the fourth man looked "like a son of the gods" (verse 25 NIV). The king then called Shadrach, Meshach, and Abednego out of the furnace and declared that no one in the kingdom was to speak against their powerful God.

SHEBA, QUEEN OF See *Queen of Sheba.*

SHEEP The primary domestic animal in both Old and New Testament times. They were used to provide food and wool, and they were often a measure of personal wealth. Sheep were frequently used as sacrifices. Because sheep need the care and protection of a shepherd, biblical writers often used sheep to symbolize people in need of God's care and protection. Isaiah wrote, "All we like sheep have gone astray; we have turned, every one, to his own way" (Isaiah 53:6).

SHEPHERD Shepherds care for sheep. Many well-known persons in the Old Testament worked as shepherds. Among them are Jacob, Joseph, Moses, and David. Jesus called himself the Good Shepherd (John 10:11). He meant that he cares for people as tenderly and as vigilantly as a shepherd cares for his sheep. Jesus told the Parable of the Lost Sheep, in which the shepherd leaves the ninety-nine sheep that are safe in the sheepfold to look for the one sheep that is missing (Luke 15:1–7).

SHIBBOLETH A password used by Jephthah (one of the judges of Israel during the period of the judges) when he was attacking the tribe of Ephraim (Judges 12). The people of Ephraim gave away their identity when they were asked to pronounce the word *shibboleth*, for they pronounced it *sibboleth*. The word *shibboleth* is now used to refer to any belief or position a person must hold in order to belong to a particular group. For example, "Some Senators feel that support of abortion is a shibboleth for a Supreme Court nominee."

SINAI, MOUNT The mountain where the Lord gave Moses the Ten Commandments (Exodus 19–20). In some passages the mountain is called Horeb. The exact site of the biblical Sinai is disputed, but the traditional location is on the Sinai Peninsula, the desolate region between Israel and Egypt (see *Exodus, the*).

SODOM AND GOMORRAH, DESTRUCTION OF During the time of Abraham and his nephew Lot, the cities of Sodom and Gomorrah, near the Dead Sea, were renowned for their wickedness. Lot lived in Sodom, and the Lord warned Abraham that he was going to destroy the cities (Genesis 18–19). Two angels who had appeared to Abraham in human form went to Lot's home in Sodom. The men of the city came to Lot's home and demanded that Lot send his guests out to be raped. Lot pleaded with the crowd, and the angels then helped Lot and his wife and daughters escape. The

Jebel Musa ("Mountain of Moses")—the traditional site of Mount Sinai

angels told them not to look back as the cities were being destroyed with fire and brimstone that rained down from the skies, but Lot's wife did look back and was turned into a pillar of salt. The term *sodomy* is derived from Sodom, because the men of Sodom wanted to homosexually rape Lot's guests.

SOLOMON The son of David and Bathsheba. He succeeded David as king of Israel (1 Kings 1–11), and he is renowned for his wisdom, wealth, and wives (he had more than 700 of them!). Solomon wrote many of the sayings in the book of Proverbs, and he is traditionally said to have written the books of Ecclesiastes and the Song of Solomon, though many scholars dispute this. Solomon built the first temple in Jerusalem, and its dedication was a high point in Israel's history. Unfortunately, Solomon started well but finished poorly. His foreign wives influenced him to worship their pagan gods. As a result of this sin, the kingdom was divided after Solomon's death. His son Rehoboam succeeded him as king, but only the tribes of Judah and Benjamin accepted Rehoboam as their king. The other ten tribes, under Jeroboam, rebelled and set up their own kingdom. This was the start of the Divided Kingdom, which included the Southern Kingdom of Judah (consisting of the tribes of Judah and Benjamin) and the Northern Kingdom of Israel (consisting of the ten northern tribes).

SOUTHERN KINGDOM (JUDAH) When the Kingdom of Israel split in two after the death of King Solomon (1 Kings 12), the two southern tribes, Judah and Benjamin, became the Kingdom of Judah. It is sometimes called the Southern Kingdom, in contrast to the Northern Kingdom of Israel.

STILL, SMALL VOICE After the prophet Elijah's mighty victory over the prophets of Baal (see *fire from heaven*), he was spiritually exhausted and discouraged. He went to Mount Sinai, and the Lord spoke to him there. The Lord caused a mighty wind, then an earthquake, then a fire to pass before Elijah, but the Lord was not in these natural phenomena. Then came a still, small voice, and Elijah recognized it as the voice of God (1 Kings 19:12). Today the expression is used to denote the inner promptings of the Holy Spirit in the life of the believer.

TABERNACLE The tent sanctuary where the Lord resided among the people of Israel from the time Moses received the Ten Commandments until King Solomon built the temple nearly 500 years later (Exodus 25–27). The tabernacle was very ornate, but it was also portable. The Israelites disassembled it and carried it with them as they traveled through the wilderness. The innermost room was called the Holy of Holies, just as in the later temple. The ark of the covenant was kept in the Holy of Holies.

TEMPLE The ornate building that was the center of worship for the Israelites from the time of King Solomon till the destruction of Jerusalem in AD 70. Solomon built the first temple in Jerusalem on the mountain where Abraham had nearly sacrificed Isaac. Solomon's temple was destroyed when the Babylonians captured Jerusalem in 586 BC. The temple was rebuilt by Zerubbabel when the Israelites first returned to their own land after the Exile. This second temple, not as glorious as Solomon's, survived until the first century BC. King Herod the Great then built a third temple. This was the temple of the New Testament period. It was destroyed in AD 70 by the armies of the Roman general Titus. By the time of Jesus, the temple had become quite a place of commerce. Since sacrifices were offered at the temple, there were many merchants selling doves, sheep, and goats. Jews came from many countries to worship at the temple, so there

Replica of the tabernacle

were money changers to exchange secular money for temple money. Jesus cleansed the temple by throwing out the money changers and merchants. Needless to say, this did not make him very popular with the religious establishment. Today there is a Muslim shrine, the Dome of the Rock, on or near the site of the temple. All that remains of Herod's temple is the western wall of the courtyard. It is often called the Wailing Wall, as for centuries the Jews have lamented the destruction of the temple.

Model of Solomon's Temple

TEMPTATION, THE When Adam and Eve were in the Garden of Eden, God told them they could eat the fruit from any tree except the tree of the knowledge of good and evil. Then the serpent came to Eve and tempted her to eat the forbidden fruit, saying that if she ate it she would be like God, knowing good from evil. This is sometimes called the Temptation. Eve ate the fruit and gave some to Adam, who also ate it. The entire event is traditionally called the fall of man.

TEN COMMANDMENTS (THE LAW) The law that Moses received from the Lord at Mount Sinai (Exodus 19–20). The Lord inscribed the commandments on two stone tablets for Moses. When Moses came down from the mountain and saw that Aaron had made a golden calf, he threw down and broke the tablets the Lord had given him. The Lord then gave him the law a second time on new tablets. The Ten Commandments were the central element in the larger structure of the Mosaic law. Jesus summarized the Ten Commandments into two simple commands when he said, "'You shall love the LORD your God with all your heart, with all your soul, and with all your mind.' This is the first and great commandment. And the second is like it: 'You shall love your neighbor as yourself.' On these two commandments hang all the Law and the Prophets." (Matthew 22:37–40).

THE TEN COMMANDMENTS

Traditional Protestant Numbering

This wording is from Exodus 20:3–17 of the New International Version.

1. You shall have no other gods before me.
2. You shall not make for yourself an image in the form of anything in heaven above or on the earth beneath or in the waters below.
3. You shall not misuse the name of the LORD your God, for the LORD will not hold anyone guiltless who misuses his name.
4. Remember the Sabbath day by keeping it holy.
5. Honor your father and your mother, so that you may live long in the land the LORD your God is giving you.
6. You shall not murder.
7. You shall not commit adultery.
8. You shall not steal.
9. You shall not give false testimony against your neighbor.
10. You shall not covet your neighbor's house. You shall not covet your neighbor's wife, or his male or female servant, his ox or donkey, or anything that belongs to your neighbor.

Note: The commandments are not actually numbered in the Bible, so the division into ten separate commandments is traditional.

Traditional Catholic Numbering

This wording, from Exodus 20:3–17 in the New American Bible (Revised Edition), is similar to the wording in Protestant translations, but Catholics and Lutherans have traditionally combined two commandments at the beginning and divided two commandments at the end of the list.

1. You shall not have other gods beside me. You shall not make for yourself an idol or a likeness of anything in the heavens above or on the earth below or in the waters beneath the earth.
2. You shall not invoke the name of the LORD, your God, in vain. For the LORD will not leave unpunished anyone who invokes his name in vain.
3. Remember the Sabbath day—keep it holy.
4. Honor your father and your mother, that you may have a long life in the land the LORD your God is giving you.
5. You shall not kill.
6. You shall not commit adultery.
7. You shall not steal.
8. You shall not bear false witness against your neighbor.
9. You shall not covet your neighbor's house.
10. You shall not covet your neighbor's wife, his male or female slave, his ox or donkey, or anything that belongs to your neighbor.

TIGRIS RIVER One of the great rivers of the Near East, it runs from present-day Turkey through present-day Iraq. It joins the Euphrates River shortly before they empty together into the Persian Gulf. The basins of the Euphrates and Tigris Rivers formed part of the Fertile Crescent of the ancient world, a region called Mesopotamia in the Bible (from the Greek word for "between the two rivers").

TITHE A gift to the Lord equal to one-tenth of one's income. The Mosaic law required that the people of Israel give a tithe (Deuteronomy 14:22–29; Malachi 3:10), partly as a means of supporting the priests and other Levites. Many Christians observe the principle of tithing by giving a tenth of their income to their church and/or other Christian organizations.

TREE OF LIFE In the very center of the Garden of Eden stood the tree of life and the tree of the knowledge of good and evil. God told Adam he could freely eat from all the trees in the Garden except the tree of the knowledge of good and evil. After Adam and Eve ate the fruit of that tree (see *fall of man*), God banished them from the Garden so they would not also eat from the tree of life and live forever. The cherubim that guarded the entrance to the Garden were placed there "to guard the way to the tree of life" (Genesis 3:24). In the book of Revelation we find the tree of life in the New Jerusalem.

TREE OF THE KNOWLEDGE OF GOOD AND EVIL The tree in the Garden of Eden from which Eve took the forbidden fruit. Adam had been told he could eat from the fruit of any tree except this one. When they did eat its fruit, "the eyes of both of them were opened, and they knew that they were naked" (Genesis 3:7). This is called the fall of man. See also *tree of life*.

TRIBES OF ISRAEL Jacob, one of the patriarchs of the people of Israel, had twelve sons. The descendants of each of these sons became a tribe (extended family) within the nation of Israel. The names of the tribes are: Asher, Benjamin, Dan, Ephraim, Gad, Judah, Issachar, Levi, Manasseh, Naphtali, Reuben, Simeon, and Zebulun. (The tribes of Ephraim and Manasseh are named for the two sons of Joseph.) Each of the tribes (except Levi) was allotted a certain portion of land when the Israelites entered the Promised Land after the Exodus

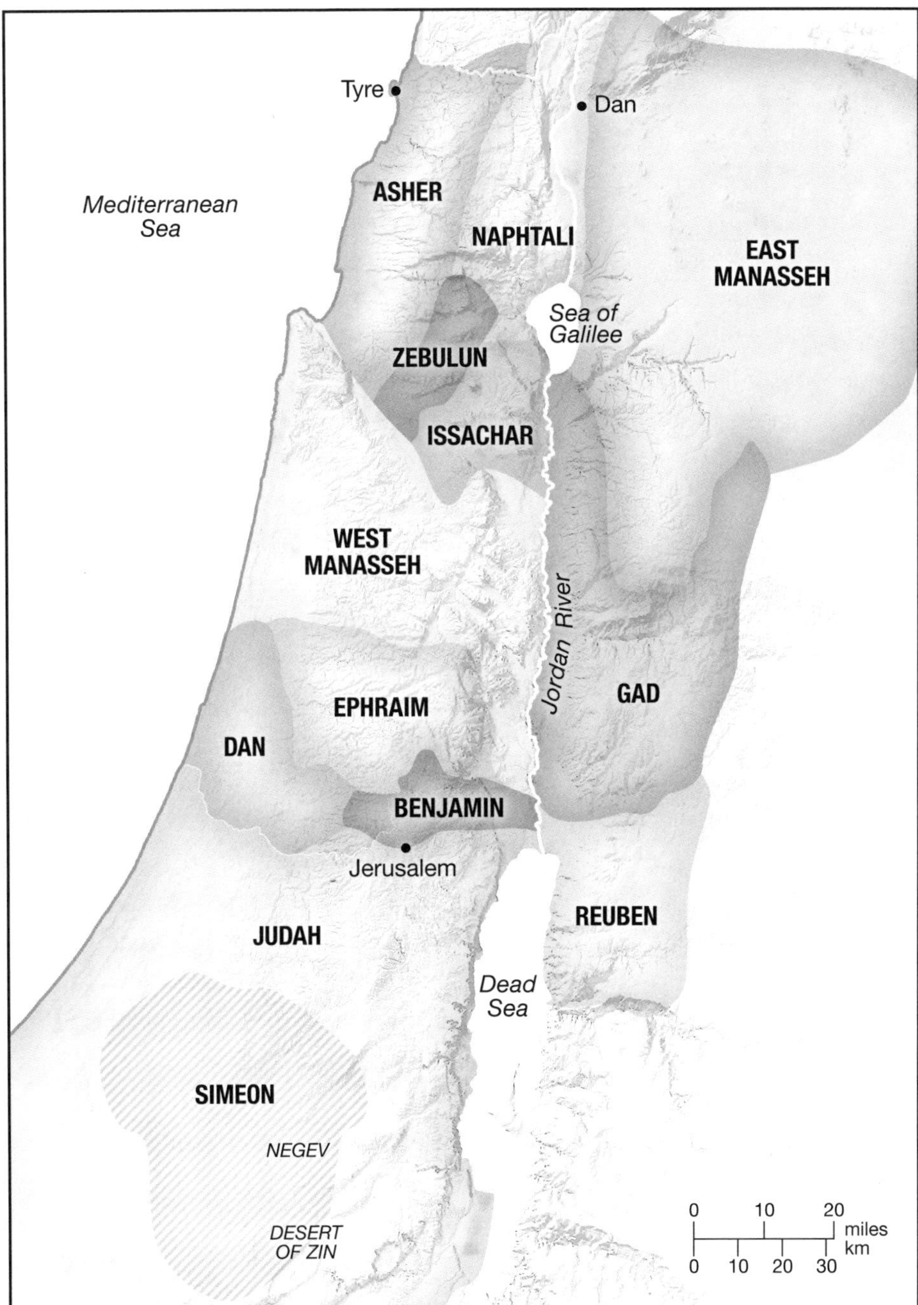

The Tribes of Israel Each of the twelve tribes of Israel (except Levi) received a territory of its own in the Promised Land. The Levites were supported by the other tribes. The tribes in the north eventually became the Northern Kingdom of Israel. Judah and Benjamin became the Southern Kingdom of Judah.

and wandering in the wilderness. The Levites, who were responsible for the tabernacle (and later the temple), did not get a territory of their own. They were supported by the tithes that the rest of the people brought to the Lord.

UNCLEAN ANIMALS According to the Mosaic law, certain animals could be eaten and all other animals could not be eaten (Leviticus 11). Those that could not be eaten, including pigs, were said to be unclean. This is part of the basis of the kosher laws still observed by many Jews.

UNLEAVENED BREAD Since it is made without leaven (yeast), unleavened bread does not rise. On the night before the Exodus, the Israelites were told to bake unleavened bread, as they would not have time to wait for the dough to rise. Ever since, unleavened bread has played an important role in the celebration of the Passover. Since Jesus and his disciples ate unleavened bread at the Last Supper (they were celebrating the Passover), unleavened bread is often used by Christians for the Communion service.

VISION A dream or dreamlike experience in which a person receives a message from God or an angel. Many people in both the Old and New Testament had visions. Jacob had a vision in which he saw angels ascending and descending a stairway that stretched between heaven and earth (see *Jacob's ladder*). The prophets often received messages in visions. An example is Isaiah's vision in the temple: "In the year that King Uzziah died, I saw the Lord" (Isaiah 6:1). Zechariah the priest (father of John the Baptist) also had a vision in the temple, when the angel Gabriel announced that Zechariah and his wife, Elizabeth, would have a son. After Jesus was born, the wise men received instructions in a dream not to tell King Herod that they had found the infant. The apostle Paul had a vision in which he was taken up into heaven, and the apostle John had an extensive vision that is recorded in the book of Revelation.

WHEAT An important grain grown for use in bread. It was also used as a sacrifice and in commercial trade. Jesus compared himself to a grain of wheat, which must die in order to produce new kernels. He also used wheat and wheat fields to symbolize the people of the world.

WILDERNESS The untamed regions in and around Israel were called the wilderness (sometimes translated "desert"). It was a dry, rocky area without much vegetation. The wilderness is an image that suggests a time of testing and learning patience. Moses lived in the wilderness for forty years before leading the Israelites out of Egypt. After the Exodus, the Israelites themselves were in the wilderness for forty years before entering the Promised Land. Centuries later, John the Baptist lived and preached in the wilderness near the Jordan River. Jesus went into the wilderness where he was tempted by Satan. The apostle Paul lived in the wilderness for a number of years after he became a Christian and before he started his active ministry. See also *temptation of Jesus* and *Paul* in the chapter "People, Places, and Events in the New Testament."

WINE The references to wine in the Bible are both positive and negative. In the Psalms, wine is listed along with many other good gifts from the Lord. Jesus turned water into wine at a marriage feast, and he and his disciples drank wine at the Last Supper. Paul encourages Timothy to "use a little wine because of your stomach and your frequent illnesses" (1 Timothy 5:23 NIV). But in both the Old and New Testaments there are warnings about the dangers of wine and of drunkenness (for example, Proverbs 23:29–35).

ZERUBBABEL In 538 BC, Zerubbabel led the first group of about 42,000 Jews from exile in Babylon back to Jerusalem (Ezra 1–6). They began rebuilding the temple, though it was not completed until 516 BC under the prompting of the prophet Haggai.

From Adam to Zerubbabel

A Quiz on People, Places, and Events in the Old Testament

Select one answer for each question.
Answers appear immediately after the quiz.

1 One of the low points of David's life was:

a. When he was thrown into the lions' den

b. When he murdered his brother

c. When he committed adultery

d. When he worshiped the golden calf

2 Who killed Abel?

a. Adam

b. The serpent

c. Cain

d. None of the above

3 Who were Abraham's sons?

a. Jacob and Esau

b. Moses and Joshua

c. Isaac and Ishmael

d. Isaac and Jacob

4 Which of the following is true of Jacob?

a. He stole his brother's birthright.

b. His name was changed to Israel.

c. He tricked Isaac.

d. All of the above

5 Who was thrown into a lions' den?

a. David

b. Daniel

c. Shadrach, Meshach, and Abednego

d. Isaiah

6 To whom did the Lord give the Ten Commandments on Mount Sinai?

a. Adam

b. Aaron

c. Abraham

d. Moses

7 Who was Moses's sister?

a. Miriam

b. Deborah

c. Elizabeth

d. Rachel

8 Leah and Rachel were:

a. Sisters

b. Wives of David

c. Naomi's daughters-in-law

d. Married to twin brothers, Esau and Jacob

9 Who was Hannah's son?

a. Cain

b. Isaac

c. Samuel

d. Solomon

10 Who was Aaron's younger brother?

a. Joshua

b. Caleb

c. David

d. Moses

11 When the Lord wanted to test Abraham's faith, what did he tell Abraham to do?

a. Lead the people of Israel across the Red Sea

b. Sacrifice his son Isaac

c. Lead the army of Israel around the walls of Jericho

d. Send Hagar and Ishmael into the wilderness

12 Which of the following is true of Noah?

a. He received the Ten Commandments on Mount Sinai.

b. The Lord told him to sacrifice his son.

c. He built an ark and survived a great flood.

d. He built a tower at Babel.

13 **Who was the second king of Israel?**

a. Saul

b. David

c. Solomon

d. Rehoboam

14 **Who was taken to heaven in a fiery chariot?**

a. Adam

b. Methuselah

c. Elijah

d. Elisha

15 **Which list shows people in the correct chronological sequence?**

a. Adam, David, Moses

b. Joshua, Isaac, Joseph

c. Esther, Ruth, Jezebel

d. Samuel, Solomon, Joash

16 **To whom did Ruth say, "Wherever you go, I will go; wherever you live, I will live"?**

a. Boaz

b. Naomi

c. Samuel

d. David

17 **Hosea was a prophet in the Northern Kingdom of Israel who:**

a. Married a prostitute

b. Married a Philistine

c. Called down fire from heaven

d. Was swallowed by a great fish

18 **Rehoboam and Joash were both:**

a. Prophets

b. Priests

c. Kings of Israel

d. Kings of Judah

19 **Who wrote many of the Psalms?**

a. Samuel

b. David

c. Deborah

d. Jeremiah

20 **Who were Judah and Benjamin?**

a. Sons of Abraham

b. Sons of Isaac

c. Sons of Jacob

d. Sons of David

21 Which sequence of events is in the correct chronological order?

a. Creation, United Kingdom, Moses in the bulrushes

b. Handwriting on the wall, Exile, Divided Kingdom

c. Fall of the Kingdom of Israel, fall of the Kingdom of Judah, Persia conquers Babylon

d. All of the above

22 How many days and nights did it rain while Noah, his family, and the animals were aboard the ark?

a. 100

b. 50

c. 30

d. 40

23 What happened in the story of the Tower of Babel?

a. God confused the languages of the people.

b. The Lord sent fire from heaven.

c. Sodom and Gomorrah were destroyed.

d. The tower fell down.

24 What happened to the cities of Sodom and Gomorrah?

a. Their walls fell down.

b. They were destroyed by fire and brimstone.

c. They were destroyed in an earthquake.

d. They were captured by King David.

25 Who dreamed of a ladder stretching up to heaven, with angels ascending and descending?

a. Jacob

b. Joseph

c. Job

d. Pharaoh

26 **Who received a coat of many colors as a sign of favoritism from his father?**

a. Isaac
b. Jacob
c. Joseph
d. David

27 **In which country was Joseph first a slave and later prime minister?**

a. Israel
b. Greece
c. Babylon
d. Egypt

28 **Who saw a burning bush in the wilderness?**

a. Abraham
b. Moses
c. Daniel
d. John the Baptist

29 **What was the Exodus?**

a. When Adam and Eve were expelled from the Garden of Eden
b. When the inhabitants of Israel were taken as captives to Assyria
c. When the inhabitants of Judah were taken as captives to Babylon
d. When the Israelites left Egypt

30 **What annual celebration memorializes the Exodus from Egypt?**

a. Passover
b. Exodus
c. Purim
d. Day of Atonement

31 **Who created the golden calf for the people of Israel to worship?**

a. Aaron
b. Samson
c. Ahab
d. The Philistines

32 **When did the Israelites conquer Jericho?**

a. Before the Exodus

b. After the period of forty years in the wilderness

c. During the life of Samson

d. During King David's reign

33 **When was the period of the judges?**

a. Before the Exodus

b. After the period of the Divided Kingdom

c. After the Israelites returned from Egypt to the Promised Land

d. After the Exile

34 **The period of the Divided Kingdom:**

a. Began during the reign of King Solomon

b. Means Israel was divided by the Jordan River

c. Preceded the period of the United Kingdom

d. Began after the reign of King Solomon

35 **Who spent three days and nights in the belly of a great fish?**

a. Jacob

b. Jonah

c. Joash

d. Jehu

36 **Who was the first king of the Northern Kingdom of Israel during the period of the Divided Kingdom?**

a. David

b. Solomon

c. Rehoboam

d. Jeroboam

37 **Why were Shadrach, Meshach, and Abednego thrown into the fiery furnace?**

a. They insisted on praying to the God of Israel.

b. They refused to bow down and worship Nebuchadnezzar's gold statue.

c. They refused to eat the rich food offered to them.

d. They were unable to interpret the king's dream.

38 **Which nation overthrew the Northern Kingdom of Israel in 722 BC?**

a. Egypt
b. Assyria
c. Babylon
d. Greece

39 **Which nation overthrew the Southern Kingdom of Judah in 586 BC?**

a. Greece
b. Rome
c. Assyria
d. Babylon

40 **Which kingdom fell immediately after the incident of the handwriting on the wall?**

a. Israel
b. Judah
c. Babylon
d. Assyria

Answers

1. c
2. c
3. c
4. d
5. b
6. d
7. a
8. a
9. c
10. d
11. b
12. c
13. b
14. c
15. d
16. b
17. a
18. d
19. b
20. c
21. c
22. d
23. a
24. b
25. a
26. c
27. d
28. b
29. d
30. a
31. a
32. b
33. c
34. d
35. b
36. d
37. b
38. b
39. d
40. c

People, Places, and Events in the New Testament

The New Testament is essentially about Jesus Christ. It starts with the four books of the Gospels, which contain parallel accounts of his life and ministry (note that although many details of Jesus's ministry are told in two or more of the Gospels, only one Bible reference is included with most of the entries in this chapter).

The Gospels are followed by the book of Acts, which starts where the Gospels end. It tells of the activities of Jesus's followers in the first thirty years after Jesus ascended into heaven.

Next come the Epistles, which are letters containing practical lessons in theology and daily living for Jesus's followers—both in the early church and today. After all, what could be more practical than a letter from a friend?

Finally, the book of Revelation is a look into the future, as the apostle John saw it in a vision. There we see Jesus enthroned in glory.

ALPHA AND OMEGA In the Greek alphabet, alpha is the first letter and omega is the last letter. In Revelation 22:13, Jesus said, "I am Alpha and Omega, the beginning and the end, the first and the last" (KJV). He meant that he had existed before anything else existed, and he would continue to exist after the heavens and the earth had been destroyed.

ANANIAS AND SAPPHIRA Husband and wife, they were members of the early church at Jerusalem. They sold some property and said they were giving the whole sum of money to the church. They actually gave only a part of the price, and they were both struck dead for their deception (Acts 5).

The Calling of John and Andrew

ANDREW One of Jesus's twelve disciples, and the brother of Peter. He was a fisherman, and he had been a disciple of John the Baptist before he met Jesus. Jesus said to Andrew and Peter, "Follow me, and I will make you fishers of men" (Matthew 4:19 KJV).

ANGELS Spiritual beings who live in heaven and serve as messengers to earth. Angels were created sinless, but the Bible says that Satan and his demons are all fallen angels who rebelled against God (2 Peter 2:4). The Bible tells of many instances in which angels interacted with humans. Perhaps the best-known example is when "a vast host of … the armies of heaven" appeared to the shepherds outside Bethlehem to announce the birth of Jesus (Luke 2:13 NLT). The concept of guardian angels comes from Jesus's statement, "Beware that you don't look down on any of these little ones. For I tell you that in heaven their angels are always in the presence of my heavenly Father" (Matthew 18:10 NLT).

ANNA An elderly woman who stayed at the temple, awaiting the arrival of the Messiah. Luke calls her a prophetess. When Joseph and Mary brought the infant Jesus to the temple to be dedicated, Anna recognized Jesus as Israel's long-awaited Messiah and told everyone that the Messiah had come (Luke 2).

ANNUNCIATION, THE The announcement by the angel Gabriel to Mary that she would become the mother of Jesus, even though she was a virgin. After the Annunciation, Mary gave a poetic response that is often called the Magnificat (Luke 1).

APOSTLE From the Greek word meaning "one who is sent"—for instance, as a missionary. The term is usually associated with Jesus's twelve disciples, all of whom (except Judas Iscariot) went out to spread the Good News about Jesus after Pentecost. Paul, the greatest missionary in the early church, was not one of Jesus's twelve disciples, but he is also called an apostle.

AQUILA AND PRISCILLA A husband and wife team who were friends and colleagues of the apostle Paul. They ministered to the young church in Ephesus for a time. Like Paul, they supported themselves by making tents (Acts 18).

ARCHANGEL A chief among angels. The only archangels named in the Bible are Michael and Gabriel. Lucifer, also known as Satan, has traditionally been identified as a fallen archangel who rebelled against God.

Basilica of the Annunciation in modern-day Nazareth

ASCENSION, THE After Jesus's crucifixion and resurrection, he was on earth forty more days. He appeared to his disciples on several occasions, gave them various instructions, and promised that the Holy Spirit would come to them. One day they went together to the Mount of Olives, just outside Jerusalem, and Jesus rose into the sky and disappeared into a cloud. Then two angels appeared to the disciples and told them that Jesus had gone to heaven (Acts 1). This is called "the Ascension."

Tower of the Church of the Ascension, Mount of Olives

AUGUSTUS The emperor of the Roman Empire at the time of the birth of Jesus. The familiar Christmas narrative from Luke 2 begins: "And it came to pass in those days, that there went out a decree from Caesar Augustus that all the world should be taxed" (KJV). Because of the census decreed by Augustus, Joseph and Mary had to journey from their home in Nazareth to Bethlehem, where Jesus was born.

BARABBAS Pontius Pilate, the Roman governor of Judea, had a custom of releasing a Jewish prisoner each year at Passover, as a gesture of goodwill to the Jewish people. After interrogating Jesus, Pilate was convinced of Jesus's innocence, so he tried to use his annual custom as a means of releasing Jesus. He offered to release either Jesus or Barabbas, a convicted murderer, assuming the crowd would respond reasonably and ask for Jesus's release. The mob chose Barabbas, and they called for Jesus to be crucified (Luke 23).

BARNABAS When Paul returned to Jerusalem after his conversion on the Damascus Road, the other believers were suspicious of him. Barnabas came to Paul's defense, explaining that Paul was now a follower of Christ. Barnabas was not one of the twelve disciples, but he was an apostle in the early church (Acts 9–15). He and Mark traveled with Paul on Paul's first missionary journey, though Mark deserted them along the way. When Paul and Barnabas were preparing for a second journey, Barnabas again wanted to take Mark with them. Paul refused, so Barnabas and Mark traveled together and Paul traveled with Silas.

BARTHOLOMEW One of the disciples of Jesus, though the Gospels tell us very little about him. Bartholomew is called Nathanael in the Gospel of John.

BEHOLD THE MAN After the trial of Jesus, the Roman soldiers put a crown of thorns on Jesus's head, and they dressed him in a purple robe and mocked him. The Roman governor Pontius Pilate hoped this would satisfy the mob, since he had found Jesus innocent. He brought Jesus out to the mob and said, "Behold the man!" (John 19:5 KJV). The Jewish leaders insisted that he be crucified, and Pilate eventually gave in to their demands.

BETHANY A small village at the foot of the Mount of Olives, just outside Jerusalem. It was the home of Jesus's friends Mary and Martha and their brother Lazarus. Jesus frequently stayed there (see map on the following page).

BETHLEHEM The small village where Jesus was born—just south of Jerusalem. A thousand years earlier Bethlehem had been the home of King David, so it was also called the city of David. When the wise men visited King Herod the Great to inquire about the newborn king of the Jews, Herod asked the chief priests and scribes where the Christ was to be born (Matthew 2). They knew instantly that such a child was to be born in Bethlehem, for Micah 5:2 foretold that a great ruler would be born in Bethlehem. A favorite Christmas carol begins, "O little town of Bethlehem, how still we see thee lie."

Modern-day Bethlehem

BREAD OF LIFE Jesus used this expression when he said, "I am the bread of life" (John 6:48). Bread was a staple element of daily food in the

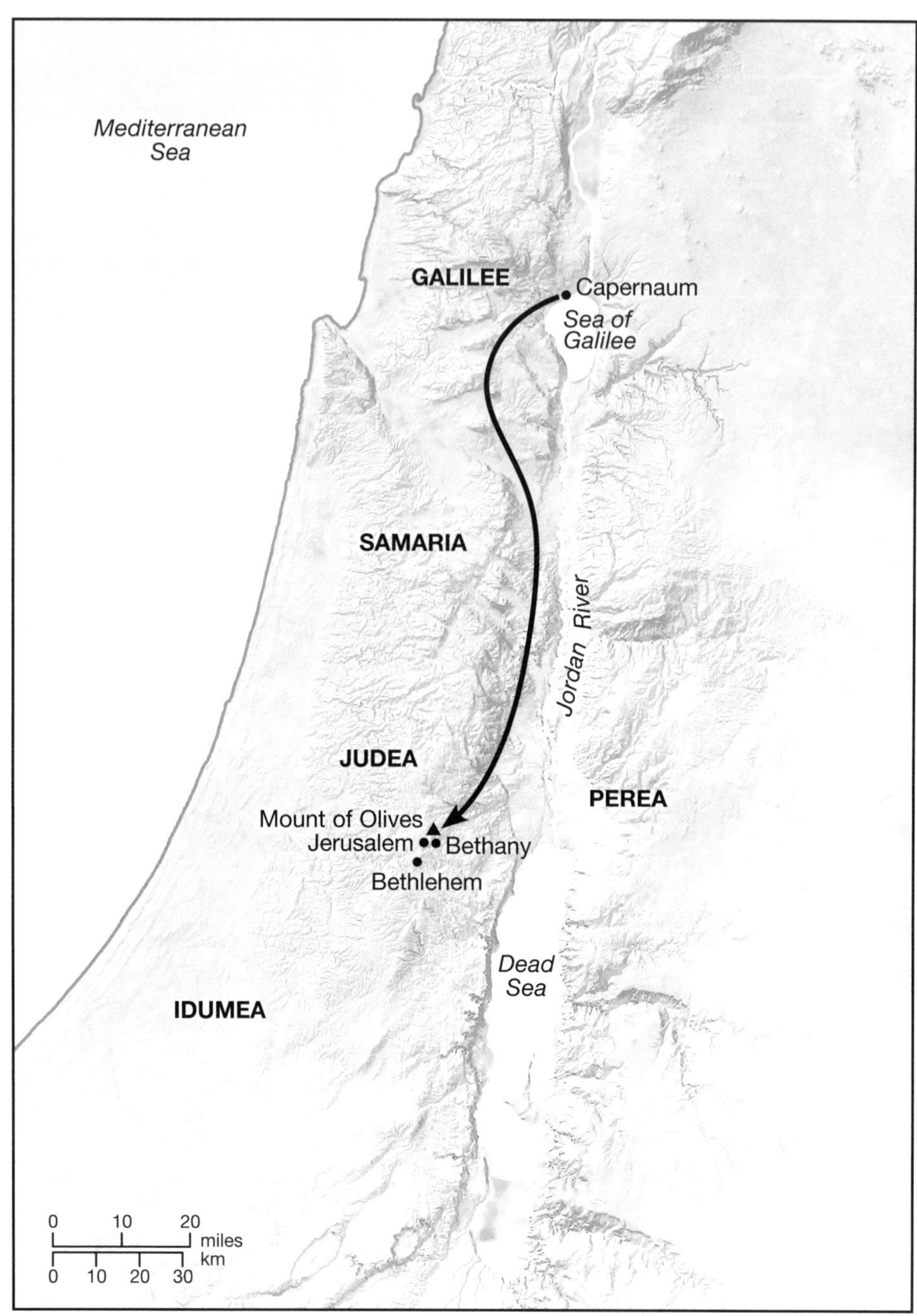

Jesus Visits Bethany After teaching throughout Galilee, Jesus returned to Jerusalem—walking eighty or more miles. He spoke in Jerusalem and then visited his friends Mary and Martha in the tiny village of Bethany on the slope of the Mount of Olives. It was here that Jesus raised Lazarus back to life.

ancient world, as it is in much of the modern world. Jesus meant that bread sustains physical life, but he himself could provide eternal life.

CAESAR A title for any of various emperors of the Roman Empire. The Caesars mentioned in the New Testament are Augustus, Tiberius, Claudius, and Nero. Augustus (reigned 30 BC to AD 14) was emperor at the time of the birth of Jesus (Luke 2:1). Tiberius (reigned AD 14–37) was emperor during the time of Jesus's ministry (Luke 3:1). Claudius (reigned AD 41–54) is mentioned in Acts 18:2 as having forced all Jews to leave Rome. Nero (reigned AD 54–68) is not identified by name, but he was the Caesar to whom Paul appealed to have his case heard (Acts 25:11). 📌 The German title *kaiser* and Russian title *czar* or *tsar* are derivatives of *Caesar*.

CAIAPHAS The high priest who presided at the trial of Jesus. The trial was a mockery, since Caiaphas was one of the leaders who had wanted Jesus arrested (Matthew 26).

CALMING THE STORM The Sea of Galilee is not large, but it lies far below sea level, and storms there can be ferocious. One day Jesus and his disciples were crossing the Sea of Galilee when a fierce storm arose (Mark 4). Jesus was sleeping in the boat, but the disciples were afraid they were going to drown. When they awoke Jesus, he said to the wind and the waves, "Peace, be still!" And the storm instantly subsided. Although the disciples had already seen Jesus perform many miracles, they were terrified at this display of power and asked one another, "Who is this? Even the wind and the waves obey him!" (verse 41 NIV).

Church of the Holy Sepulchre (foreground)—the traditional site of Calvary

CALVARY The place outside the city of Jerusalem where Jesus was crucified (see *crucifixion*). Calvary is also called Golgotha. 📌 Today the term *Calvary* is often used to refer to the entire event and purpose of Jesus's crucifixion (for example, there is a gospel song called "Calvary Covers

It All"). The popular hymn "The Old Rugged Cross" begins with the words, "On a hill far away stood an old rugged cross." The hill in that song is Calvary.

CAPERNAUM A town in Galilee, on the shore of the Sea of Galilee. At the start of Jesus's ministry, after he was rejected by the people in his hometown of Nazareth, he went to Capernaum and was warmly welcomed (Luke 4). Much of Jesus's public ministry took place in the vicinity of Capernaum.

CENTURION A Roman military commander who had one hundred soldiers under his command. Several centurions are mentioned in the New Testament, including Cornelius, who believed in Jesus under Peter's teaching.

CHIEF PRIESTS See *Sanhedrin.*

CHRIST A title for Jesus. It comes from a Greek word and is the equivalent of the Hebrew word that means "Messiah," or "anointed one." In the Old Testament, individuals

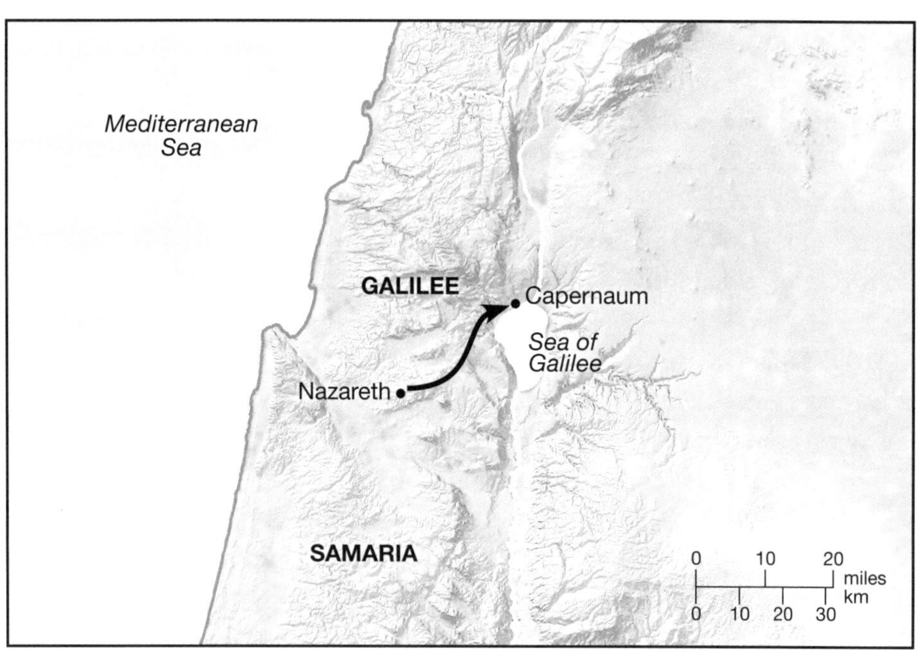

Capernaum Jesus and his disciples moved on to Capernaum after he was rejected in his hometown of Nazareth. Capernaum was a small village on the shore of the Sea of Galilee. Ruins of an ancient synagogue (likely built on top of the very synagogue where Jesus taught) can be seen there today.

were anointed with oil to show that they had been selected as the king. Jesus is the ultimate king. In contemporary usage, most people use the names Jesus, Christ, and Jesus Christ interchangeably.

CORNELIUS A Roman centurion who had a vision in which he was told to send for the apostle Peter (Acts 10). After hearing Peter preach, Cornelius became a believer in Jesus, and he and everyone in his household were baptized. This caused a dispute among the church leaders as to whether gentiles who became believers also had to convert to Judaism. The issue was resolved at the Council at Jerusalem (see *Jerusalem, Council at*).

CROSS When Jesus Christ was sentenced to death by Pontius Pilate, he was crucified on a cross (Mark 15:20–32). A cross consisted of a wooden crosspiece attached to an upright post. The victim's arms were stretched out on the crosspiece and tied or nailed in place, and the feet were tied or nailed to the upright post. The cross was lifted up and inserted into a hole in the ground, and the victim was left to hang there until he died, usually by suffocation. The cross of Christ has become a symbol of his death, and particularly his atonement for the sins of mankind, bringing redemption. See also *crucifixion*.

CROWN OF THORNS After Jesus was betrayed by Judas Iscariot, he was tried and condemned by the Sanhedrin (Jewish ruling council) and then taken to Pontius Pilate for sentencing (see *trial of Jesus*). Pilate interrogated Jesus but found him not guilty. Nonetheless, to appease the Jewish leaders, Pilate had Jesus savagely beaten. In the process of carrying out this punishment, the soldiers made a crown of thorns and forced it on Jesus's head. They also put a purple robe on him and mocked him as the king of the Jews.

CRUCIFIXION A form of capital punishment in the Roman Empire. The criminal's hands and feet were tied or nailed to a wooden cross, which was then lifted up and inserted into a hole in the ground.

Crucifixion was excruciatingly painful, and a person could survive on the cross for several days before finally dying. The victim's legs were sometimes broken to keep him from lifting himself up to breathe. This then led to death by suffocation. After Jesus was betrayed, he was tried by the Sanhedrin (see *trial of Jesus*), which found him guilty of blasphemy. The penalty for blasphemy was death, so Jesus was taken to Pontius Pilate, the Roman governor of Judea, for formal sentencing. Pilate interrogated Jesus and found him not guilty, but to appease the Jewish leaders he sentenced Jesus to death on a cross. The crucifixion of Jesus is an important aspect of Christian doctrine, because Jesus paid the penalty for our sins by his death (see *atonement* in the chapter "Church Life and Theology"). Tradition tells us that the apostle Peter was crucified, but that he asked to be crucified headdownward because he felt unworthy to die as Jesus had died.

Christ on the Cross

DAMASCUS ROAD Saul, later known as the apostle Paul, was traveling from Jerusalem to Damascus (the capital of Syria) to persecute Christians when he had his conversion experience (Acts 9:1–19) (see *Paul*). Today the expression "Damascus Road experience" refers to a conversion experience.

DEMONS Evil spirits. Demons are probably fallen angels who joined Satan in his rebellion against God. They help Satan tempt people to sin, and they have great destructive power. The New Testament contains numerous accounts of people who were demon-possessed. As the Son of God, Jesus cast out many. Exorcism, the act of casting the demon(s) out of a person who is demon-possessed, involves calling upon the name and power of Jesus against the demon. The Greek word translated "demon" in modern translations was translated "devil" in the King James Version.

Liberal theology tends to discount the existence of demons and of Satan, but the recent increase in spiritism and the occult would seem to validate the traditional understanding that demons are indeed real.

DISCIPLES Any follower or learner can be called a disciple, but the term is used specifically for the Gospel accounts of Jesus's twelve closest followers. They are sometimes called The Twelve. Their names were Simon Peter, James and John (sons of Zebedee), Andrew, Bartholomew (also called Nathanael), James (son of Alphaeus), Judas Iscariot, Matthew (also called Levi), Philip, Simon the Zealot, Thaddaeus (also called Judas, son of James), and Thomas. The disciples are also called the apostles (persons who are sent out to proclaim the gospel), because after Jesus's resurrection and ascension they went throughout the known world to tell others the Good News about Jesus. The Bible does not give many details about their deaths (except for Judas Iscariot, who hanged himself, and James son of Zebedee, who was put to death by King Herod Agrippa), but tradition says that most of the apostles died as martyrs (see *martyr* in the chapter "Church History").

DORCAS A Christian woman known for her acts of mercy who was brought back to life when the apostle Peter prayed for her (Acts 9). Many believed in the Lord as a result of this miracle.

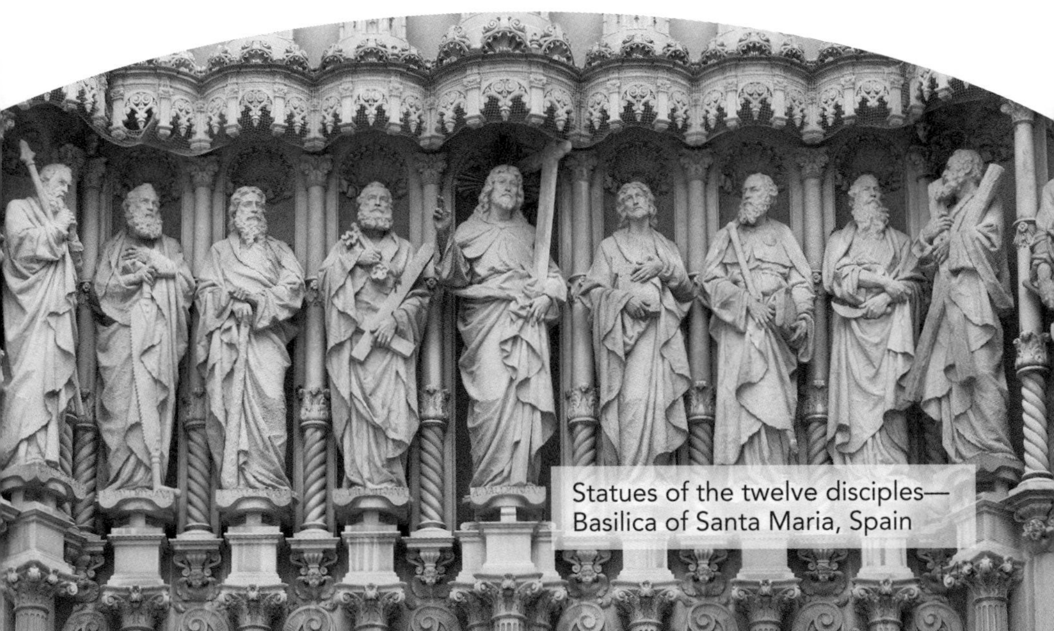
Statues of the twelve disciples—Basilica of Santa Maria, Spain

DOUBTING THOMAS See *Thomas.*

DOVE A bird mentioned in both the Old and New Testaments. It was used as food and also as an acceptable sacrifice. The Holy Spirit came down in the form of a dove at the baptism of Jesus. In church history, up to the present, the dove has come to symbolize peace, love, and the church.

ELIZABETH (ALSO SPELLED ELISABETH) The wife of Zechariah the priest and mother of John the Baptist (Luke 1). She was a cousin of Mary, the mother of Jesus. John's birth was foretold by an angel who appeared to Zechariah while he was carrying out his priestly duties in the temple. While Mary was pregnant, she visited Elizabeth, who was also pregnant. When Elizabeth heard Mary's greeting, "Elizabeth's child leaped within her" (Luke 1:41 NLT). She greeted Mary by saying, "Blessed are you among women, and blessed is the fruit of your womb!" (Luke 1:42).

EMMANUEL See *Immanuel.*

EMPTY TOMB A reference to Jesus's resurrection. Roman guards had been posted at Jesus's tomb to make sure no one stole his body (Matthew 27). When some of the women among Jesus's followers went to the tomb early on Sunday morning, however, they found the tomb was empty. Jesus had come back to life!

"He is risen! He is not here." (Mark 16:6)

EUTYCHUS A young man who fell asleep and fell out a window while the apostle Paul was preaching. He died, but Paul prayed for him and he came back to life (Acts 20).

FLIGHT TO EGYPT King Herod the Great was furious when he discovered that the wise men had gone home without telling him where to find the newborn king of the Jews (Matthew 2). In order to kill the child, he ordered the death of all the boys in Bethlehem who were two years of age or younger. An

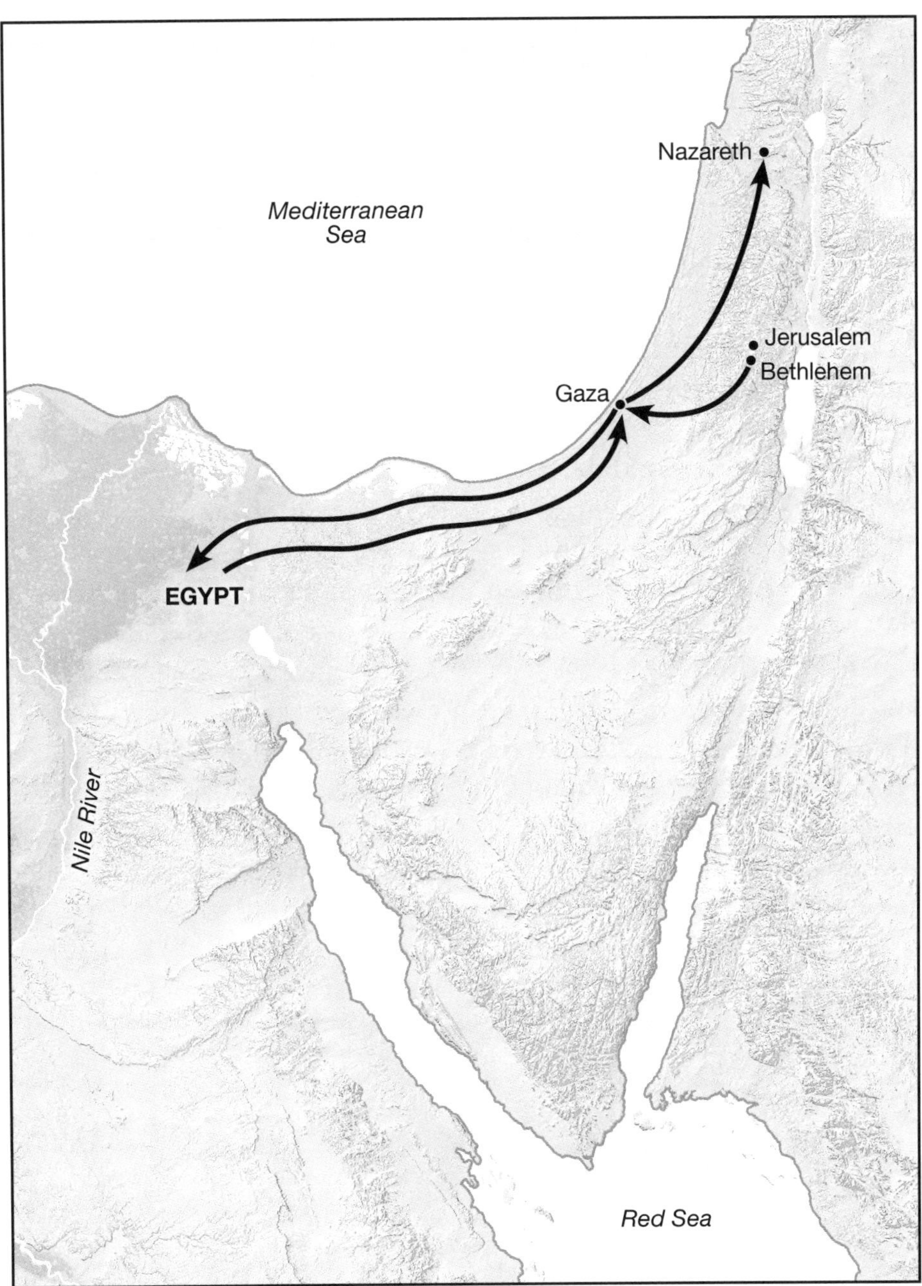

The Flight to Egypt King Herod planned to kill the baby Jesus, whom he perceived to be a future threat to his position. Warned of this treachery in a dream, Joseph took Mary and Jesus to Egypt and stayed until Herod's death, which occurred a year or two later. They planned to return to Judea, but God led them instead to Nazareth in Galilee.

angel appeared to Mary's husband, Joseph, in a dream and told him to take Mary and Jesus to Egypt, where they would be safe. They fled immediately and stayed there until Herod's death, about two years later. The holy family then returned to Nazareth, the village in Galilee where Joseph and Mary had grown up.

GABRIEL An archangel who served as a messenger from God. He appeared to the prophet Daniel, Zechariah (father of John the Baptist), the Virgin Mary, and Joseph (husband of Mary). His announcement to Mary (see *Annunciation*) was that she would give birth to a son who would be the Son of God, even though she was a virgin.

GALILEE The northern region of the Holy Land, between the Mediterranean Sea and the Sea of Galilee. Jesus grew up in the village of Nazareth, which is in Galilee, and much of his public ministry took place in Galilee. The region of Samaria was south of Galilee, between Galilee and Judea.

GALILEE, SEA OF A medium-sized lake (about seven miles across) on the eastern border of the region of Galilee. Peter, Andrew, James, and John were all fishermen on the Sea of Galilee, and much of Jesus's ministry took place in that area. Jesus's miracles of walking on water and calming the storm both took place here. The Jordan River flows into the Sea of Galilee and then out to the Dead Sea.

Sea of Galilee

GENEALOGY A listing of ancestors or descendants. The Israelites took great care to preserve their genealogies to show their standing as descendants of Abraham, thus their participation in God's covenant to Abraham. There are many genealogies in the Bible, including genealogies of Jesus in Matthew 1 and Luke 3. In the King James Version, the genealogy of Jesus in Matthew 1 makes repeated use of the word *begat*, which means "became the father of." It begins, "Abraham begat Isaac; and Isaac begat Jacob; and Jacob begat Judas and his brethren."

Olive trees, garden of Gethsemane

GETHSEMANE, GARDEN OF A garden at the foot of the Mount of Olives, just outside Jerusalem. After the Last Supper, Jesus and his disciples went to Gethsemane to pray, as they frequently did. On this night, Jesus prayed, "Father, if you are willing, take this cup from me; yet not my will, but yours be done" (Luke 22:42 NIV). As a man, he preferred not to go through with the suffering that lay just ahead, but as the Son of God he wanted God's will to be done. It was immediately after this that Judas Iscariot came to Gethsemane and betrayed Jesus to the Jewish leaders.

GOLD, FRANKINCENSE, AND MYRRH Three precious gifts that the wise men brought to Jesus (Matthew 2). As in our world today, gold was a precious commodity then. Frankincense and myrrh were aromatic substances used as perfumes. The gifts were valuable, fitting as gifts for a king. Joseph and Mary may have used the gold to finance their unexpected escape to Egypt (see *flight to Egypt*).

GOLDEN RULE A teaching of Jesus from his Sermon on the Mount (Matthew 7:12). A popular rendition is "Do unto others as you would have them do unto you." Much of civilized behavior is based on the principle of the Golden Rule. Many religions other than Christianity also have teachings similar to the Golden Rule.

GOLGOTHA The place outside Jerusalem where Jesus was crucified (see *crucifixion*). The name means "the place of the skull." In the King James Version it is called Calvary (Luke 23:33). 📌 Today there are two locations in Jerusalem that are identified as possible sites of Golgotha and the empty tomb: the Church of the Holy Sepulchre and the Garden Tomb.

Bedrock resembling a skull near the Garden Tomb, Jerusalem

GOOD SAMARITAN, PARABLE OF THE When Jesus told a lawyer to love his neighbor as himself, the lawyer asked, "Who is my neighbor?" Jesus responded by telling the Parable of the Good Samaritan (Luke 10:25–37): A Jewish man was traveling along the road to Jericho and was attacked by bandits who beat him up and robbed him. A Jewish priest came by but did nothing to help the man. Then a Levite (a temple worker) came by and also did nothing to help the man. Finally, a Samaritan, who was despised by the Jews, came along and helped the man. He dressed his wounds, took him to an inn, and paid the innkeeper to care for the man. Jesus asked the lawyer, "Which of the three was a neighbor to the man?" The lawyer answered, "The one who showed pity." Jesus responded, "Go and do likewise." 📌 Today a Good Samaritan is anyone who goes out of his way to help someone in distress.

GOOD SHEPHERD Jesus called himself the Good Shepherd (John 10). He meant that he loves and cares for his followers, just as a shepherd cares for his sheep. See also *Lost Sheep, Parable of the.*

GREAT COMMISSION Jesus's instruction to his disciples to preach the gospel throughout the world: "Go and make disciples of all nations, baptizing them in the name of the Father and of the Son and of the Holy Spirit, and teaching them to obey everything I have commanded you" (Matthew 28:19–20 NIV). A slightly different version is recorded in Mark 16:15: "Go into all the world and preach the gospel to every creature" (see *gospel* in the chapter "Church Life and Theology").

Ancient ruins of Corinth in modern-day Greece

GREECE A country in southeastern Europe on the major peninsula that juts into the Mediterranean Sea east of Italy. It was the center of the Greek Empire, which flourished during the period between the Old and New Testaments. By the first century AD, Greece was part of the Roman Empire. The apostle Paul visited Greece several times and started churches there (for example, in Corinth and Philippi). Greek was the trade language of the portions of the Roman Empire that had previously been conquered by Alexander the Great, and the New Testament was written in *Koiné* ("common") Greek.

HEROD In the New Testament, four generations of rulers named Herod are mentioned. This is confusing to many Bible readers, because in most instances the text simply refers to "Herod."

- *Herod the Great*, a ruthless ruler, was king of the entire New Testament region of Israel from 40–4 BC. He was responsible for many building projects, including the third temple in Jerusalem. He was king at the time of the birth of Jesus. The wise men naturally went to see King Herod to inquire about the newborn king of the Jews (Matthew 2). Herod was insanely jealous of anyone who might try to take his throne, so he told the wise men to let him know when they found this new king. When they returned home without reporting back to him, Herod was furious and ordered the death of all the boys in Bethlehem under the age of two. (This event is sometimes called the "Slaughter of the Holy Innocents.") In a dream, an angel warned Mary's husband, Joseph, of this danger, so he and Mary escaped to Egypt to protect their baby son. Herod the Great died in 4 BC, so Jesus's birth may have been as early as

6 BC. When Herod the Great died, his kingdom was divided among three of his sons. Judea and Samaria went to Archelaus, Galilee and Perea (east of the Jordan River) went to Herod Antipas, and the northeastern portions of the kingdom went to Herod Philip I. When Joseph, Mary, and Jesus returned from Egypt, they bypassed Judea and went to Galilee when they heard that the wicked Archelaus had succeeded Herod the Great in Judea (Matthew 2).

Herod Antipas

- *Herod Antipas* (also called Herod the Tetrarch), the ruler in Galilee, participated in the trial of Jesus (Luke 23). He was visiting in Jerusalem at the time, so Pontius Pilate sent Jesus to him. Herod asked Jesus many questions to which Jesus gave no reply. Herod and his soldiers then mocked Jesus, put a kingly robe on him, and sent him back to Pilate. Herod Antipas was also responsible for the death of John the Baptist (see *Herodias*; *Salome*).
- *Herod Agrippa*, a grandson of Herod the Great, is mentioned briefly in Acts 12, where he is called King Herod. As his grandfather had been, Herod Agrippa was king over the entire region. He was responsible for the death of the apostle James (son of Zebedee), and he imprisoned the apostle Peter. He died suddenly after receiving praise from the people of the cities of Tyre and Sidon, who shouted, "[This is] the voice of a god and not of a man!" (Acts 12:22). Herodias, who wanted to execute John the Baptist, was his sister.
- *Herod Agrippa II*, the son of Herod Agrippa and great-grandson of Herod the Great, is called King Agrippa in Acts 25. He was king over the northern and eastern region of the Holy Land. He interrogated the apostle Paul after Paul's appeal to Caesar. Secular history tells

us that Agrippa's sister Bernice was his mistress. Another sister, Drusilla, married Felix, the Roman governor of Judea at that time, who heard Paul's case (Acts 24).

HERODIAS A granddaughter of Herod the Great and sister of Herod Agrippa I. She married her uncle, Herod Philip I. Later she married another uncle, Herod Antipas. John the Baptist kept saying it was wrong for Herod Antipas to marry the wife of Herod Philip, and Herodias got revenge by arranging for John's death: At a wild birthday party for Herod Antipas, Herodias's daughter, Salome, danced and pleased the king and his guests (Mark 6). Herod told Salome she could have anything she requested. After consulting with her mother, Salome asked for the head of John the Baptist on a platter.

HOLY FAMILY Joseph, Mary, and Jesus are called the holy family.

HOSANNA During Jesus's Triumphal Entry into Jerusalem, the crowds shouted, "Hosanna to the Son of David!" (Matthew 21:9). *Hosanna* is a Hebrew expression meaning "Save!" It became an expression of praise.

IMMANUEL The prophet Isaiah said, "Behold, a virgin shall conceive, and bear a son, and shall call his name Immanuel" (Isaiah 7:14 KJV). Matthew 1:23 quotes this prophecy and shows that it was fulfilled by Jesus's birth. Matthew also tells us what the Hebrew name means: "God with us." The name is spelled *Emmanuel* in the King James Version.

JAMES (BROTHER OF JESUS) During Jesus's ministry, his brothers did not believe he was the Messiah. After Jesus's death, resurrection, and ascension, however, his brother James became one of the leaders of the church in Jerusalem (Acts 15). Many scholars believe he wrote the letter that we know as the book of James. ➧ There are several references in the New Testament to Jesus's brothers and sisters. Matthew 13:55 lists four brothers: James, Joseph (sometimes spelled Joses), Simon, and Jude (sometimes spelled Judas). Some people prefer to call them half-brothers of Jesus, since God was Jesus's father. The tradition in the Roman Catholic Church, which holds that Mary was a virgin her whole life, is that they were cousins of Jesus or possibly Joseph's children from an earlier marriage.

JAMES (SON OF ALPHAEUS) One of Jesus's twelve disciples. The Bible gives us no other details about him.

James the Greater (son of Zebedee)

JAMES (SON OF ZEBEDEE) A fisherman who became one of Jesus's twelve disciples. James, his brother John, and Peter were the three disciples who were closest to Jesus. James was present at the Transfiguration of Jesus and was also with Jesus in the garden of Gethsemane. He was the first of the disciples to be martyred when he was put to death by King Herod Agrippa (Acts 12).

JERUSALEM, COUNCIL AT The first church council was held in Jerusalem in about AD 50 to decide whether gentiles had to become converts to Judaism in order to become Christians (Acts 15). Peter told the church leaders in Jerusalem that the Holy Spirit had come upon Cornelius and the other gentile believers in Christ. The conclusion of the Council was that gentiles did not have to be circumcised in order to be Christians.

JESUS Also called Jesus Christ, he is the central figure in the New Testament. His life and ministry are the subject of each of the four Gospels. The name Jesus means "he will save" and is the same name as the Hebrew Joshua. Jesus is often referred to as the founder of the Christian religion. Actually, it was his disciples and the other apostles who spread the gospel (the Good News of Christ's salvation) and started churches after Jesus's ascension to heaven. Jesus's mother, Mary, was a virgin, and his birth was announced to shepherds by angels. He was born in Bethlehem, was taken to Egypt to escape the wrath of King Herod, and grew up in the Galilean village of Nazareth as a carpenter's son. He performed many miracles during his public ministry, was betrayed by one of his disciples, was crucified by the Roman government, came back to life again in three days, and ascended into heaven. The exact years of Jesus's birth and death are uncertain. Scholars believe he was born no later than 4 BC, which is the year Herod the Great died. Luke 3:23 tells us that Jesus "was about thirty years old when he began his ministry" (NIV). The events recorded in the Gospels suggest that his earthly ministry lasted about three years, so he would have been about thirty-three when he was crucified. He died during the period that Pontius Pilate was governor of Judea, which was AD 26–36. Christians accept Jesus as the Son of God, the Messiah promised to the people of Israel in the Old Testament. Most Jews do not accept Jesus as their Messiah, viewing him instead as simply a good teacher. To Muslims, Jesus is an important prophet.

JOHN (THE DISCIPLE) One of Jesus's closest disciples. John refers to himself as "the disciple whom Jesus loved" (John 13:23 NIV). Before meeting Jesus, he was already a disciple of John the Baptist. He wrote the Gospel of John, which is an eyewitness account of the life and ministry of Jesus. After Jesus ascended to heaven, Peter and John became leaders of the early church. John wrote the New Testament epistles (letters) we call 1 John, 2 John, and 3 John. He may also have written the book of Revelation.

JOHN THE BAPTIST John was the son of Zechariah the priest

Byzantine-era mosaic of Jesus

and his wife, Elizabeth, and he was a second cousin of Jesus. His role was to announce the coming of the Messiah. John lived in the wilderness and ate locusts and wild honey. When he preached, great crowds came out to hear him, and he baptized them in the Jordan River (see *baptism* in the chapter "Church Life and Theology"). When Jesus came to be baptized, John said, "Behold! The Lamb of God who takes away the sin of the world!" (John 1:29). John was beheaded by Herod Antipas (see *Herodias*; *Salome*).

Excavation at "Bethany Beyond the Jordan," a possible site where John baptized (John 1:28)

JOSEPH (HUSBAND OF MARY) The earthly father of Jesus. Very little is known about Joseph, except that he was a carpenter and a descendant of King David. He was a man of upright principles, as evidenced by his plan not to marry Mary when he found out she was pregnant. An angel told him in a dream that Mary's child had been conceived by the Holy Spirit and that he should marry her (Matthew 1). Presumably he died before Jesus began his public ministry.

JOSEPH OF ARIMATHEA After Jesus died on the cross, Joseph of Arimathea asked Pontius Pilate for permission to bury the body (John 19). Joseph and Nicodemus then embalmed Jesus's body and laid it in Joseph's own rock-hewn tomb. Along with Nicodemus, Joseph was a member of the Sanhedrin and had become a follower of Jesus.

JUDAS (SON OF JAMES) Another name for Thaddaeus, one of Jesus's twelve disciples. The Bible tells us very little about him.

JUDAS ISCARIOT One of Jesus's twelve disciples—the one who betrayed him to the Jewish leaders for thirty pieces of silver (Matthew 26). After Jesus's last Passover meal with the disciples (the Last Supper), Judas led the Jewish leaders to the garden of Gethsemane and betrayed Jesus there by greeting him with a kiss. When he saw that Jesus was actually condemned to death, Judas committed suicide.

JUDEA During the New Testament period, this term was used specifically for the Roman province of Judea, which was south of the region of Samaria. Jerusalem was the capital of Judea. Pontius Pilate was the Roman governor of Judea during the years of Jesus's public ministry.

KING OF KINGS In Revelation 19, Jesus is described as a great warrior on a white horse who destroys the beast (the Antichrist) and the kings and nations that follow the beast. On Jesus's robe and on his thigh is written this title: KING OF KINGS AND LORD OF LORDS. It means that Jesus is more powerful than all other kings, no matter how powerful they may appear. 📌 The "Hallelujah Chorus" from Handel's *Messiah* includes the refrain, "King of Kings and Lord of Lords."

KING OF THE JEWS When the wise men visited King Herod the Great, they asked where they could find the newborn king of the Jews (Matthew 2). They expected to find the infant king in the royal palace. After Pontius Pilate condemned Jesus to death by crucifixion, the Roman soldiers flogged (whipped) Jesus. Then they clothed him in a purple robe and put a crown of thorns on his head. They knelt down in mockery and said, "Hail, King of the Jews!" (John 19:3). When Jesus was nailed to the cross, the soldiers put a sign above his head that said, in Aramaic, Latin, and Greek: JESUS OF NAZARETH, THE KING OF THE JEWS (verse 19). The chief priests objected to the wording of the sign and asked Pilate to change it to "He said, 'I am the King of the Jews'" (verse 21), but Pilate refused to change it. 📌 Crucifixes often show a sign above Jesus's head that says "INRI." This is an abbreviation for the Latin words *Iesus Nazarenus Rex Iudaeorum* ("Jesus of Nazareth, King of the Jews").

LAMB OF GOD Once when John the Baptist saw Jesus approaching, John said, "Behold! The Lamb of God who takes away the sin of the world!" John meant that Jesus was like a sacrificial lamb. He was the perfect sacrifice sent by God to atone for the sins of mankind. John went on to say, "I have seen and testified that this is the Son of God" (John 1:29, 34).

LAST SUPPER, THE At the end of Jesus's public ministry, he and his disciples celebrated the Passover together (Luke 22). When Jesus blessed the bread and gave it to his disciples, he said, "This is my body given for you; do this in remembrance of me." Then he took a cup of wine and said, "This cup is the new covenant in my blood, which is poured out for you" (verses 19–20 NIV). While they were eating, Judas Iscariot left to betray Jesus to the chief priests. After supper, Jesus and the other disciples went to the garden of Gethsemane to pray, and Jesus was arrested shortly thereafter. He was crucified the next day. In accordance with Jesus's command, Christians celebrate the Lord's Supper, or Holy Communion, to commemorate his death. One of the most famous works of Renaissance art is Leonardo da Vinci's painting called *The Last Supper*.

LAZARUS The brother of Mary and Martha, and one of Jesus's close friends (John 11). When Lazarus died, Jesus waited several days before going to Bethany, where Lazarus lived. When Jesus finally arrived, he asked Mary and Martha to take him to the tomb and to roll the stone away from the opening. Martha responded, "Lord, he has been dead for four days. The smell will be terrible" (verse 39 NLT). But when they opened the tomb, Jesus prayed and called out to Lazarus. Lazarus then came back to life and came out of the grave, still wrapped in his graveclothes.

LEVI See *Matthew*.

The Cenacle, a Crusader-era structure in Jerusalem, commemorates the traditional location of the Last Supper.

LOAVES AND FISHES, MIRACLE OF THE On two different occasions Jesus miraculously provided food for a huge crowd of people who had been listening to him teach (Mark 6:30–44; Mark 8:1–10). Once there were 5,000 men (not to mention the women and children), and another time there were 4,000 men. In the first instance, a boy in the crowd gave the disciples five small loaves of bread and two dried fishes. Jesus took the loaves and fishes, blessed them, and began dividing them among the disciples for distribution to the crowd. The food was miraculously multiplied, and the entire crowd was fed. The feeding of the five thousand is the only one of Jesus's many miracles that is reported in each of the four Gospels (Matthew 14:13–21; Mark 6:30–44; Luke 9:10–17; John 6:1–13).

LOST SHEEP, PARABLE OF THE Jesus told this parable to show that God cares for and seeks out each person (Luke 15). If a shepherd had 100 sheep and lost one of them, he would leave the 99 and search for the one that was lost. In the same way, God searches for each of us, even for notorious sinners. See also *Good Shepherd*.

LUKE The writer of the Gospel of Luke and of the book of Acts. He was a physician who wanted to write an orderly account of all he had learned about Jesus and about the activities of the apostles and the growth of the early church. He was a close companion of the apostle Paul and probably observed firsthand much of what is recorded in the book of Acts.

MAGI See *wise men*.

MAGNIFICAT The poetic response that the Virgin Mary gave after the angel Gabriel announced to her that she would be the mother of Jesus, the Messiah (Luke 1:46–55). *Magnificat* is Latin for "magnifies" and is the first word in the Latin text of the Magnificat. It has been repeated by Christians for centuries, in both Latin and modern languages, and also set to music in many variations. In the English Standard Version, it begins,

My soul magnifies the Lord,
and my spirit rejoices in God my Savior,
for he has looked on the humble estate of his servant.
For behold, from now on all generations will call me blessed.

MAMMON The King James Version uses this word in Matthew 6:24, part of Jesus's Sermon on the Mount: "No man can serve two masters.... Ye cannot serve God and mammon." *Mammon* means money or wealth.

MANGER A simple wood or stone structure that holds hay for livestock to eat. Jesus was born in a stable because Mary and Joseph arrived in Bethlehem and found "there was no lodging available for them." His mother "wrapped him snugly in strips of cloth and laid him in a manger" (Luke 2:7 NLT). Perhaps the manger was the cleanest spot she could find.

MARK The writer of the Gospel of Mark. Also called John Mark, he traveled with the apostles Paul and Barnabas on their first missionary journey, but he deserted them and returned to Jerusalem. When Barnabas recommended that they again take Mark on their second journey, Paul flatly refused (Acts 15), so Barnabas took Mark, and Paul traveled with Silas. But later Paul welcomed Mark back into his ministry.

MARTHA See *Mary and Martha.*

MARY (MOTHER OF JESUS) She is often called the Virgin Mary, because she was a virgin when Jesus was born. She was a young woman, perhaps about fourteen at the time of her engagement to Joseph. While she was still engaged, the angel Gabriel told her (see *Annunciation*) that she would have a son, and that she was to name him Jesus (Luke 1). She asked how this could be, since she was a virgin. The angel replied, "The Holy Spirit will come upon you, and the power of the Most High will overshadow you. So the baby to be born will be holy, and he will be called the Son of God" (verse 35 NLT). Joseph wanted to break their engagement when he found out that Mary was pregnant, but the angel appeared to him in a dream and told him to marry her. We do not know much about Mary after the birth of Jesus, though she was still living at the time of Jesus's death. 📌 The doctrine of the Roman Catholic Church is that Mary remained a virgin for her entire life. Many Protestants do not accept this doctrine, since the Gospel accounts name several of Jesus's brothers and refer to his sisters. For a comment about varying interpretations of the term "Jesus's brothers," see *James (brother of Jesus)*. Other dogmas of the Roman Catholic Church include the Immaculate Conception (the doctrine that Mary was conceived without original sin) and the Assumption of Mary (the doctrine that she was taken bodily to heaven without dying). She is often called the Mother of God by Catholics (see *Hail Mary* in the chapter "Church Life and Theology").

MARY AND MARTHA With their brother, Lazarus, these sisters were Jesus's close friends. Once when Jesus visited in their home, Mary sat at Jesus's feet and listened to his teaching while Martha worked in the kitchen, preparing the meal (Luke 10). Martha complained that Mary was not doing her share of the work, but Jesus responded, "Mary has chosen what is better" (verse 42 NIV). Shortly before Jesus was betrayed and killed, Mary poured costly perfume on his feet and wiped his feet with her hair as an act of devotion.

Ruins of an ancient synagogue in Magdala, the possible hometown of Mary Magdalene

MARY MAGDALENE A follower of Jesus, she was present at Jesus's crucifixion and was one of the women who first found out that Jesus had been raised back to life (Luke 24). Tradition says that she had been a prostitute before meeting Jesus, but the Gospels do not say so. It is clear, however, that Jesus cast seven demons out of her.

MATTHEW One of Jesus's disciples. He had been a tax collector, a despised occupation, before Jesus called him, saying, "Follow me" (Matthew 9:9). Matthew is traditionally regarded as the writer of the book of Matthew. He is also called Levi in the Gospel accounts.

MATTHIAS After the suicide of Judas Iscariot, the remaining disciples selected Matthias to take Judas's place as a witness of the resurrection of Jesus. He is described as a person who had been with Jesus and the disciples throughout Jesus's ministry (Acts 1), but the actual process of selecting between two candidates was done by casting lots (like throwing dice) so God would direct the decision.

MESSIAH Late in the period of the Old Testament, the Jews began looking for Messiah (which means "the anointed one"), the great king who would be their liberator and savior (Daniel 9:25–26). His coming had been foreshadowed as early as the time of Adam and Eve. In the New Testament era, the term *Christ* is equivalent to *Messiah*. Jesus was accepted by many as the Messiah that the Scriptures foretold would be born from David's royal line, but others chose not to believe that he was the redeemer God had promised. Christians accept Jesus as the Messiah, the one anointed by God as the Savior; most Jews do not accept Jesus as the Messiah. One of the great works of sacred music is called *Messiah*, by George Frideric Handel. It presents great prophetic passages from the Old Testament, then uses New Testament texts to present the birth, death, and resurrection of Jesus the Messiah.

MICHAEL Michael and Gabriel are archangels (chiefs among angels) and are the only angels mentioned by name in the Bible. In Daniel 10, Michael is seen engaged in warfare against the prince of Persia, which was evidently an evil spirit power. In Revelation 12, Michael and his angels defeat the dragon (Satan) in a great battle in heaven.

MIRACLES Supernatural events caused by the power of God, often functioning as a sign from God. The Bible is filled with miracles, from the parting of the Red Sea to fire from heaven to walking on water. In a sense, of course, any interaction between God and man is miraculous. Some of the key miracles in the life of Christ are the Virgin Birth, the raising of Lazarus, the Resurrection, and the

Ascension. Evangelical Christians tend to take at face value the accounts of miracles in the Bible. Christians of a more liberal persuasion are often uncomfortable with the concept of miracles, looking instead for natural explanations for events that are presented in the Bible as miracles.

MISSIONARY JOURNEYS OF PAUL The apostle Paul took three extended trips through the areas that are in present-day Turkey and Greece. His ministry was "to Jews, and also to Greeks" (Acts 20:21), and he shared the Good News about Jesus Christ everywhere he went. Groups of believers (churches) sprang up in many of the cities he visited, including Ephesus and Galatia (in present-day Turkey) and Philippi, Thessalonica, and Corinth (in present-day Greece). The epistles (letters) Paul later sent to these churches are the biblical books of Ephesians, Galatians, Philippians, 1 and 2 Thessalonians, and 1 and 2 Corinthians. Barnabas traveled with Paul on his first journey, and Silas traveled with Paul on his second journey. In 2 Corinthians 11, Paul

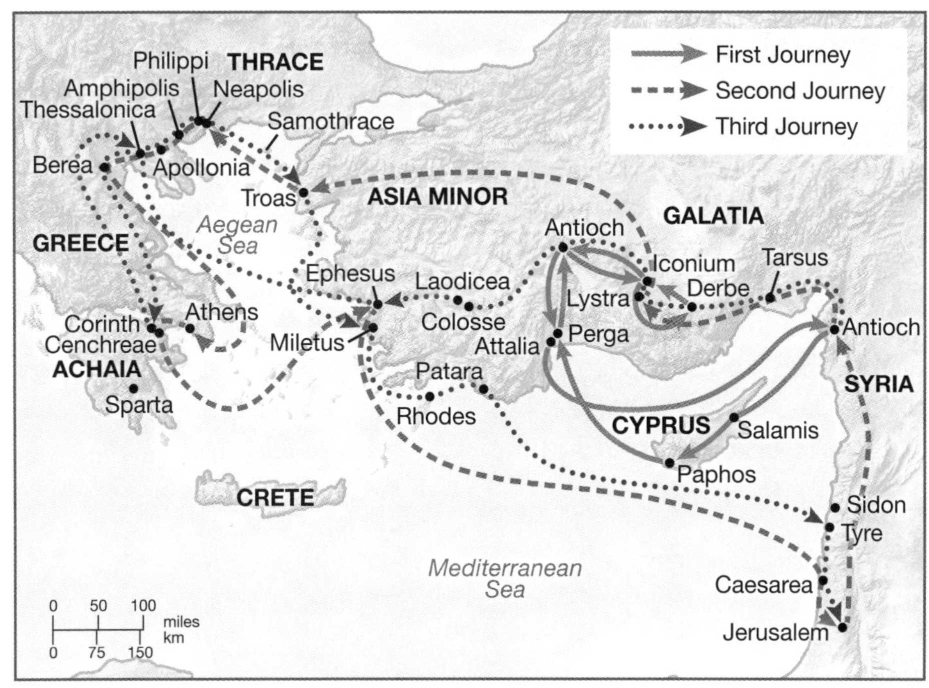

Paul's First, Second, and Third Missionary Journeys
See Acts 13:1–14:28; 15:36–18:22; 18:23–21:16.

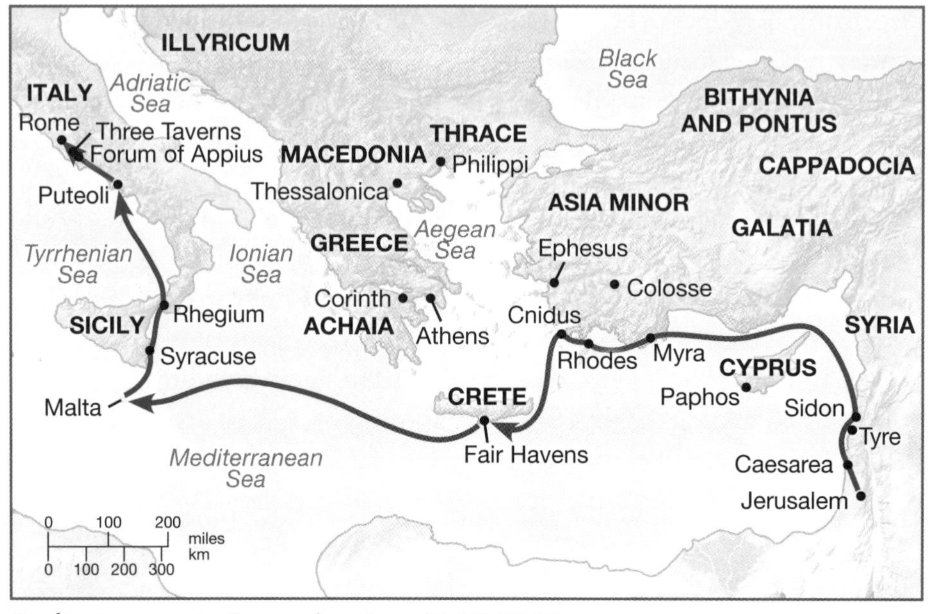

Paul's Journey to Rome See Acts 21:17–28:31.

described his numerous tribulations. Among other hardships, he was imprisoned, flogged, beaten with rods, stoned, and lashed with thirty-nine lashes on five different occasions. He was shipwrecked three times, and he spent a night and a day in the open sea. Tradition tells us that Paul also made a trip to Spain near the end of his life, but this journey is not recorded in the book of Acts.

MONEY CHANGERS At the time of Jesus, there were money changers at the temple who exchanged government-issued money for temple currency. Only temple currency, with no image on the coins, could be used at the temple to buy animals used for sacrifice. The money changers made an unfair profit in the transaction, and on two occasions Jesus cleansed the temple by turning over the tables of the money changers. He said they had turned the temple into a den of thieves (Matthew 21:13).

MOUNT OF OLIVES See *Olives, Mount of.*

NATHANAEL Another name for Bartholomew, one of Jesus's twelve disciples. Before Nathanael had met Jesus, the disciple Philip told Nathanael he had found the one Moses and the prophets had written about—Jesus of Nazareth. Nathanael retorted, "Nazareth! ... Can anything good come from Nazareth?" When Jesus met Nathanael, he called him "a genuine son of Israel—a man of complete integrity" (John 1:45–47 NLT).

NATIVITY, THE The birth of Jesus (*nativity* means "birth"). The story of the Nativity is one of the best-known stories in the Bible. It begins with the Annunciation (Luke 1)—the angel Gabriel's message to Mary that she would become pregnant even though she was a virgin, and that her son would be the Son of God. The angel also gave Mary's husband, Joseph, a message, assuring him that Mary's child was the result of a miraculous conception. When Joseph and Mary went to Bethlehem to be enrolled in the census, there was no room in the inn, and they had to stay in a stable. It was there that Jesus was born, and Mary laid him in a manger. An angel appeared to the shepherds in the nearby fields to give them the glorious news that the savior, Christ the Lord, had been born in Bethlehem. The Nativity has been the subject of thousands of works of art and songs through the centuries. Many familiar Christmas carols, including "Silent Night" and "O Come, All Ye Faithful," take us back to the events in Bethlehem 2,000 years ago.

NAZARETH The village where Jesus grew up. It is in the region of Galilee, about seventy miles north of Jerusalem and Bethlehem. The familiar Nativity narrative in Luke 2 says "Joseph also went up from Galilee, out of the city of Nazareth, into Judea, to the city of David, which is called Bethlehem" (verse 4). Although Joseph and Mary were traveling south, they "went up" to Bethlehem, which is in the hill country of Judea and substantially higher in altitude than Nazareth. Jesus was born in Bethlehem, but his family returned to Nazareth after their unexpected escape to Egypt (see *flight to Egypt*). Since he grew up in Nazareth, he was called a Nazarene. There was a Roman army garrison in Nazareth, which may have been one reason the residents of Nazareth were looked down on by other Jews. When Jesus's disciple Nathanael had first heard about Jesus, he said, "Can anything good come out of Nazareth?" (John 1:46). Jesus returned to Nazareth after he had started his public ministry, but the people there refused to accept him as the long-awaited Messiah. Jesus responded, "A prophet is not without honor except in his own country and in his own house" (Matthew 13:57).

Nicodemus

NICODEMUS A Pharisee and a member of the Sanhedrin, the Jewish ruling council. He paid a secret visit to Jesus one night to find out more about Jesus and his teachings. Jesus told him, "Unless you are born again, you cannot see the Kingdom of God" (John 3:3 NLT). Jesus went on to tell Nicodemus, as recorded in John 3:16, "For God so loved the world that he gave his one and only Son, that whoever believes in him shall not perish but have eternal life" (NIV). Nicodemus evidently became a believer, because he later spoke up in Jesus's defense in the Sanhedrin. After Jesus's crucifixion, Nicodemus joined Joseph of Arimathea in asking Pontius Pilate for Jesus's body for burial.

NO ROOM IN THE INN When Joseph and Mary traveled from Nazareth to Bethlehem to register in the census, they found that there was no room available in the village inn (Luke 2). They ended up staying in a stable—where Jesus was born. But most modern scholars say that the Greek word traditionally translated here as "inn" is better translated as "guest room." So the New International Version says that "there was no guest room available for them" (verse 7).

OLIVES, MOUNT OF The hill immediately to the east of Jerusalem. The garden of Gethsemane is at the foot of the mount. Bethany, the home of Mary, Martha, and Lazarus, was on the far side of the Mount of Olives. Jesus and his disciples were on the Mount of Olives when he ascended into heaven. The Mount of Olives is sometimes called Olivet.

ONESIMUS A slave who ran away from his master, Philemon. The apostle Paul befriended Onesimus, who became a believer in Christ under Paul's teaching. Paul sent him back to Philemon with a letter in which Paul asked Philemon to accept Onesimus back as a brother. We know this letter as the book of Philemon.

PARABLE A story with a deeper meaning than is readily apparent. Jesus frequently taught in parables. Sometimes he explained his parables to his disciples to make sure they understood him (for example, the Parable of the Sower, Matthew 13:1–23). The Parable of the Prodigal Son shows that God continues to love us, no matter how far we roam from fellowship with him. He always awaits our return and welcomes us back. The Parable of the Lost Sheep shows that God loves every one of us. In the Parable of the Pearl of Great Price, Jesus said the kingdom of heaven is like a pearl that is more valuable than any other possession. See the list "Ten Parables of Jesus" on the next page.

PASSION OF CHRIST The events of the last week of Jesus's ministry are called the Passion of Christ. As observed in the church today, Passion Week (also called Holy Week) begins on Palm Sunday and ends a week later, before daybreak on Easter Sunday. Passion plays are elaborate plays that portray the events in the last week of Jesus's life, culminating in his crucifixion and resurrection. Perhaps the most famous is the Passion play in Oberammergau, Germany, which is presented every ten years.

Olive grove on the Mount of Olives

TEN PARABLES OF JESUS

1. The sower and the four types of soil (Matthew 13:1–23)
2. The pearl of great price (Matthew 13:45–46)
3. The lost sheep (Matthew 18:12–14)
4. The unforgiving debtor (Matthew 18:21–35)
5. The Good Samaritan (Luke 10:25–37)
6. The rich fool who died (Luke 12:13–21)
7. The Prodigal Son (Luke 15:11–32)
8. The obedient and disobedient sons (Matthew 21:28–32)
9. The marriage feast to which no one came (Matthew 22:1–14)
10. The money (talents) loaned for investment (Matthew 25:14–30)

PAUL Often called Saint Paul or the apostle Paul, he was the first great missionary and theologian in Christian history. He lived during the mid-first-century AD and wrote many of the letters that became books of the New Testament. His story is told in the book of Acts, where he is initially called Saul (his Hebrew name). Paul was a member of the devout Jewish sect called the Pharisees, and he was ferocious in persecuting Christians during the first years of the early church. Once when he was on his way to Damascus (see *Damascus Road*) to persecute the Christians there, he was blinded by a bright light from heaven and heard the voice of Jesus asking, "Saul! Saul! Why are you persecuting me?" (Acts 9:4 NLT). Saul was blind for several days, until Ananias, a Christian leader, was prompted by the Holy Spirit to go and see him. Ananias laid hands on Saul, and Saul's sight was restored and he received the Holy Spirit. From that point forward

Saul, now called Paul, was a fearless witness of the power of Christ and an intelligent defender of the gospel. He was beaten, stoned, flogged, arrested, and thrown in prison because of his faith, but he was not deterred. At the end of his life he was imprisoned in Rome, where, according to tradition, he was martyred during the reign of Emperor Nero.

PEARL OF GREAT PRICE, PARABLE OF THE Jesus said the kingdom of heaven is like a very expensive pearl. A pearl merchant will sell everything he has to purchase a choice pearl. In the same way, we should be willing to give up all earthly treasures to obtain entrance to the kingdom of heaven (Matthew 13:45–46).

PENTECOST In the Old Testament, the Feast of Pentecost was celebrated fifty days after Passover (the word *Pentecost* originates from the Greek for "fiftieth day"). Also called the Feast of Weeks, it was a time to celebrate and praise God for the wheat harvest (Exodus 34:22; Leviticus 23:15–21). By the period of the New Testament, Pentecost also commemorated the giving of the Law to Moses. A week after Jesus's ascension into heaven, at the time of the Feast of Pentecost, Jesus's followers were all together in a room in Jerusalem. Suddenly a sound like a mighty, rushing wind filled the house, and what seemed to be tongues of fire came and rested on their heads. They were filled with the Holy Spirit, and they

Dungeon in Mamertine Prison—the traditional site of Paul's final Rome imprisonment

began speaking in tongues—speaking languages they had not learned. The apostle Peter then gave a powerful public message connecting this amazing event to scriptural prophecies of the Messiah, and about 3,000 people believed in Jesus that day (Acts 2). 📌 Pentecost is celebrated by Jews today as "Shavuot," the Hebrew word for "weeks." 📌 In the church year, Pentecost (also called Whitsunday) is a celebration of the coming of the Holy Spirit. 📌 The term *Pentecost* has come to be associated with the coming of the Holy Spirit. The term *Pentecostal* has been adopted by various denominations that emphasize the supernatural gifts of the Holy Spirit, especially speaking in tongues.

PETER One of Jesus's twelve disciples, he was also called Simon and Cephas. Both Peter (Greek) and Cephas (Aramaic) mean "rock." Like the disciples James and John, Peter was a fisherman, and the three of them were in Jesus's inner circle of followers. Peter was the first of the disciples to recognize that Jesus was the Messiah. He said to Jesus, "You are the Christ, the Son of the living God" (Matthew 16:16). After Jesus was betrayed and arrested, Peter denied knowing him three different times, but then was stricken with grief (see *Get behind me, Satan* in the chapter "Famous Sayings from the Bible"). After the ascension of Jesus, Peter became one of the leaders of the early church (Acts 1–12). He wrote the books of 1 Peter and 2 Peter. 📌 The Roman Catholic Church points to Peter as the first head of the church, with all popes (bishops of Rome) being his successors. 📌 Saint Peter is popularly said to be the keeper of the keys to heaven, with authority to determine who can enter and who cannot enter (see Matthew 16:19).

Statue of Peter

PHARISEES An important religious group within Judaism during the period of the New Testament.

They were experts in the Mosaic law and in the hundreds of additional laws devised to ensure that the people kept the laws in the Books of Moses. Jesus was very critical of the Pharisees. He called them hypocrites because they were concerned about tiny infractions of their own rules while they themselves did not live by the spirit of the laws of Moses. Nicodemus and Paul were both Pharisees who became followers of Jesus.

PHILEMON A friend of the apostle Paul, to whom Paul wrote the letter that we know as the book of Philemon. Philemon's slave, Onesimus, had run away, but he became a believer in Christ under Paul's teaching. Paul sent Onesimus back to Philemon with a letter in which he asked Philemon to accept Onesimus as a brother.

PHILIP (THE DISCIPLE) One of Jesus's twelve disciples. We do not know much about him except that he introduced Nathanael (also called Bartholomew) to Jesus, and Nathanael then became one of Jesus's twelve disciples (John 1:43–51). Note that he is not the same Philip (see the next entry) who met the Ethiopian eunuch on the Gaza road.

PHILIP (THE EVANGELIST) One of the seven men selected by the apostles to serve the Jerusalem church in practical ways. Philip took the Good News of Christ to Samaria, where many people became believers. One day Philip was sent by an angel to the desert road to Gaza (Acts 8:26–40). There Philip met an Ethiopian eunuch who was reading prophecies from the book of Isaiah but without understanding them. Philip helped him understand that Jesus was the person about whom Isaiah had been prophesying. The Ethiopian was delighted to hear the Good News and, when he saw some water, asked Philip to baptize him.

The Baptism of the Eunuch

PILATE, PONTIUS The Roman governor of Judea at the time of Jesus's ministry. Secular history tells us that Pilate was governor during the years AD 26–36. When Jesus was betrayed by Judas Iscariot and then put on trial by the Jewish leaders, he was taken to Pilate for sentencing. Pilate questioned him, sent him to Herod Antipas, questioned him again, and announced that Jesus was not guilty. He had a custom of releasing one Jewish prisoner each Passover, so he offered to set Jesus free, but the people and their leaders asked for the release of the murderer Barabbas instead. To appease the Jewish leaders, Pilate sentenced Jesus to death by crucifixion. Before doing so, however, he publicly washed his hands as a symbol of his innocence regarding Jesus's death (Matthew 27). See also *Caiaphas*; *trial of Jesus.* Today, if a person "washes his hands" of a situation, he is disclaiming responsibility for it.

First-century inscription bearing the name *Pontius Pilate*

PRINCE OF PEACE A title for the Messiah, as prophesied in Isaiah 9:6. See also *Unto us a child is born* in the chapter "Famous Sayings from the Bible."

PRISCILLA See *Aquila and Priscilla.*

PRODIGAL SON, PARABLE OF THE To illustrate God's love for those who are lost or who reject him, Jesus told this parable (paraphrased from Luke 15): A man had two sons, the younger of whom demanded his portion of their inheritance. His father agreed, and the son left home and squandered his money in riotous living. Finally, penniless and friendless and hungry, he decided to return to his father. He was sure his father would not accept him as a son, but perhaps he could be a servant in his father's household. The father, who had been mourning for him, saw him coming and ran and embraced him. The son apologized and said he was no longer worthy to be called a son, but the father told his servants to prepare a celebration feast. The older brother was angry that the father was celebrating the return of the wayward son. "I've worked hard for you all these years, and you've never put on a celebration for me," he exclaimed. But the father replied, "It is right to celebrate. Your brother was lost, but now he is found." The word *prodigal* means recklessly extravagant, but by extension from the parable it has come also to mean a person who returns home after a period of rebellion.

RABBI A Jewish teacher, scholar, and religious leader. Jesus was called a rabbi by some of his followers.

RESURRECTION, THE After Jesus was crucified, his body was laid in a rock-hewn tomb donated by Joseph of Arimathea. At the request of the chief priests, Roman guards were posted to ensure that Jesus's disciples would not steal his body and claim that he had come back to life. Early on Sunday morning, Mary Magdalene and several other women went to the tomb to anoint Jesus's body with spices. They found the tomb was empty, and an angel told them that Jesus had come back to life again (Matthew 28). *Resurrection* means coming back to life after having died. Jesus appeared to his disciples and many other followers during the forty days following his resurrection. He was then taken up into heaven (see *Ascension*). Christians around the world celebrate the resurrection of Jesus on Easter. Also, most Christians observe their day of rest on Sunday rather than Saturday (see *Sabbath* in the chapter "People, Places, and Events in the Old Testament") because the Resurrection occurred on Sunday.

Traditional site of Jesus's tomb, inside the Church of the Holy Sepulchre

ROMAN EMPIRE At the height of its power during the New Testament period, the Roman

Empire encompassed most of Europe and the lands surrounding the Mediterranean Sea. It stretched from Spain to the Holy Land, and from England to northern Africa. The Roman Empire consisted of a number of provinces, including Judea, Samaria, and Galilee. Christianity spread rapidly through the Roman Empire during the first several centuries after Christ. The Roman government was a very present part of life during the time of Jesus. Mary and Joseph traveled from Nazareth to Bethlehem because of a census decreed by Emperor Caesar Augustus. The Zealots were a Jewish political party whose aim was to overthrow the rule of Rome in the Jewish territories. Pontius Pilate was the Roman governor of Judea at the time of Jesus's public ministry.

ROME The central city of the Roman Empire, which governed the land of the Bible during the time of Jesus. The name "Rome" is sometimes used to refer to the entire Roman Empire or the government of the empire, just as we sometimes use "Washington" and "Moscow" to refer to the governments of the USA and Russia, respectively. After the apostle Paul was arrested in Jerusalem and spent time in prison in Caesarea, he finally went to Rome to appeal his case to Caesar (Nero). While he was there under house arrest, he wrote several of his epistles that are now books of the New Testament. See also *Rome* in the chapter "Church History."

SADDUCEES An influential priestly party in Judaism during the period of the New Testament.

Ancient ruins amid modern Rome

The Sadducees accepted only the Books of Moses as their Scripture. The New Testament and the historian Josephus tell us that the Sadducees did not believe in the supernatural or the resurrection of the dead. The Pharisees disagreed with the Sadducees on many theological points, but both groups generally rejected Jesus. Jesus, in turn, warned his followers not to be deceived by the teachings of the Pharisees and the Sadducees.

SALOME Although she is not mentioned by name in Mark 6, she is the daughter of Herodias and the stepdaughter of King Herod Antipas, whose story is told in the Gospels. Salome danced at a wild birthday party for Herod, who was so pleased that he offered her anything she requested, up to half his kingdom. She consulted with her mother, who suggested that she ask for the head of John the Baptist. This saddened Herod, but he felt he could not go back on his promise, so he had John beheaded. Secular history tells us that Salome married Herod Philip II (a son of Herod the Great). He was her uncle on her father's side and her great-uncle on her mother's side. A different woman named Salome was with Mary Magdalene when they went to Jesus's tomb and found that Jesus had been raised from the dead.

SAMARIA, SAMARITANS The city of Samaria, about forty miles north of Jerusalem, was one of the capitals of the Northern Kingdom of Israel. It was destroyed by the Assyrians in 722 BC after a three-year siege. This marked the end of the Northern Kingdom (2 Kings 17). During New Testament times, the region south of Galilee and north of Judea was called Samaria. The people who lived there—the Samaritans—were of mixed ancestry, part Jewish and part gentile. As a result, the Jews of Jesus's time considered the Samaritans inferior. Jews would not travel through their land or even speak to them (John 4:9). This provides the setting for Jesus's Parable of the Good Samaritan (Luke 10), where neither the priest nor the Levite (a temple worker) stopped to help the man who had been beaten, but a despised Samaritan stopped and helped him. Jesus told his listeners to be like the Samaritan, the one who had acted in a neighborly manner. Jesus shocked his disciples by traveling through Samaria and by speaking with a woman at the well, who was a Samaritan (John 4).

SANHEDRIN The supreme religious and legal council of the Jews during the New Testament period. The Sanhedrin had a great deal of civil authority under the rule of the Roman Empire, but it did not have the authority to give the death sentence. For that reason, Jesus was taken to Pontius Pilate for sentencing after he was tried and found guilty by the Sanhedrin. The members of the Sanhedrin were priests, Pharisees, Sadducees, and scribes, and the high priest served as president. The term *chief priests* is frequently used in the Gospels to refer to the priests who served in the Sanhedrin as well as other members of prominent priestly families.

SAPPHIRA See *Ananias and Sapphira.*

SAUL The Hebrew name of Paul, the great apostle. In the book of Acts he is referred to first as Saul of Tarsus, then as Paul.

SAVIOR Jesus is called the Savior because his death paid the penalty for our sins (see *atonement* in the chapter "Church Life and Theology"). In this way he saves us from eternal punishment. The British spelling, as used in the King James Version, is Saviour.

SCRIBES The professional interpreters of the Law during the period of the New Testament. Many of the scribes were Pharisees. Like the Pharisees and the Sadducees, most of the scribes rejected Jesus. Jesus called them hypocrites, for they insisted that the people follow every detail of the Law, but they themselves missed the spirit of the Law.

SEA OF GALILEE See *Galilee, Sea of.*

SEPULCHRE A tomb. The King James Version uses this word for the tomb in which Jesus's body was laid after he was crucified. Modern translations tend to use the word *tomb*. It was a small chamber carved in a hillside with a large rock to cover the entrance. See also *empty tomb*.

SERMON ON THE MOUNT Many of Jesus's key teachings are contained in the Sermon on the Mount. It is recorded in chapters 5–7 of the Gospel of Matthew. The Sermon on the Mount includes the Beatitudes, the Lord's Prayer, the Golden Rule, and teachings that are expressed in phrases like "Ask, and it will be given to you" and "Go the second mile." One of the hallmarks of the Sermon on the Mount is the way Jesus reinterprets and applies key teachings from the Mosaic law. For instance, Jesus said, "You have heard that it was said, 'Love your neighbor and hate your enemy.' But I tell you, love your enemies and pray for those who persecute you" (Matthew 5:43–44 NIV).

SEVEN LAST WORDS OF CHRIST The term *words* is confusing, since the expression actually refers to the seven statements of Jesus while he was on the cross. The seven statements are compiled from the Gospels, though none of the Gospels mentions all seven of them. Today these statements have been put to music in numerous settings, and Good Friday services often include a meditation on this aspect of the Passion of Christ.

SILAS The apostle Paul's coworker on his second missionary journey. Paul and Silas were thrown into jail in Philippi, and through their ministry the jailer became a Christian (Acts 16).

SIMEON An old man who waited expectantly to see the Messiah. On

THE SEVEN LAST WORDS OF CHRIST

1. Father, forgive them, for they do not know what they do. (Luke 23:34)
2. *To the thief on the cross:* Truly I tell you, today you will be with me in paradise. (Luke 23:43 NIV)
3. *To Mary:* Woman, behold your son! *To John:* Behold your mother! (John 19:26–27)
4. My God, my God, why have you forsaken me? (*Eli, Eli, lema sabachthani?*) (Matthew 27:46 NIV)
5. I thirst! (John 19:28)
6. Father, into your hands I commit my spirit. (Luke 23:46 NIV)
7. It is finished! (John 19:30)

the day that Mary and Joseph took the infant Jesus to the temple to present him to the Lord, Simeon went to the temple and recognized Jesus as the Messiah. After holding the child and praising God, Simeon said, "Lord, now let your servant die in peace.... I have seen your salvation" (Luke 2:29–30 NLT).

SIMON OF CYRENE A visitor in Jerusalem at the time of Jesus's crucifixion. Jesus was too weak to carry his own cross to the execution site because he had been terribly whipped and beaten by the Roman soldiers. When the soldiers saw a man named Simon of Cyrene, they forced him to carry Jesus's cross to Golgotha for him (Luke 23:26).

Simon of Cyrene Helps Jesus Carry His Cross

SIMON PETER See *Peter*.

SIMON THE ZEALOT One of Jesus's disciples. Little else is known about him, but the designation "the Zealot" suggests that he may have been a member of the Zealots, a Jewish political group that resisted Roman rule.

SON OF DAVID When Jesus entered Jerusalem on a donkey (see *Triumphal Entry*), the crowds shouted, "Hosanna to the Son of David!" (Matthew 21:9). When they called him the Son of David, they did not simply mean that he was a direct descendant of King David (which he was). They were hailing him as the Messiah, the great deliverer whose entrance into Jerusalem in this way had been foretold in the Old Testament (Zechariah 9:9).

SON OF GOD A title for Jesus. The New Testament is very clear that Jesus was not just "a" son of God; he was the "only begotten" or "one and only" Son of God—the second person of the Trinity. See also *God the Son* in the chapter "Church Life and Theology."

SON OF MAN Jesus frequently referred to himself as the Son of

Man. While the term seems to emphasize his humanity, Jesus was alluding to the "Son of Man" mentioned in Daniel 7. He used the term to show that he was indeed the Messiah. For instance, Mark 8:31 says, "He began to teach them that the Son of Man must suffer many things, and be rejected by the elders and chief priests and scribes, and be killed, and after three days rise again."

SOWER, PARABLE OF THE Jesus told this parable (Matthew 13) to illustrate that people respond differently when they hear the gospel—the Good News of God's kingdom: When a sower (farmer) scattered seed, some fell on a path, and the birds ate it up. Some fell on rocky soil and sprouted quickly, but the seedlings died in the strong sunshine because their roots had no depth. Some fell among thorns, which grew up and choked out the good plants. And some fell on good soil and grew and yielded an abundant harvest. Jesus told his disciples what the parable meant: The seed is the Good News. The path represents the hardened hearts of those who are not receptive to the Good News. The evil one comes and snatches away what has been planted there. The rocky soil is the person who receives the Good News eagerly, but his newfound faith withers since it has no spiritual roots. The thorny soil is the person who receives the Good News, but the cares of this life spring up and crowd out the spiritual things. Finally, the good soil is the person who is ready to receive the Good News and grow spiritually by committing his or her heart to Christ and living by faith in him.

STEPHEN One of the first group of deacons (people who serve the church in practical ways) appointed by the apostles after Pentecost, and the first Christian martyr (Acts 7). Stephen performed many miracles, but he was arrested when some Jewish leaders lied about him. He presented a lengthy defense showing that Jesus was the Messiah foretold in the Scriptures. When he accused the Jewish leaders of having murdered the Messiah, they stoned him to death. The first mention of Saul of Tarsus (Paul) is that he was present when Stephen was stoned.

SWADDLING CLOTHES When Jesus was born, his mother wrapped him in "swaddling clothes" (Luke 2:7 KJV). It's an old-fashioned term, but it simply means strips of cloth that are wrapped around a baby. In the ancient world, the custom of wrapping a baby in swaddling clothes was to ensure that its bones would grow straight.

SYNAGOGUE A meeting of Jews for worshiping God; also, the building where such meetings take place. In New Testament times the synagogue building functioned also as a school. A synagogue is comparable in function to a Christian church. When Jesus traveled around Galilee and Judea, he often taught in synagogues.

Ruins of the Capernaum synagogue

TALENTS, PARABLE OF THE One of Jesus's parables was about a man who gave each of his three servants sums of money ("talents") to invest (Matthew 25). To one he gave five talents, to another two talents, and to another one talent. (A talent was equal to 75 pounds, so this amount of gold or silver was very valuable.) The servants who received five and two talents invested theirs wisely and doubled their money. The servant who received only one talent buried his in the ground. The master praised the first two as faithful servants, but he called the third one a wicked and lazy servant for not having wisely used what was entrusted to him. Jesus meant that we are to use wisely all that has been entrusted to us, for we never know when we will be called to account for our life. 📌 Today the use of the word *talent* to mean a special ability or natural aptitude is a figurative extension of *talent* (a monetary value) as it is used in the parable.

TAX COLLECTORS In the Gospel accounts, tax collectors (the King James Version uses the term *publicans*) were at the lowest level of society. They were Jews, but they were hated by their countrymen for several reasons: (1) they often cheated tax-paying citizens, (2) they worked for the oppressive Roman government, and (3) they had frequent contact with gentiles. Jesus made the Pharisees furious when he spent time with tax collectors and other sinners (Luke 5:30). Matthew was a tax collector who became one of Jesus's twelve disciples (Matthew 9:9). Zacchaeus was another tax collector who became a follower of Jesus (Luke 19).

Mount of Temptation near Jericho—the traditional site of the temptation of Jesus

TEMPTATION OF JESUS After Jesus was baptized by John the Baptist, he went into the wilderness (or desert) for forty days. There he fasted and prayed and was tempted by Satan. The Gospel accounts (for example, Luke 4) tell of three specific temptations. In each instance, Jesus refuted Satan by quoting from the Scriptures: Jesus was hungry after fasting so long, and Satan tempted him to turn stones into bread. Jesus quoted from Deuteronomy 8:3 as he responded, "It is written, 'Man shall not live by bread alone, but by every word of God'" (Luke 4:4). Satan then took Jesus to a high mountain and showed him all the kingdoms of the world. Satan said, "If you worship me, it will all be yours" (verse 7 NIV). Jesus quoted from Deuteronomy 6:13 as he responded, "You must worship the LORD your God and serve only him" (verse 8 NLT). Finally, Satan took Jesus to the highest point on the temple and tempted him to jump down and show himself to be the Son of God. Satan quoted from Psalm 91:11–12, which says that "angels ... will lift you up in their hands, so that you will not strike your foot against a stone" (NIV). Jesus responded by quoting from Deuteronomy 6:16 as he said, "The Scriptures also say, 'You must not test the LORD your God'" (verse 12 NLT).

THADDAEUS One of Jesus's twelve disciples. Very little is known about him. Luke 6:16 calls him by a different name: "Judas the son of James."

THIEF ON THE CROSS Jesus was crucified between two criminals who were also being crucified. One of them hurled insults at him: "'Aren't you the Messiah? Save yourself and us!' But the other criminal rebuked him. 'Don't you fear God? ... We are getting what our deeds deserve. But this man has done nothing wrong.' Then he said, 'Jesus, remember me when you come into your kingdom.' Jesus answered him, 'Truly I tell you, today you will be with me in paradise'" (Luke 23:39–43 NIV).

THIRTY PIECES OF SILVER When Judas Iscariot agreed to betray Jesus to the Jewish leaders, they gave him thirty pieces of silver (Matthew 26). After Jesus was arrested, Judas repented and threw the money onto the floor of the temple. He then committed suicide. The priests used the money to buy a field to be used as a cemetery for foreigners. ➧ Today this term has come to mean any price paid for murder.

THOMAS (THE DISCIPLE) One of Jesus's twelve disciples. He is sometimes called Doubting Thomas because of an incident that occurred after Jesus's resurrection (John 20): He had not been present when Jesus appeared to the other disciples, and he did not believe that Jesus was actually alive. He said, "I won't believe it unless I see the nail wounds in his hands, put my fingers into them, and place my hand into the wound in his side." Eight days later, Jesus again appeared to the disciples, including Thomas. He told Thomas, "Put your finger here, and look at my hands. Put your hand into the wound in my side. Don't be faithless any longer. Believe!" Thomas exclaimed, "My Lord and my God!" (verses 25, 27, 28 NLT). ➧ Today a Doubting Thomas is a person who must see something to believe it.

TIMOTHY A young pastor whose mentor in the Christian faith was the apostle Paul. The books of 1 Timothy and 2 Timothy were letters Paul wrote to Timothy.

TRANSFIGURATION, THE One day Jesus took Peter, James, and John with him up a high mountain. While they were there, Jesus's divinity suddenly showed—he was transfigured. The disciples were allowed to see in advance his Resurrection glory. His face shone like the sun, and his clothes became as white as light. Then Moses and Elijah appeared with him. A bright cloud covered them, and the voice of God spoke from the cloud: "This is my beloved Son, in whom I am well pleased" (Matthew 17:5 KJV). This event, called the Transfiguration, showed Jesus to be the Son of God.

TRIAL OF JESUS After Judas Iscariot betrayed Jesus to the Jewish leaders, Jesus was taken to a midnight trial before Caiaphas, the high priest. Caiaphas and the Sanhedrin found Jesus guilty of blasphemy, a crime punishable by death according to the Mosaic law. Under Roman law, however, the Jewish authorities could not impose the death penalty. So the Jewish leaders took Jesus to Pontius Pilate, the Roman governor of Judea. He questioned Jesus but found him innocent. Herod Antipas, the king in the region of Galilee, happened to be in Jerusalem, so Pilate sent Jesus (who was a Galilean) to Herod for questioning. Herod also found Jesus innocent, and he sent him back to Pilate. Pilate had Jesus flogged, and the Roman soldiers put a crown of thorns and a purple robe on him. Pilate then tried to release Jesus, since he had a custom of releasing one Jewish prisoner each year at the time of the Passover, but the Jewish leaders insisted that Jesus be crucified. Pilate finally gave in, and he authorized the death sentence, though he publicly washed his hands to show that he was innocent of Jesus's death. Each of the Gospels includes an account of Jesus's trial, though none of them contains all the details. See Matthew 27, Mark 15, Luke 23, and John 18–19.

TRIUMPHAL ENTRY, THE A week before his crucifixion, Jesus entered Jerusalem on a donkey. The crowds recognized this as the fulfillment of an ancient prophecy: "See, your

Jesus Is Led from Herod to Pilate

king comes to you, righteous and victorious, lowly and riding on a donkey" (Zechariah 9:9 NIV). The crowd spread palm branches on the road ahead of him and shouted, "Hosanna to the Son of David!" (Matthew 21:9). They were acclaiming him as the Messiah. Five days later, however, the mob demanded that Pilate crucify Jesus. ➧ In the church today, the Triumphal Entry is commemorated on Palm Sunday.

The Entrance of Christ into Jerusalem

TURNING WATER INTO WINE Jesus performed his first miracle at a wedding feast in the village of Cana in Galilee (John 2). When the master of ceremonies ran out of wine, Jesus told the servants to fill six large jars with water. Then he told them to draw some out for tasting. The water had become delicious wine, and the master of the feast complimented the bridegroom on serving such good wine.

TWELVE DISCIPLES, THE See *disciples.*

VIRGIN BIRTH Mary was still a virgin when Jesus was born, so his birth is called the Virgin Birth, and Mary is sometimes called the Virgin Mary. The fact that Mary was a virgin fulfilled the prophecy in Isaiah 7:14: "The virgin will conceive and give birth to a son, and will call him Immanuel" (NIV). (Immanuel means "God with us.") Mary was engaged but not yet married to Joseph when the angel Gabriel appeared to her (see *Annunciation*) and told her she would give birth to a son. "'How will this be,' Mary asked the angel, 'since I am a virgin?' The angel answered, 'The Holy Spirit will come on you, and the power of the Most High will overshadow you. So the holy one to be born will be called the Son of God'" (Luke 1:34–35 NIV). ➧ The doctrine of the Roman Catholic Church is that Mary remained a virgin throughout her life.

VIRGIN MARY See *Mary (mother of Jesus)*

WALKING ON WATER Close to dawn on the day after Jesus multiplied the loaves and fishes, Jesus's twelve disciples were in a boat on the Sea of Galilee. A storm arose, and Jesus went out to them, walking on the water. They were terrified that he was a ghost, but he told them not to be afraid. Peter then jumped out of the boat and began walking on the water toward Jesus. Suddenly his faith faltered and he began to sink, so Jesus reached out to keep him from sinking. When they got in the boat, the wind died down (Matthew 14). 📌 Today the expression "walking on water" is sometimes used to describe something that is not humanly possible. A person may be very talented, but "he can't walk on water."

WISE MEN These men, also called Magi (Greek for "wise men"), were astrologers (perhaps from Babylon or Persia) who saw a special star and came to Jerusalem looking for the newborn king of the Jews (Matthew 2). King Herod the Great was distraught when he heard of their quest, for he wanted no rival. He inquired of the Jewish teachers and learned that the Messiah was to be born in Bethlehem. Herod gave the wise men this information and said, "Go to Bethlehem and search carefully for the child. And when you find him, come back and tell me so that I can go and worship him, too!" (verse 8 NLT). The wise men went to Bethlehem, found Jesus with his mother, and worshiped him. They gave him precious gifts of gold, frankincense, and myrrh. The wise men were warned in a dream not to return to King Herod, so they returned to their own land by a different way. Herod was furious when he learned that he had been tricked, and he ordered the death of all the boys in Bethlehem under the age of two. 📌 It has traditionally been assumed there were three wise men, and tradition has even supplied them with names—Caspar, Melchior, and Balthazar—but the Bible does not include this information.

The Magi Journeying

WOMAN AT THE WELL When Jesus was traveling from Judea

back to Galilee, he went through Samaria. Outside the village of Sychar he stopped at the village well and asked a woman there to give him a drink. The woman, whose name is not mentioned in the biblical account, expressed surprise that a Jewish man would even speak to a Samaritan woman, much less ask for a drink. Jesus responded that she would have asked him for living water if she had known who he was. Then Jesus told her to get her husband, and she said she didn't have a husband. Jesus responded, "You're right! You don't have a husband—for you have had five husbands, and you aren't even married to the man you're living with now" (John 4:17–18 NLT). After some further conversation, the woman said, "'I know that Messiah' (called Christ) 'is coming. When he comes, he will explain everything to us.' Then Jesus declared, 'I, the one speaking to you—I am he.'" She then left her water jug and ran into the village and told everyone, "Come, see a man who told me everything I ever did. Could this be the Messiah?" (verses 25–26, 29 NIV).

WORD, THE The Gospel of John begins with the words, "In the beginning was the Word, and the Word was with God, and the Word was God." The Word was the Son of God, the second person of the Trinity, who had existed from the very beginning. In the Incarnation,

Early photo of Jacob's Well—the traditional site of Jesus's encounter with the Samaritan woman

he was Jesus—the personification of God's message to mankind. But more than that, he was God himself in human form.

ZACCHAEUS A wealthy tax collector who wanted to see Jesus when he passed through Jericho (Luke 19). Zacchaeus was too short to see over the crowds when Jesus came along the road, so he climbed a sycamore tree. When Jesus came to that spot, he looked up and told Zacchaeus he wanted to have dinner at his house. Like other tax collectors, Zacchaeus charged as much as he could, thereby cheating the public. When he listened to Jesus's teaching, he knew he had done wrong, and he pledged to give half his possessions to the poor and restore four times what he had taken from others.

ZEALOTS A Jewish political party in the first century AD. They were opposed to paying taxes to Rome, and they sought to free Israel from the rule of Rome. One of Jesus's twelve disciples was called Simon the Zealot, which may indicate an association with that party.

ZECHARIAH (ALSO SPELLED ZACHARIAS) A priest who was the husband of Elizabeth and the father of John the Baptist. One day when he was performing his priestly duties in the temple, the angel Gabriel appeared to him to tell him that his wife would have a son, and they were to name him John (Luke 1). Zechariah did not believe the angel, because his wife was too old to have a child. As a result of his disbelief, Zechariah was unable to speak until the baby was born.

ZION The mountain in Jerusalem where the temple was built. By extension, Jerusalem and all of Israel are sometimes called Zion in the Bible. The Zionist movement of the late nineteenth century was the force behind the migration of Jews from other lands back to the Holy Land, culminating in the establishment of the modern state of Israel in 1948.

From Andrew to Zacchaeus

A Quiz on People, Places, and Events in the New Testament

Select one answer for each question. Answers appear immediately after the quiz.

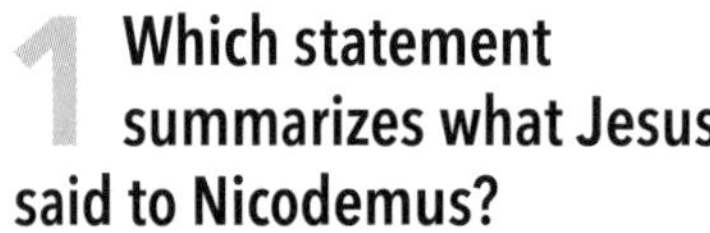

1 Which statement summarizes what Jesus said to Nicodemus?

a. Sell all you have and give the money to the poor.

b. This day you shall be with me in paradise.

c. No one can see the kingdom of heaven unless he is born again.

d. Arise, take up your bed, and walk.

2 When the apostle John was an old man, he had a vision. In which book of the New Testament is his vision recorded?

a. Gospel of John

b. Revelation

c. 1 John

d. Romans

3 What elderly woman recognized the infant Jesus as the Messiah when Joseph and Mary took him to the temple?

a. Anna

b. Elizabeth

c. Dorcas

d. Priscilla

4 Who was emperor in Rome when Jesus was born?

a. Caesar Augustus

b. Julius Caesar

c. Nero

d. Herod

5 **Who was the mother of John the Baptist?**

a. Mary
b. Miriam
c. Anna
d. Elizabeth

6 **What was Cornelius's occupation?**

a. Tentmaker
b. Tax collector
c. High priest
d. Roman centurion

7 **Who ordered that all boys in Bethlehem under the age of two be killed?**

a. Herod the Great
b. Pharaoh
c. Pontius Pilate
d. Caiaphas

8 **Who was Onesimus?**

a. A centurion
b. A slave
c. A tax collector
d. One of Jesus's disciples

9 **When Herod Antipas told Salome she could have anything she requested, what did she ask for?**

a. That Herod marry her
b. Thirty pieces of silver
c. The head of John the Baptist
d. Half the kingdom

10 **Who was the brother of James (son of Zebedee)?**

a. Peter
b. Paul
c. Andrew
d. John

11 **Which two people were struck dead when they lied to Peter about some property they had sold?**

a. Aquila and Priscilla
b. Mary Magdalene and Lazarus
c. Ananias and Sapphira
d. Judas Iscariot and Caiaphas

12 After the wise men visited Jesus, an angel appeared to Joseph in a dream. What did the angel tell him?

a. To take Mary and Jesus to Egypt

b. To take Jesus to the temple

c. That Jesus was the Son of God

d. That Joseph should marry Mary

13 Who was the high priest who presided at the trial of Jesus?

a. Caiaphas

b. Aaron

c. Barnabas

d. Ezra

14 What does the Bible tell us about Joseph of Arimathea?

a. His father gave him a multicolored coat.

b. He was the husband of the Virgin Mary.

c. He carried Jesus's cross to Golgotha.

d. He owned the tomb in which Jesus was buried.

15 Who were four of Jesus's disciples?

a. Matthew, Mark, Luke, John

b. Matthew, Mark, Peter, John

c. Matthew, Judas Iscariot, Andrew, John

d. Peter, James, John, Paul

16 The brother of Mary and Martha died, but Jesus brought him back to life. What is his name?

a. Cornelius

b. Simon

c. Ananias

d. Lazarus

17 Who betrayed Jesus with a kiss?

a. Pontius Pilate

b. Simon the Sorcerer

c. Judas Iscariot

d. Mary Magdalene

18 Which three disciples were closest to Jesus?

a. Peter, Andrew, and James

b. Peter, John, and Paul

c. Peter, James, and John

d. Matthew, Mark, and Luke

19 **Saul of Tarsus was present when one of these men was stoned to death. Which one was it?**

a. Peter

b. Saul

c. John

d. Stephen

20 **Thomas is sometimes called Doubting Thomas because he did not believe that:**

a. Peter had walked on water.

b. Jesus had calmed the storm.

c. Peter had been released from prison.

d. Jesus had come back to life.

Answers

1. c
2. b
3. a
4. a
5. d
6. d
7. a
8. b
9. c
10. d
11. c
12. a
13. a
14. d
15. c
16. d
17. c
18. c
19. d
20. d

King of Kings and Lord of Lords

A Quiz on the Life and Ministry of Jesus

Select one answer for each question. Answers appear immediately after the quiz.

1 What is the Ascension?

a. When Jesus came back to life again on the third day

b. When Jesus raised Jairus's daughter back to life

c. When Jesus rose into heaven forty days after the Resurrection

d. When the angel Gabriel appeared to the Virgin Mary to tell her she would have a son

2 On what day do Christians commemorate the Triumphal Entry?

a. Christmas

b. Good Friday

c. Palm Sunday

d. Pentecost Sunday

3 What was the town on the Sea of Galilee where much of Jesus's ministry took place?

a. Capernaum

b. Jerusalem

c. Bethlehem

d. Jericho

4 *Christ* (from a Greek word) and *Messiah* (from a Hebrew word) both mean the same thing. What do they mean?

a. Bread of Life

b. God with us

c. Anointed One

d. Prophet

5 What term is used to describe Jesus's death on the cross?

a. The Ascension

b. The Crucifixion

c. The Resurrection

d. The Transfiguration

6 Where was Jesus born?

a. Jerusalem

b. Bethlehem

c. Capernaum

d. Nazareth

7 In the Parable of the Sower, what does the seed represent?

a. The plentiful harvest

b. The cares of this world

c. Seven years of plenty

d. The Good News of God's kingdom

8 What is the Nativity?

a. The birth of Jesus

b. The manger where Mary laid the baby Jesus

c. The death of Jesus

d. The angels' announcement to the shepherds that the Savior had been born

9 Who brought gifts of gold, frankincense, and myrrh to Jesus?

a. The shepherds

b. The angels

c. The wise men

d. King Herod

10 What parable did Jesus tell in response to the question, "Who is my neighbor?"

a. Parable of the Good Samaritan

b. Parable of the Lost Sheep

c. Parable of the Prodigal Son

d. Parable of the Pearl of Great Price

11 Which event is called the Annunciation?

a. When Jesus rose from the tomb three days after he died

b. When Jesus died on the cross

c. When the angel Gabriel told the Virgin Mary that she would have a baby who was the Son of God

d. When Moses and Elijah appeared with Jesus on a mountaintop

12 Which of these expressions is called the Great Commission?

a. I am the Alpha and the Omega.

b. Behold the Lamb of God.

c. Go into all the world and preach the gospel to every creature.

d. Train up a child in the way he should go.

13 Who said, "Behold! The Lamb of God ..."?

a. Isaiah

b. Peter

c. Paul

d. John the Baptist

14 What were Jesus and his disciples celebrating at the Last Supper?

a. The fall of Rome

b. The Passover

c. The Day of Atonement

d. The Feast of Tabernacles

15 Where did Jesus go to pray with his disciples after the Last Supper?

a. Garden of Gethsemane

b. Garden of Eden

c. Bethlehem

d. Capernaum

16 Where did Joseph and Mary live before Jesus was born?

a. Jerusalem

b. Egypt

c. Nazareth

d. Bethany

17 Which term refers to Jesus's coming back to life after his death on the cross?

a. The Nativity

b. The Crucifixion

c. The Resurrection

d. The Second Coming

18 What was the name of the hill where Jesus was crucified?

a. Mount Sinai

b. Mount of Olives

c. Mount of Transfiguration

d. Golgotha

19 According to the Gospels, what was Jesus's first miracle?

a. Walking on water

b. Healing a blind man

c. Multiplying the loaves and fishes

d. Turning water into wine

20 Which saying of Jesus is not found in the Sermon on the Mount?

a. Go into all the world and preach the gospel to every creature.

b. Love your enemies.

c. Ask, and it will be given to you.

d. Go the second mile.

Answers

1. c
2. c
3. a
4. c
5. b
6. b
7. d
8. a
9. c
10. a
11. c
12. c
13. d
14. b
15. a
16. c
17. c
18. d
19. d
20. a

Church History

This chapter features entries for the most significant events, people, and terms related to the history of the church after the book of Acts.

It includes the great church councils at Nicaea and Chalcedon and important movements in church history, such as the Reformation, the Great Awakening, and Pentecostalism.

You will also find terms related to current events that are shaping modern church history, such as *freedom of religion* and *First Amendment rights.*

Examples of those who have played key roles in church history include Augustine of Hippo, John Wycliffe, Martin Luther, Ignatius of Loyola, Richard Allen, Pope John XXIII, and Billy Graham.

Also included are denominational movements such as Methodism and the Anabaptist movement, as well as names of the largest American denominations.

AD In the Western world, history is divided into two eras—the years before Christ (BC) and the years after Christ (AD). AD is an abbreviation for the Latin phrase *Anno Domini* ("the year of the Lord"). For those who prefer not to use terms with a specifically Christian connotation, CE ("Common Era") is used instead of AD. The year AD 1 is theoretically the first year in the life of Christ, but most historians now agree that Jesus was born prior to 4 BC, the year in which Herod the Great died.

AFRICAN METHODIST EPISCOPAL CHURCH (AME) An African-American denomination with roots in what is now the United Methodist Church. The church began in 1787 when a group of Black people under the leadership of Richard Allen left St. George's Church in Philadelphia, where they had been subject to segregation and humiliation. The AME Church is one of the larger denominations in the USA (see list at the entry for *denominations*).

AFRICAN METHODIST EPISCOPAL ZION CHURCH (AME ZION) Another African-American denomination with roots in what is now the United Methodist Church. The church began in 1796 when a group of Black people left the John Street Methodist Episcopal Church in New York City. Many prominent nineteenth-century abolitionists, including Harriet Tubman and Frederick Douglass, were members of the AME Zion Church. The AME Zion Church is one of the larger denominations in the USA (see list at the entry for *denominations*).

ALLEN, RICHARD (1760–1831) An influential Black church leader in America in the years following the Revolutionary War. He founded the African Methodist Episcopal Church in Philadelphia when he and other Black Christians were humiliated in white churches.

Richard Allen

AMISH An Anabaptist group that emphasizes peaceful living and community and family values. The Old Order Amish are remarkable because they reject most modern conveniences, including automobiles, televisions, telephones, and mechanized farm equipment. They dress in plain clothing of the style of several centuries ago, and men wear long beards. They try to keep to a minimum any contact with outsiders. They are an offshoot of the Mennonites, who are less conservative than the Amish. The group originated in Switzerland at the end of the seventeenth century, though most now live in the USA.

ANABAPTIST MOVEMENT A movement that began in Switzerland in the 1520s. It emphasized the necessity of baptism for adult believers and opposed infant baptism. Members of the movement were called Anabaptists (which means "baptism again") because if they had been baptized as infants, they were baptized again as adult believers. The Anabaptists were radicals of the Reformation, both for their views on baptism and because they rejected the involvement of the church in government. ➧ Church groups today that trace their roots back to the original Anabaptist movement include the Mennonites and the Amish.

ANGLICAN CHURCH A term that refers to the Church of England and various self-governing churches around the world (such as the Episcopal Church) that have ties to the Church of England and share a common heritage in the Book of Common Prayer and the episcopal form of church government.

AQUINAS, THOMAS (c. 1225–74) A medieval theologian whose writings, including *Summa Theologica* ("a summation of theology"), have influenced theologians and theological thinking over the last 700 years. At a time when the influence of Greek thought was undermining faith in revelation, Aquinas synthesized Aristotelian reason and Christian faith. Building on Aristotle's philosophy, Aquinas concluded that God is the first cause—the uncaused cause. His definition of many Christian doctrines (including transubstantiation) became authoritative in the church. He is generally still viewed as the most authoritative theologian for the Roman Catholic Church.

ARCHAEOLOGY The study of sites and artifacts from cultures and civilizations of an earlier era. Archaeologists carefully excavate sites of cities, battles, graves, temples, and so on, to understand the culture that created the site. In the Near East, cities were often rebuilt upon ruins of earlier cities, so some sites contain as many as ten or more levels that might span several thousand years. Today these ruins form mounds called "tells." Artifacts at an archaeological site might include tools, jewelry, coins, pottery, religious objects, skeletal remains, or foundations of buildings. During the past century, archaeologists have found archaeological evidence of many cultural details mentioned in the Bible—including details previously thought by some scholars to be unreliable.

ARIANISM See *Nicaea, Council of.*

ARMINIANISM Doctrines based on the teachings of Dutch theologian Jacob Arminius (1560–1609). In contrast to Calvinism, with its emphasis on God's sovereign election, Arminianism sees no conflict between election and man's free will. Predestination is seen as God's foreknowledge of the way each person will freely choose to accept or reject Christ. Methodist theology is in the Arminian tradition.

ASCETIC A person who voluntarily abstains from the comforts and pleasures of this life in order to combat vice and cultivate personal holiness. Monasticism, with its emphasis on poverty, chastity, and obedience, is an ascetic lifestyle.

ASSEMBLIES OF GOD A denomination that emphasizes

Archaeological site of Tell es-Sultan in Jericho

speaking in tongues and affirms baptism in the Holy Spirit as a second blessing subsequent to becoming a Christian. It is one of the largest Pentecostal denominations in the USA.

ATHANASIUS (c. 293–373) Bishop of Alexandria (Egypt) and a participant in the Council of Nicaea. He was a strong defender of orthodoxy, particularly against the heresy (see *heresy* in the chapter "Church Life and Theology") of Arianism, which held that Jesus was the Son of God but was a created being and not coeternal with God. A letter written by Athanasius in 367 contains a list of New Testament books. It is the earliest list that includes only the twenty-seven books that came to be accepted as the New Testament canon (see *New Testament canon established*).

AUGUSTINE OF CANTERBURY (?–604) The first archbishop of Canterbury. Pope Gregory I sent Augustine from Rome to take the gospel to England. Under his preaching, thousands of people in England were converted, including Ethelbert, the king of Kent.

AUGUSTINE OF HIPPO (354–430) Bishop of Hippo (in modern-day Algeria). He is often considered the greatest thinker in Christian antiquity and the most important theologian in the Western church during the 1,200 years from Paul to Thomas Aquinas. His theology was foundational for the sixteenth-century Reformers. *Confessions*, his autobiography, is a classic account of a conversion from paganism to Christianity. His book *The City of God* (411) played an important role in establishing Christianity as the major religious power after the fall of Rome.

Augustine of Hippo

BAPTIST A general term designating the denominations in which adult believers are baptized, but infants are not baptized (see *baptism* in the chapter "Church Life and Theology"). Worship in Baptist churches tends to be plain and non-liturgical, with an emphasis on the sermon. See also *National Baptist Convention*; *Southern Baptist Convention*.

BARTH, KARL (1886–1968) Barth (pronounced *Bart*) was a Swiss theologian who was a proponent of a movement called neoorthodoxy, which was a reaction to the theological liberalism of the early twentieth century. He is considered by many to be the foremost theologian of the twentieth century.

BC In the Western world, history is divided into two eras—the years before Christ (BC) and the years after Christ (AD). BC is simply an abbreviation for "Before Christ." For those who prefer not to use terms with a specifically Christian connotation, BCE ("Before the Common Era") is used instead of BC. 📌 The year 1 BC is theoretically the last year before the birth of Jesus, but most historians now agree that Jesus was born earlier than 4 BC, the year in which Herod the Great died.

BECKET, THOMAS (1118–70) A twelfth-century archbishop of Canterbury. As head of the church in England (this was before the establishment of the Church of England), he opposed King Henry II's attempts to limit the authority of the church. Becket was murdered in the Canterbury Cathedral by four knights who were supporters of the king. He was canonized a few years after his death (see *canonization* in the chapter "Church Life and Theology"). 📌 After Becket's death, many pilgrims visited his tomb in Canterbury. The travelers in Chaucer's *Canterbury Tales* were on their way to Canterbury to visit Becket's tomb. 📌 *Murder in the Cathedral* by T. S. Eliot and *Becket* by Jean Anouilh are twentieth-century plays about Becket's murder.

Murder of Thomas Becket

BENEDICT XVI, POPE (reigned 2005–13) He brought a fairly conservative position to church affairs. He retired in 2013 rather than serving until his death (in 2022).

Pope Benedict XVI

BENEDICT OF NURSIA (c. 480–547) Founder of the Benedictines, an early monastic order (see *monasticism*). The Benedictines combine prayer, study, and work as a way of life. Benedict's "Rule" for monastic living gave detailed descriptions of all aspects of life in the monastery. It became the pattern for other monastic orders in the centuries that followed.

BENEDICTINES Members of a religious order founded by Benedict of Nursia in the sixth century. It was one of the earliest monastic orders (see *monasticism*). The motto of the Benedictines is "Pray and Work." Benedict's "Rule" for his order became the pattern for other monastic orders in the centuries that followed.

BERNARD OF CLAIRVAUX (1090–1153) A French preacher and theologian who was an adviser to popes, bishops, and kings, and was instrumental in launching the Second Crusade (see *Crusades*). His emphasis on grace was influential four centuries later for Martin Luther and John Calvin. 📌 His influence reaches us today through several hymns, including "O Sacred Head, Now Wounded" and "Jesus, Thou Joy of Loving Hearts."

BIBLE BELT The areas in the United States, especially in the South, where Christianity and belief in the Bible are more predominant than in other parts of the country. The term is sometimes used disparagingly, and it usually connotes religious and social conservatism.

BONHOEFFER, DIETRICH (1906–45) A Lutheran pastor in Germany who was active in the anti-Hitler movement. He was hanged by the Nazis in 1945. His major works include *The Cost of Discipleship* (1937) and *Letters and Papers from Prison* (1951).

BOOK OF CONCORD Published in 1580, the *Book of Concord* contains all the documents generally accepted by the Lutheran Church as fundamental to its tradition. It includes the Apostles' Creed, Luther's Large and Small Catechisms, the Augsburg Confession, and the Formula of Concord (developed to settle doctrinal controversies that arose within Lutheranism after Martin Luther's death).

CALVIN, JOHN (1509–64) A great leader of the Reformation in Switzerland. He was younger than Martin Luther and Ulrich Zwingli and represented the next generation of Reformers. His teachings emphasized the sovereignty of God and election. He wrote *Institutes of the Christian Religion*, the most important and influential treatise on Protestant doctrine from the Reformation era. The Reformed traditions stem from Calvin and Calvinism. Calvin was French, but he became the leader of the church in Geneva, Switzerland, which had enormous influence in the affairs of state. Like the other Reformers, Calvin taught that people are saved by grace rather than by good works. Nonetheless, he also stressed virtue and the importance of Christian influence in government and public policy. Adultery, blasphemy, and heresy were punishable by death in Geneva. Calvin had a significant impact on the development of Protestantism. The presbyterian form of church government derives from Calvin's teaching. In France, his followers were known as Huguenots. In England, Scotland, and America his followers formed the various Presbyterian churches.

John Calvin

CALVINISM The doctrines based on the teachings of John Calvin, one of the great leaders of the

Protestant Reformation. One of the distinctive features of Calvinism is the sovereignty of God over the affairs of people, especially in election, and that justification and sanctification are inseparable in the life of the believer. The doctrine of election holds that only the elect—those persons chosen by God—will be saved. Churches established by Calvin's followers are known as Reformed churches and follow a presbyterian form of church government. In America, Calvinist theology has also influenced Congregational, Baptist, and independent churches.

CANON OF THE NEW TESTAMENT See *New Testament canon established.*

CANTERBURY, ARCHBISHOP OF The spiritual head of the Church of England. In this role, he influences the Anglican churches around the world. He is appointed by the ruling monarch of Great Britain, who is titular head of the Church of England.

CAREY, WILLIAM (1761–1834) A British missionary to India in the early nineteenth century who is known as the "Father of Modern Missions." One of his legacies is the development of voluntary mission societies that send missionaries out to evangelize in the far corners of the world. Carey was a gifted linguist and personally involved in translating the Bible into thirty-six languages of South Asia.

William Carey

CATHOLIC When capitalized, *Catholic* means Roman Catholic (Catholic schools, Catholic doctrine). When not capitalized, *catholic* means universal, as used in the Apostles' Creed: "I believe in ... the holy catholic church ..."

CATHOLIC CHURCH See *Roman Catholic Church.*

CATHOLICISM The faith, practice, or system of the Roman Catholic Church.

CHALCEDON, COUNCIL OF (451) The church council in Chalcedon (located in present-day Turkey; pronounced *KAL-si-don*) addressed the issue of the two natures of Christ. The council affirmed that Christ was both God and man, and that the deity and humanity of Christ exist "without confusion, without change, without division, without separation." The definition accepted by the council has been the measure of orthodoxy on this subject ever since.

CHARISMATIC MOVEMENT Also called "charismatic renewal," this movement emphasizes baptism in the Holy Spirit and speaking in tongues. Many charismatics (as they are often called) see baptism in the Holy Spirit as a "second blessing"—the coming of the Holy Spirit into a believer's life at some time subsequent to his or her conversion. Although charismatics share many views in common with those who attend Pentecostal churches, they tend to be part of non-Pentecostal churches (see *Pentecostalism*). The movement began about 1960, and now there are several million charismatics in Protestant and Catholic churches throughout the world.

CHARLEMAGNE (c. 742–814) The first emperor of what came to be known as the Holy Roman Empire, a European empire that existed in name for 1,000 years until it was finally dismantled by Napoleon. Charlemagne was initially king of what is today France and Germany, and he was a friend and defender of Christianity in all his conquered territories. He was crowned emperor as he knelt at the altar in Saint Peter's Basilica on Christmas Day in the year 800. This surprise coronation by Pope Leo III suggested the supremacy of the church over the state and set the stage for many church-state struggles for centuries to come.

CHIEF END OF MAN See *What is the chief end of man?*

CHINA INLAND MISSION One of the earliest independent mission agencies of the modern missionary movement. It was founded by J. Hudson Taylor in 1866 for the evangelization of China. It was subsequently called Overseas Missionary Fellowship, and now OMF International.

CHRIST IS RISEN/HE IS RISEN INDEED In the early church, as in many churches today, believers

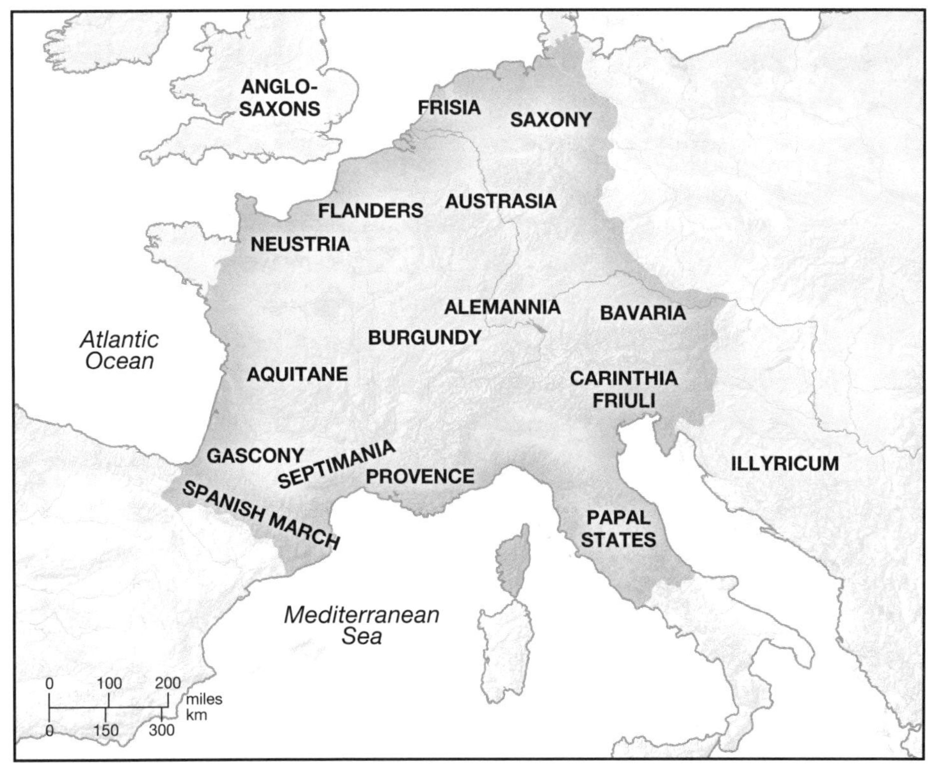

Charlemagne's Empire, 814

greeted one another on Easter by saying, "Christ is risen," to which the others would respond, "He is risen indeed."

CHRISTENDOM The entire Christian church around the world. The word can refer to all Christian people or to all lands in which Christianity predominates.

CHRISTIAN SCIENCE An organization founded by Mary Baker Eddy in 1879. Its official name is the Church of Christ, Scientist. Christian Science does not accept many of the tenets of orthodox Christianity, including the Trinity. One of the features of Christian Science is the belief that matter and flesh do not really exist. Only that which is "mind" possesses reality. Accordingly, Christian Scientists tend to reject many aspects of modern medicine as inconsequential. *The Christian Science Monitor* is a widely respected news outlet with widespread circulation.

CHRISTOPHER, SAINT (third century) He may have been a martyr about the year 250. He is the patron saint of travelers because of the tradition that he once carried the Christ child across a river (the name Christopher means "Christ-bearer"). Many people wear Saint Christopher medals for protection as they travel. 📌 In 1969 the Roman Catholic Church removed Christopher's feast from the calendar of saints because of lack of historical evidence of his existence, but he is still revered as a saint.

CHURCH COUNCILS In the early church, significant theological conflicts were resolved at church councils—gatherings of church leaders from around Christendom. The first church council was held in Jerusalem in about AD 50, to decide whether gentile converts to Christianity must first become converts to Judaism (Acts 15). Other significant councils were held over the course of the next several centuries. The Council of Nicaea (325), called by Constantine the Great, was the first great ecumenical council (see *ecumenical* in the chapter "Church Life and Theology"), followed by the Council of Constantinople (381) and the Council of Chalcedon (451). In response to the Protestant Reformation, the Roman Catholic Church convened the Council of Trent (1545–63). The Vatican I council (1869–70) defined the dogma of papal infallibility. Vatican II (1962–65) adopted sweeping changes in the Roman Catholic Church. For Protestants, doctrines formulated by ecumenical councils may be true and may unify Christians, but they are not

Council of Trent

infallible. For Roman Catholics, the decisions are infallible and irrevocable.

CHURCH FATHERS The orthodox theologians of the church during the first several centuries after Christ. Included in such a list are Justin Martyr, Origen, Athanasius, John Chrysostom, Jerome, and Augustine of Hippo.

CHURCH HISTORY The record of the Christian church from the time of Christ to the present. There are numerous strands, of course, in a subject so complex. The list on the next page shows twenty-five of the most important events.

CHURCH OF ENGLAND The state church of England, also called the Anglican Church. The Church of England split away from the Roman Catholic Church in 1534 since King Henry VIII would not accept the pope's ruling that Henry could not divorce his wife. The ruling monarch of England is titular head of the church, though the archbishop of Canterbury is recognized as the spiritual head of the church. The Episcopal Church in the USA and the Anglican Church in North America are direct descendants of the Church of England.

CHURCH OF GOD IN CHRIST The largest Pentecostal denomination in the USA. Like other Pentecostal groups, it emphasizes the baptism in the Holy Spirit and holiness as the standard for Christian living. Its membership is primarily Black, whereas membership of the Assemblies of God is primarily White.

Mormon Temple in Salt Lake City

CHURCH OF JESUS CHRIST OF LATTER-DAY SAINTS The religious group founded by Joseph Smith in 1830, also called the Mormons. Joseph Smith wrote *The Book of Mormon*, which he said was the translation of a divinely inspired text on gold plates that he found in New York. After Smith's death, his followers split into several factions, and Brigham Young became leader of the group that is

MOST IMPORTANT EVENTS IN CHURCH HISTORY

YEAR	EVENT
70	Destruction of Jerusalem by Titus
313	Edict of Milan
325	Council of Nicaea
367	New Testament canon in its present form is recognized
386	Augustine of Hippo converted
406	Jerome completes translation of the Vulgate
451	Council of Chalcedon
540	Benedict establishes the monastic "Rule"
988	Christianization of Russia
1054	The Great Schism (the East-West Split)
1095	Crusades launched by Pope Urban II
1272	Thomas Aquinas completes *Summa Theologica*
1378	The Papal Schism
1455	Gutenberg Bible printed
1517	Luther posts Ninety-Five Theses
1525	Anabaptist movement begins
1534	King Henry VIII and the Act of Supremacy
1536	Calvin's *Institutes of the Christian Religion* published
1545	Council of Trent begins
1611	King James Version of the Bible published
1735	Great Awakening begins
1738	John and Charles Wesley converted
1792	William Carey helps form Baptist Missionary Society
1906	Azusa Street Revival propels Pentecostalism forward
1962	Vatican II opens

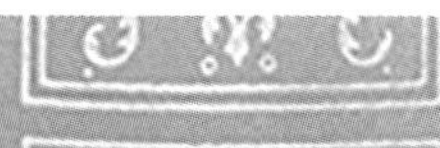

now the Church of Jesus Christ of Latter-day Saints. Young led his followers to Utah, where they founded Salt Lake City, now the central city of the church. Mormons are known for clean living and a dedication to their families. The doctrines of the Mormon Church differ from orthodox Christianity in numerous respects. Mormons deny the Trinity and believe that mankind's destiny is to evolve to Godhood. Mormon theology also says that God continues to give revelations to men, specifically to the leaders of their organization, and that these revelations have a standing equal to or even above that of the Bible.

CITY OF GOD, THE An important book by Augustine of Hippo, in which he interpreted human history as a struggle between God's people, living in the city of God, and the pagans living in the city of the world. Those in the city of God receive eternal life, but those in the city of the world receive eternal punishment. The book was written in 411 and was motivated by Augustine's reflection upon the significance of the sack of Rome by the pagan Visigoths in 410.

CONFESSIONS The autobiography of Augustine of Hippo. It was written in about 400 and tells of Augustine's spiritual struggles and triumphs. He describes his indulgent lifestyle as a young man, his struggle with the claims of Christianity, and his conversion to Christianity. It begins with the affirmation, "You made us for yourself, and our hearts are restless until they find their rest in you." Few other books have been as influential in Christian history.

CONGREGATIONAL A form of church government that puts ultimate authority in the hands of the congregation rather than the pastor, the elders, or a bishop. Baptist churches, Congregational churches, and many independent churches have congregational forms of government. For comparison, see *episcopal*; *presbyterian.*

CONSTANTINE THE GREAT (c. 280–337) First emperor of the Roman Empire to become a Christian. The story of his conversion is fascinating. When Constantine prayed to the God of the Christians the day before a strategic battle, he had a vision of a flaming cross in the sky and the words "In this sign conquer." His soldiers carried the symbol of the cross on their shields the next day, and they were indeed victorious. Shortly thereafter, in 313, Constantine issued the Edict of Milan, in which he legalized Christianity and recognized the right of churches to own property. Constantine convened the Council of Nicaea (see *Nicaea, Council of*) in 325 to unite the church against the heresy of Arianism. In 330 he moved the capital of the empire from Rome to Byzantium, which he renamed Constantinople (now Istanbul, Turkey). He was baptized a Christian on his deathbed.

CONSTANTINOPLE Present-day Istanbul, the great city on the Bosporus Straits. In the year 330, Constantine the Great moved the capital of the Roman Empire from Rome to Byzantium, the city at the crossroads between Europe and Asia. He renamed it Constantinople—the City of Constantine. When the Roman Empire was split into two parts in 395, Constantinople remained capital of the eastern empire, which came to be known as the Byzantine Empire. Long before the Great Schism in 1054, Constantinople was the center of the church in the East. It retained this position until the fall of Constantinople to the Muslim Turks in 1453. The Basilica of Hagia Sophia in Constantinople was the central church building of the Eastern Orthodox Church. The Council of Constantinople was held in 381 to combat numerous heresies and to affirm the earlier work of the Council of Nicaea.

Istanbul, Turkey—formerly Constantinople

COUNCILS, CHURCH See *church councils.*

COUNTER-REFORMATION A reform movement in the Roman Catholic Church during the period of the Protestant Reformation. It included inquisitions (see *Spanish Inquisition*) to rid the church of heresy and abuses, but it also included elements of theological reform and missionary zeal. Ignatius of Loyola founded the Society of Jesus (see *Jesuits*) during this time. Much of the Counter-Reformation was based on the reforms established by the Council of Trent.

CRANMER, THOMAS (1489–1556) The Church of England broke with the Roman Catholic Church because the pope would not sanction King Henry VIII's divorce from his first wife, Catherine of Aragon. However, the real architect of Anglican doctrine and liturgy was Thomas Cranmer. King Henry appointed him archbishop of Canterbury, and it was Cranmer who urged Henry to authorize distribution of the Bible in English (see *Tyndale, William*). Cranmer changed the liturgy of the church from Latin to English when he wrote and compiled the Book of Common Prayer. He wrote the Forty-Two Articles (later reduced to Thirty-Nine Articles), the doctrinal anchor for the Church of England. One of the ironies of Henry's divorce from Catherine was played out when Cranmer was burned at the stake as a heretic by Mary, the Catholic daughter of Henry and Catherine.

Remains of a Crusader fortress in northern Israel

CRUSADES, THE The Crusades were a series of religious wars in which armies from Christian Europe attempted to take control of the Holy Land away from the Muslims. The period of the eight crusades spanned about 200 years, from 1095–1291. The third Crusade was led by Richard the Lion-Hearted of England. Others were led by kings of France, Germany, and the Holy Roman Empire. The

Crusades were largely unsuccessful in dislodging the Muslims from the Holy Land, but they expanded trade between Europe and the Middle East.

Charles Darwin

DARWIN, CHARLES (1809–82) A British naturalist who first expounded the theory of evolution. His book *The Origin of Species* (1859) rejects the traditional concept that plants and animals as we know them today were created by a divine act of creation. The emergence and acceptance of the theory of evolution had a profound impact on the religious world, as it caused many biblical scholars to reexamine their understanding of Scripture. If the story of the creation was not literally true, one might also disbelieve many other doctrines that had previously been accepted without question. Charles Darwin and Abraham Lincoln were born on the same day, February 12, 1809.

DENOMINATIONS Almost from the very beginning of the church there have been differences in theology and church governance between various groups. Today the Christian church is divided into three major branches: Roman Catholic, Eastern Orthodox, and Protestant. Within Protestantism, there are hundreds of denominations—groups of churches associated with one another through common beliefs and governance. Some American denominations are direct descendants of European state churches, and others have come into existence when a group within an established denomination becomes disillusioned with the theology or practices of the denomination. They then break away and form a new denomination. Some denominations, such as the Southern Baptist Convention, include millions of members and thousands of congregations. Other denominations are relatively small, with only dozens of congregations and thousands of members.

TEN LARGEST CHRISTIAN BODIES IN AMERICA

1. Catholic	62 million
2. Baptist	25–30 million
3. Nondenominational	21 million
4. Methodist	12 million
5. Pentecostal	10 million
6. Lutheran	6.5 million
7. Churches of Christ	3 million
8. Reformed/Presbyterian	2 million
9. Anglican/Episcopal	1.75 million
10. Orthodox (Greek, Russian, Coptic, etc.)	1.2 million

Numbers are approximate and represent adherents. Source: *Christian Denominations*, copyright © 2024 by Rose Publishing.

DIET OF WORMS A formal assembly of princes (called a "diet") that took place in Worms, Germany (pronounced *Vōrms*), in 1521. The Reformer Martin Luther was called there to recant his teachings because they were considered heretical. He responded, "Here I stand; I can do no other. God help me. Amen."

DISPENSATIONALISM A method of biblical interpretation that divides human history into seven ages, or dispensations. In each dispensation, people are tested to determine their response to God's revealed truth. Salvation is always by God's grace, but the faith required of humans is different in each dispensation. The present dispensation, the sixth, is the age of the church. Dispensationalists hold to a literal interpretation of the Bible and a premillennial view of the Second Coming of Christ (see *Millennium* in the chapter "Church Life and Theology").

Dispensationalism arose in the nineteenth century and flowered in twentieth-century fundamentalism. It was promoted and popularized through the notes in the *Scofield Reference Bible* and by Dallas Theological Seminary.

DOMINICANS Members of a Christian religious order that was founded in 1216. The Dominicans were originally itinerant preachers, and their vows include poverty. The order has produced many influential theologians and missionaries. Thomas Aquinas and Girolamo Savonarola were both Dominicans.

EARLY CHURCH The church as it existed during the first several hundred years after the life of Christ. Since many of Jesus's disciples and the other early apostles left Jerusalem after Pentecost to spread the gospel of Christ, the center of Christianity moved westward from Jerusalem to southern Europe, particularly Rome. As the gospel spread, heresies quickly arose, and many of the New Testament epistles (letters) were written to counter various false teachings. Some key figures in the early church, besides the disciples and the apostle Paul, include Clement, Justin Martyr, Origen, Constantine the Great, Athanasius, John Chrysostom, Jerome, and Augustine of Hippo.

EASTERN ORTHODOX CHURCH The family of churches that make up one of the three great branches of Christianity, along with the Roman Catholic Church and Protestant churches. Historically, there was a natural division in the church. The church in the East, centered in Constantinople, used Greek as its liturgical language, while the church in the West, centered in Rome, used Latin. The Eastern Orthodox Church split from the Roman Catholic Church in the Great Schism of 1054. It rejects the papacy (the office of the pope), and its worship is more mystical than that of the Roman Catholic Church. The Orthodox churches are the primary churches in Greece (Greek Orthodox Church), Russia (Russian Orthodox Church), and several other Eastern European countries.

EAST-WEST SPLIT See *Great Schism (the East-West split).*

EDDY, MARY BAKER (1821–1910) The founder of Christian Science. She emphasized the use of the mind in healing, claiming that her teachings came by direct revelation of

God. Her writings are accepted by Christian Scientists as having equal authority with the Bible.

EDWARDS, JONATHAN (1703–58) A Congregational minister who became one of the most influential theologians and preachers in American history. His preaching was an important factor in the Great Awakening in New England. He was one of the most learned scholars of his generation, and shortly before his death he became president of the college that later became Princeton University. One of his best-known sermons is "Sinners in the Hands of an Angry God."

Jonathan Edwards

EPISCOPAL A form of church government with a hierarchy of bishops, in which ultimate authority in the local church resides with the bishop rather than with the pastor, the representative bodies, or the congregation. The Roman Catholic Church, the Eastern Orthodox Church, the Episcopal Church, and the United Methodist Church all have episcopal forms of government. For comparison, see *congregational*; *presbyterian*.

EPISCOPAL CHURCH A mainline denomination in the USA that is a direct descendant of the Church of England. As an Anglican church, the governmental structure and liturgies of the Episcopal Church are very similar to those of the Church of England. Both churches use the Book of Common Prayer.

ERASMUS (1466–1536) A Dutch Renaissance scholar who prepared the way for the Reformers. His Greek New Testament, published in 1516, was an important source for Martin Luther in his German translation, and also for Stephanus, who prepared the Textus Receptus in 1550.

EUSEBIUS OF CAESAREA (c. 265–339) The "Father of Church History." His histories of the church have provided one of the few windows on the church in ancient times. His great work was *Historia Ecclesiastica*. Eusebius was a contemporary of Constantine the Great, of whom he wrote a biography, and he participated in the Council of Nicaea.

EVANGELICAL The evangelical movement arose in the USA after World War II as a refinement of fundamentalism and as an alternative to the trends in mainline Protestantism. Evangelicals uphold the fundamentals of the faith (see *fundamentalism*), but they also believe they should be involved with the culture in which they live. Like fundamentalists, evangelicals emphasize the necessity of a personal relationship with Christ as Savior and Lord. They often use the term *born again* to describe their relationship with God. More broadly, the term *evangelical* refers to revival movements since the Great Awakening. The term is also used of a renewal and missionary movement in the Church of England that began in the late eighteenth century. In a survey of adult Americans by the Gallup organization in 2018, 41 percent responded yes to the question, "Would you describe yourself as a born-again Christian?"

EVANGELICAL LUTHERAN CHURCH IN AMERICA A mainline denomination that is the largest of several Lutheran denominations in the USA. It is the result of a merger in 1987 of two large Lutheran denominations. All Lutheran churches trace their roots back to Martin Luther. See also *Lutheran Church, Missouri Synod.*

FIRST AMENDMENT RIGHTS The First Amendment to the US Constitution provides for freedom of religion and freedom of speech and of the press. The actual text of the amendment begins, "Congress shall make no law respecting an establishment of religion, or prohibiting the free exercise thereof..." In the second half of the twentieth century, the Supreme Court tended to interpret the First Amendment as calling for a strict separation of church and state. Judicial conservatives tend to think that this interpretation of the First Amendment is incorrect, and that the original intent was simply that Congress must not institute a state church, as many European countries had done at the end of the eighteenth century. More recently, the Supreme Court has taken a more moderate perspective on issues related to the separation of church and state.

FISH, SIGN OF THE When they are all put together, the initial letters of the Greek words for "Jesus Christ, Son of God, Savior" spell *ichthus*, the Greek word for "fish." The Christians in the early church used the word *ichthus* and a simple sign of a fish to identify themselves as Christians. This was particularly important when they were being persecuted, since they could identify one another with a sign that looked innocent to those who did not understand it.

FOX, GEORGE See *Friends, Society of.*

FRANCIS, POPE (reign 2013–). He is the first pope from the Americas. He tends to be more liberal than his predecessor, Pope Benedict. He pronounced that the church could bless same-sex couples, though he was clear that the church does not allow for same-sex marriages. He took the name Francis in honor of Saint Francis.

FRANCIS OF ASSISI (c. 1181–1226) A saint, and founder of the Franciscan Order. Francis had a wealthy upbringing, but he left his wealth in order to become a poor itinerant preacher. His preaching and lifestyle included an appreciation of God's creation and love of all living things. He started the practice of using nativity scenes (crèches) to focus on Christmas as a celebration of the birth of Jesus.

FRANCISCANS Members of a Christian religious order founded by Francis of Assisi. It is the largest order in the Roman Catholic Church, and it includes both men and women. As Saint Francis did, Franciscans take a vow of poverty.

FREE CHURCH TRADITION Churches formed by breaking away from state churches. Churches stemming from Anabaptist, Brethren, and Pietist traditions, as well as English Baptists and Quakers, fall into this broad category.

FREEDOM OF RELIGION The freedom to choose a religion (or no religion at all) and to worship freely and openly without fear of persecution. Many early immigrants, including the Pilgrims, came to America because there was not sufficient freedom of religion in England or Europe in the seventeenth century. The US Constitution guarantees freedom of religion in the First Amendment (see *First Amendment rights*).

FRIENDS, SOCIETY OF Better known as Quakers, the Friends include several groups, all of whom trace their roots to the teachings of George Fox (1624–91). Seeking religious enlightenment that he did not find in other churches in England, Fox came to rely on "the inner light of the living Christ." Some groups ("meetings") of Friends have no formal ceremonies, creeds, or clergy. Other groups have pastors and conventional worship services. Friends are pacifists and are known for social action.

FUNDAMENTALISM A conservative theological movement that arose in the United States at the turn of the twentieth century in reaction to liberalism in church and society. Fundamentalists identify certain "fundamentals" of the faith that they feel are required in true believers. These fundamentals include belief in the deity of Christ, the Virgin Birth, the sacrificial death of Christ, the resurrection and ascension of Jesus, the inspiration and inerrancy of Scripture, and the bodily return of Jesus Christ (see *Second Coming* in the chapter "Church Life and Theology"). In contrast to evangelicals, fundamentalists are often separatist. Many fundamentalists follow a dispensationalist interpretation of Scripture (see *dispensationalism*). 📌 Because fundamentalists have often been perceived as being reactionary in their conservatism, the term *fundamentalist* is often used in the media to describe any conservative and reactionary religious group, including conservative Muslims and conservative Hindus.

Billy Graham

GRAHAM, BILLY (1918–2018) An American evangelist who held evangelistic crusades and preached the gospel to millions of people in countries around the world. He came to national and international prominence in the early 1950s with successful and long-running crusades in large cities such as New York and London. Graham was the most prominent and widely respected evangelical leader in America for many years. He preached a simple biblical message of repentance, often punctuating his messages with the statement, "The Bible says ..."

GRAIL, HOLY The cup used by Jesus at the Last Supper, a meal he ate with his disciples the night before his crucifixion. In medieval legends, the Holy Grail was also used to catch Jesus's blood while he was hanging on the cross, and it became the object of quests by King Arthur's knights. 📌 By extension, a grail can be anything that is the object of a long and arduous search.

GREAT AWAKENING A spiritual revival that spread across colonial America in the 1730s and 1740s. Its leaders included the popular preachers Jonathan Edwards and George Whitefield. There was a great increase in the establishment of Congregational, Presbyterian, Methodist, and Baptist churches as a result of the Awakening.

GREAT SCHISM (THE EAST-WEST SPLIT) The split between the Eastern and Western churches that occurred in 1054. From the time of the early church there were natural divisions between the Latin-speaking churches in the West, centered in Rome, and the Greek-speaking churches of the East, centered in Constantinople. The split finally occurred over theological differences. The pope in Rome excommunicated the patriarch in Constantinople, and vice versa (see *excommunication* in the chapter "Church Life and Theology"). The Eastern church became the Eastern Orthodox Church, and the Western church eventually was known as the Roman Catholic Church. The Papal Schism began in 1378 regarding the office of the pope, and it is also sometimes called the Great Schism, or the Great Western Schism.

GREEK ORTHODOX CHURCH The Greek Orthodox Church in the USA is related to the Greek Orthodox Church in Greece. It was brought to America by Greek immigrants and is the largest of various Orthodox churches in the USA. Church services tend to be elaborate and liturgical. See also *Eastern Orthodox Church*.

GUTENBERG BIBLE When Johannes Gutenberg invented movable type in the mid-1400s, one of the first books he printed was the Bible. The text in the Gutenberg Bible was the Latin Vulgate (see *Vulgate* in the chapter "Bible Overview"). There are twenty-one complete Gutenberg Bibles preserved in museums today.

HENRY VIII, KING (1491–1547) The king of England who broke with the Roman Catholic Church and established the Church of England. His first wife, Catherine of Aragon, was the daughter of King

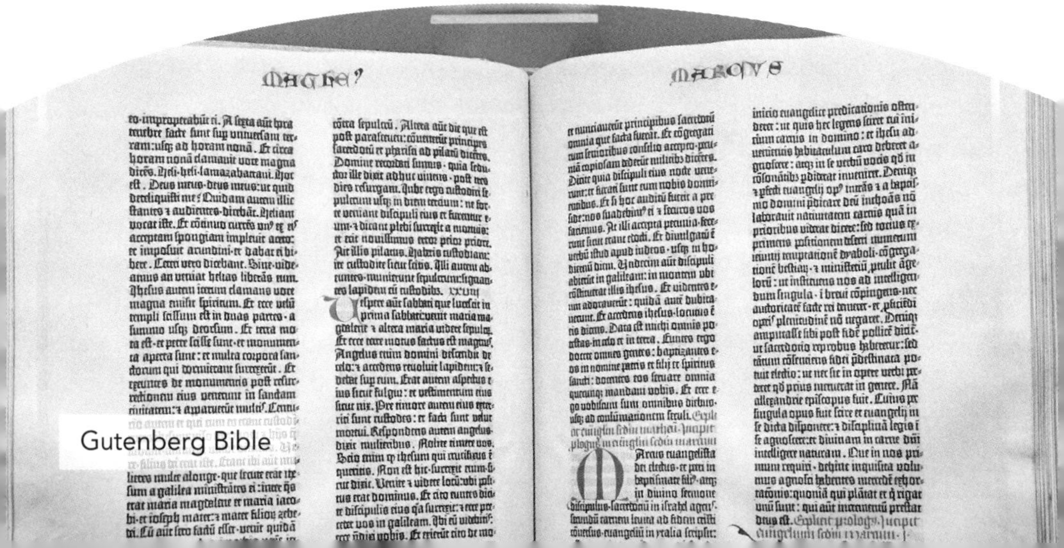

Gutenberg Bible

Ferdinand and Queen Isabella of Spain (who sponsored Christopher Columbus). Catherine bore a daughter, Mary (later to be known as Bloody Mary for her persecution of Protestants), but Henry wanted a divorce because he felt he needed a son. His proposed divorce was not sanctioned by Pope Clement VII, so in 1534 Parliament passed the Act of Supremacy, which established the Church of England with the king as head of the church. Henry was eventually married six times. After a brief reign by Henry's son, Edward VI, Henry's daughter Mary became queen. She was a Roman Catholic like her mother and tried to bring England back under the authority of Rome. After Mary's death, Henry's daughter Elizabeth I began her long reign.

HERE I STAND; I CAN DO NO OTHER When Reformer Martin Luther was called to recant his teachings at the Diet of Worms (a formal assembly of princes held in Worms, Germany), he refused, saying, "Here I stand; I can do no other. God help me. Amen."

HOLY GRAIL See *Grail, Holy*.

HOLY ROMAN EMPIRE See *Charlemagne*.

HUGUENOTS (pronounced *HYOO-geh-nots*) French Protestants of the sixteenth century who followed John Calvin's teachings. They were persecuted in their Roman Catholic homeland, the worst atrocities being committed in 1572, when thousands of Huguenots were murdered. They received certain freedoms and protection for a time under the Edict of Nantes, but even those freedoms were later removed by King Louis XIV. Many Huguenots fled to America.

Historic French Huguenot church

HUMANISM A philosophy that elevates mankind to a preeminent position and celebrates man's freedom. When humanism is nontheistic, dismissing the significance of God, it is often referred to as secular humanism. Secular humanism is a prominent philosophy in America today.

HUS, JAN (c. 1370–1415) A Czech reformer whose attacks on the abuses in the church preceded the Protestant Reformation by more than a century. Hus was influenced by John Wycliffe, who lived a generation earlier in England. Hus was tried at the Council of Constance (the same church council that ended the Papal Schism) and was burned at the stake as a heretic.

ICHTHUS See *fish, sign of the.*

IGNATIUS OF LOYOLA (1491–1556) The founder of the Society of Jesus, the religious order commonly called the Jesuits. As a young man, Ignatius was badly wounded in battle. While recuperating, he read about the life of Christ and was inspired to become a soldier for Christ. He was briefly imprisoned by the Spanish Inquisition because of his religious views.

INDULGENCES In the Roman Catholic Church, a grant for the removal of part or all of the temporal punishment for sin. Indulgences are granted both for the living and for those in purgatory. Prior to the Reformation, indulgences could be obtained in exchange for certain good works, pilgrimages, or donations to the church. The sale of indulgences was one of the practices to which the Reformer Martin Luther objected.

INNOCENT III, POPE (1160–1216) One of the greatest of the medieval popes, he reigned 1198–1216. He convened the Fourth Lateran Council, at which the dogma of transubstantiation was defined. Innocent supported the Fourth Crusade, and he asserted the power of the papacy over kings and emperors. He forced King John of England (of Magna Carta fame) to acknowledge that the English throne served to promote the pope's interests.

INQUISITION See *Spanish Inquisition.*

INSTITUTES OF THE CHRISTIAN RELIGION The classic summary of the Christian faith (1536) by John Calvin, one of the great leaders of the Protestant Reformation. Frequently referred to simply as Calvin's *Institutes*, it is a theological handbook that lays the biblical foundations of Reformed Protestantism.

JAMES I, KING (1566–1625) The king of England who, under pressure from the Puritans, authorized the Bible translation known as the Authorized Version, more popularly known as the King James Version. First published in 1611, it is still widely used today. James was first crowned King James VI of Scotland when he succeeded his mother—Mary, Queen of Scots—while still a boy. He was crowned James I of England in 1603.

JEHOVAH'S WITNESSES A religious movement that began in the nineteenth century and is still active today. Their founder first predicted that Christ would return to earth in 1914. Jehovah's Witnesses deny the doctrine of the Trinity, and they practice strict separation from the government and from anyone who is not a member of their church. They do not accept blood transfusions, and they are known for their aggressive door-to-door proselytizing.

JEROME (c. 347–419) Translator of the Hebrew Old Testament and the Greek New Testament into Latin. His translation came to be called the Vulgate (from the Latin word for "common" or "popular") because it was written in the "vulgar," or common, language. It was the predominant translation in the Roman Catholic Church for the next 1,500 years.

JERUSALEM, DESTRUCTION OF (AD 70) Jerusalem was destroyed by the Roman general Titus in AD 70. This forced the scattering of the young church, which

The Siege and Destruction of Jerusalem

had been centered in Jerusalem, throughout the Roman Empire. The destruction of Jerusalem was prophesied by Jesus (Luke 19:41–44), but it is not otherwise mentioned in the Bible.

JESUITS Members of the Society of Jesus, a religious order of men founded by Ignatius of Loyola in the sixteenth century. Many Jesuits are teachers or missionaries. The order operates hundreds of schools and colleges around the world. 📌 The term *jesuitical* has a negative connotation: being prone to intrigue or deviousness. This is because the Jesuits often wielded power behind the scenes in the governments of Europe.

JOAN OF ARC (c. 1412–31) A French peasant girl who, at the age of seventeen, led a French army to victory over the English army during the Hundred Years' War. She claimed she received instructions from several deceased saints, which led to her trial as a heretic. She was burned at the stake, though the verdict was later overturned. She was canonized by the Roman Catholic Church in 1920.

JOHN XXIII, POPE (1881–1963) Although he was pope for only five years (1958–63), his influence on the Roman Catholic Church was profound. He convened the Second Vatican Council (see *Vatican II*), which introduced sweeping changes in the church and in the everyday life of Roman Catholics.

JOHN PAUL II, POPE (1920–2005) He was pope from 1978–2005. Polish by nationality, he was the first non-Italian to be elected since the sixteenth century. He reinforced conservative Catholic positions in both dogma and social issues. His support of the pro-democracy movement in Poland helped topple Communism throughout Eastern Europe.

JOSEPHUS (c. 37–100) A Jewish historian whose writings give tremendous insight into the history and everyday life of first-century Judaism. His best-known work is *Antiquities.*

JUSTIN MARTYR (c. 100–165) An apologist (see *apologetics, apologist* in the chapter "Church Life and Theology") who defended Christianity against charges of treason and atheism, accusations which were frequently leveled by the government of Rome against Christians. He tried to convince the Romans that Christianity was not contrary to their philosophies, but that their philosophies pointed the way to Christianity. He was martyred for his beliefs during the reign of Emperor Marcus Aurelius.

Martin Luther King Jr.

KING, MARTIN LUTHER JR. (1929–68) A Black Baptist pastor who led the civil rights movement in America. He supported a nonviolent approach, and his work was instrumental in the passage of important civil rights legislation. His famous "I Have a Dream" speech was presented at a great civil rights march in Washington, DC, in 1963. He was assassinated in 1968 at the age of thirty-nine. 📌 Dr. King's birthday is now celebrated as a holiday throughout the United States.

KNOX, JOHN (c. 1514–72) A Reformer and leader of the Protestant Reformation in Scotland who founded the (Presbyterian) Church of Scotland. He was heavily influenced by John Calvin's teachings.

LATIN The official language of the Western church (see *Roman Catholic Church*) for most of its history. The Latin Vulgate translation of the Bible was prepared by Jerome in the fourth century, and it was the main translation used by the church for 1,500 years. Until the Vatican II Council, the Roman Catholic Mass was always in Latin, and official pronouncements of the church are still presented in Latin.

LATTER-DAY SAINTS After Joseph Smith's death, his Mormon followers split into several groups. The group that called itself the Church of Jesus Christ of Latter-day Saints, under the leadership of Brigham Young, moved to Utah. Another group, which called itself the Reorganized Church of Jesus Christ of Latter-day Saints, moved to Missouri.

LEO X, POPE (1475–1521) Pope from 1513–21, the period when the Reformation began. Although he excommunicated Martin Luther, he never thought Luther was a serious threat to the church. Leo was a great patron of the arts. One of his projects was the rebuilding of Saint Peter's Basilica, a huge job in which Renaissance artists Raphael and Michelangelo were both involved.

LEWIS, CLIVE STAPLES (C. S.) (1898–1963) C. S. Lewis was a great Christian writer and apologist of the twentieth century. He was a professor first at Oxford and then at Cambridge. He wrote fiction for adults (the Space Trilogy, 1938–45) and for children (the Chronicles of Narnia, 1950–56). His other works include *The Problem of Pain* (1940), *The Screwtape Letters* (1945), *Mere Christianity* (1952), and his autobiography, *Surprised by Joy* (1955). ➧ Lewis died on November 22, 1963, the same day President John F. Kennedy was assassinated.

LIBERALISM A theological movement that began in the late nineteenth century. It emphasized freedom, progress, and new ways of thinking, including new ways of looking at the Bible and at Jesus. Liberalism does not accept the traditional view that Scripture is inspired by God (see *Scripture, inspiration of* in the chapter "Church Life and Theology"), and it tends not to accept the deity of Jesus. Fundamentalism and neoorthodoxy were twentieth-century reactions against liberalism.

LIVINGSTONE, DAVID (1813–73) A British missionary and explorer in Africa in the nineteenth century. When Livingstone had been out of touch with European civilization for some time, the journalist Sir Henry Stanley went to search for him. When they finally met, Stanley gave his famous greeting, "Dr. Livingstone, I presume?"

David Livingstone

LUTHER, MARTIN (1483–1546) The "Father of the Protestant Reformation." Luther was a monk in Germany who became convinced that the doctrines of the church were not consistent with Scripture. In particular, he felt that the church ignored the biblical teaching of justification by grace, through faith. In 1517 he posted his Ninety-Five Theses on the door of the Wittenberg church. In this document he set forth his disagreements with the Roman authorities in the church, particularly with regard to the sale of indulgences. His rallying cries became *sola fide* ("by faith alone"), *sola gratia* ("by grace alone"), and *sola Scriptura* ("by Scripture alone"). By *sola fide* he meant that a person could be saved only through faith, not by indulgences granted by the church. In 1520 he was excommunicated by Pope Leo X, and in 1521 he received a hearing in Worms, Germany (see *Diet of Worms*). He was asked to recant his teachings, but he refused, saying, "Here I stand; I can do no other. God help me. Amen." One of his great contributions to the Protestant movement was his translation of the Bible into German. This helped establish a standard for translating the Bible into the common language of the people. The Luther translation is used to this day in Germany, and it has had an effect on German culture and language similar to that of the King James Version in English. Luther's followers came to be known as Lutherans, and his teaching formed the foundation for the Lutheran churches.

LUTHERAN The church tradition that grew out of the teachings of Martin Luther. The Lutherans "protested" against various doctrines dictated by the Roman authorities in the church, hence the name "Protestant" for their movement. Historically, Lutheran doctrines were represented by the terms *sola Scriptura* ("by Scripture alone"), *sola gratia* ("by grace alone"), and *sola fide* ("by faith alone"). The Lutheran Church became the state church in Germany and Scandinavia. See also *Book of Concord*; *Lutheran Church, Missouri Synod*; *Evangelical Lutheran Church in America*.

LUTHERAN CHURCH, MISSOURI SYNOD A major Lutheran denomination in the USA that is theologically conservative. Like all Lutheran churches, it traces its roots to Martin Luther. See also *Evangelical Lutheran Church in America*.

MAINLINE DENOMINATIONS The large established denominations in the USA that historically have played a culture-shaping role in American society. They include the Episcopal Church, the United Methodist Church, the Presbyterian Church (USA), the Evangelical Lutheran Church in America, and the United Church of Christ. Their leaders tend to be theologically and culturally liberal. Since World War II, evangelicals have tended to distinguish themselves from mainline churches. Membership in mainline denominations has been steadily slipping since the mid-1960s, while membership in evangelical denominations has generally been growing.

MARTYR A person who is killed because of his or her faith. The first Christian martyr was Stephen (Acts 7), and tradition says that most of the apostles suffered martyrdom. Literally millions of Christians have been killed for their faith during the last 2,000 years. During the years of the early church, many Christians were killed by being thrown to the lions.

MAYFLOWER COMPACT Before the Pilgrims established their colony in Massachusetts in 1620, they wrote the Mayflower Compact, an agreement that the members of the community would work together and would submit themselves to the laws that were to be adopted "for the general good of the colony." It was the first agreement for self-government in America. Its opening words are, "In the name of God, Amen."

MENNONITES A Protestant group that emphasizes peaceful living and community and family values. It dates back to the Anabaptist movement during the Reformation era. The name comes from Menno Simons (c. 1496–1561), one of the early leaders. Mennonites are known for their leadership in the peace movement and for their social work in fighting hunger and poverty.

METHODISM, METHODIST The revival movement within the Church of England spearheaded by John and Charles Wesley in the eighteenth century. The movement was characterized by an emphasis on personal holiness, prayer, good works, and strict discipline. The Methodists eventually broke away from the Church of England but retained an episcopal form of church structure. The United Methodist Church in America is a direct descendant of the early Methodist movement. The African

Methodist Episcopal Church (AME) and the AME Zion Church are Black denominations that are offshoots of the Methodist Church.

MILAN, EDICT OF The decree of Constantine the Great in 313 that legalized Christianity in the Roman Empire. It did not make Christianity the official religion of the empire, but it protected Christians from government persecution and ensured an equal legal footing for Christianity alongside the other religions.

MONASTICISM An ascetic way of life in which people (both men and women) live according to a religious rule. Most monastic life is communal and celibate. Some, but not all, religious orders are monastic. Monks and nuns who join a monastic order take vows of poverty, chastity, and obedience.

MOODY, DWIGHT L. (1837–99) An American evangelist who held great crusades throughout America and England. He was a forerunner in holding the types of crusades later held by Billy Sunday and Billy Graham. Moody was also the founder of the Moody Bible Institute in Chicago.

MORE, THOMAS (1478–1535) An English statesman and influential leader of the Roman Catholic Church during the reign of King Henry VIII. Henry elevated More to the position of lord chancellor, but More would not support the king's plan to divorce Catherine of Aragon in defiance of the pope. More was accused of high treason, and Henry had him beheaded. He is considered by the Roman Catholic Church to be a martyr, and he was canonized in 1935. *A Man for All Seasons* is a popular play and movie about Sir Thomas More.

Sir Thomas More

MORMONS This term refers to members of the Church of Jesus Christ of Latter-day Saints. See also *Smith, Joseph*; *Young, Brigham*.

NATIONAL BAPTIST CONVENTION The two largest Black denominations in the USA are the National Baptist Convention of America and the National Baptist Convention, USA, Inc. Between them they have more than 11 million members. They both trace their history to 1880, and the two groups split in 1915. In theology, both groups are similar to other Baptist denominations.

NATIONAL COUNCIL OF THE CHURCHES OF CHRIST IN THE USA An ecumenical association of Christian churches in the United States. For the most part, the National Council of Churches is made up of Protestant denominations with relatively liberal theology, as well as several Eastern Orthodox churches. A smaller, evangelical counterpart is the National Association of Evangelicals. See also *World Council of Churches.*

NEOORTHODOXY A theological movement of the twentieth century. Karl Barth and Reinhold Niebuhr are names particularly associated with neoorthodoxy (neo/"new" + orthodoxy). It was a reaction against liberalism and was an attempt to regain some of the orthodox truths of the Reformation. In contrast to fundamentalism, neoorthodoxy did not see the Bible as infallible (see *Scripture, inerrancy of* in the chapter "Church Life and Theology"), but believed that God speaks through the Bible.

NEW TESTAMENT CANON ESTABLISHED The canon is the official list of books included in

The Council of Nicaea

the Bible. The New Testament contains twenty-seven books—the four Gospels, the Acts of the Apostles, twenty-one Epistles, and Revelation. The books of the New Testament were written over a period of about fifty years, from AD 40–90. The Gospels were written to provide an account of the life and ministry of Jesus, and the Epistles are letters that were written (mostly by the apostle Paul) to specific churches or groups of Christians. These letters were widely copied and circulated, and over time the letters written by the apostles or immediate disciples of the apostles were accepted by the church as having divine authority and having been inspired by God. There was no single point in history when the canon was officially established. Over the first several hundred years of church history, various groupings of Gospels and letters were given prominence. The New Testament canon in its present form was largely in place by about 200, and the first exact listing of the twenty-seven books we now know as the New Testament was included in a letter written by the church leader Athanasius in 367. The same list was published shortly thereafter by two different church councils.

NICAEA, COUNCIL OF (325) At a church council called by Constantine in Nicaea (pronounced *nigh-SEE-uh*; in present-day Turkey), church leaders from around Christendom dealt with various heresies that had arisen in the 300 years since the time of Christ. In particular, the council was convened to combat Arianism, a heresy that stated that Jesus Christ, the Son, was created by the Father and was not of the same essence as the Father. The Council adopted a creed (later adapted to the form of the Nicene Creed as we know it today) as a universal statement and affirmation of the orthodox beliefs of the Christian church. See *Nicene Creed* in the chapter "Church Life and Theology."

NICHOLAS, SAINT (fourth century) A bishop in Asia Minor (present-day Turkey); he is said to have attended the Council of Nicaea. He is the patron saint of children, and one of the most popular saints of the church. His feast day is December 6, a holiday that is widely celebrated in Europe by giving gifts to children. The Dutch form of Saint Nicholas is *Sinterklaas*, from which we get the contemporary name Santa Claus.

NINETY-FIVE THESES The document that Martin Luther posted to the door of the Castle Church in Wittenberg, Germany, in 1517. In it he set forth his various disagreements with the Roman authorities in the church, especially regarding the sale of indulgences. The document was written in Latin, but it was soon translated into German and widely distributed. The posting of the Ninety-Five Theses is generally considered the start of the Protestant Reformation.

NONCONFORMISTS Also called dissenters, Nonconformists are persons who do not conform to the practices of a state church. The English Baptists, Congregationalists, and Presbyterians of the 1600s were considered Nonconformists because they rejected certain practices of the Church of England.

ORIGEN (c. 185–c. 254) A great theologian and apologist of the early church who tried to reconcile Greek philosophy with Christian theology. His works of theology laid the foundation for other leaders who followed him.

ORTHODOX CHURCHES See *Eastern Orthodox Church.*

PAPAL SCHISM From 1378–1415, there were two and then three competing popes. One pope was in Rome, the traditional seat of the popes, and the other was in Avignon, France, where the papacy had been located since 1309. The schism was finally ended by action of the Council of Constance, which deposed all three of the then-reigning popes. (The same council burned Jan Hus at the stake as a heretic and ordered that John Wycliffe's body be exhumed and burned.) The Papal Schism is also known as the Great Western Schism.

Blaise Pascal

PASCAL, BLAISE (1623–62) A French mathematician, philosopher, and religious thinker. Much of his religious philosophy is found in *Pensées*, a book of collected writings that was published after his death. It includes his famous wager on the existence of God.

Saint Patrick

PATRICK, SAINT (c. 385–c. 461) By tradition, Patrick was the missionary who first took the gospel of Christ to Ireland, and under whose preaching Ireland was converted to Christianity. He is the patron saint of Ireland. ➷ Saint Patrick's Day, his feast day, is March 17. It is particularly celebrated by persons with Irish heritage, who wear green on that day.

PATRON SAINT A saint from whom a person, a group of people, a church, or an institution claims special prayers and protection. For instance, Saint Christopher is the patron saint of ferrymen and travelers, Saint Patrick is the patron saint of Ireland, etc. A person with the same name as a saint may consider the saint to be his or her patron saint.

PAUL VI, POPE (1897–1978) He was pope from 1963–78, and he continued the reforms begun by his predecessor, Pope John XXIII. He confirmed the Roman Catholic Church's ban on contraception in his controversial 1968 letter to the church, *Humanae Vitae*. He was the first pope to travel widely around the world.

PEALE, NORMAN VINCENT (1898–1993) Pastor and author. His book *The Power of Positive Thinking* (1954) is one of the best-selling books in American publishing history.

PENTECOSTALISM The twentieth-century movement that emphasizes baptism in the Holy Spirit as a second blessing, one of the signs of which is speaking in tongues and other charismatic gifts. Pentecostal churches tend to be conservative in theology, and there are varying styles of church government. Their churches were among the first to ordain and promote the ministry of women. Two of the largest denominations in America are Pentecostal: the Assemblies of God and the Church of God in Christ. Beginning in the 1960s, the charismatic movement, which has many similarities to classical Pentecostal teaching and experience, began moving through the Roman Catholic Church and mainline Protestant denominations.

PILGRIMS A small group of English separatists who established the first settlement in Massachusetts (they were heading for Virginia but were blown off course) in 1620. They came to North America in search of freedom of religion, which they had not experienced in England. They came on a small ship called the Mayflower. Their harvest celebration in the fall of 1621 was the first Thanksgiving.

PIUS XII, POPE (1876–1958) Pope from 1939–58, a period including World War II and the rise of Communism in Eastern Europe. Pius was actively involved in international affairs. During his reign the dogma of the bodily assumption (taking up) of the Virgin Mary into heaven was defined.

POLYCARP (?–167) Bishop of Smyrna (in present-day Turkey). Tradition says he was a disciple of the apostle John and was burned at the stake because he would not renounce Christ.

Polycarp

PRESBYTERIAN A form of church government that puts ultimate authority in a series of representative bodies, starting with elected elders in the local church, then a regional group (a presbytery), and a national or international group. The Presbyterian Church (USA) has a presbyterian form of government. For comparison, see *congregational*; *episcopal*.

PRESBYTERIAN CHURCH (USA) A mainline denomination formed in 1983 as a reunion of the (northern) United Presbyterian Church and the (southern) Presbyterian Church, US, which had been separate since the Civil War. The

PC (USA) is relatively liberal theologically and culturally. A more conservative offshoot is the Presbyterian Church in America.

PROTESTANT One of the three great branches of Christianity, along with the Roman Catholic Church and the Eastern Orthodox Church. There are hundreds of Protestant denominations, all of which come directly or indirectly from the Protestant Reformation of the sixteenth century. Baptist, Episcopal, Congregational, and Pentecostal churches are all Protestant. There is tremendous theological diversity between Protestant churches, from ultraliberal to ultraconservative.

PURITANS A seventeenth-century religious party in England. Their intent was to purify (hence the name Puritan) the Church of England along the lines of Calvinism. The Puritans emphasized personal piety and upheld the Bible as the sole authority in doctrine, liturgy, *and* church government. Many Puritans, including the separatist Pilgrims, emigrated to New England, where their influence was pervasive. The Puritans influenced King James I to authorize a new English translation of the Bible—known today as the King James Version. The Puritan movement gained such prominence in England that the Puritans, under Oliver Cromwell, engaged in the English Civil War and took control of the government from 1649–60. Because of the Puritans' stress on personal piety, the term *puritanical* has taken on a negative sense of

The Landing of the Pilgrim Fathers

self-righteous adherence to strict moral standards. H. L. Mencken described Puritanism as having "the haunting fear that someone, somewhere, may be happy."

QUAKERS See *Friends, Society of.*

REFORMATION There have been two times in church history when Christendom seemed to be divided all the way to the roots. The first was the Great Schism (the East-West split) of 1054, when the Eastern Orthodox Church and the Roman Catholic Church split apart. The second began in 1517, when Martin Luther ignited the Protestant Reformation. For hundreds of years, individuals and groups within the Western church (for example, the Waldensians, John Wycliffe, and Jan Hus) had been urging reform of the various abuses that had crept in. Following their example, Luther also cried out for reform—but this time the protest drew wide attention. A movement began that would have a result Luther had never anticipated: The Western church would be divided. The sixteenth century was an age of developing nations, and soon German-speaking Switzerland under Ulrich Zwingli, French-speaking Switzerland under John Calvin, and England under King Henry VIII and Thomas Cranmer took up the banner of reform. Thus was born Protestantism, the third great branch of Christendom. The Reformers emphasized the Bible as the supreme authority in matters of faith and practice.

Reformer Martin Luther

REFORMED CHURCHES The Protestant churches born out of the Reformation that are Calvinist in theology and church government, as opposed to Lutheran, Anglican, or Anabaptist. Examples would be the Presbyterian Church (USA), the Christian Reformed Church, and the Reformed Church in America.

REFORMERS A general reference to the key figures of the Reformation movement. The Reformers include

Martin Luther, Ulrich Zwingli, John Calvin, and John Knox.

ROMAN CATHOLIC CHURCH One of the three great branches of the Christian church, along with the Eastern Orthodox Church and the Protestant churches. For the first 1,000 years after Christ, the church was catholic (universal) and unified. With the Great Schism of 1054, the Eastern and Western churches split apart. The Western church, under the bishop of Rome, the pope, was the sole church throughout Europe for nearly 500 more years. Then came the Protestant Reformation, and Martin Luther and others were excommunicated. Various Protestant churches were formed, and the church that continued under the authority of the pope came to be known as the Roman Catholic Church. The Roman Catholic Church claims that Peter was the first pope, with a continuous succession of popes over the past 1,900 years. The pope is the head of the Roman Catholic Church, and he is assisted and counseled by clergymen called cardinals. The top clergymen around the world are the bishops and archbishops. The Roman Catholic Church has a long and rich tradition, but significant changes were adopted by the Vatican II Council, including the celebration of the Mass in the vernacular (common) language (rather than the traditional Latin). The Roman Catholic Church is today the largest body of Christians in the USA, and it is the dominant church throughout Latin America, Southern Europe, and Poland. The Catholic church in the USA tends to be theologically and culturally more conservative than the mainline Protestant churches.

ROME The central city of the Roman Empire for centuries, it became one of the centers of the early church. As the church developed, the bishop of Rome—the pope—played an increasingly dominant role. As a result, Rome became the central city of the Western church. By the time of the Reformation, the term *Rome* was often used to refer to the pope and the entire leadership of the church. See also *Rome* in the chapter "People, Places, and Events in the New Testament."

SALVATION ARMY An international social service organization that also functions as a Protestant denomination. While it has an emphasis on evangelism, it is best known to the general public for its social work with the poor. During the Christmas season, representatives of the Army solicit donations for their work by ringing bells in shopping malls and on street corners. The Army was founded in the 1860s by William Booth, an evangelical crusader who worked in the slums of London. Salvationists, as members of the Army are called, do not observe any sacraments.

SAVONAROLA, GIROLAMO (1452–98) A Dominican friar and fiery preacher who tried to introduce reforms in the Western church shortly before the Protestant Reformation. He was a contemporary of Leonardo da Vinci. He was a popular figure in Florence, Italy, as he railed against the immorality of Pope Alexander VI and the corruption of the Medici rulers of Florence. He claimed to have special revelation from God, and he was excommunicated when he disregarded the pope's order that he stop preaching. Shortly thereafter he was hanged and burned as a heretic.

SCHISM, GREAT See *Great Schism (the East-West split)*. See also *Papal Schism*.

SCOPES TRIAL A famous trial in Tennessee in 1925, also called the Monkey Trial. Tennessee law forbade teaching the theory of evolution in public schools, and John Scopes, a high school teacher, purposely broke this law he felt was a violation of academic freedom. The prosecuting attorney was William Jennings Bryan, and Clarence Darrow defended Scopes. The much publicized trial highlighted the growing debate between fundamentalist Christianity and secular science. Scopes was convicted and fined, but the issue of the appropriateness and constitutionality of the Tennessee law was left unresolved. After the trial, fundamentalists increasingly became outsiders to sophisticated modern culture.

John T. Scopes

SEPARATION OF CHURCH AND STATE Many immigrants came to America in the seventeenth and eighteenth centuries to find freedom of religion and escape the repression of the state churches of Europe. When the US Bill of Rights was adopted, the First Amendment insured both the freedom of religion and that the government would not establish a religion (see *First Amendment rights*). Over the years, the "establishment clause" of the First Amendment has been interpreted by the Supreme Court to mean that the government at all levels, and all governmental agencies (including public schools), must maintain a strict separation from any religious activity, lest they be construed as "establishing" a religion.

SEVENTH-DAY ADVENTISTS A Protestant denomination that places special importance on the Bible's commandment, "Remember the Sabbath day, to keep it holy" (Exodus 20:8). Their name comes from their belief that Saturday, not Sunday, is the proper day for observing the Sabbath. Seventh-day Adventists are also active in supporting the separation of church and state. Growing out of a movement that predicted Christ's second coming would occur in 1844, the church was formed in 1863.

SMITH, JOSEPH (1805–44) Founder of the Mormon church in 1830. He wrote *The Book of Mormon*, which he claimed was the translation of a divinely inspired text on gold plates he found in New York. He was murdered by a mob while imprisoned in Illinois. See also *Church of Jesus Christ of Latter-day Saints*; *Young, Brigham.*

Joseph Smith

SOCIAL GOSPEL A movement in Protestant churches from about 1875–1930, in which principles from both the Old and New Testaments were brought to bear on the social problems of the day. Since many who promoted this social gospel were influenced by liberalism, conservatives tended to reject the validity of the social gospel. To conservatives, the social gospel was simply a new form of a "good works" theology. Washington Gladden, a Congregationalist minister, has been called the "Father of the Social Gospel." Charles Sheldon's immensely popular book, *In His Steps*, contains many examples of the practical outworking of the social gospel.

SOLA FIDE, SOLA GRATIA, SOLA SCRIPTURA Latin for "by faith alone," "by grace alone," and "by Scripture alone." These were favorite expressions of the Reformer Martin Luther's, since they expressed his belief that a person could be saved only by God's grace, not by works or penance or indulgences, and that this grace is received through faith (see *justification by grace, through faith* in the chapter "Church Life and Theology"). *Sola Scriptura* expressed Luther's belief that all doctrine had to be validated by holding it against the standard of Scripture.

SOUTHERN BAPTIST CONVENTION The largest Protestant denomination in the USA. Although they predominate in the South, Southern Baptist churches can be found throughout the country. There are various theological factions within the convention, but in general it is evangelical in theology. Like all Baptists, Southern Baptists baptize and receive into membership only adults and young people who can make a profession of faith (as opposed to infant baptism). Worship is nonliturgical, but it often features a gospel "invitation" to receive Christ as Savior and Lord after the sermon.

SPANISH INQUISITION A reform movement in Spain at the end of the fifteenth century. Sponsored by King Ferdinand and Queen Isabella (who also sponsored Christopher Columbus's voyages), the purpose of the Inquisition was to eliminate heretics and to rid the church and society of undesirable elements. The leading inquisitor was Tomás de Torquemada, who burned more than 2,000 heretics and expelled more than 200,000 Jews from Spain. The term *inquisition* has come to mean a harsh questioning without regard for an individual's rights.

SPURGEON, CHARLES HADDON (1834–92) One of the

great Baptist preachers of the nineteenth century. He was the pastor of the Metropolitan Tabernacle in London. More than 3,000 of his sermons have been published, and he is still frequently quoted by preachers today.

STATE CHURCH A church established by civil authorities; also called an established church. In England, the Church of England is the state church, and the reigning monarch is titular head of the church. In Scandinavian countries, the Lutheran Church is the state church. Citizens are not required to be members of the state church, but in most instances the church is supported financially by the government. In that context, a "free church" is a church independent of ties to the state or the state church. The First Amendment to the US Constitution specifically prohibits the United States government or any state from establishing a state church (see *separation of church and state*).

SUMMA THEOLOGICA (Latin for "a summation of theology") The great theological work written by Thomas Aquinas. He synthesized the philosophy of Aristotle and Christian faith, including an examination of the existence of God. He concluded that God is the uncaused cause. *Summa Theologica* was completed in 1272 and has influenced the development of Roman Catholic theology over the past 750 years.

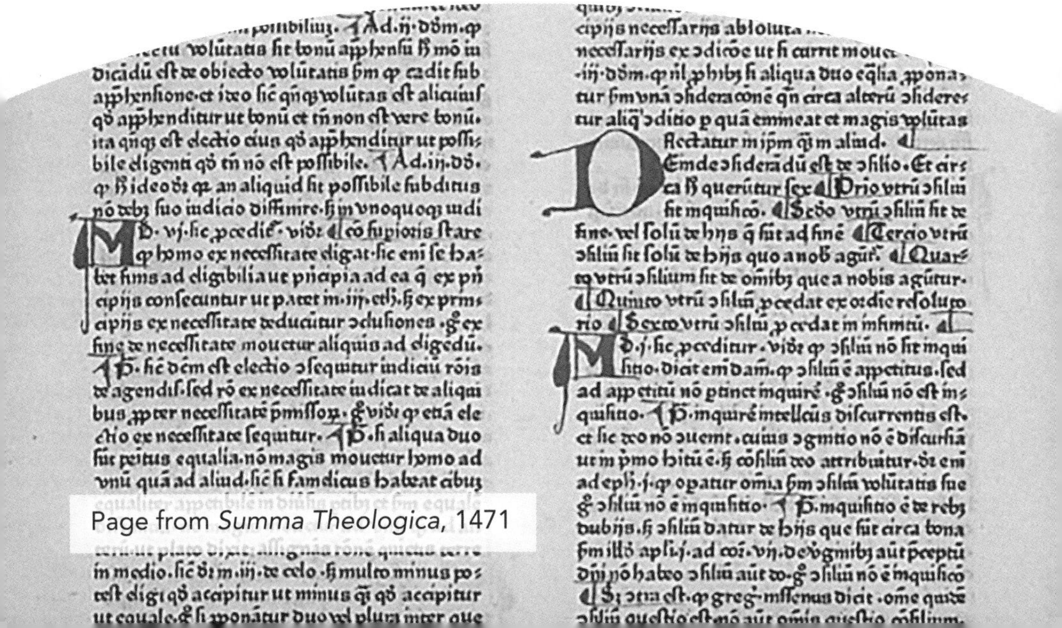

Page from *Summa Theologica*, 1471

SUNDAY, BILLY (1862–1935) A popular evangelist who held great rallies in large cities and small towns across America. Sunday had been a professional baseball player before becoming a revival preacher. It has been estimated that he preached to 100 million people during his lifetime and had one million converts. His revival ministry can be compared to that of Dwight L. Moody in the nineteenth century and that of evangelist Billy Graham in the second half of the twentieth century.

TAYLOR, J. HUDSON (1832–1905) One of the first missionaries to China and the founder of the China Inland Mission in 1865, which is now called OMF International. Taylor was also an early proponent of "faith missions"—organizations that rely on God to provide their financial resources.

TERESA, MOTHER (1910–97) A Roman Catholic nun who worked among the poor in the slums of Calcutta, India. She founded a religious order called the Missionaries of Charity. Even after her death, she is still internationally known for her tireless efforts on behalf of the downtrodden. In 1979 she received the Nobel Peace Prize, and in 2016 she was canonized as a saint.

Mother Teresa

THIRTY-NINE ARTICLES The statement of faith of the Church of England, written in 1563. It was adapted from an earlier document, the Forty-Two Articles, written by Thomas Cranmer.

THROWN TO THE LIONS During the first several centuries after Christ, Christians were persecuted by the Roman government. Sometimes they were thrown to hungry lions in the Colosseum as a type of public sport. The Romans did not invent this savagery, however, as we see in the story of Daniel in the lions' den. ➘ By extension, anyone who feels defenseless against a fierce opponent might say, "I am being thrown to the lions."

TORQUEMADA, TOMÁS DE (1420–98) A Spanish Dominican who was appointed by King Ferdinand and Queen Isabella as inquisitor general (see *Spanish Inquisition*). Under his ruthless direction, 2,000 heretics were burned, and more than 200,000 Jews were expelled from Spain.

TOURS, BATTLE OF By 732, Muslim armies had conquered North Africa, had marched across Spain, and had crossed the Pyrenees Mountains into southern France. They were turned back by Charles Martel (Charlemagne's grandfather) at the Battle of Tours. This was an important turning point in the expansion of Islam, as it allowed Europe to maintain its status as a Christian continent.

TRAPPISTS Members of a religious order of monks. Trappist monks have traditionally been known for taking vows of silence, under which they were rarely allowed to speak to one another.

TRENT, COUNCIL OF (1545–63) A church council in Trent (northern Italy) called by the pope in response to the growing influence of the Protestant Reformation. The actions of this council substantially defined the Roman Catholic Church in the post-Reformation era. Among other subjects, the council decreed that Scripture and church tradition are equal sources of truth, and that the interpretation of Scripture comes solely through the church.

William Tyndale

TYNDALE, WILLIAM (c. 1494–1536) A contemporary of Martin Luther and, like Luther, a great Bible translator. Tyndale's English translation of the New Testament was not the first such translation (he followed John Wycliffe by 150 years), but his was the first English translation to be printed (1526) and widely distributed. Tyndale said he wanted to translate the Scriptures so every plowboy could read them in his own language. He lived and worked in exile in Europe because his translation work was not acceptable to King Henry VIII and the religious establishment in the days before Henry broke with Rome. Tyndale was tried as a heretic and burned at the stake because of his translation. His work was completed by Miles Coverdale, whose complete Bible was printed in 1535 and later widely distributed with King Henry's blessing! Tyndale House Publishers, which was founded by Kenneth Taylor (who paraphrased *The Living Bible*), is named after William Tyndale.

UNITED METHODIST CHURCH The second-largest Protestant denomination in the USA, after the Southern Baptist Convention. The United Methodist Church is a mainline denomination whose leadership is relatively liberal theologically and culturally. It was among the first denominations to allow the ordination of women, and social concerns play a large role in its agenda. The present denomination is the result of various splits and mergers over the years, but its history dates back to the work of John Wesley and George Whitefield. See also *Methodism, Methodist*.

VATICAN The administrative center of the Roman Catholic Church. The Vatican (or Vatican City) is the world's smallest independent state; it is located inside the city of Rome. The pope is both head of the Roman Catholic Church and head of the government of the Vatican.

The Vatican

The Vatican covers substantially less than one square mile in area, and it is dominated by Saint Peter's Basilica. It is home to many art treasures, including the Sistine Chapel and Michelangelo's *Pietà*. The term *Vatican* is often used to refer to the pope and the administration of the Roman Catholic Church, just as Washington and Moscow are used to refer to the governments of the USA and Russia.

VATICAN II (SECOND VATICAN COUNCIL) A council of the Roman Catholic Church, convened by Pope John XXIII in 1962. Its expressed purpose was to update the church, and it did indeed bring significant changes into the life of the church. There were gestures of reconciliation between the Roman Catholic Church and the Eastern Orthodox Church and also with Protestant churches. Personal Bible reading by regular church members was encouraged, and the Mass was now to be said in vernacular (common) languages (such as English) rather than in Latin.

WESLEY, CHARLES (1707–88) Brother of John Wesley and, with John, one of the founders of Methodism. Charles was a musician and wrote more than 5,000 hymns, including "Christ the Lord Is Risen Today," "Hark! The Herald Angels Sing," "Soldiers of Christ, Arise," and "Jesus, Lover of My Soul."

John Wesley

WESLEY, JOHN (1703–91) One of the founders of Methodism, and a great evangelist. He was one of the great preachers of the eighteenth century. John Wesley was ordained in the Anglican Church, but he had a significant conversion experience at the age of thirty-five while attending a meeting where Martin Luther's Commentary on Romans was being read. Wesley wrote later, "I felt my heart strangely warmed. I felt I did trust in Christ, Christ alone for salvation." John's brother Charles Wesley worked side by side with him.

WESTMINSTER SHORTER CATECHISM A series of questions and answers whose purpose is to provide instruction to children in the essentials of the Christian faith. The first question is, "What is the chief end of man?"

WHAT IS THE CHIEF END OF MAN? The first question in the Westminster Shorter Catechism. The answer is: "The chief end of man is to glorify God and enjoy him forever."

WHITEFIELD, GEORGE (1714–70) A popular preacher who was influential both in England and in the American colonies. With the Wesley brothers, he worked for revival in the church, but he parted with the Wesleys because of his Calvinist theology. His preaching tours in America helped kindle the Great Awakening.

WILBERFORCE, WILLIAM (1759–1833) A brilliant member of Britain's Parliament and an evangelical who championed social reform. He was influential in the establishment of numerous Christian works, including the British and Foreign Bible Society. Perhaps his greatest contribution was his campaign to end slavery in England and throughout the British Empire. Wilberforce died four days after Parliament passed the Emancipation Act in 1833, which freed more than 800,000 slaves.

William Wilberforce

WILLIAMS, ROGER (c. 1603–83) A Puritan leader who was expelled from Massachusetts because his separatist views were seen as disruptive. He founded Rhode Island and established it as a colony that guaranteed democracy, freedom of religion, and separation of church and state.

WORLD COUNCIL OF CHURCHES An international, ecumenical association of Protestant and Orthodox churches seeking to advance Christian unity. Its involvement in and support of liberal causes has tended to overshadow its theological and social contributions. An evangelical counterpart is the World Evangelical Fellowship. See also *National Council of the Churches of Christ in the USA*.

WYCLIFFE, JOHN (c. 1330–84) An early English Reformer who, like Luther 150 years later, rejected some aspects of doctrine in the Western church. His teachings influenced Jan Hus and laid the foundations for the Protestant Reformation in Europe. His name is associated with a translation of the New Testament from Latin into English. He started the translation, which was finished after his death by his followers. In 1415, the Council of Constance (the same church council that ended the Papal Schism and found Jan Hus guilty of heresy) ordered that Wycliffe's body be exhumed and burned. Wycliffe Bible Translators, an organization dedicated to the translation of the Bible into all the languages of the world, was named for John Wycliffe.

YOUNG, BRIGHAM (1801–77) After Joseph Smith's death, the Mormons split into several factions. Brigham Young led his group to Utah, where they founded Salt Lake City in 1847. This group is now known as the Church of Jesus Christ of Latter-day Saints. Brigham Young University, in Salt Lake City, is named after him.

ZWINGLI, ULRICH (1484–1531) An early leader of the Reformation in Switzerland. He was a dynamic Bible expositor and was pastor of the largest church in Zurich. He was a contemporary of Martin Luther, but differences in their views of the Eucharist (Holy Communion) kept them from joining forces. John Calvin, in Geneva, represented the next generation of Reformation leadership in Switzerland.

Ulrich Zwingli

Saints and Sinners, Past and Present

A Quiz on Church History

Select one answer for each question. Answers appear immediately after the quiz.

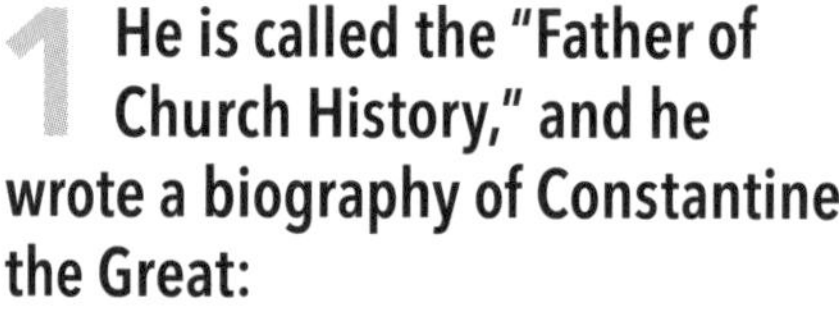

1 He is called the "Father of Church History," and he wrote a biography of Constantine the Great:

a. William Tyndale

b. Augustine of Hippo

c. Jerome

d. Eusebius of Caesarea

2 What was the purpose of the Edict of Milan, which was issued by Roman emperor Constantine the Great in 313?

a. To move the capital from Rome to Byzantium and rename it Constantinople

b. To establish the New Testament canon

c. To legalize Christianity in the Roman Empire

d. To mandate that all Roman citizens had to become Christians

3 His autobiography, *Confessions*, is a classic account of a conversion from paganism to Christianity:

a. Augustine of Hippo

b. Thomas Aquinas

c. Billy Graham

d. C. S. Lewis

4 Who created the Latin translation of the Bible that is called the Vulgate?

a. Eusebius of Caesarea

b. Jerome

c. Martin Luther

d. Erasmus

5 The result of the Great Schism of 1054 was:

a. The establishment of Protestantism

b. The separation of the Roman Catholic Church and the Eastern Orthodox Church

c. That two competing popes excommunicated each other

d. The separation of the Church of England from the Roman Catholic Church

6 What was the purpose of the Crusades?

a. To consolidate the power of the Holy Roman Empire

b. To allow Germany to adopt Protestantism

c. To gain control of the Holy Land by removing it from the Muslims

d. To stop the Muslims from advancing into Europe

7 This archbishop of Canterbury was murdered in the cathedral in 1170 because he resisted King Henry II's attempts to limit the authority of the church:

a. Augustine of Canterbury

b. Thomas Becket

c. Thomas More

d. Girolamo Savonarola

8 This Czech reformer attacked abuses in the church a century before the start of the Protestant Reformation:

a. John Wycliffe

b. John Wesley

c. Ulrich Zwingli

d. Jan Hus

9 This Reformer announced his disagreements with the Roman Catholic Church by posting his Ninety-Five Theses on the door of the Castle Church in Wittenberg, Germany:

a. William Tyndale

b. John Calvin

c. Martin Luther

d. Ulrich Zwingli

10 Which British monarch established the Church of England?

a. King Henry II

b. King Henry VIII

c. Queen Elizabeth I

d. King James I

11 Which of the following was not a martyr?

a. William Tyndale

b. Thomas More

c. Girolamo Savonarola

d. Martin Luther

12 He was a leader of the Reformation in Switzerland and the author of *Institutes of the Christian Religion*:

a. John Calvin

b. Martin Luther

c. John Knox

d. Jan Hus

13 Who was one of the founders of Methodism?

a. John Knox

b. John Wesley

c. John Calvin

d. Thomas Cranmer

14 This sixteenth-century movement denounced infant baptism and accepted only the baptism of those old enough to understand the meaning of faith:

a. Methodism

b. Anabaptist movement

c. Great Awakening

d. Southern Baptist Convention

15 Which pioneer missionary founded the China Inland Mission in 1866?

a. David Livingstone

b. William Carey

c. J. Hudson Taylor

d. Mother Teresa

16 Dietrich Bonhoeffer is best known for:

a. His role in the development of neoorthodoxy

b. Helping Martin Luther establish the Lutheran Church

c. Speaking out against Hitler and the Nazis during World War II

d. His role in the ecumenical movement

17 **A conservative theological movement that arose early in the twentieth century; among other essentials, it stressed the inerrancy of Scripture:**

a. Great Awakening

b. Neoorthodoxy

c. Methodism

d. Fundamentalism

18 **The twentieth-century movement that emphasized baptism in the Holy Spirit as an individual experience:**

a. Pentecostalism

b. Lutheranism

c. Arminianism

d. Anabaptist movement

19 **A twentieth-century evangelist who preached to millions of people:**

a. George Whitefield

b. Billy Graham

c. Martin Luther

d. Karl Barth

20 **Who was elected pope in 1978?**

a. Pius XII

b. John XXIII

c. Paul VI

d. John Paul II

Answers

1. d	5. b	9. c	13. b	17. d
2. c	6. c	10. b	14. b	18. a
3. a	7. b	11. d	15. c	19. b
4. b	8. d	12. a	16. c	20. d

Church Life and Theology

This chapter is about everyday church life—terms that relate to the church year, to liturgy, to sacraments and ordinances, and to offices in the church. Also included are significant "religious" quotations that are not directly from the Bible but are used in everyday life. Quotations taken from the Bible are found in the next chapter, "Famous Sayings from the Bible."

Theology is the study of God and his relationship to the world. Many people feel that theology is only for ministers and theologians, but theology touches people in everyday life. For those who believe in God—particularly those who believe in a personal relationship with God—theology helps them define what they believe. The Apostles' Creed, which is recited by millions of Christians every week, is a statement of theology. In fact, it contains many theological terms that are directly or indirectly included in this chapter.

In addition, this chapter contains many familiar terms that are used in everyday conversation. It also contains technical terms that are not necessarily used frequently, but they describe important aspects of the Christian faith. This chapter also includes terms that relate to the book of Revelation.

666 In the book of Revelation, the mark of the beast is the number 666. Each person living at that time will have to receive the mark on his or her forehead or right hand in order to buy or sell anything (Revelation 13:16–17). See also *mark of the beast.*

ADVENT The period beginning on the fourth Sunday before Christmas and ending on Christmas Eve. Advent means "coming," and it is a time of preparation for Christmas—the celebration of Christ's first coming. Advent also looks ahead to the Second Coming. Many Christians commemorate Advent with special devotional readings each day. Many also use an Advent wreath, which contains five candles. One candle is lit on the first Sunday of Advent and each day that week. The next week a second candle is lit, until all four candles are lit during the week before Christmas. Then on Christmas Day the fifth candle, the Christ Candle, is lit. The first Sunday of Advent is the beginning of the liturgical church year.

AGAPE There are several different Greek words that are translated "love" in English. One of these words, *agape* (pronounced *ah-GAH-pay*), refers to a willful, other-centered love. God's love is agape love, and the Bible teaches Christians to love God and one another with this type of love (Matthew 22:37–40). *Agape* is translated "charity" in some passages in the King James Version.

AGNOSTIC A person who doesn't know if there is a God, and may believe it is impossible ever to know. In contrast to an agnostic, a

Advent wreath

theist believes there is a God, and an atheist believes there is no God.

ALL SAINTS' DAY This holy day is celebrated on November 1 by Christians in liturgical churches. It honors all the saints, especially those who are not otherwise honored in the church year. 📌 Halloween, the night before All Saints' Day, was originally called All Hallows' Eve ("the eve of all holy ones' day").

AMEN An expression of affirmation often spoken at the end of a prayer. It comes from a Hebrew word that means "it is true."

ANOINTING OF THE SICK See *last rites*.

ANTICHRIST Anyone who is against Christ is an antichrist, but many Christians believe the book of Revelation teaches that a final Antichrist will appear in the end times. He will be a magnetic but totally evil person who carries out Satan's plans in the world. He will unite the world under his leadership (Revelation 13, where he is called the beast). Finally, he will gather all his armies for a battle against Christ, but he will be defeated at the Battle of Armageddon (Revelation 16, 19) and will be thrown into the lake of fire (see *hell*). 📌 Christians have identified various evil rulers through the centuries as the Antichrist, but none of them has fulfilled the role described for the Antichrist in Revelation.

APOLOGETICS, APOLOGIST Apologetics is the logical defense and proof of Christianity. An apologist is a Christian intellectual who specializes in presenting the Christian faith in a way that is understandable to his or her contemporary culture.

APOSTASY The deliberate denial and abandonment of the faith; a turning away from the faith. A heretic rejects some aspect of orthodoxy but retains the name Christian. An apostate turns away entirely and rejects identification with the faith.

APOSTLES' CREED A statement of faith used in both Roman Catholic and Protestant churches, dating from about 150. Although it is an accurate statement of the beliefs of the apostles, it is highly unlikely that any of Jesus's disciples were involved in composing it.

THE APOSTLES' CREED

I believe in God the Father almighty,
Maker of heaven and earth,
And in Jesus Christ, his only Son, our Lord,
Who was conceived by the Holy Spirit,
Born of the Virgin Mary,
Suffered under Pontius Pilate,
Was crucified, dead, and buried;
He descended into hell.
The third day he rose again from the dead.
He ascended into heaven
And is seated at the right hand of God the Father almighty.
From there he shall come to judge the living and the dead.
I believe in the Holy Spirit,
The holy catholic [universal] church,
The communion of saints,
The forgiveness of sins,
The resurrection of the body,
And the life everlasting.

ARCHBISHOP A high-ranking bishop, and the highest-ranking clergyman in an archdiocese (see the next entry). An archbishop has limited authority over the work of the other bishops in his province.

ARCHDIOCESE The territorial jurisdiction of an archbishop. Most archdioceses are major metropolitan areas. See also *diocese.*

ARMAGEDDON According to Revelation 16:16, a great battle between good and evil will be fought at "the place that in Hebrew is called Armageddon" (NIV). If this will be a literal battle, the location is uncertain, but it may mean the plains of Megiddo, an area in northern Israel. In the battle, God triumphs over the forces of evil that are backed by Satan. 📌 Figuratively, "Armageddon" is any great battle or war, but particularly a battle or any other event that is anticipated to have dire or final consequences.

ASH WEDNESDAY The first day of Lent. Christians who observe Ash Wednesday participate in special services, which includes putting ashes on one's forehead as a sign of repentance for sin. See also *Mardi Gras*.

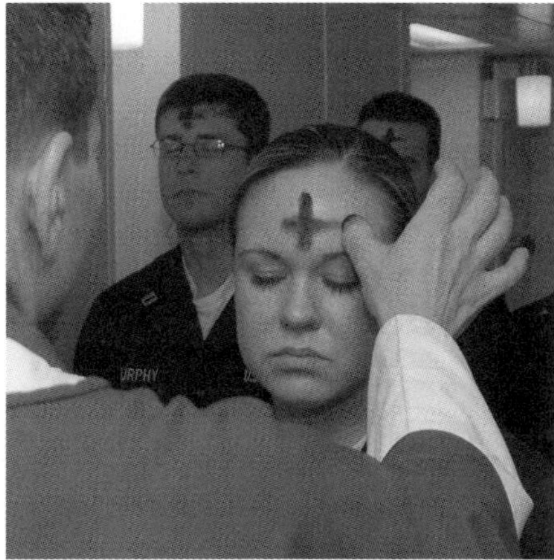

ASHES TO ASHES In the burial service presented in the Book of Common Prayer, the minister says as the earth is put on the casket, "Earth to earth, ashes to ashes, dust to dust." It is a reminder to all present that all of us are mortal. As God said to Adam, "Dust you are, and to dust you shall return" (Genesis 3:19).

ATHEIST A person who believes there is no God. This is in contrast to a theist, who believes there is a God, and an agnostic, who does not know if there is a God or believes it is impossible ever to know. 📌 Madalyn Murray O'Hair was a prominent American atheist of the late twentieth century who worked to ban religious practices in schools and other public arenas.

ATONEMENT One of the central teachings of Christianity, referring to the reconciliation between God and sinners. This reconciliation is brought about through the death of Christ as a substitute for sinful mankind. Romans 6:23 says that "the wages of sin is death." But God has provided a way for people to be reconciled to him without having to pay the prescribed penalty of eternal death (eternal separation from God). Christ satisfied divine justice by his suffering and death in the place of sinners (see also *forgiveness*). Under the old covenant of the Mosaic law, the Israelites offered animal sacrifices to atone for their sin. The New Testament points out, however, that "it is not possible that the blood of bulls and goats could take away sins" (Hebrews 10:4). God applied the benefits and efficacy of the work of Christ to the people in the Old Testament who by faith offered sacrifices that foreshadowed the final sacrifice of Christ.

AVE MARIA A prayer to the Virgin Mary that has been repeated by Roman Catholics for centuries. Ave Maria is Latin for "Hail Mary," the greeting given to Mary by the angel Gabriel, who told her she would be the mother of Jesus, the Messiah (see *Annunciation* in the chapter "People, Places, and Events in the New Testament"). The Ave Maria has been set to music in numerous variations. For the English text, see *Hail Mary*.

BAPTISM, BAPTIZE The sacrament or ordinance that shows publicly that the individual is a member of the "body of Christ," the church. As a rite of initiation into the Christian church, baptism binds the candidate to be a responsible follower of Christ. There are two modes of baptism—infant baptism and adult (or believer's) baptism. When an infant is baptized, his parents and/or godparents pledge to see that the child "is brought up in the Christian faith and life" (the Book of Common Prayer). Normally the baptism is then confirmed when the child is old enough to make his or her own affirmation of faith (see *confirmation*). When older children or adults are baptized, they make their own profession of faith. *Infant baptism* emphasizes God's electing grace (see *election*) and is understood to be the sign of the new covenant (replacing circumcision, the sign of the old covenant); *believer's baptism* emphasizes the human response to God. Baptism is performed by sprinkling or pouring water on the head or, as done in Baptist churches, immersing the candidate completely in water. In most instances the minister or priest says, "I baptize you in the name of the Father, and of the Son, and of the Holy Spirit."

BAPTISM IN THE HOLY SPIRIT After the Resurrection, Jesus told his disciples, "Wait for the gift my Father promised, which you have heard me speak about. For John baptized with water, but in a few days you will be baptized with the Holy Spirit" (Acts 1:4–5 NIV). The Holy Spirit did indeed come upon and dwell in the disciples—on the day of Pentecost. With the coming of the Spirit, a new era in the relationship between God and mankind was initiated. The church—the mystical "body of Christ"—was established, and God's Spirit came to live in the minds and hearts of his people (1 Corinthians 3:16). The "fruit of the Spirit" is evidence of the Spirit that dwells within the believer. Christians in the Pentecostal tradition see the baptism in the Holy Spirit as a second blessing that can occur to individuals after conversion. They tend also to expect the miraculous gifts of the Holy Spirit (particularly speaking in tongues) as a manifestation of the baptism in the Holy Spirit.

BELIEVER A Christian; a person who believes in and professes Jesus as the Son of God who died to forgive his or her sins, bringing peace with God and the promise of eternal life.

BENEDICTION A blessing, usually pronounced by the minister at the end of a church service.

BISHOP The highest-ranking clergyman in a diocese or other unit of church government. A bishop oversees the work of other clergy within the diocese. See also *archbishop*.

BLASPHEMY Insulting or mocking God, or detracting from him in any way. It can include using God's name in vain, which is prohibited in the Ten Commandments. Blasphemy was punishable by death in the Old Testament. See also *unpardonable sin*.

BLOOD OF CHRIST Under the Mosaic law, a system of animal sacrifices was established that foreshadowed the sacrifice of Christ. The blood showed that the animal had died as a provisional atonement for the sins of the person making the sacrifice. Under the new covenant, Jesus was the perfect sacrifice that, once for all, secured atonement for sins. As with the Old Testament sacrifices, the blood of Christ represented his sacrificial death. In the Eucharist (Holy Communion), the wine (the cup) signifies the blood of Christ. See also *body of Christ*.

BODY OF CHRIST In the Eucharist, the bread (the host)

signifies the body of Christ. At the Last Supper, Jesus took bread, gave thanks and broke it, and gave it to his disciples. He said, "This is my body given for you; do this in remembrance of me" (Luke 22:19 NIV) (see also *blood of Christ*; *transubstantiation*; *consubstantiation*). In another sense, the church is called the body of Christ (Colossians 1:18). In 1 Corinthians 12, Paul describes the church as a single body made up of many individual parts, each of which plays an important but different role. The city name "Corpus Christi" (in Texas) comes from the Latin *corpus Christi*, "body of Christ."

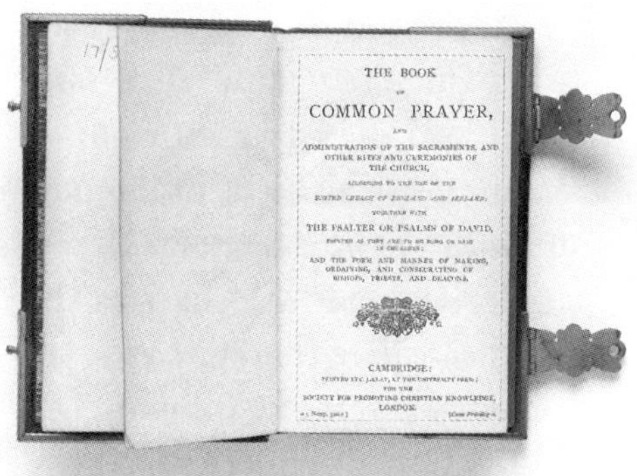

BOOK OF COMMON PRAYER, THE The official book containing the liturgy of the Anglican churches. It contains the order of worship, including prayers for special occasions, wedding ceremonies, and funeral services. A revised edition was adopted by the Episcopal Church in the USA in 1979. See also *Cranmer, Thomas* in the chapter "Church History."

BOOK OF LIFE A record kept in heaven listing the names of all who have eternal life. In a description of the Judgment Day, Revelation 20:15 says, "Anyone whose name was not found written in the book of life was thrown into the lake of fire" (NIV).

BORN AGAIN This term comes from Jesus's conversation with Nicodemus. Jesus told him, "Unless you are born again, you cannot see the Kingdom of God" (John 3:3 NLT). Nicodemus thought Jesus meant a second physical birth, but Jesus meant a spiritual rebirth. Jesus went on to say, "For God so loved the world that he gave his one and only Son, that whoever believes in him shall not perish but have eternal life" (John 3:16 NIV). Thus, the term means the act in which the Holy Spirit gives eternal life to a person dead in sin. Through the centuries, most Christians have identified rebirth or regeneration with baptism. All Christians, by definition, are born again. Many Christians are uncomfortable with the term, however, since it has a connotation of theological conservatism. The media often use the term *born-again Christian* to call attention to a person's own identification as being born again. The term gained prominence during the US presidency of Jimmy Carter, who identified himself as a born-again Christian.

BRIDE OF CHRIST The church is sometimes referred to as the bride of Christ. While that specific term is not used in the New Testament, Ephesians 5:21–33 suggests that Christ is the husband and the church is his bride. Husbands are to love their wives just as Christ loves the church.

CANON LAW The body of laws governing a church—particularly the Roman Catholic Church.

CANONIZATION, CANONIZE The process by which a person is officially recognized as a saint by the Roman Catholic Church. To become a saint, a person must have lived an exemplary life, and four miracles must be associated with him or her. Saints are revered by the Roman Catholic Church around the world. In the Catholic tradition, saints go directly to heaven when they die rather than going first to purgatory. Saints are then able to intercede in heaven on behalf of the faithful. The term also refers to the process in which the church fathers recognized the New Testament writings as being the inspired Word of God (see *New Testament canon established* in the chapter "Church History").

Cardinals at the Vatican

CARDINAL A high-ranking bishop in the Roman Catholic Church. As of 2024 there are 236 cardinals worldwide, and collectively they comprise the Sacred College of Cardinals. Cardinals assist the pope and rank just below him within the church. Cardinals are appointed by the pope, and the College of Cardinals selects the new pope when a pope dies. Most cardinals serve as heads of archdioceses. Others have administrative positions in the Vatican. There are presently fifteen cardinals in the USA and Canada. Two well-known cardinals of the 1990s were John Cardinal O'Connor of New York and Cardinal Joseph Bernardin of Chicago.

CATECHISM A formal series of questions and answers designed to teach children and other Christians the basic beliefs of the Christian faith. In many churches, a child must go to catechism classes before being confirmed (see *confirmation*). See also *Westminster Shorter Catechism* in the chapter "Church History."

CHARITY The Greek word *agape* (pronounced *ah-GAH-pay*) is sometimes translated "charity" in the King James Version. In that sense it means self-giving, other-centered love. The thirteenth chapter of 1 Corinthians contains a beautiful description of this type of love. It ends with the statement, "And now abideth faith, hope, charity, these three; but the greatest of these is charity." Today the more common meaning of *charity* is simply giving money to those who are less fortunate.

CHRISTENING The process of naming an infant at the time of its baptism. The minister or priest asks what the child's name is, and the parents or godparents respond with the child's Christian (given) name. The minister then baptizes the child, saying, "(Name), I baptize you in the name of the Father, and of the Son, and of the Holy Spirit." By extension, ships are "christened" when first launched.

CHRISTIAN One who believes in and professes Jesus as the Son of God who died to forgive his or her sins, bringing peace with God and the promise of eternal life. One who is identified with Christ and his church, usually through baptism. As an adjective, *Christian* is used broadly to designate the influence of Christianity in the world (the Christian West, Christian civilization, Christian culture). More narrowly, it is used by evangelicals to describe their cultural initiatives (Christian music, Christian books, Christian colleges). In contemporary usage, *Christian* is sometimes used simply to describe any Western person who is not an adherent of another religion.

CHRISTIANITY The religion of all those who profess Jesus Christ as the Son of God and the Savior of mankind. It is one of the great faiths in the world today. There are three major branches of Christianity: (1) the Roman Catholic Church, (2) the Eastern Orthodox Church, and (3) all Protestant churches. The Christian church in its entirety is sometimes called Christendom, or simply the church.

CHRISTMAS December 25, the celebration of the birth of Jesus. Christians around the world celebrate Christmas by attending special church services and giving gifts to one another. See also *Advent*. The secular celebration of Christmas makes little reference to the birth of Jesus, focusing instead on Santa Claus (see *Nicholas, Saint* in the chapter "Church History"), reindeer, snowmen, and gift giving.

CHURCH The word *church* has several related meanings: (1) The body of all Christians, living and dead. Those who are alive are sometimes called the church militant—fighting against sin and for righteousness. Those who are dead and in the presence of God are called the church triumphant. (2) The worldwide body of Christians—all persons in every nation who profess faith in Christ as the Son of God and Savior (see *body of Christ*). (3) A denomination or major division of the universal church (such as the Church of England, the United Methodist Church, the Roman Catholic Church, or the Eastern Orthodox Church). (4) A local congregation of Christians that gathers for service and worship of God. (5) A building in which a congregation meets for worship.

CHURCH YEAR The church year, also called the liturgical year or the Christian year, begins in late November or early December, on the first Sunday of Advent. The church year provides a systematic way of celebrating important events in Christian history. Highlights of the church year are Christmas, Epiphany, the Sundays of Lent, Easter, Ascension Day, Pentecost

(Whitsunday), and Trinity Sunday. Many days of the year are named in honor of one or more of the saints (see *All Saints' Day*). Many churches that are less liturgical observe only major holidays.

CIRCUMCISION, CIRCUMCISE Cutting the foreskin from the penis of a man or, more typically, an infant boy. When the Lord made a covenant with Abraham, promising that Abraham would be the father of many nations, he also instituted the ceremony of circumcision (Genesis 17). All the males in Abraham's family and among his descendants were to be circumcised as a sign of the covenant. Boys were to be circumcised when they were eight days old. Ever since, Jewish males have been circumcised. In the New Testament, Paul uses the ceremony of circumcision as a paradigm for the whole system of the Law. He argues that Christians are no longer bound to the Mosaic law because of the redemption freely offered through Christ's death. Although circumcision may not have religious significance for Christians, many Christian parents still choose to have their sons circumcised. Baptism is often seen as the sign of the new covenant with Christ, replacing circumcision, the sign of the old covenant (Colossians 2:11–12).

CLERGY Persons who have been ordained for Christian ministry. Clergymen have often been called "men of the cloth" because of their traditionally distinctive dress.

COLLECT (pronounced *KAH-lekt*) A short prayer used in the liturgy of many churches.

COMMUNION A sacrament or ordinance in which believers eat bread (the host) and drink wine or grape juice (the cup), according to Jesus's command at the Last Supper (see *Do this in remembrance of me* in the chapter "Famous Sayings from the Bible"). There are various beliefs regarding the meaning of Communion. Roman Catholics believe that when the priest blesses the bread and wine (called the "elements"), they change substance and become the actual body and blood of Christ. This is called transubstantiation. Lutherans traditionally affirm consubstantiation, believing that the body and blood of Christ are present with the bread and wine. Reformed churches affirm that Christ is spiritually present with the elements. In the Free church tradition, the bread and wine are seen as symbolic of the body and blood of Christ. This is called the memorialist view. Nearly all Christians take Communion occasionally, and in many denominations it is a weekly observance. In the Roman Catholic Mass, the laypeople (see *layman, laywoman, layperson*) usually receive the host but not the cup. Protestant laypeople receive both the host and the cup. Communion is also called Holy Communion, the Eucharist, the Lord's Supper, or the Lord's Table. See also *First Communion.*

CONFESSION In general, the act of stating that one has sinned and is remorseful. The Bible says, "If we confess our sins, he [God] is faithful and just and will forgive us our sins and purify us from all unrighteousness" (1 John 1:9 NIV). In the Roman Catholic Church, as part of the sacrament of penance, individuals confess their sins to a priest, expressing sorrow for having sinned. The priest may assign an act of penance or restitution; then, as God's representative, the priest extends absolution (forgiveness). Since the Vatican II Council, confession to a priest has become a less prominent part of everyday life for most Roman Catholics.

CONFIRMATION The ceremony in which a child who has been baptized and has reached a certain age confirms publicly that he or she is a believer and promises by the grace of God to live as a Christian. In many churches a child must go to a confirmation, communicant's, or catechism class prior to confirmation. Confirmation is one of the seven sacraments in the Roman Catholic Church.

Elements of Communion

CONGREGATION A body of people assembled for public worship.

CONSCIENTIOUS OBJECTOR A person who refuses to serve in the military because of a moral objection to the military and to warfare. Most conscientious objectors claim religious grounds for taking such a stand. The United States recognizes the conscientious objector as having a valid position, though it is difficult to prove conscientious objection if the individual does not belong to a church that is registered as objecting to military service. Many nations with mandatory military service allow conscientious objectors to perform alternate community service.

CONSUBSTANTIATION In Lutheran doctrine, there is a real presence of the body and blood of Christ with the bread and wine in the Eucharist. This is in contrast to the Roman Catholic dogma of transubstantiation, which asserts that the bread and wine become the actual body and blood of Christ. A third view, which John Calvin taught, is that the bread and wine remain actual bread and wine, but those taking Communion receive the body and blood of Christ in a spiritual manner.

CONVENT A residence for nuns. The popular image of a convent is of an isolated and secluded community, but today many convents are modern dwellings in cities.

Gorny Convent—Jerusalem

CONVERSION The act or process of adopting a religion. Conversion sometimes entails switching from one religion to another, as when a Muslim becomes a Christian. The term is also used when a person turns from nonbelief or nominal belief to an active faith. Two famous conversions are those of Saul of Tarsus (see *Damascus Road* in the chapter "People, Places, and Events in the New Testament") and Augustine of Hippo.

COVENANT A solemn agreement between two parties, in which one or both promise to perform certain actions. In the Old Testament, God entered into covenants with Noah, Abraham, Moses and the people of Israel, and David. God promised to give Abraham descendants as numerous as the stars in the heavens, and he promised to give them the land of Canaan, from the Nile River to the Euphrates River. Circumcision was instituted as the sign of the covenant. At Mount Sinai, the Lord said to Moses and Israel, "If you will obey me and keep my covenant, you will be my own special treasure from among all the peoples on earth" (Exodus 19:5 NLT). The Lord then gave Moses the Ten Commandments as the moral standard for the people. When Christ came, he established the new covenant, as promised in Jeremiah 31:31. This "new covenant" is new in the sense that it is the final and complete revelation of God's covenant with mankind. At the Last Supper, Jesus took the cup of wine and said, "This is my blood, which confirms the covenant between God and his people. It is poured out as a sacrifice to forgive the sins of many" (Matthew 26:28 NLT). He meant that his death on the cross would make atonement for people's sins. Under the new covenant, a person's responsibility is to have faith that the finished work of Christ provides for his or her salvation. The Greek word translated "testament," as used in *Old Testament* and *New Testament*, is also commonly translated "covenant." So the Old Testament is the "old covenant" and the New Testament is the "new covenant."

CREATION SCIENCE A modern attempt to merge a literal, biblical understanding of the creation with modern science (see *evolution*). Adherents of creation science attempt to show scientific proof for the creation as it is described in the book of Genesis.

CREATIONISM The belief that the creation took place literally as it is described in the book of Genesis. This includes the creation of the world and all animals and mankind as the willful and deliberate act of God. Creationists do not accept the theory of evolution as a valid explanation for the development of life and the diversity of species. Many creationists believe the creation took place in six literal, twenty-four-hour days, and that the earth is relatively young. Many Christians, however, hold to a doctrine of creation without accepting all aspects of creationism.

CREED A formal statement of belief (the word comes from the Latin *credo*, which means "I believe"). The best-known Christian creeds are the Apostles' Creed and the Nicene Creed.

CROSS, SIGN OF THE Making the sign of the cross (also called crossing oneself) is an act of piety. Many Christians cross themselves when they pray. In the Western tradition, the sign of the cross is made by touching the fingers of the right hand to the forehead, then below the chest, then the left shoulder and right shoulder.

CRUCIFIX An emblem that shows the body of Jesus hanging on a cross. Crucifixes can be large or small. They are often worn on chains as necklaces, and Roman Catholic churches often display large crucifixes.

CUP In the Eucharist (Holy Communion), the wine or juice is called the cup. See also *host*.

DAMNATION When a person is convicted of an offense, he or she is punished. The punishment for sin is sometimes referred to as damnation—spiritual death, or spiritual separation from God. Christians have traditionally believed that anyone who is not saved by God's grace, through faith in Christ's atonement on his or her behalf, is condemned to eternal damnation in hell.

DEACON In the early church, deacons were selected by the apostles to care for the widows and administer the daily distribution of food (Acts 6). The requirement was that they be wise, full of the Holy Spirit, and well thought of by the rest of the church. Two of the first deacons were Stephen and Philip (the evangelist). Many churches have deacons today. In Roman Catholic and Anglican churches, a deacon has taken holy orders (see *holy orders*) and may progress to the priesthood. Deacons in some

Protestant churches have spiritual responsibility under the leadership of the pastor. In other churches, the deacons have responsibility primarily for the physical assets of the church, such as the church building, the parsonage (the pastor's home, provided by the church), and the money. See also *elder*; *trustee*.

DEARLY BELOVED, WE ARE GATHERED TOGETHER The opening words of the traditional wedding service, as found in older editions of the Book of Common Prayer.

DEISM A rationalistic philosophy that includes belief in God as a Supreme Being, but he is like a master clockmaker who created the universe but then left it to run by itself. He does not intervene in human affairs. Deism (the term comes from the Latin *deus*, "god") excludes belief in the Trinity, the Incarnation, the Atonement, and miracles. Deism was a prominent religious philosophy among the elite leaders of the eighteenth century. Benjamin Franklin and Thomas Jefferson considered themselves deists.

DEPRAVITY, TOTAL A doctrine that describes the extent to which human nature is corrupted as a result of Adam and Eve's sin (see *fall of man* in the chapter "People, Places, and Events in the Old Testament"). Total depravity does not mean that there is no goodness in a person or in mankind generally, nor does it mean that nonbelievers cannot do good. It does mean, however, that every aspect of human nature has been affected by sin. No one can do anything acceptable to God or claim a right standing with God on his or her own merits. It is only by God's grace that people can achieve reconciliation with him, through faith in Christ's atonement.

DEVIL Satan, the angelic being who was the first to rebel against God. He became the chief antagonist of God and God's people. The caricature of the devil as a red-suited person with horns, a pointed tail, and a pitchfork is unfortunate, since it trivializes the existence and superhuman power of the devil. See also *demons* in the chapter "People, Places, and Events in the New Testament."

DIOCESE The territory in which a bishop has governmental authority. See also *archdiocese*.

DISCIPLE, DISCIPLESHIP Any follower of Jesus Christ can be called a disciple. The process of mentoring another person to be a disciple of Jesus is often called discipleship.

DOCTRINE Teachings of Scripture; teachings that define and explain various aspects of Scripture, theology, and creeds of the faith. A doctrine that has become the official teaching of a church or denomination may be called dogma.

DOGMA A doctrine officially taught by a church or denomination. Some dogmas (for example, the dogma of the Trinity) are held throughout the church, while others are accepted in only part of the church. The dogma of the Immaculate Conception, for instance, is accepted only by the Roman Catholic Church. The Protestant view is that all dogma must be validated by Scripture. The Roman Catholic view is that dogma is God's objective truth defined by the church, and that the dogmas of the church are infallible.

DOXOLOGY A short hymn of praise to God. This doxology, written in the seventeenth century, is frequently sung in churches today:

Praise God, from whom
all blessings flow;
Praise him all creatures
here below;
Praise him above, ye
heavenly host;
Praise Father, Son, and
Holy Ghost.

EASTER The Sunday on which Christians celebrate the resurrection of Jesus. It is often considered the most significant event of the church year because of the apostle Paul's statement that "if Christ has not been raised, then your faith is useless and you are still guilty of your sins" (1 Corinthians 15:17 NLT). In the Western tradition, Easter is always in late March or early April—on the first Sunday after the first full moon following the spring equinox. 📌 The secular celebration of Easter makes no reference to the Resurrection, focusing instead on the Easter bunny, candy, and decorated eggs: symbols of fertility and springtime.

ECUMENICAL, ECUMENISM An ecumenical movement promotes unity among diverse Christian bodies. Ecumenical movements in recent years have attempted to unite several Protestant denominations, or to reunite the Roman

Catholic Church and the Anglican Church. The National Council of the Churches of Christ in the USA and the World Council of Churches promote ecumenism. The great church councils of the fourth and fifth centuries are called ecumenical councils because they represented all of Christendom. The Roman Catholic Church uses the term *ecumenical council* for additional councils (including the Council of Trent and Vatican II) that are not accepted by Protestants or the Eastern Orthodox Church as being ecumenical.

ELDER A position of leadership for a layperson in a church. In most churches, the elders have some spiritual responsibility for the congregation, either in their own right or under the leadership of the pastor. See also *deacon*; *trustee*.

ELECTION The doctrine that God chooses the people who will receive salvation. Those who are chosen are called the elect. Two of the great advocates of this doctrine were Augustine of Hippo and John Calvin. Calvin did not profess to know who had been chosen, but he saw certain actions as indicators that a person was among the elect—a public profession of faith, water baptism, participation in the Lord's Supper, and a moral life (see *Calvinism* in the chapter "Church History"). See also *sovereignty of God*; *predestination*.

ENCYCLICAL A letter from the pope addressed to the bishops of the Roman Catholic Church. Encyclicals set out guidelines for the application of the church's dogmas, and Catholics must accept the doctrinal teachings contained in them. Encyclicals are named or known by the opening words of the Latin text. For example, Pope Paul VI's controversial encyclical regarding birth control is known as *Humanae Vitae*.

EPIPHANY A church holiday celebrated on January 6, observed to commemorate the coming of the wise men to Jesus in Bethlehem. Epiphany also celebrates the coming of Christ for the gentiles.

ESCHATOLOGY The doctrine of the "last things." The term is often used in relation to events at the end of the world, including the Rapture, the Tribulation, Armageddon, the Second Coming, and Judgment Day. There are various and conflicting views of eschatology.

ETERNAL LIFE A phrase used in the Bible to describe the kind of life given by Jesus. The term describes more than just the duration of life; it speaks also to the quality of life that one experiences. The Bible tells us in Romans 6:23 that "the wages of sin is death, but the gift of God is eternal life in Christ Jesus our Lord." In a prayer recorded in John 17:3, Jesus said, "Now this is eternal life: that they know you, the only true God, and Jesus Christ, whom you have sent" (NIV).

ETHICAL RELATIVISM The theory in ethics that there is no fixed standard for right and wrong. Each situation can be judged on its own merits according to the views of the individual and the cultural and historical context. ➧ Joseph Fletcher's book *Situation Ethics* (1966) played a key role in establishing this view.

ETHICS The branch of philosophy that deals with the distinction in human conduct between right or wrong, good or evil. Christian doctrines provide an excellent basis for ethics, although Christians often disagree over the morality of such things as war, abortion, and divorce.

EUCHARIST Another name for Holy Communion. The literal meaning of Eucharist is thanksgiving.

EUTHANASIA The act of choosing how and when a person will die, as opposed to letting nature take its course. Assisted suicide and mercy killing are two forms of euthanasia. The issues surrounding euthanasia become increasingly complex as modern medicine is able to prolong life far beyond the point that death would naturally occur. In its most insidious form, as in the Holocaust, euthanasia becomes murder according to an arbitrary standard of who should and should not be allowed to live. The word *euthanasia* comes from Greek words meaning "good death."

EVANGELISM, EVANGELISTIC Evangelism is the act of spreading the gospel, the Good News about eternal life through Jesus Christ. The terms *evangel* (of Greek origin) and *gospel* (of Old English origin) both mean "good news." Evangelism can take place on a personal level, or in great evangelistic outreaches or crusades like those of Billy Graham, or in the form of traditional missionary work. Evangelicals, whether members of mainline or other denominations, tend to be interested in evangelism.

EVANGELIST An evangelist is a person who proclaims the gospel, the Good News about eternal life through Jesus Christ. The term is usually used in reference to someone like Billy Graham, who conducted large public meetings, or crusades. Television evangelists (often called televangelists) have come under substantial criticism in recent years because of their sometimes flamboyant lifestyles and exaggerated claims. The writers of the biblical Gospels are sometimes called the Evangelists.

EVIL Wickedness; the opposite of goodness; that which has been tainted by sin and is contrary to the nature and will of God. The Bible does not reveal the origin of evil, except to say that Satan was the first to commit it. The Bible does affirm, however, that God has it under his control.

EVOLUTION The theory that higher life forms evolved from lower forms over billions of years. According to this theory, the first living organism was only a single cell. That organism reproduced and mutated and, through a long sequence of constructive mutations and natural selection, higher life forms (including human beings) evolved. This theory was first made popular by Charles Darwin in his book *The Origin of Species* (1859). The theory of evolution is broadly accepted by scientists, and it is taught in public schools as the definitive view of the origin of life on earth. Many Christians believe that this theory contradicts the account of the creation presented in the book of Genesis. Others believe that the Bible explains *who* created life and *why* it was created, and that science explains *how* it was created.

EX CATHEDRA A Latin phrase that means literally "from the throne." When the pope speaks *ex cathedra*, he is making a pronouncement with the authority of the church. According to Roman Catholic dogma, the pope is infallible when he speaks *ex cathedra* on matters of faith or morals (see *papal infallibility*). A cathedral, the principal church within a diocese, is the church that contains the bishop's cathedra ("throne"). But many people mistakenly think that any large church with Gothic architecture is a cathedral.

EXCOMMUNICATION The most severe form of church discipline, in which a person is excluded from the communion of a church because of his or her stubborn sinfulness. In the Roman Catholic Church, a person who has been excommunicated is denied the sacraments and a Christian burial, but is not seen as being outside the grace of God. Other forms of church discipline include suspension from the sacraments without excommunication, and defrocking (removing from office) an ordained minister.

EXTREME UNCTION See *last rites.*

FAITH Confidence or active trust in something that cannot be objectively proven or disproven. In Christian theology, faith entails belief in God and in his offer of forgiveness of sin through Jesus Christ. Faith also entails quiet confidence in God as a believer prays for God's will to be done in his or her life, expecting that God will also provide for personal needs along the way. Faith manifests itself in action, as in James 2:20, which says that "faith without works is dead." The word *faith* also refers to a religion in its entirety (the Hindu faith, the Christian faith), or to a denomination or other major group within a religion. In this context, a marriage between a Roman Catholic and a Protestant might be called an interfaith marriage.

FASTING The discipline of going without food for a period of time in order to devote one's time and energy to meditation and prayer. Jesus Christ fasted in the wilderness for forty days and nights.

FATHER (GOD THE FATHER) See *God the Father.*

FIRST COMMUNION In the Roman Catholic Church a child first participates in the Eucharist at about age six. This is called the child's First Communion. Parents and friends often celebrate the event with gifts for the child.

FOR RICHER, FOR POORER An expression in the traditional wedding vows. See *to have and to hold.*

FORGIVENESS Pardon for an offense or a wrong; also called remission of sins. Because all humans are sinful (see *fall of man* in the chapter "People, Places, and Events in the Old Testament"), they are separated spiritually from God unless they receive God's forgiveness through faith in the atoning death and resurrection of Jesus Christ. God continues to forgive believers when they confess their sins (1 John 1:9). The Bible states that God forgets their sin when he forgives them, removing their offenses as far as the east is from the west (Psalm 103:12). Christians are also instructed to forgive one another: "Be kind and compassionate to one another, forgiving each other, just as in Christ God forgave you" (Ephesians 4:32 NIV).

FOUR HORSEMEN OF THE APOCALYPSE In Revelation 6, John's vision includes four horses that represent various aspects of God's future judgment upon mankind. The first horse is white. Its rider is a conqueror and seems to represent a short period of imperial rule. The second horse is red and represents warfare and bloodshed. The third horse is black and represents famine. The fourth is a pale horse and represents death and hell.

FREE WILL There are differing views among Christians as to the extent to which fallen sinners are free to respond to God's grace. The Arminian view is that humans are free and able to choose whether or not to obey God's commands and accept God's grace. The Reformed view is that humans can embrace Christ only as God works in their hearts. Whatever the extent of free will, it seems to be contradicted by the sovereignty of God. If God already planned and knows everything that will happen, how can man freely do anything, good

Four Horsemen of the Apocalypse

or bad? Are people not bound to do whatever God has foreordained, whether or not they recognize they are being guided by his invisible will? One answer is that people have free will as they see things *from their finite (limited) human perspective*. From that vantage point, they can choose whether to obey God and accept his grace. Therein lies free will.

FRUIT OF THE SPIRIT In his letter to the Galatians, the apostle Paul writes, "The fruit of the Spirit is love, joy, peace, forbearance, kindness, goodness, faithfulness, gentleness and self-control" (Galatians 5:22–23 NIV). These virtues are the result when the Holy Spirit is living in and dominating the life of a believer. The preceding verses contain a list of sinful activities that are the natural result when a person is dominated by the sinful nature (see *depravity, total*).

GIFTS OF THE HOLY SPIRIT The New Testament teaches that the Holy Spirit gives special gifts or abilities to all Christians. Different gifts are given to different individuals, but all are to be used to strengthen the "body of Christ," the church. The gifts of the Holy Spirit include faith, healing, working miracles, speaking in tongues, interpreting what has been spoken in tongues, serving, teaching, encouraging, leading, and contributing money. However, the apostle Paul makes it very clear in 1 Corinthians 13 (the love chapter) that love should be valued more than any of the spiritual gifts.

GLORIA PATRI The Latin name of an ancient Christian hymn. *Gloria patri* is Latin for "Glory be to the Father." It is usually sung in English:

> *Glory be to the Father,*
> *And to the Son,*
> *And to the Holy Ghost.*
> *As it was in the beginning,*
> *Is now, and ever shall be,*
> *World without end. Amen, amen.*

GLORIFICATION The transformation that will take place when believers enter the future kingdom of heaven. They will be given imperishable, glorious, spiritual bodies instead of their present perishable bodies (1 Corinthians 15:35–57).

GLORIFY, GLORY To glorify God is to honor him, worship him, and praise him. One aspect of God's glory is simply the revelation to mankind of his being and his nature, especially in the person and atoning work of Jesus Christ. Hebrews 1:3 says, "The Son is the radiance of God's glory and the exact representation of his being, sustaining all things by his powerful word" (NIV). Adam was created to reflect the image and glory of God, but he fell short of that destiny, which has been fulfilled in Christ. In another sense, the glory of God is reflected by the church, the "body of Christ"—even though it is very imperfect. The visible manifestation of God's invisible presence and glory is sometimes called the "Shekinah." An example is the pillar of cloud and fire that protected and led the Israelites in the wilderness (Exodus 13:21).

GOD The name most frequently used for the eternal, holy, all-powerful, all-knowing, ever-present personal spirit who created and sustains the universe (for more names of God, see the next page). To use Thomas Aquinas's concept, God is the uncaused cause. Christians believe that God exists in three persons—God the Father, God the Son, and God the Holy Spirit (see *Trinity*). The Westminster Shorter Catechism says God is a Spirit who is "infinite, eternal, and unchangeable in his being, wisdom, power, holiness, justice, goodness, and truth." The term *god* (not capitalized) is used to refer to any supernatural spirit or power that people worship. Some religions (for example, Hinduism) have many gods. The first of the Ten Commandments says, "You shall have no other gods before me" (Exodus 20:3 NIV).

GOD IS GREAT, GOD IS GOOD, AND WE THANK HIM FOR OUR FOOD A prayer that many Christians say before a meal. To pray before eating is to "say grace."

Saying grace

GOD THE FATHER According to the doctrine of the Trinity, God exists eternally in three persons: God the Father, God the Son, and God the Holy Spirit. God the Father, in eternity past, planned all things, including a wonderful

SOME OF THE NAMES FOR GOD IN THE BIBLE

NAME	MEANING
ABBA	Aramaic: "father" or "dear father." Jesus used this term when he was praying in the garden of Gethsemane.
ADONAI	Hebrew: "the LORD, the superior one"
EL SHADDAI	Hebrew: "God Almighty"
ELOHIM	Hebrew: "The supreme or sovereign God"; it can also mean "god" in a more generic sense.
FATHER	God the Father, one of the persons of the Trinity; this name shows God's fatherly love.
JEHOVAH	An alternate form of *Yahweh*
LORD	Many English translations use LORD (with small capital letters) to translate *Yahweh*.
YAHWEH	The personal name used only of Israel's God; it means "I Am That I Am," or "I Am the One Who Is." This name was too holy for the Israelites to pronounce, so *Adonai* was substituted in public reading.

plan of salvation for sinful humanity because of his great love. This plan involved sending his Son, Jesus Christ, into the world as the Redeemer for all those who would believe in him.

GOD THE HOLY SPIRIT According to the doctrine of the Trinity, God exists eternally in three persons: God the Father, God the Son (Jesus Christ), and God the Holy Spirit. After Jesus ascended into heaven, God the Holy Spirit, also called "the Helper" (John 14:26), came to dwell permanently in the hearts of believers. In this way, God lives in and among his people. The Holy Spirit convicts them of sin, prays for them, and helps them in every way to do God's will.

GOD THE SON According to the doctrine of the Trinity, God exists eternally in three persons: God the Father, God the Son, and God the Holy Spirit. God the Son existed with the Father before the foundation of the world, and he carries out his Father's plan of redemption. God the Son was incarnated as Jesus Christ. His mother, Mary, was a virgin, and Christ lived as a perfect man who never sinned. He was crucified, died, and was buried. His death was the perfect atonement for humanity's sin. After three days, he rose from the dead and later ascended into heaven, where he sits at the right hand of God the Father. Someday he will return to earth in triumph and glory. See also *Incarnation*; *Second Coming*.

GODFATHER, GODMOTHER, GODPARENTS Terms for adults who participate in a child's baptism and pledge to take a role in looking out for the spiritual well-being of the child.

GOOD FRIDAY The Friday before Easter, when Christians remember the crucifixion of Jesus. The name Good Friday seems like a misnomer, since it commemorates Jesus's death. It was a good day, however, in the sense that Christ provided atonement for sins when he died.

GOOD NEWS An angel appeared to the shepherds in the fields outside Bethlehem on the night of Jesus's birth, saying, "Do not be afraid, for behold, I bring you good tidings of great joy which will be to all people. For there is born to you this day in the city of David a Savior, who is Christ the Lord" (Luke 2:10–11). The Good News is exactly the news the angels told the shepherds—that God sent a Savior to earth to save people from their sin. The word *gospel* (Matthew 4:23) comes from an Old English word meaning "good news."

GOSPEL A term for the Good News about Jesus Christ—that he is the Son of God, that he died to secure atonement for humanity's sin, and that he rose from the dead, thereby conquering death (1 Corinthians 15:20–23). The first four books of the New Testament are called the Gospels because they contain the Good News about Jesus. 📌 By extension, the word *gospel* has also come to mean anything that is accepted as infallible truth. The word *gospel* comes from *godspell*, an Old English word meaning "good news." A popular musical from the 1970s is called *Godspell*. It is a contemporary retelling of the gospel, based on the Gospel of Matthew.

GRACE Something that is freely given, that cannot be earned. In Christian theology, grace is the unmerited favor of God bestowed on sinners. Its highest expression is in the redemption provided by Christ's death. God's grace is freely extended to all people because of his great love for his own creation. The apostle Paul said, "While we were still sinners, Christ died for us" (Romans 5:8 NIV). We are forgiven and justified by God's grace, through faith in what Christ did. While not all people are recipients of God's *special* grace of personal redemption in Christ, all are recipients of God's *common* grace—the natural blessings he bestows on all mankind through creation.

HADES In the New Testament, the Greek word *Hades* refers to the place of the dead. For a fuller explanation, see *hell*.

HAIL MARY A popular name for the prayer to the Virgin Mary that is often repeated by Roman Catholics. It is also called the Ave Maria.

Hail Mary, full of grace,
The Lord is with thee.
Blessed art thou among women,
And blessed is the fruit of thy
  womb, Jesus.
Holy Mary, Mother of God,
Pray for us sinners,
Now and at the hour of our
  death.

"Hail Mary" has also come to mean a prayer uttered in a moment of desperation. In football, a "hail Mary" pass is a pass thrown in desperation, in hopes that a receiver will be able to catch it.

HANUKKAH (also spelled Chanukah; both spellings are pronounced *HAH-nuh-kuh*) The Jewish celebration that commemorates the cleansing and rededication of the Jewish temple after it was desecrated by the Syrian king Antiochus during the time of the Maccabees (164 or 165 BC), a Jewish family who led the revolt. Also called the Festival of Lights, Hanukkah is celebrated in late November or December, depending on where it falls on the Hebrew calendar that year. On each night of the eight-day festival, an additional candle is lit in a special candelabrum called a Hanukkah menorah.

Hanukkah menorah

HEAVEN The dwelling place of God. It is very real, but it is not a physical place we can discover with our physical senses. It exists in a spiritual realm. Jesus used the analogy of a house when he told his disciples, "My Father's house has many rooms; if that were not so, would I have told you that I am going there to prepare a place for you? And if I go and prepare a place for you, I will come back and take you to be with me that you also may be where I am" (John 14:2–3 NIV). Jesus came to earth from heaven, and forty days after his resurrection, he ascended and returned to heaven. The book of Revelation contains various descriptions of heaven. We see God seated on a throne, with millions of angels bowing down in worship before him. Also in Revelation we see John's vision of a holy city, the New Jerusalem, coming down from heaven to be the eternal home of God and of those who have eternal life. It is described as a city with streets of gold and gates made of pearls (see *pearly gates*). It is a glorious place with no crying, no sadness, and no death. Many Christians use the word *heaven* to describe this eternal home.

HELL The future dwelling place of Satan and his demons. Also the place of future punishment for wicked, unredeemed people. It is a place of fire and eternal torment. In Revelation 20:10, 15 it is called the lake of fire. In Mark 9:48, Jesus described hell as a place "where 'their worm does not die and the fire is not quenched.'" In some ways, hell is the opposite of heaven. The biblical references to hell are confusing, in part because there are three different words that are all translated "hell" in the King James Version. The Hebrew word *Sheol* and the Greek word *Hades* refer to a place where the dead have only a shadowy existence; these words are often translated "death," "the grave," or "Destruction" in modern translations. The Greek *Gehenna* is usually rendered "hell" in modern translations and refers to the fires of hell.

HERESY Adherence to a religious belief that is contrary to church dogma. It is the opposite of orthodoxy. There have been and continue to be many heresies that plague the church. Some of the early heresies were Gnosticism, Docetism, and Arianism. Gnosticism included the belief that matter is evil and spirit is good, and that salvation comes through the acquisition of secret knowledge (gnosis). Docetism included the belief that Jesus was not really a man, but just seemed to be a man. Arianism included the belief that Christ had been created by God the Father, so Christ was not coequal and coeternal with the Father. Adherents of heresies are called heretics.

HERETIC A person who adheres to a religious belief contrary to church dogma (see *heresy*). In the history of the church, many heretics have been burned at the stake or otherwise executed. In some cases, people burned as heretics by the rulers of their day were seen by later generations as martyrs or even saints. An example is Joan of Arc.

HERMENEUTICS The science and art of biblical interpretation. Most Christians affirm the divine inspiration and authority of Scripture, but they disagree on how the Scriptures should be interpreted. In general, the goal of hermeneutics is to discern the original and authentic meaning of the biblical text. This is done by helping the reader understand the cultural and historical context in which the Bible was written, as well as the cultural context in which it is being read.

HOLY The word *holy* has several related meanings: (1) "Set apart" or "separate." (2) To be without sin, or separate from sin. (3) Sacred. (4) Christians are said to be holy because they are cleansed by God through the atoning death of Christ. (5) One aspect of salvation is sanctification, the ongoing development of holiness in the life of the Christian. 📌 The expression "holier than thou" is disdainfully said about people who seem to flaunt their goodness, or "holiness."

HOLY COMMUNION Another name for the Eucharist, or Communion.

HOLY GHOST Another name for the Holy Spirit. See *God the Holy Spirit.*

HOLY ORDERS A sacrament in the Roman Catholic Church by which a man is ordained to special service in the church as a deacon, priest, or bishop.

HOLY SEE The seat of government, or jurisdiction, of the pope; the Vatican. The word *see* comes from a Latin word that means "seat."

HOLY SPIRIT The third person of the Trinity. See *God the Holy Spirit.*

HOST In the Eucharist, the bread is called the host. The term derives from a Latin word for "sacrifice." See also *cup.*

HYPOCRITE A person who says one thing but does another. Jesus frequently called the scribes and Pharisees hypocrites (see *strain out a gnat and swallow a camel* in the chapter "Famous Sayings from the Bible"). 📌 Many people say they do not want to follow Christ because of all the hypocrites in the churches. There are indeed many hypocrites, but that simply shows human sinfulness and underscores the need all people have for sanctification.

I AM THAT I AM When Moses met God at the burning bush, Moses asked God what his name was. God responded, "I AM WHO I AM" (Exodus 3:14). In Hebrew the name is spelled YHWH, or Yahweh. In the several centuries before Christ, Jews were not allowed to pronounce the name because it was holy. When they came to the name in the Scripture, they said *Adonai* ("the Lord"). See the list of names for God near the entry *God the Holy Spirit.*

I BELIEVE IN GOD THE FATHER ALMIGHTY The first phrase of the Apostles' Creed. For the complete text, see *Apostles' Creed.*

IHS An ancient Christian symbol that is still frequently seen in churches. It is taken from the first three letters of *IHSOUS*, the Greek spelling of *Jesus.*

IMMACULATE CONCEPTION The dogma of the Roman Catholic Church that the Virgin Mary was free of original sin from the moment she was conceived in her mother's womb. This doctrine should not be confused with the virgin birth of Jesus, which means that Mary was a virgin when Jesus was born.

IMPRIMATUR The official approval, given by a representative of the Roman Catholic Church, that a book may be printed. *Imprimatur* is Latin for "let it be printed." ✎ More broadly, an *imprimatur* can be any type of endorsement by a person in authority.

IN JESUS'S NAME Many Christians end their prayers by saying, "In Jesus's name, Amen." This tradition comes from Jesus's teaching, as recorded in passages such as John 14:13–14: "I will do whatever you ask in my name, so that the Father may be glorified in the Son. You may ask me for anything in my name, and I will do it" (NIV).

IN SICKNESS AND IN HEALTH An expression in the traditional wedding vows. See *to have and to hold.*

INCARNATION, THE The act through which the eternal Son of God, the second person of the Trinity, united himself with human flesh in the person of Jesus (the word *incarnation* means "in flesh"). Jesus was fully man and fully God simultaneously. Matthew 1:23 says, "Look! The virgin will conceive a child! She will give birth to a son, and they will call him Immanuel, which means 'God is with us'" (NLT). Through the Incarnation, God is indeed with us. The Incarnation is an important aspect of Christian theology because God the Son came to earth and became the perfect sacrifice on behalf of sinful people to atone for sin (see *atonement*). Furthermore, Hebrews 4:15 is a reminder that Jesus sympathizes with all our weaknesses, for he has been tempted in every way we are tempted, though he did not sin.

INFANT BAPTISM See *baptism.*

INRI See *king of the Jews* in the chapter "People, Places, and Events in the New Testament."

INVOCATION A prayer at the beginning of a worship service or other public gathering, asking God to be present and to bless the meeting.

JEHOVAH A name for God. The name *Jehovah* comes from combining two Hebrew names for God—the consonants of YHWH, the name that was too sacred to pronounce, and the vowels of Adonai (see the list of names for God near the entry *God the Holy*

Spirit). Some English translations translate Yahweh as "Jehovah", while others translate it "Lord."

JUDGMENT DAY A term for the final day of reckoning, when God settles all accounts, judging evil and rewarding faith; also called the Day of the Lord. The books of Daniel and Revelation both contain vivid descriptions of the final judgment. Each person will stand before God, the books will be opened, and the individual will be judged according to his deeds recorded in the books. Anyone whose name is not recorded in the Book of Life will be thrown into the lake of fire. Some theologians see separate judgments for believers (2 Corinthians 5:10) and unbelievers (Revelation 20:11–15).

JUSTICE Doing what is right for another person, or ensuring that what is right takes place. The Old Testament prophets spoke much about the need for justice, and Israel and Judah were both criticized for not treating widows and orphans justly. The prophet Micah gave this prescription for right living: "He has shown you, O mortal, what is good. And what does the LORD require of you? To act justly and to love mercy and to walk humbly with your God" (Micah 6:8 NIV). In a stricter sense, justice means giving a person what he deserves as a result of his actions. Scripture is very clear that "all have sinned and fall short of the glory of God" (Romans 3:23) and that "the wages of sin is death" (Romans 6:23). According to God's justice, all peo-

The Last Judgment

ple deserve eternal separation from God. Thankfully, God provided a way of atonement and redemption for those who believe in Christ.

JUSTIFICATION God's act of forgiving sinners and declaring them righteous, not because they deserve it but because of the righteousness of Christ. Justification is God's free gift for those who accept it (see next entry). God justified sinners in the Old Testament in the same way, though justification was based upon the righteousness of the Christ who had not yet come. The people demonstrated their faith by offering animal sacrifices that foreshadowed the sacrifice of Christ.

JUSTIFICATION BY GRACE, THROUGH FAITH A rallying cry of the Reformers, who emphasized that God alone saves sinners (Romans 3:23–24). Nothing people "do" can make them right with God—not good works, not church affiliation, not even having faith by itself. As Paul taught, our salvation is God's gift to us: "By grace you have been saved through faith, and that not of yourselves; it is the gift of God" (Ephesians 2:8).

KINGDOM OF GOD, KINGDOM OF HEAVEN One of the central themes of Jesus's teaching as recorded in the synoptic Gospels. There are varying views regarding the "kingdom of heaven." It often refers to the sphere in which Christ rules over mankind. In the beginning of his ministry, Jesus preached, "Repent, for the kingdom of heaven is at hand!" (Matthew 3:2). Christians see both present and future aspects to that kingdom, as well as spiritual and earthly aspects. In some of his parables, Jesus used everyday situations to describe various aspects of the kingdom of heaven. For instance, he said, "The kingdom of heaven is like a mustard seed.... The kingdom of heaven is like yeast.... The kingdom of heaven is like treasure hidden in a field" (Matthew 13 NIV).

LAST RITES The popular name for the anointing of the sick, a sacrament in the Roman Catholic Church. It was formerly called extreme unction. When a person is near death a priest anoints him or her with holy oil and prays for the person's physical and spiritual healing.

LAYMAN, LAYWOMAN, LAYPERSON A person in a church who is not ordained as a minister or member of the clergy.

LENT A period of penitence and fasting before Easter, beginning on Ash Wednesday. Lent lasts for forty days, not counting Sundays. Many Christians observe Lent by giving up some daily food or activity to help them remember Christ's suffering.

LIMBO In Roman Catholic tradition, the final resting place of souls who are not sent to hell but are also not allowed entrance into heaven (unbaptized infants, for example). The concept of limbo is not held by Protestants. By extension, the term *limbo* has come to mean any in-between position, or a state of uncertainty.

LITANY A repetition of prayers, or a prayer consisting of supplications by the leader and alternate responses by the congregation. An example is a litany in the Book of Common Prayer in which the people repeatedly respond, "Have mercy upon us."

LITURGY The established order or format of public worship. All churches follow some pattern in public worship. On the "low church" side, Pentecostals favor an unstructured, spontaneous format. On the "high church" side, Roman Catholics follow a more highly structured service centered on the Eucharist. Worship is often considered "liturgical" to the degree it features the sacrament of Communion.

LORD There are several Hebrew and Greek words in the Bible that are translated "Lord" in English. In the New Testament, Jesus was often called Lord, from *kyrios*, a Greek word that could also be translated "Master." In the Old Testament, the personal name Yahweh is also translated "Lord." Many English translations print this particular sense of the Old Testament word in small capitals (LORD) to show that it is a translation of Yahweh and to distinguish it from *Lord* as a translation of other Hebrew words.

LORD'S DAY Sunday, the day Christians have traditionally observed as a day of rest. See also *Sabbath* in the chapter "People, Places, and Events in the Old Testament."

LORD'S SUPPER Another name for Communion or the Eucharist (the term is used by the apostle Paul in 1 Corinthians 11:20). It is called the Lord's Supper because it commemorates Jesus's death. As

Jesus gave his disciples the bread at the Last Supper, he said, "This is my body, which is given for you. Do this in remembrance of me" (1 Corinthians 11:24 NLT).

LOVE In the New Testament, several different Greek words are translated "love." One of those words, *agape* (pronounced *ah-GAH-pay*), means a willful, other-centered love that is unmerited and does not require anything in return. God loves all people with this type of love, and Christians are encouraged also to love one another in this manner. Jesus said, "This is my commandment: Love each other in the same way I have loved you. There is no greater love than to lay down one's life for one's friends" (John 15:12–13 NLT). Another Greek word in the New Testament is *philia*, which is an emotional love (from which the name *Phila*delphia is derived—"the city of brotherly love"). A closely related word means "friend."

LUCIFER A name sometimes used for Satan, the devil. It means "light bearer" and may refer to his attributes before his rebellion and fall. The name Lucifer is used only once in the King James Version (Isaiah 14:12), and it is not used at all in most other translations.

MARDI GRAS The Tuesday before Ash Wednesday. It is also called Shrove Tuesday. *Mardi Gras* is French for "fat Tuesday." It was traditionally a celebration of feasting before the beginning of Lent, but it has now become secularized and is simply a day for partying. The most famous celebration of Mardi Gras is in New Orleans. In Latin America the comparable celebration is called *carnival.*

MARK OF THE BEAST Revelation 13 describes a terrible beast who is given power by Satan to rule over the entire earth. All except those whose names are written in the Book of Life will worship the beast. He will require each person to receive a mark on his or her forehead or right hand in order to buy or sell. The mark of the beast is the number 666. Christians differ in their identification of the beast. Many see him as a political or religious figure of the future. See also 666.

A Catholic Mass

MASS The celebration of the sacrament of the Eucharist. In the Roman Catholic Church, the entire service is also called the Mass. It typically includes prayers, readings from Scripture, a sermon (homily), and the Eucharist. The liturgy of the Mass can be sung or spoken. Traditionally it included the Gregorian chants, sung in Latin: the *Kyrie* (short for *Kyrie eleison*, "Lord have mercy"), *Gloria* ("Glory"), *Credo* ("I believe"), Sanctus (short for *Sanctus, sanctus, sanctus*, "Holy, holy, holy"), and *Agnus Dei* ("Lamb of God"). The Mass has been celebrated in the vernacular (for example, English) rather than in Latin only since the Vatican II Council.

MATRIMONY Marriage, in which a man and woman pledge themselves to one another for life. In the Roman Catholic and Eastern Orthodox churches, matrimony is a sacrament.

MAUNDY THURSDAY The Thursday before Easter, when Christians commemorate the Last Supper. Also called Holy Thursday. The name comes from *maundy*, an old English custom in which the king washed the feet of poor people, as Jesus had washed the feet of his disciples at the Last Supper (John 13).

MERCY Kindness, leniency, tender compassion, pardon, pity in action. When the tax collector in Luke 18:13 stood in the temple and prayed, "God, be merciful to me a sinner," he was acknowledging his sin but was asking God to forgive him and view him as though he had no sin.

MESSIANIC JEW Going all the way back to the time of Jesus, most

Jews have not seen Jesus as the Messiah. Those who do are called Messianic Jews.

MILLENNIUM, THE Revelation 20 says Satan will be bound and thrown into an abyss for 1,000 years. Because Revelation is not an easy book to interpret, Christians differ as to the precise meaning of the 1,000 years. Premillennialists and postmillennialists both tend to interpret this period of time in a literal sense, with Christ reigning on earth for a millennium (Latin for "one thousand years"). The premillennial perspective sees the Second Coming of Christ as an event immediately *before* Christ establishes his thousand-year reign. The postmillennial perspective sees the Second Coming *after* a thousand-year period of peace on earth. Amillennialists, on the other hand, tend to interpret the time period as a figure of speech that refers to the kingdom of God between Christ's first coming and the Second Coming.

MINISTER A Protestant clergyman. Most ministers are ordained (see *ordain*). In most churches, only ordained ministers, often called pastors, are authorized to administer the sacraments or ordinances.

MISSION, MISSIONARY SOCIETY An organization that sends missionaries to other cultures (see next entry). A handful of missionary societies date back to the nineteenth century, and many have changed their names over the years (for example, China Inland Mission, founded in 1865 by J. Hudson Taylor, was renamed Overseas Missionary Fellowship, and is now known as OMF International). But many others were founded in the 1950s or more recently (for example, Pioneers, founded in 1979).

MISSIONARY A person commissioned to take the gospel of Christ to another culture. The apostle Paul was one of the first missionaries (see *missionary journeys of Paul* in the chapter "People, Places, and Events in the New Testament"). He traveled throughout Asia Minor (modern-day Turkey) and Greece, founding churches. Saint Patrick was a missionary who took the gospel to Ireland. The Jesuits have a history of missionary work on behalf of the Roman Catholic Church. Three great Protestant missionaries were William Carey in India, David Livingstone in Africa, and J. Hudson Taylor in China. Today there are hundreds of missionary societies that support thousands of missionaries. One of the great changes in the missionary movement today is that non-Western churches (for instance, in Korea) are sending out many missionaries.

J. Hudson Taylor

MONK A man who is a member of a religious order and who lives in a cloistered community called a monastery. The popular image of a monastery is an ancient stone structure in a rural setting, but today some monasteries are modern dwellings in cities.

MONOTHEISM The belief in one God. In Deuteronomy 6:4, Moses proclaims, "Hear, O Israel: The LORD our God is one LORD" (KJV). Judaism, Christianity, and Islam are the three great monotheistic religions. See also *polytheism*.

MORTAL SIN The dogma of the Roman Catholic Church traditionally divides sin into two categories—venial sin and mortal sin. Mortal sin is more serious than venial sin. It involves a serious sin, undertaken after sufficient reflection and with full consent. It is an act of turning away from God, making the sinner spiritually dead and subject to everlasting punishment. A person who repents and confesses can be forgiven of mortal sin, but one who dies in mortal sin is damned (see *damnation*).

NEW COVENANT God's covenant with mankind is his great and unified plan of forgiveness and salvation. Under the Old Testament covenant with Moses, the people of Israel were to believe God and follow the Mosaic law, including circumcision and the system of animal sacrifices. In the New Testament, Jesus Christ established the new covenant. Instead of animal sacrifices for atonement, Jesus was the one and only sacrifice whose death could atone for people's sins once and for all (Hebrews 7:27). Under the new covenant, God promises to accept those who believe in Jesus as their Redeemer and Savior (Hebrews 9:15).

NEW JERUSALEM According to the book of Revelation, God will destroy the present heaven and earth and will create a new heaven and a new earth. Part of the new creation will be a holy city, the New Jerusalem, that will come down to earth. This will be the dwelling place of God with those who have eternal life. In that place there will be no more crying or death or mourning or pain. The city and its streets will be made of pure gold, and the twelve gates of the city will each be made of a single pearl (see *pearly gates*). The New Jerusalem is also identified with the church, which is the bride of Christ.

NICENE CREED An ancient creed that articulates Christian orthodoxy. It was developed from an earlier creed adopted at the Council of Nicaea, so it contains language specifically designed to combat the heresy of Arianism, which held that Jesus was not of the same essence as God. The Nicene Creed is still confessed in many churches today. The version presented here is taken from the current edition of the Book of Common Prayer.

NUN A woman who is a member of a religious order. In many orders, nuns live in communities called convents. Many nuns are teachers, social workers, nurses, etc.

Nuns with Pope Francis at the Vatican

OMNIPOTENCE OF GOD One of the attributes of God. It means that God is all-powerful.

OMNIPRESENCE OF GOD One of the attributes of God. It means that God is present everywhere.

OMNISCIENCE OF GOD One of the attributes of God. It means that God is all-knowing.

ORDAIN, ORDINATION When a person is formally commissioned by a church or denomination for

THE NICENE CREED

We believe in one God,
the Father, the Almighty,
maker of heaven and earth,
of all that is, visible and invisible.

We believe in one Lord, Jesus Christ,
the only-begotten Son of God,
eternally begotten of the Father,
God from God, Light from Light,
true God from true God,
begotten, not made,
of one Being with the Father;
through him all things were made.
For us and for our salvation he came down from heaven,
was incarnate from the Holy Spirit and the Virgin Mary,
and was made man.
For our sake he was crucified under Pontius Pilate;
he suffered death and was buried.
On the third day he rose again
in accordance with the Scriptures;
he ascended into heaven
and is seated at the right hand of the Father.
He will come again in glory to judge the living and the dead,
and his kingdom will have no end.

We believe in the Holy Spirit, the Lord, the giver of life,
who proceeds from the Father [and the Son],
who with the Father and the Son is worshiped and glorified,
who has spoken through the prophets.
We believe in one holy catholic and apostolic Church.
We acknowledge one Baptism for the forgiveness of sins.
We look for the resurrection of the dead,
and the life of the world to come. Amen.

This text is taken from the 2019 edition of the Book of Common Prayer.

a particular ministry, he or she is ordained. The individual is usually tested first for knowledge of the Scriptures and the doctrines of the particular church or denomination. In many ordination services, other ordained persons lay hands on and pray for the person being ordained. The ordination of women is not allowed in the Roman Catholic Church nor in most conservative Protestant denominations.

ORDINANCE A formal act or rite celebrated by the church. Various churches observe various ordinances, but most include baptism and Communion. Some churches refer not to *ordinances* (commands) but to *sacraments* (holy things).

ORIGINAL SIN The doctrine that all persons are inherently guilty of sin and have a corrupt human nature. Sin entered the human race at the fall of man, when Adam disobeyed God and ate the forbidden fruit. The Bible teaches that all people share Adam's guilt and miserable condition. As a result, all people are born in a state of alienation from God. Romans 5:12 says, "Just as sin entered the world through one man, and death through sin, and in this way death came to all people, because all sinned" (NIV).

ORTHODOX, ORTHODOXY Adherence to the accepted teachings of a religion. Christian orthodoxy is measured both by Scripture and by the long history of church teaching. The Apostles' Creed and the Nicene Creed are both basic guides by which to measure orthodoxy, as they are accepted by both Protestants and Catholics. If a particular belief (for example, that Jesus was not really the Son of God) runs counter to one of the ancient creeds, it is not orthodox.

OUR FATHER A popular name for the Lord's Prayer, particularly among Roman Catholics. It is also called the *Paternoster* (from the Latin for "our Father"). For the complete text, see *Lord's Prayer* in the chapter "Famous Sayings from the Bible."

PACIFIST A person who believes war is morally wrong. Most pacifists also avoid violence of any kind. Mennonites and other Anabaptist groups, Quakers, and Jehovah's Witnesses are pacifists. See also *conscientious objector*.

PALM SUNDAY The Sunday before Easter, when Christians remember Jesus Christ's Triumphal Entry into Jerusalem. It is called Palm Sunday because the crowd spread palm branches in front of Jesus as he rode into the city on a donkey.

PAPACY The reign of a pope; the succession of popes; the administration and function of the pope.

PAPAL INFALLIBILITY According to Roman Catholic dogma, the pope is infallible (without error) when he speaks *ex cathedra* (with the authority of the church) on matters of faith or morals. Papal infallibility was defined in 1870 in a decree of the First Vatican Council. Only two recent papal statements have been presented as infallible: the Immaculate Conception of Mary (defined in 1854) and the bodily assumption (taking up) of Mary to heaven (defined in 1950).

PARADISE The word *paradise* has several related meanings, all of which suggest a place of perfection: (1) The Garden of Eden. (2) The place believers go immediately after death (see *thief on the cross* in the chapter "People, Places, and Events in the New Testament"). (3) Heaven. Two great works of literature have themes involving paradise: John Milton's *Paradise Lost* and Dante's *Divine Comedy*, with a major part called "Paradiso."

PARISH The local area served by an Anglican or Roman Catholic Church. A member of a parish is called a parishioner. Roman Catholics are encouraged to participate in their own parish church rather than traveling to a church in another parish.

Palm Sunday celebration in Jerusalem

PASTOR The spiritual leader of a congregation. In Protestant churches the pastor is often called the minister. In the Roman Catholic Church the pastor is a priest.

PATERNOSTER The Latin name for the Lord's Prayer. *Paternoster* comes from *pater noster* ("our Father"), the first words of the Lord's Prayer in Latin.

PEARLY GATES In Revelation 21:21, each of the gates of the New Jerusalem is described as being made of a single pearl. The term *pearly gates* has come to mean the entrance into heaven.

PENANCE A sacrament in the Roman Catholic Church in which a person is repentant, expresses an intention not to continue sinning, and confesses the sins to a priest. The priest may require penance (for example, prayer, fasting, or abstinence) and/or restitution (making things right), depending on the nature of the sin. Then, as God's representative, the priest extends absolution (forgiveness). Catholics are expected to participate in the sacrament of penance (which is also called the Rite of Reconciliation) at least once a year.

POLYTHEISM Belief in many gods, in contrast to monotheism. Hinduism, for example, is a polytheistic religion. The Roman Empire at the time of Christ was home to many forms of polytheism.

PONTIFF Any Roman Catholic bishop, though the term is usually used specifically for the pope.

POPE The head of the Roman Catholic Church. The pope has absolute jurisdiction in the church, though substantial responsibilities are delegated to the cardinals and bishops, who are appointed by the pope. Roman Catholics believe the pope is infallible when he speaks *ex cathedra*—that is, when he speaks for the entire church on matters of faith and morals. The pope lives in the Vatican, an independent principality located in the city of Rome. He is head of the government of the Vatican. The pope is acknowledged as a world leader because of his tremendous influence on Roman Catholics around the world. The Roman Catholic Church claims that the apostle Peter was the first pope, and that there is an unbroken line of popes who have succeeded him. Recent popes have been Pius XII (1939–58), John XXIII (1958–63), Paul VI (1963–78), John

Paul I (1978), John Paul II (1978–2005), Benedict XVI (2005–13), and Francis (2013–).

Pope Francis

PRAY, PRAYER Talking with God. Prayer can be formal, as in reciting a litany from a prayer book, or it can be as informal as a quick thought addressed to God while stopped at a traffic light. It can be silent or spoken, private or public. The apostle Paul said, "Pray without ceasing" (1 Thessalonians 5:17).

PREDESTINATION The doctrine that pertains to God's plans for creation and humankind from before the foundation of the world. Christians hold two different views regarding predestination in salvation. The Arminian view understands predestination of certain people based on God's prior knowledge of who would decide to believe in Christ (see *free will*). The Calvinist (or Reformed) tradition understands predestination as being based upon God's own good will and pleasure, not on human decision (see *election*).

PRIEST In Roman Catholic, Orthodox, and Anglican churches, the pastor is called a priest. Roman Catholic priests must follow the rule of celibacy, which means they cannot marry. See also *priest* in the chapter "People, Places, and Events in the Old Testament."

PROVIDENCE (DIVINE PROVIDENCE) God's general care and provision for all his creatures. In theism, the providence of God regulates the universe. 📌 Providence, Rhode Island, was so named by its founder, Roger Williams, because of his sense of God's direction and provision.

PSALTER A book containing the Psalms arranged for liturgical or devotional use. Some churches read the Psalter responsively; in others, psalms are put to music.

PURGATORY In Roman Catholicism, the place of spiritual

cleansing after death, usually imagined to involve punishment and suffering. According to this doctrine, Christians go to purgatory to be purified of venial sins that were unconfessed and unforgiven on earth. After the appropriate cleansing has taken place, the soul is ready to be received into heaven. Indulgences, masses, and prayers for the dead can speed the cleansing process and reduce the time in purgatory. A popular misconception is that purgatory is a place where people go who are neither good enough for heaven nor bad enough for hell. 📌 The second section of Dante's *Divine Comedy* is "Purgatorio" ("Purgatory").

PURIM The contemporary Jewish celebration of the rescue of the Jews in the time of Esther.

Purim celebration in Jerusalem

R.I.P. These initials stand for *requiescat in pace*, or its English equivalent, "rest in peace." The initials are frequently seen on tombstones.

RAPTURE A phrase used by premillennialists (see *Millennium*) to describe the event of the members of Christ's body, the church, being "caught up" in the air to meet Christ. They base this upon 1 Thessalonians 4:16–17, which says, "The dead in Christ will rise first. Then we who are alive and remain shall be caught up together with them in the clouds to meet the Lord in the air. And thus we shall always be with the Lord." Premillennialists are divided over whether the Rapture occurs before, during, or after the Tribulation. Not all systems of eschatology include the Rapture as a distinct event.

REDEEMER, REDEMPTION To redeem something is to buy it back or rescue it. In Christian theology, all of creation, including mankind, originally belonged to God—because he created it all. But with the fall of man, sin entered the world, and all people born since then have inherited a corrupt nature and are guilty of sin. God, who is holy, requires an atonement for sin. Jesus Christ, through his suffering and death, paid the price of freedom to rescue all who believe. It is in this sense that Jesus is called the Redeemer.

RELIGIOUS ORDER A group of men or women who take religious vows, usually including obedience (to a superior as well as to God), poverty, and chastity (sexual purity). A woman in a religious order is a nun. A man in a religious order is a monk if he lives in a monastery. Men in religious orders who are not priests are called brothers. Most religious orders are Roman Catholic or Eastern Orthodox. Benedictines, Dominicans, Franciscans, Jesuits, and Trappists are all members of religious orders. Mother Teresa, who worked among the poor in Calcutta, India, founded an order called the Missionaries of Charity.

REPENTANCE Changing one's mind about the wrong one has done and then turning away from it. It is an important concept in Christian theology, because we must repent of our sinfulness before we are likely to seek salvation. Repentance is an important part of the Christian life—both in the Roman Catholic sacrament of penance and in the Protestant view of justification and sanctification. Once Jesus referred to some people who had recently been killed, and he said to his audience, "Unless you repent you will all likewise perish" (Luke 13:5).

REVIVAL A religious awakening that sweeps through a congregation or community or even an entire nation. A revival is characterized by fervor in worship, an awareness of personal sin, an eagerness to seek forgiveness from God and from other people, and an eagerness to share one's experience with others. The Great Awakening was an important revival in American history. The Jesus People movement of the 1960s and 1970s was a revival among young people. The term is also used, particularly in Baptist churches, for any special evangelistic meeting.

RIGHTEOUS Being and doing what is right in God's sight. Because of original sin and depravity, no one is truly righteous. But God declares his people righteous because the righteousness of Christ is counted on their behalf. See also *original sin*; *justification*.

ROSARY A string of fifty beads used by Roman Catholics to assist them in repeating a litany that includes the Apostles' Creed, the Our Father, and the Hail Mary. To "say the rosary" is to meditate on sacred mysteries from the life of Christ while saying Hail Marys.

SACRAMENT A formal act or rite celebrated by the church. According to the catechism in the Book of Common Prayer, "sacraments are outward and visible signs of inward and spiritual grace." Various churches observe various sacraments, but all include baptism and Communion. The Roman Catholic Church and the Eastern Orthodox Church observe seven sacraments, including confirmation, penance, matrimony, holy orders, and the anointing of the sick (also called holy unction, or extreme unction, or last rites). Some churches refer not to *sacraments* (holy things) but to *ordinances* (commands).

SACRED That which is holy, or set apart for religious usage. The term is also used in contrast to that which is secular (for example, sacred music).

SAINTS In the Roman Catholic Church and the Eastern Orthodox Church, a saint is a person who has died and has been officially recognized for unusual holiness (see *canonization*). Several miracles must be attributed to the person before he or she can be made a saint. More broadly, a saint is any holy person. In some contexts, all Christians are called saints. 📌 The Spanish words for saint are *san* (masculine) and *santa* (feminine), as in San Francisco, San Antonio, and Santa Barbara, all of which are cities named for saints. In Portuguese the word is *são*, as in São Paulo, Brazil, which is named for Saint Paul.

SALVATION The act or process of being delivered from sin and its consequences. In Christian theology, salvation refers broadly to God's actions in securing deliverance for sinners—including justification, sanctification, and glorification. According to the New Testament, people receive salvation as a free gift when they acknowledge their need for God and trust in Jesus's death to pay for their sin.

SANCTIFICATION The ongoing development of holiness in the life of the Christian. The Holy Spirit dwells within believers, convicting them of sin and changing their character. As they recognize sin, they can call upon the power of God to help them overcome it. The apostle Paul wrote, "Those who are dominated by the sinful nature think about sinful things, but those who are controlled by the Holy Spirit think about things that please the Spirit (Romans 8:5 NLT).

SATAN A name for the devil, the supremely evil spirit who is the enemy of God and the enemy of

BIBLE VERSES THAT SHOW THE WAY TO SALVATION

- † *All have sinned and fall short of the glory of God.* (Romans 3:23)
- † *The wages of sin is death, but the gift of God is eternal life in Christ Jesus our Lord.* (Romans 6:23)
- † *God demonstrates his own love for us in this: While we were still sinners, Christ died for us.* (Romans 5:8 NIV)
- † *God so loved the world that he gave his one and only Son, that whoever believes in him shall not perish but have eternal life.* (John 3:16 NIV)
- † *If you declare with your mouth, "Jesus is Lord," and believe in your heart that God raised him from the dead, you will be saved. For it is with your heart that you believe and are justified, and it is with your mouth that you profess your faith and are saved.* (Romans 10:9–10 NIV)

Christians. He is not God's opposite, however, for he was created by God, is under God's control, and will ultimately be defeated by God. Satanism, the cult of Satan worship, is not a new phenomenon, but it is more visible today than it has often been in the past.

SCRIPTURE, INERRANCY OF The doctrine that the original Bible manuscripts were without error. The *original* manuscripts no longer exist, however, and inerrancy does not claim that the early manuscripts we do have are without error. Nor does it claim that any particular translation of the Bible is without error.

SCRIPTURE, INSPIRATION OF The doctrine that the biblical writers were guided by God as they wrote his intended message (2 Peter 1:20–21), although they did not know their writings would later become part of the Bible. A familiar verse that refers to the inspiration of Scripture is 2 Timothy 3:16: "All Scripture is God-breathed and is useful for teaching, rebuking, correcting and training in righteousness" (NIV). The inspiration of Scripture is one of the tenets of fundamentalism.

SECOND COMING The New Testament teaches that Jesus will come to earth a second time. This is called the Second Coming. Jesus himself said he would return: "If I go and prepare a place for you, I will come back and take you to be with me that you also may be where I am" (John 14:3 NIV). At the time of Jesus's ascension into heaven, two heavenly messengers told the disciples, "This same Jesus, who has been taken from you into heaven, will come back in the same way you have seen him go into heaven" (Acts 1:11 NIV). Jesus did not specify when he would return. Christians in the early church expected him to return during their lifetime, and believers ever since have hoped that the Second Coming was imminent. For varying views regarding the Second Coming, see *Millennium*.

SECULAR Anything that is not sacred is secular. The term is often used specifically to distinguish between two things, one of which is sacred and the other of which is secular (for example, sacred music and secular music).

SERMON The exposition of a lesson from Scripture during a church service. In Protestant churches, the sermon is usually the centerpiece of the entire service. A short sermon can be called a homily.

SEVEN DEADLY SINS In church tradition, the seven deadly sins are pride, covetousness (greed), lust, envy, gluttony, anger, and sloth (laziness). They are "deadly" because they are so common—and so easy to fall into. They are also called capital sins.

SHEOL In the Old Testament, the Hebrew word *Sheol* refers to the place of the dead. For a fuller explanation, see *hell.*

SHROVE TUESDAY See *Mardi Gras.*

SIN An offense against God; disobedience to God's holy standards. According to the Bible, sin entered the world when Adam and Eve ate the forbidden fruit (see *fall of man* in the chapter "People, Places, and Events in the Old Testament"). As a result, all people are born with innate sin. But sin is also a willful disobedience of God's laws, either by not doing what we should do or by doing what we should not do. Jesus Christ, the Son of God, secured atonement for sin through his sacrificial death in place of sinners. See also *original sin*; *mortal sin*; *venial sin*; *seven deadly sins*; *unpardonable sin*; *atonement.*

📌 Many actions and attitudes are clearly defined as sin in the Bible, but many people choose to define sin according to contemporary cultural standards rather than according to the standards found in the Bible. For example, one of the Ten Commandments says, "You shall not commit adultery." Yet contemporary culture tends not to see adultery as a sin, and even glamorizes it in movies, novels, and television.

SON (GOD THE SON) See *God the Son.*

SOUL The terms *soul* and *spirit* are often used interchangeably to refer to the total spiritual (nonphysical) part of a person that lives on after physical death. The Bible does not clearly specify what happens to the soul when the body dies, but a predominant Protestant belief is that the soul of the believer passes immediately to heaven (2 Corinthians 5:8). The Roman Catholic understanding is that most souls destined for heaven go first to purgatory. At the time of the resurrection of the dead, the physical body will be raised up and made perfect, enabling the glorified and reunited body and soul to enjoy God forever (1 Corinthians 15:42–44).

SOVEREIGNTY OF GOD The doctrine that God has absolute authority and control over all things, including the details of human life. This doctrine is an important aspect of Calvinism. See also *omnipotence of God.*

SPEAK NOW OR FOREVER HOLD YOUR PEACE A popular paraphrase of a statement in the traditional wedding ceremony. The actual sentence is, "If any man can show just cause, why [these two persons] may not lawfully be joined together, let him now speak, or else hereafter forever hold his peace."

SPEAKING IN TONGUES One of the gifts of the Holy Spirit; also called glossolalia. This gift enables a person to speak in a language he or she has not learned. When this ability was first given to the disciples at Pentecost, they spoke languages that were understood by visitors in Jerusalem who came from many different countries. Pentecostal and charismatic churches emphasize the gift of speaking in tongues as a sign of baptism in the Holy Spirit. The contemporary manifestation tends to be an unknown "prayer language" for the benefit of the individual rather than a known human language for the benefit of others. In some traditions, speaking in tongues is rejected as invalid for the church today.

SPIRIT The vital force that gives life to the physical body. When God created Adam, God "breathed into his nostrils the breath of life, and the man became a living being" (Genesis 2:7 NIV). When there is no spirit, the body dies. The distinction between soul and spirit has been a matter of ongoing debate; many use the terms interchangeably. The term *spirits* is also used to refer to angels and demons, those supernatural beings who do not have physical bodies. When capitalized, *Spirit* usually refers to the Holy Spirit.

SPIRIT OF THE LORD See *Holy Spirit* and *God the Holy Spirit.*

SPIRITUAL GIFTS See *gifts of the Holy Spirit.*

STATIONS (WAY) OF THE CROSS It consists of a series of fourteen meditations (stations) commemorating events in the

Passion of Christ (see *Passion of Christ* in the chapter "People, Places, and Events in the New Testament"). Depictions of these scenes are found in many Roman Catholic churches. Stations of the Cross are also located along the Via Dolorosa, a street in the Old City of Jerusalem, where they commemorate the traditional spots where each event actually happened.

SUNDAY Most Christians treat Sunday as a special day—a day of rest and a day for worship. Sunday replaces Saturday as the Sabbath because Jesus's resurrection occurred on a Sunday. It is sometimes called the Lord's Day.

SUNDAY SCHOOL A church program of Christian education for children. The Sunday school movement began in the eighteenth century. In Protestant churches, Sunday school is traditionally held for an hour on Sunday morning, before or after the worship service.

TESTIMONY A personal statement of what one has seen or experienced. It is often used by Christians in the sense of recounting a person's own pilgrimage of faith and God's faithfulness in his or her life.

THANKSGIVING An American holiday on which families traditionally gather to celebrate and thank God for all his blessings. The first Thanksgiving was held by the Pilgrims in 1621, when they held a three-day feast to celebrate the successful harvest. Thanksgiving

Stations of the cross are located along the *Via Dolorosa* in Jerusalem.

is celebrated in the USA on the fourth Thursday of November (in Canada it is the second Monday of October).

THEOLOGIAN A person who studies theology. Great theologians in history include Augustine of Hippo, Thomas Aquinas, and John Calvin. Twentieth-century theologians include Karl Barth, Paul Tillich, J. I. Packer (all Protestants), and Karl Rahner (Roman Catholic).

THEOLOGY The study of God and his relationship to the world. More broadly, theology is a rational interpretation of religious faith. Thousands of books have been written expounding various aspects of Christian theology. The Apostles' Creed and the Nicene Creed, however, are very succinct summaries of orthodox theology.

TILL DEATH US DO PART An expression in the traditional wedding vows. In the newest edition of the Book of Common Prayer, the phrase is "until we are parted by death." See also the entry for *to have and to hold.*

TO HAVE AND TO HOLD A phrase in the bride's and groom's vows. The following words are spoken in the traditional wedding service, as found in the Book of Common Prayer:

> "I, (name), take you, (name), to be my wife [husband], to have and to hold from this day forward, for better for worse, for richer for poorer, in sickness and in health, to love and to cherish, until we are parted by death. This is my solemn vow."

TOTAL DEPRAVITY See *depravity, total.*

TRANSUBSTANTIATION In Roman Catholic doctrine, the elements of the Eucharist (Holy Communion), when consecrated, change from the substance of bread and wine to the substance of the actual body and blood of Christ. This is in contrast to the Lutheran doctrine of consubstantiation, which asserts the real presence of the body of Christ *with* the elements. A third view, which John Calvin taught, is that the bread and wine remain actually bread and wine, but those taking Communion receive the body and blood of Christ in a spiritual manner.

TRIBULATION, THE The church has experienced tribulation

(hardship, persecution) from the earliest days after the resurrection and ascension of Christ. Millions of Christians have been persecuted and killed because of their faith. According to the books of Daniel and Revelation, there will be a terrible period of tribulation in the future. This Great Tribulation will be worse than any before (Matthew 24:21). There are various interpretations of how long it will last, when it will take place (for example, before or after the Rapture), and whether passages that describe the Tribulation (for example, Luke 21:5–24) are symbolic or literal.

TRINITY, THE Christians believe that God is a Trinity, or three persons in one nature: God the Father, God the Son, and God the Holy Spirit. All three are one God, the same in properties and attributes, and equal in power and glory. Although the word *trinity* is not found in the Bible, God progressively revealed himself as a Trinity through the Father's work of creation, the incarnation of the Son, and the outpouring of the Holy Spirit at Pentecost. The New Testament writers reflect a consciousness of the Trinity, as seen in the Great Commission: "Go and make disciples of all nations, baptizing them in the name of the Father and of the Son and of the Holy Spirit" (Matthew 28:19 NIV). The doctrine of the Trinity was developed by the early church and is clearly reflected in the Apostles' Creed and the Nicene Creed. Belief in the Trinity is a prime test of Christian orthodoxy.

TRINITY SUNDAY See *church year*.

TRUSTEE A position of leadership held by laypeople in some churches (see *layman, laywoman, layperson*). Trustees are usually responsible for the physical assets of the church.

UNPARDONABLE SIN Jesus said, "Truly I tell you, people can be forgiven all their sins and every slander they utter, but whoever blasphemes against the Holy Spirit will never be forgiven; they are guilty of an eternal sin" (Mark 3:28–29 NIV). This unpardonable sin is not a singular event for which a person later feels remorse. It is an ongoing, willful, and active rejection of the testimony of the Holy Spirit concerning the person and truth of Christ, and it can only be committed by an unbeliever. Those who commit it, because of the hardness of their hearts, decisively reject Christ, ridicule that which is holy, and are generally unconcerned about their souls. Christians who *fear* they have committed the unpardonable sin demonstrate by their repentance that they have not done so, and the forgiveness of God is freely offered to them.

VENIAL SIN The dogma of the Roman Catholic Church traditionally divides sin into two categories—venial sin and mortal sin. Venial sin is less serious than mortal sin. It must, however, be confessed and turned from, and penance must be done, either in this life or in purgatory. The distinction between mortal and venial sin is not often made today.

WE HAVE LEFT UNDONE THOSE THINGS WHICH WE OUGHT TO HAVE DONE A statement from the general confession in the Book of Common Prayer. The confession goes on to say, "and we have done those things which we ought not to have done." These sins are also called sins of omission and sins of commission.

WHITSUNDAY See *church year.*

WITNESSING Evangelicals often use the term in the sense of personal evangelizing—sharing the Good News about Jesus Christ with another person.

A Christian worship service

WORSHIP To ascribe honor and worth to someone or something. Christians and Jews are expected to worship God and only God (see *Ten Commandments* in the chapter "People, Places, and Events in the Old Testament"). The worship of God is the essence of the life of the church and the life of the Christian. Many churches call their public gatherings *worship* services.

YAHWEH This is the personal name of God in Hebrew. When God spoke to Moses from the burning bush, he said that his name was Yahweh (Exodus 3:13–14). It means "I Am That I Am" or "I Will Be What I Will Be." This personal name was so sacred that the Jews in the centuries before Christ would not even pronounce it. When they came to the name *YHWH* (Yahweh) in the Torah, they pronounced it *Adonai. Yahweh* is usually translated "Lord" in English, and many translations put this name in small capital letters (LORD) to show that it is a translation of *Yahweh* (see the list of names for God near the entry *God the Holy Spirit*).

YESHUA This Aramaic name is translated into English as both Joshua and Jesus. It means "Yahweh saves." It is presumed that Jesus spoke Aramaic, which was the everyday language in Israel during the first century, so Jesus was probably called *Yeshua* during his life on earth. Today there are occasional references to Jesus as Yeshua, especially by Messianic Jews.

YHWH This is a transliteration of the personal name of God in Hebrew. It is sometimes called the tetragrammaton ("four letters"). In English it is usually spelled *Yahweh* or *Jehovah*.

YOM KIPPUR The contemporary Jewish celebration of the biblical Day of Atonement. It is the holiest day in the Jewish calendar.

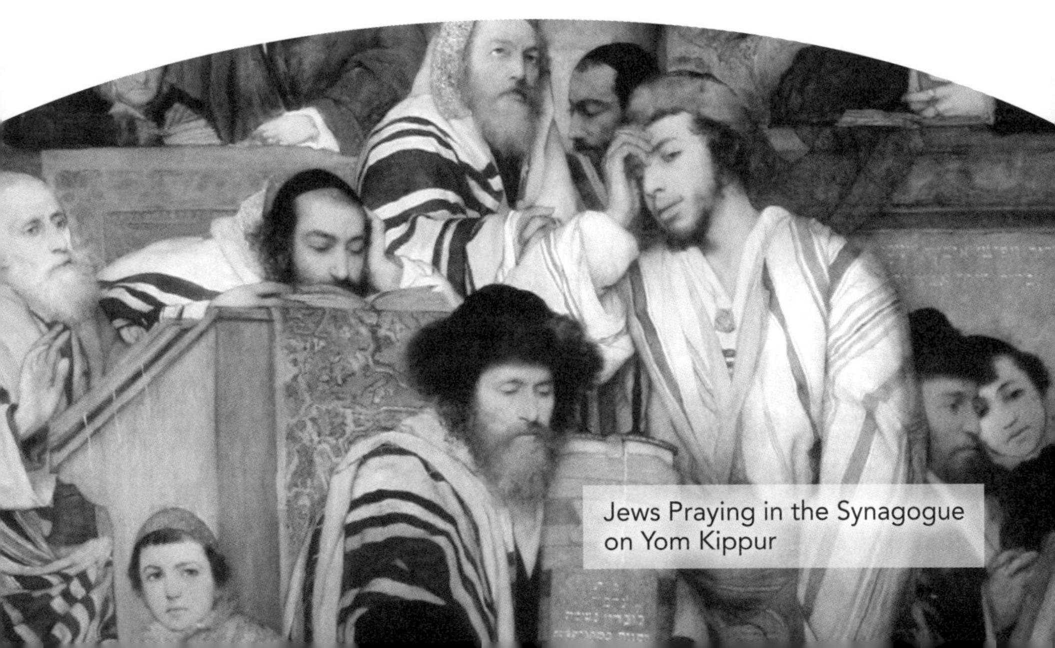

Jews Praying in the Synagogue on Yom Kippur

A Few Theological Terms

A Quiz on Theology in Everyday Life

Select one answer for each question.
Answers appear immediately after the quiz.

1 What is conversion?

a. The process of being recognized as a saint
b. Moving from nonbelief or nominal belief to an active faith
c. Stubborn sinfulness
d. The act of confession

2 What is blasphemy?

a. Turning away from the faith
b. Gossiping
c. Another term for adultery
d. Insulting or mocking God

3 What is sanctification?

a. The ongoing development of holiness in the life of the Christian
b. The act of becoming a Christian
c. The inspiration of Scripture
d. Speaking in tongues

4 Which of these Bible verses best reflects the doctrine of original sin?

a. The wages of sin is death, but the gift of God is eternal life in Christ Jesus our Lord. (Romans 6:23)
b. God demonstrates his own love for us in this: While we were still sinners, Christ died for us. (Romans 5:8 NIV)
c. Just as sin entered the world through one man, and death through sin, and in this way death came to all people, because all sinned. (Romans 5:12 NIV)
d. God so loved the world that he gave his one and only Son, that whoever believes in him shall not perish but have eternal life. (John 3:16 NIV)

5 The omnipotence of God means:

a. God is all-powerful.

b. God is present everywhere.

c. God is all-knowing.

d. God is unchangeable.

6 What is an agnostic?

a. A person who believes there is no God

b. A person who does not know if there is a God

c. A person who believes in God

d. A person who commits adultery

7 Which statement most closely reflects the traditional Protestant view of doctrine?

a. Doctrine must be validated by Scripture.

b. Doctrine is God's objective truth defined by the church.

c. The validity of doctrine is dependent on the historical and cultural context.

d. It does not matter what an individual believes as long as he or she is sincere.

8 Yahweh is:

a. The food that miraculously appeared each morning while the Israelites were in the wilderness

b. A Hebrew name for God

c. The community that created the Dead Sea Scrolls

d. A Greek word for "love"

9 What is heresy?

a. Detracting from God in any way, such as by mocking him

b. A deliberate denial and abandonment of the faith

c. Adherence to a belief that is contrary to church dogma

d. Saying one thing but doing another

10 Justification is God's action of declaring sinners righteous because of Christ. According to the New Testament, how are we justified?

a. Through sacrifices

b. By the grace of God, through faith

c. By following the Golden Rule

d. By meditating

11 **The term *rapture* is related to:**

a. Agape love

b. Eschatology

c. The transfiguration of Christ

d. The glory of God

12 **What is the mark of the beast?**

a. The mark of Cain

b. Original sin

c. An icon

d. The number 666

13 **In the Eucharist (Holy Communion), what does the wine or juice signify?**

a. The fruit of our labor

b. The body of Christ

c. The sins of mankind

d. The blood of Christ

14 **What is the fall of man?**

a. The first sin committed by each person

b. Original sin

c. Adam's disobedience by eating the forbidden fruit

d. Jesus's descent into hell after the Crucifixion

15 **Which of the following is a gift of the Holy Spirit, as described in the New Testament?**

a. Faith

b. Speaking in tongues

c. Teaching

d. All of the above

16 **According to Roman Catholic dogma, what is purgatory?**

a. The eternal resting place of the souls of unbaptized infants

b. A place where a person is purified of venial sins unforgiven on earth

c. A place of everlasting punishment for those who have committed mortal sins

d. None of the above

17 **Which of the following relates to the doctrine that God exists in three persons?**

a. The Immaculate Conception

b. The Trinity

c. The Incarnation

d. The omnipotence of God, the omnipresence of God, and the omniscience of God

18 Which term indicates the basis for reconciliation between God and sinners through the death of Christ?

a. Canonization
b. Sanctification
c. Atonement
d. Transubstantiation

19 Assisted suicide and mercy killing are examples of:

a. Ecumenism
b. Euthanasia
c. Polytheism
d. Heresy

20 Which term relates to the doctrine that God chooses the people who will receive salvation?

a. Free will
b. Consubstantiation
c. Filioque
d. Election

Answers

1. b
2. d
3. a
4. c
5. a
6. b
7. a
8. b
9. c
10. b
11. b
12. d
13. d
14. c
15. d
16. b
17. b
18. c
19. b
20. d

Famous Sayings from the Bible

English literature is filled with biblical quotations, including many titles of books (for example, Steinbeck's *East of Eden*). One can scarcely read a magazine or newspaper without finding phrases or words from the Bible, and everyday speech is peppered with sayings from the Bible.

This chapter contains many of these well-known sayings. Some entries are direct quotes, while others are paraphrased or based on biblical language or content. Most of the direct quotations are taken from the New King James Version or the original King James Version, since several instantly recognizable biblical phrases still use wording from that stately translation, even in this day of modern translations.

A HOUSE DIVIDED AGAINST ITSELF CANNOT STAND Once when Jesus cast out a demon, the scribes said he was possessed by Beelzebub (Satan). Jesus responded, "How can Satan cast out Satan? If a kingdom is divided against itself, that kingdom cannot stand. And if a house is divided against itself, that house cannot stand" (Mark 3:23–25). Abraham Lincoln quoted Jesus when he said in 1858, three years before the start of the Civil War, "'A house divided against itself cannot stand.' I believe this government cannot endure permanently half slave and half free. I do not expect the Union to be dissolved—I do not expect the house to fall—but I do expect it will cease to be divided."

A PROPHET IS NOT WITHOUT HONOR EXCEPT IN HIS OWN COUNTRY Jesus said this when he was rejected in his hometown of Nazareth after having received great acclaim in other parts of the country (Matthew 13:57). See also *Physician, heal thyself.*

A SOFT ANSWER TURNS AWAY WRATH The complete proverb reads, "A soft answer turns away wrath, but a harsh word stirs up anger" (Proverbs 15:1).

A TIME TO BE BORN, AND A TIME TO DIE One of the cycles of life mentioned in Ecclesiastes 3, which begins, "To everything there is a season, a time for every purpose under heaven."

ALL HAVE SINNED, AND FALL SHORT OF THE GLORY OF GOD This verse, Romans 3:23, means that no one measures up to God's standard of perfection. We are all sinners (see *original sin* in the chapter "Church Life and Theology"). But see the promise at the end of Romans 6:23: "The wages of sin is death, but the gift of God is eternal life in Christ Jesus our Lord."

ALL THINGS TO ALL MEN When the apostle Paul said in 1 Corinthians 9:22 that he was "all things to all men," he meant that he wanted to find common ground with each person he met so he could tell others about Christ. Perhaps this is the biblical equivalent of "When in Rome, do as the Romans do," except that Paul had a specific purpose in mind. When the phrase is used today, it often suggests that a person is wishy-washy.

ALL THINGS WORK TOGETHER FOR GOOD The complete verse (Romans 8:28) reads as follows in the King James Version: "And we know that all things work together for good to them that love God, to them who are the called according to his purpose." It does not mean that only good things will happen to those who love God, but that God will use every circumstance in their lives and turn it into something for their good.

ALL WE LIKE SHEEP HAVE GONE ASTRAY A phrase from Isaiah 53:6, in which the prophet Isaiah described the people of Israel as having wandered away from God, just as sheep tend to wander away from the shepherd.

ALL WHO LIVE BY THE SWORD SHALL DIE BY THE SWORD A paraphrase of Jesus's statement to Peter in the garden of Gethsemane, spoken after Peter drew his sword and cut off the ear of the high priest's servant (Matthew 26:52). Jesus then touched the man's ear and healed it.

AM I MY BROTHER'S KEEPER? After Adam and Eve's son Cain had killed his brother, Abel, God asked Cain where Abel was. Cain retorted, "Am I my brother's keeper?" (Genesis 4:9). The expression has come to be used in any situation in which a person

is disclaiming responsibility for another person. The title and theme of Jodi Picoult's novel *My Sister's Keeper* is a play on this biblical expression.

BE FRUITFUL AND MULTIPLY God's instruction to Adam and Eve (Genesis 1:28), telling them to populate the earth. God gave the same instruction to Noah and his family after the Flood (see *Noah* in the chapter "People, Places, and Events in the Old Testament").

BEAT THEIR SWORDS INTO PLOWSHARES This description of "the last days" is found in Isaiah 2:4 and Micah 4:3: "They will beat their swords into plowshares and their spears into pruning hooks. Nation will not take up sword against nation, nor will they train for war anymore" (NIV). This means that weapons of war will no longer be needed; they will be changed into tools used in peaceful life. In Joel 3:10, the phrase is turned around. The nations of the world are warned about the coming judgment of the Lord, and they are told, "Beat your plowshares into swords and your pruning hooks into spears." In other words, prepare yourselves; don't be complacent, and prepare to meet God.

BEATITUDES Eight concise teachings of Jesus, found in the Sermon on the Mount. The word *beatitude* is from the Latin word meaning "blessed," and each of the Beatitudes begins with the word *blessed*. In most of these statements,

Mount of Beatitudes—the traditional site of the Sermon on the Mount

Jesus took common wisdom and turned it upside down to show that man's natural perspective is usually different from God's perspective. Here is the entire text (Matthew 5:3–10 NIV):

Blessed are the poor in spirit,
for theirs is the kingdom of heaven.
Blessed are those who mourn,
for they will be comforted.
Blessed are the meek,
for they will inherit the earth.
Blessed are those who hunger and thirst for righteousness,
for they will be filled.
Blessed are the merciful,
for they will be shown mercy.
Blessed are the pure in heart,
for they will see God.
Blessed are the peacemakers,
for they will be called children of God.
Blessed are those who are persecuted because of righteousness,
for theirs is the kingdom of heaven.

BEHOLD, I STAND AT THE DOOR AND KNOCK The complete verse (Revelation 3:20) reads as follows in the King James Version: "Behold, I stand at the door, and knock: if any man hear my voice, and open the door, I will come in to him, and will sup with him, and he with me." The rendering in the New Living Translation is more contemporary: "Look! I stand at the door and knock. If you hear my voice and open the door, I will come in, and we will share a meal together as friends." The door is a metaphor for people's lives. Jesus wants to enter into our lives and have fellowship with us.

"Behold, I stand at the door and knock." (Revelation 3:20)

BLESS THE LORD, O MY SOUL A phrase found in several of the Psalms (the NIV translates it "Praise the LORD, my soul"). A very familiar passage is found in the opening verses of Psalm 103 (KJV):

Bless the LORD, O my soul: and all that is within me, bless his

holy name.
Bless the LORD, O my soul, and
forget not all his benefits.

BLESSED ARE THE MEEK, FOR THEY SHALL INHERIT THE EARTH One of the Beatitudes of Jesus (Matthew 5:5). People who are meek are usually shoved aside by those who are powerful, but Jesus was teaching that meekness is a higher value than worldly power.

BLESSED ARE THE PEACE-MAKERS, FOR THEY SHALL BE CALLED SONS OF GOD One of the Beatitudes of Jesus (Matthew 5:9). Great warriors and generals have always captured the respect and admiration of people, but Jesus was pointing out that peacemaking is one of the highest of virtues.

BLIND LEADING THE BLIND Jesus said the Pharisees were blind guides, meaning that they were spiritually blind. He also said, "Can the blind lead the blind? Will they not both fall into a pit?" (Luke 6:39 NIV). He meant that people should be careful not to choose as teachers and leaders those who are themselves spiritually blind.

BUT AS MANY AS RECEIVED HIM, TO THEM HE GAVE THE RIGHT TO BECOME CHILDREN OF GOD From John 1:12, this means that anyone who receives Jesus, whether Jew or gentile, becomes a child of God.

BY THE SKIN OF MY TEETH An expression from the book of Job. After Job had suffered many hardships, he said, "I have been reduced to skin and bones and have escaped death by the skin of my teeth" (Job 19:20 NLT). The saying describes barely escaping death or some other calamity.

BY THEIR FRUITS YOU WILL KNOW THEM A saying of Jesus from the Sermon on the Mount. He was giving a warning about false prophets. He described how people are like fruit trees: Just as bad trees yield bad fruit and good trees yield good fruit, people's motives can be judged by observing their actions.

Jesus concluded, "Therefore by their fruits you will know them" (Matthew 7:20). See also *wolf in sheep's clothing*.

CAST THE FIRST STONE The Pharisees tried to trick Jesus by bringing to him a woman who had been caught in the act of adultery. According to the Mosaic law, both the woman and the man should have been stoned to death (one wonders where the man went!). The Pharisees asked Jesus what they should do. If he said not to stone her, they would accuse Jesus of breaking the law. If he said they should stone her, he would be breaking the law of Rome, under which the Jews were not allowed to pronounce their own death penalty. Jesus saw the trap, and he also had compassion for the woman. He responded, "He that is without sin among you, let him first cast a stone at her" (John 8:7 KJV). One by one her accusers slipped away, for they all recognized sin in their own lives. When Jesus saw that her accusers had all left, he said to the woman, "Neither do I condemn you; go and sin no more" (John 8:11). In saying this, he was not excusing her sin, for he told her to sin no more. Instead, he offered a promise of forgiveness for sin. The story of the adulterous woman is not included in the earliest and most reliable Greek manuscripts. This does not necessarily mean that the event never happened. It simply means that John probably did not write the verses (John 7:53–8:11) that tell about it.

CAST YOUR BREAD UPON THE WATERS An expression in the book of Ecclesiastes (11:1). The entire verse in the New King James Version says, "Cast your bread upon the waters, for you will find it after many days." It is an admonition to faith and to generosity. This verse is paraphrased in *The Living Bible*, "Give generously, for your gifts will return to you later."

CHILDREN, OBEY YOUR PARENTS An admonition from the apostle Paul in his letters to the Ephesians (6:1) and the Colossians (3:20). This statement is a paraphrase of one of the Ten Commandments: "Honor your father and your mother."

COME TO ME, ALL YOU WHO ARE WEARY Jesus said, "Come to me, all you who are weary and burdened, and I will give you rest" (Matthew 11:28 NIV). He meant that he wanted to provide peace of mind and the confidence that comes from doing the will of God. He also meant that it was no longer necessary to work at keeping the Mosaic law to achieve salvation. Through Jesus's death and resurrection, there would be a new way for people to be reconciled with God.

CONSIDER THE LILIES OF THE FIELD In the Sermon on the Mount, Jesus taught his followers not to worry about things such as food, drink, or clothing since God would take care of their physical needs. Instead, they should seek the kingdom of heaven. He said, "Why are you anxious about clothing? Consider the lilies of the field, how they grow: they neither toil nor spin, yet I tell you, even Solomon in all his glory was not arrayed like one of these. But if God so clothes the grass of the field, which today is alive and tomorrow is thrown into the oven, will he not much more clothe you, O you of little faith?" (Matthew 6:28–30 ESV).

CUP OF COLD WATER Jesus said, "If you give even a cup of cold water to one of the least of my followers, you will surely be rewarded" (Matthew 10:42 NLT).

DO NOT CAST YOUR PEARLS BEFORE SWINE Jesus said this as part of the Sermon on the Mount (Matthew 7:6). He meant that it is useless to try to teach holy things to unholy or unbelieving people.

DO THIS IN REMEMBRANCE OF ME Jesus said this at the Last Supper (Luke 22:19). He was instructing his disciples—and all Christians—to observe the Lord's Supper as a reminder of his death. Nearly 2,000 years later, Christians around the world do so every time they take Communion. These words are often carved on tables used for Communion in Protestant churches.

DO TO OTHERS WHAT YOU WOULD HAVE THEM DO TO YOU A paraphrase of one of Jesus's teachings in the Sermon on the Mount. Matthew 7:12 in the New Living Translation phrases it, "Do to others whatever you would like them to do to you." Also called the Golden Rule, this teaching is central to much of what is considered civilized behavior in Western cultures.

DUST THOU ART, AND UNTO DUST SHALT THOU RETURN When Adam and Eve sinned, God banished them from the Garden of Eden and pronounced a curse upon the earth. He said to Adam, "Dust thou art, and unto dust shalt thou return" (Genesis 3:19 KJV). He was reminding Adam that he had been created from "the dust of the ground" (Genesis 2:7), and he was telling Adam that he and his descendants would all die because of their sin (see *fall of man* in the chapter "People, Places, and Events in the Old Testament"). In the traditional Christian funeral service, the minister sprinkles soil (dust) on the casket before it is buried and says, "Earth to earth, ashes to ashes, dust to dust." This is a reminder to those present that all will die and "return to dust."

EARTH WAS WITHOUT FORM, AND VOID The first two verses of the book of Genesis, read as follows in the New King James Version: "In the beginning God created the heavens and the earth. The earth was without form, and void; and darkness was on the face of the deep." The account then goes on to describe the creation.

EAT, DRINK, AND BE MERRY An expression from the book of Ecclesiastes (8:15). Solomon advises people to seek out and enjoy the good things in life as they carry out their daily responsibilities.

Communion table

EYE FOR EYE, TOOTH FOR TOOTH According to the Mosaic law (Deuteronomy 19:21), the penalty for gouging out a person's eye was that the offender's eye was to be gouged out. Similarly, knocking out a tooth resulted in loss of a tooth for the offender. This concept of justice called for a penalty equal to—but not greater than—the offense. Jesus made reference to this law when he said, "You have heard that it was said, 'Eye for eye, and tooth for tooth.' But I tell you, do not resist an evil person. If anyone slaps you on the right cheek, turn to them the other cheek also" (Matthew 5:38–39 NIV). See also *Turn the other cheek*; *Heap coals of fire on his head.*

EYE OF A NEEDLE A rich man asked Jesus what he could do to get eternal life. Jesus told him to keep the commandments, sell his possessions, give to the poor, and follow him. The man went away sad, because he had great wealth. "Jesus said to his disciples, 'I tell you the truth, it is very hard for a rich person to enter the Kingdom of Heaven. I'll say it again—it is easier for a camel to go through the eye of a needle than for a rich person to enter the Kingdom of God!' The disciples were astounded. 'Then who in the world can be saved?' they asked. Jesus looked at them intently and said, 'Humanly speaking, it is impossible. But with God everything is possible'" (Matthew 19:23–26 NLT). Even rich people can get into heaven if God brings them in, but wealth is a liability, not an asset, in one's spiritual journey. This "eye of a needle" has often been defined as a small doorway that a camel could get through only with great difficulty. There is no historical evidence that such doors were called eyes of a needle, and such an interpretation seems contrary to the intent of Jesus's teaching.

FAITH AS SMALL AS A MUSTARD SEED Jesus used a mustard seed, which is tiny, as an example of the power of even a small amount of faith. He said, "If you have faith as small as a mustard seed, you can say to this mountain, 'Move from here to there,' and it will move. Nothing will be impossible for you" (Matthew 17:20 NIV).

FAITH, HOPE, AND LOVE The beautiful thirteenth chapter of 1 Corinthians ("the love chapter") stresses the importance of love (it is translated "charity" in the King James Version). The chapter ends with the statement, "These three remain: faith, hope and love. But the greatest of these is love" (verse 13 NIV).

FATHER, FORGIVE THEM; FOR THEY KNOW NOT WHAT THEY DO Jesus spoke these words as he was suffering on the cross (Luke 23:34 KJV). He was referring to those who were responsible for his crucifixion. See also *seven last words of Christ* in the chapter "People, Places, and Events in the New Testament."

FISHERS OF MEN Jesus's first disciples were Andrew and Peter, James and John, all of whom were commercial fishermen on the Sea of Galilee. Jesus said to them, "Follow me, and I will make you fishers of men" (Matthew 4:19 KJV). He meant they would be able to spend their time spreading the Good News of salvation to others rather than simply catching fish.

FOLLOW ME Jesus said this to Peter and Andrew and James and John when he invited them to be his disciples. Since they were all fishermen, he also said, "I will make you fishers of men" (Matthew 4:19) (see *fishers of men*).

FOR GOD SO LOVED THE WORLD The phrase that begins John 3:16, one of the best-known and best-loved verses in the Bible. The complete text, as found in the King James Version: "For God so loved the world, that he gave his only begotten Son, that whosoever believeth in him should not perish, but have everlasting life."

FOR SUCH A TIME AS THIS Esther was a Jewish woman who had been selected because of her beauty to become the wife of King Ahasuerus (Xerxes) of Persia. When her older cousin and foster father, Mordecai, heard that the prime minister, Haman, had launched a plan to kill all the Jews in the kingdom, he urged Esther to ask the king to countermand the plan. Mordecai sent her a message that said, "Who knows but that you have come to your royal position for such a time as this?" (Esther 4:14 NIV). The entire story is told in the book of Esther. 📌 The expression can be used today in a situation where a person seems uniquely suited to carry out a difficult task. See also *If I perish, I perish.*

FORGIVE US OUR TRESPASSES This is a phrase from the Lord's Prayer, as it is printed in the Book of Common Prayer. The complete sentence is, "Forgive us our trespasses, as we forgive those who trespass against us." An alternate reading, often used in public worship, is, "Forgive us our debts, as we forgive our debtors" (Matthew 6:12). It is a request that God forgive us for having sinned against him, just as we forgive those who sin against us. But it is also a challenge to be forgiving, for the converse of this request is that God will forgive us only a little if we forgive others only a little.

GET BEHIND ME, SATAN Jesus said these words on two different occasions. During the temptation of Jesus, Satan took Jesus to the top of a high mountain and showed him all the kingdoms of the world. Then Satan said he would give all this to Jesus if Jesus would bow down and worship him. Jesus responded, "Get behind Me, Satan! For it is written, 'You shall worship the LORD your God, and Him only you shall serve'" (Luke 4:8). He was quoting from Deuteronomy 6. Toward the end of his ministry on earth, Jesus told his disciples that he would be killed, but that he would come back to life again in three days. Peter took him aside and told him he should not say such things. Jesus rebuked Peter by saying, "Get behind me, Satan!" (Matthew 16:23 NIV). He meant that Peter was being used as Satan's instrument. Jesus went on to say that Peter was looking at the situation only from a human point of view, not a divine point of view. 📌 Today a related phrase—"Not today, Satan"—is also used. It expresses a determination not to allow Satan to frustrate, hinder, or wreck God's agenda for our day and our lives.

GIVE TO CAESAR WHAT BELONGS TO CAESAR The Pharisees wanted to trap Jesus, so they asked him whether it was right to pay taxes to Rome. Jesus perceived their trick, so he took a coin and asked whose image was on it. When they responded that it was Caesar's, he said, "Give to Caesar what belongs to Caesar, and give to God what belongs to God" (Mark 12:17 NLT). He meant that although people are obligated to pay earthly possessions to earthly governments, their very lives belong to God, so they should submit themselves to God.

GIVE US THIS DAY OUR DAILY BREAD A phrase from the Lord's Prayer. It is a request that God provide us with daily food. The Lord's Prayer is found in Matthew 6:9–13.

GLORIA IN EXCELSIS DEO Latin for "Glory to God in the highest." This was the chorus of the angels who appeared to the shepherds outside Bethlehem on the night of Jesus's birth (Luke 2:14).

GLORY TO GOD IN THE HIGHEST, AND ON EARTH PEACE, GOOD WILL TOWARD MEN The chorus of the angels who announced the birth of Jesus to the shepherds in the fields outside Bethlehem (Luke 2:14). The Latin text is also familiar from Christmas carols: *Gloria in excelsis Deo*. The familiar Christmas narrative from the Gospel of Luke is presented in the entry for *Nativity* in the chapter "People, Places, and Events in the New Testament."

GO AND SIN NO MORE See *Cast the first stone*.

GO INTO ALL THE WORLD The first phrase of the Great Commission, in which Jesus instructed his disciples to preach the gospel throughout the world (Mark 16:15).

GO THE SECOND MILE In the days of Jesus, Roman soldiers could require common citizens to carry their gear for them. In the Sermon on the Mount, Jesus taught his listeners to go an extra mile if a soldier compelled them to go one mile: "If anyone forces you to go one mile, go with them two miles" (Matthew 5:41 NIV). The saying can be applied to any situation in which a person willingly goes beyond what is required.

GOD CREATED MAN IN HIS OWN IMAGE The account of the creation in Genesis includes this poetic description of the creation of the first man and woman (Genesis 1:27 NIV): "So God created mankind in his own image, in the image of God he created them; male and female he created them." This does not mean that God is human in form. Adam and Eve were created in the image of God in the sense that they had intelligence and free will and were capable of loving God and each other.

GOD IS LOVE The apostle John wrote to the early Christians, "Dear friends, let us love one another, for love comes from God. Everyone who loves has been born of God and knows God. Whoever does not love does not know God, because God is love" (1 John 4:7–8 NIV).

GOOD SAMARITAN Jesus responded to the question "Who is my neighbor?" by telling the story of the Good Samaritan (Luke 10:25–37). A Jewish man was attacked by thieves and was badly injured. Two religious leaders walked past him without stopping to help. Then a Samaritan man stopped and took the injured man to an inn and paid for his medical

Remains of an ancient Roman road. Jesus said, "If anyone forces you to go one mile, go with them two miles" (Matthew 5:41 NIV).

care. The Samaritans were seen by the Jews as an inferior class of people, so Jesus was showing that anyone can and should be a neighbor to someone who is in need. Today the term *Good Samaritan* is used in reference to anyone who stops to help a person in need.

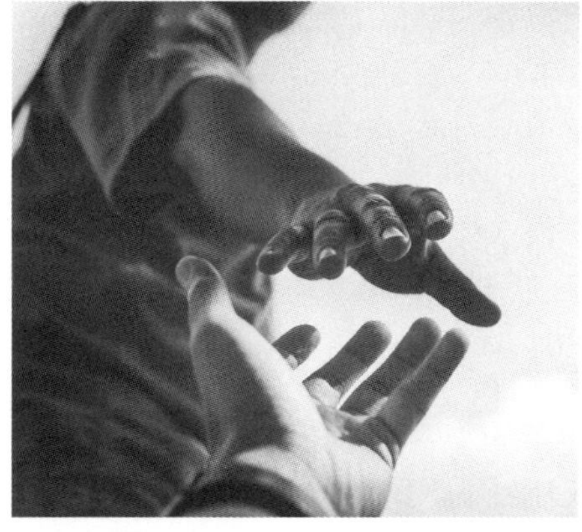

GOOD TIDINGS OF GREAT JOY When the angel appeared to the shepherds to announce the birth of Jesus, he said, "Do not be afraid, for behold, I bring you good tidings of great joy which will be to all people. For there is born to you this day in the city of David a Savior, who is Christ the Lord" (Luke 2:10–11).

HE THAT IS NOT WITH ME IS AGAINST ME Jesus said this to show that there is no middle ground—either a person believes in Jesus or is his enemy. The quotation is found in Matthew 12:30.

HEAP COALS OF FIRE ON HIS HEAD In Romans 12:20, Paul quoted from Proverbs 25:22 in teaching that we are not to avenge ourselves: "If your enemy is hungry, feed him; if he is thirsty, give him a drink; for in so doing you will heap coals of fire on his head." In other words, he will feel ashamed of himself for what he has done. Today the expression is used in any situation in which a person will feel ashamed because of kindness shown to him after he has been unkind.

HEAR, O ISRAEL: THE LORD OUR GOD IS ONE LORD (KJV) This great declaration of monotheism is found in Deuteronomy 6:4. Belief in one God was one feature that distinguished the people of Israel from those in the nations around them.

HONOR YOUR FATHER AND YOUR MOTHER One of the Ten Commandments (Exodus 20:12). It does not require explanation—except to children!

I AM THE LIGHT OF THE WORLD As recorded in the Gospel of John, Jesus frequently used light as a metaphor for his role in the world. Jesus said, "I am the light of the world. Whoever follows me will never walk in darkness, but will have the light of life" (John 8:12 NIV). See also *You are the light of the world*; *Your word is a lamp to my feet.*

I AM THE RESURRECTION AND THE LIFE After Lazarus had died, Jesus went to Bethany, where he said to Martha, "Your brother will rise again." She responded, "Yes ... he will rise when everyone else rises, at the last day." Jesus then said, "I am the resurrection and the life. Anyone who believes in me will live, even after dying. Everyone who lives in me and believes in me will never ever die" (John 11:23–26 NLT). Jesus was predicting his own death and resurrection, and he meant that anyone who believed in him would be raised again to eternal life. Jesus then went to Lazarus's tomb and raised him back to physical life.

I AM THE WAY, THE TRUTH, AND THE LIFE Jesus told his disciples he was going to his Father's house (by which he meant heaven), and that they would join him there. Thomas said, "'Lord, we don't know where you are going, so how can we know the way?' Jesus answered, 'I am the way and the truth and the life. No one comes to the Father except through me'" (John 14:5–6 NIV).

I WILL NEVER LEAVE YOU OR FORSAKE YOU The book of Hebrews (13:5) makes this statement, quoting from the book of Deuteronomy. Moses was preparing the people of Israel for their entrance into the Promised Land, where they would fight the Canaanites. Moses said, "Be strong and courageous. Do not be afraid or terrified because of them, for the LORD your God goes with you; he will never leave you nor forsake you" (Deuteronomy 31:6 NIV).

IF I PERISH, I PERISH Esther was a Jewish woman who had been selected because of her beauty to become a member of the harem of

King Ahasuerus (Xerxes) of Persia. She later became queen. When her cousin and foster father, Mordecai, heard that Haman had launched a plan to kill all the Jews in the kingdom, he urged Esther to ask the king to countermand the plan. Although she was the queen, she could be put to death for approaching the king without being invited. Before going in to see the king, she said, "If I perish, I perish!" (Esther 4:16). The king agreed to see Esther, and the plan to exterminate the Jews was reversed. The entire story is told in the book of Esther. The Jewish holiday of Purim commemorates this rescue of the Jews. See also *for such a time as this.*

IF YOU LOVE ME, KEEP MY COMMANDMENTS Jesus was speaking to his disciples when he said this (John 14:15). It is part of a lengthy discourse that occurred after the Last Supper while they were still together in the Upper Room (see *Last Supper* in the chapter "People, Places, and Events in the New Testament.").

IN MY FATHER'S HOUSE ARE MANY MANSIONS Jesus spoke these words in telling his disciples that he would soon be returning to his Father in heaven and that he would prepare a place for them there (John 14:1–4). Modern translations use the word *rooms* rather than *mansions*, but the size of our abode there is not significant. The important point is that we will be with God in heaven.

IN THE BEGINNING The opening words of the book of Genesis and the Gospel of John. The first verse of Genesis reads: "In the beginning God created the heavens and the earth." John purposely began his Gospel with a parallel statement: "In the beginning was the Word, and the Word was with God, and the Word was God." John meant that Jesus, the Word, had existed in the very beginning with God.

INTO YOUR HANDS I COMMIT MY SPIRIT One of the seven last words of Christ as he hung on the cross (Luke 23:46). He was speaking to God the Father.

IT IS FINISHED Jesus's last words before he died on the cross, as recorded in John 19:30. See also *seven last words of Christ* in the chapter "People, Places, and Events in the New Testament."

IT IS MORE BLESSED TO GIVE THAN TO RECEIVE In one of the apostle Paul's sermons in the book of Acts (20:35), he quoted this as a saying of Jesus, although it is not recorded as such in any of the Gospels.

JOHN 3:16 If a person has memorized only one verse from the Bible, it is probably John 3:16: "For God so loved the world that he gave his one and only Son, that whoever believes in him shall not perish but have eternal life" (NIV).

JUBILATE DEO Latin for "O be joyful in the Lord." This is a translation of the opening phrase of Psalm 100. See also *Make a joyful noise unto the Lord.*

JUDGE NOT, THAT YOU BE NOT JUDGED A saying of Jesus from the Sermon on the Mount (Matthew 7:1). He was reminding his listeners that everyone sins, and those who point out the sin in others will have their own sins pointed out. See also *Cast the first stone.*

KILL THE FATTED CALF A fatted calf is a calf that is ready to be slaughtered and eaten as part of a special feast. In Jesus's Parable of the Prodigal Son (Luke 15), the father tells his servants to "bring the fatted calf here and kill it" and prepare a feast in honor of his son who has returned (Luke 15:23–24). Today the expression can refer to preparation for any gala event.

LAY NOT UP FOR YOURSELVES TREASURES UPON EARTH This is part of Jesus's teaching from the Sermon on the Mount: "Do not lay up for yourselves treasures on earth, where moth and rust destroy and where thieves break in and steal; but lay up for yourselves treasures in heaven, where neither moth nor rust destroys and where thieves do not break in and steal. For where your treasure is, there your heart will be also" (Matthew 6:19–21).

LEAD US NOT INTO TEMPTATION A phrase from the Lord's Prayer, found in Matthew 6:9–13. It is a request that God protect the believer from falling into temptation. 📌 In 2017 Pope Francis suggested that a better English translation might be "Do not let us fall into temptation." This is similar to the New Living Translation: "Don't let us yield to temptation."

LET MY PEOPLE GO When Moses went to Pharaoh (king of Egypt) to demand that he release the Israelites from slavery, he said, "Let my people go" (Exodus 5:1 NLT). God sent plagues upon Egypt to encourage Pharaoh to respond, but Pharaoh steadfastly refused. He finally relented when God sent the final plague, the death of the firstborn in every household in Egypt (see *plagues of Egypt* in the chapter "People, Places, and Events in the Old Testament"). The Israelites then left Egypt, an event called the Exodus. 📌 The slavery of Black people in America has often been compared to the Israelites' slavery in Egypt. For that reason, Abraham Lincoln, the Great Emancipator, is sometimes likened to Moses. Harriet Tubman, a leader in the Underground Railroad and formerly enslaved herself, was nicknamed Moses.

LET THE DEAD BURY THEIR DEAD One of Jesus's followers said he wanted to bury his father before following Jesus. Jesus responded, "Follow me; and let the dead bury their dead" (Matthew 8:22 KJV). He meant that those who were spiritually dead could care for their own dead, but he expected his followers to put obedience to him above earthly concerns.

LET THERE BE LIGHT In the Genesis account of the creation, God created light with the command, "Let there be light" (Genesis 1:3).

LORD'S PRAYER When Jesus's disciples asked him how they should pray, he taught them a prayer that is recorded in Matthew 6:9–13 (compare Luke 11:2–4). It is recited regularly in many Protestant and Roman Catholic churches. Some churches say "Forgive us our debts," and some say "Forgive us our trespasses." Catholics do not usually include the last two lines of the prayer. Some churches use modern translations. Here is one form of the prayer:

Our Father in heaven,
hallowed be your name.
Your kingdom come,
your will be done,
on earth as it is in heaven.
Give us this day our daily bread,
and forgive us our debts,
as we also have forgiven our debtors.
And lead us not into temptation,
But deliver us from evil.
For yours is the kingdom, and the power,
and the glory, forever. Amen.

LOVE CHAPTER (1 CORINTHIANS 13) In the New King James Version, this beautiful chapter begins, "Though I speak with the tongues of men and of angels, but have not love, I have become sounding brass or a clanging cymbal." The last verse reads, "And now abide faith, hope, love, these three; but the greatest of these is love." (A passage from the love chapter is presented in three different translations near the entry for *translation* in the chapter "Bible Overview.")

LOVE THE LORD YOUR GOD WITH ALL YOUR HEART, SOUL, AND MIND See *You shall love the Lord your God with all your heart, with all your soul, and with all your mind.*

LOVE YOUR ENEMIES In the same discourse as the Beatitudes, Jesus again took common wisdom and turned it upside down to show that human wisdom is often contrary to God's wisdom: "I say to you, love your enemies, bless those who curse you, do good to those who hate you, and pray for those who spitefully use you and persecute you" (Matthew 5:44). See also *Turn the other cheek*; *Heap coals of fire on his head.*

LOVE YOUR NEIGHBOR AS YOURSELF In Luke 10:25–29, a lawyer asked Jesus what he must do to gain eternal life. Jesus responded by asking him what was written in the Law. The man said, "'You shall love the LORD your God with all your heart, with all your soul, with all your strength, and with all your mind,' and 'your neighbor as yourself.'" The man was not quoting directly from the Ten Commandments, but was paraphrasing from several passages in Exodus and Leviticus. Jesus responded, "Do this and you will live." When the man then asked, "Who is my neighbor?" Jesus responded by telling the Parable of the Good Samaritan.

MAKE A JOYFUL NOISE UNTO THE LORD The opening phrase of Psalm 100 (KJV): "Make a joyful noise unto the LORD, all ye lands. Serve the LORD with gladness: come before his presence with singing." See also *Jubilate Deo.*

MAN SHALL NOT LIVE BY BREAD ALONE During the temptation of Jesus in the wilderness, when he was very hungry after fasting for forty days and nights, Satan tempted him to turn stones into bread. Jesus responded by quoting from Deuteronomy 8:3: "It is written, 'Man shall not live by bread alone, but by every word that proceeds from the mouth of God'" (Matthew 4:4). 📌 Today the saying is still relevant, but it can also refer to a person's need for emotional and spiritual sustenance.

MANY ARE CALLED, BUT FEW ARE CHOSEN Jesus said this to illustrate that God calls all people to respond to him, but relatively few choose to follow him (Matthew 22:14). See also *Wide is the gate and broad is the way that leads to destruction.*

MY CUP RUNS OVER A line from the Twenty-Third Psalm. David, the psalmist, used this metaphor to mean that he was filled with joy. For the complete text of the psalm, see *Twenty-Third Psalm*.

MY GOD, MY GOD, WHY HAVE YOU FORSAKEN ME? Jesus said this while he was suffering on the cross (Matthew 27:46 NIV). He was quoting the first verse of Psalm 22. Jesus had never sinned, yet he was dying as a sacrifice to make atonement for the sins of all people. For a brief period of time (until he was raised from the dead), Jesus was separated from the presence of God the Father. That was more painful to him than the excruciating physical pain of hanging on the cross.

NO ONE CAN SERVE TWO MASTERS A teaching of Jesus from the Sermon on the Mount (Matthew 6:24 NIV). He went on to say, "You cannot serve both God and money." Jesus meant that a person cannot make wealth his primary pursuit and also seek a right relationship with God. One or the other will win out as "master" and the guiding force in a person's life.

NOTHING NEW UNDER THE SUN An expression from the book of Ecclesiastes (1:9). In the three thousand years since the days of Solomon, millions of inventions have been created. Our lives are very different now, even compared to the days of our grandparents. But many aspects of life have not changed: Both good and evil exist in the world; there is work to be done; and there is love in our hearts for friends and family. In those respects, there is "nothing new under the sun."

OF MAKING MANY BOOKS THERE IS NO END If this was true in Solomon's day (Ecclesiastes 12:12), then how much more is it true today!

OUR FATHER WHICH ART IN HEAVEN The beginning of the Lord's Prayer, as quoted from the King James Version. For a contemporary version of the complete text, see *Lord's Prayer*.

PHYSICIAN, HEAL THYSELF When Jesus returned to his hometown of Nazareth after performing many miracles in other towns, he anticipated that his friends and neighbors would demand that he perform miracles for them also: "You will undoubtedly quote me this proverb: 'Physician, heal yourself'—meaning, 'Do miracles here in your hometown like those you did in Capernaum'" (Luke

4:23 NLT). He went on to say, however, that a prophet is not without honor except in his own country.

REMEMBER THE SABBATH DAY, TO KEEP IT HOLY One of the Ten Commandments (Exodus 20:8). By the time of Jesus, the Pharisees had added hundreds of laws to the Mosaic law, including many laws concerning the Sabbath. Jesus said, "The Sabbath was made to meet the needs of people, and not people to meet the requirements of the Sabbath" (Mark 2:27 NLT).

SALT OF THE EARTH A saying of Jesus in the Sermon on the Mount: "You are the salt of the earth. But what good is salt if it has lost its flavor?" (Matthew 5:13 NLT). He used salt as a metaphor to mean that his followers are to influence the world around them, just as salt adds flavor whenever it is added to food. Salt can also be used as a preservative. The expression "salt of the earth" is now used to refer to a good, decent, hardworking person—the sort of person one would want as a neighbor.

SEEK AND YOU WILL FIND One of the teachings of Jesus from the Sermon on the Mount (Matthew 7:7). He was teaching that God wants to give good gifts to anyone who asks him for them. The entire quotation is, "Ask and it will be given to you; seek and you will find; knock and the door will be opened to you" (NIV).

SEPARATING THE SHEEP FROM THE GOATS Jesus once described the Judgment Day as a time when God will separate the sheep from the goats. The sheep, representing people who showed God's love to others, will receive an eternal reward. The goats, representing those who did not show God's love to others, will receive eternal punishment. Another frequent interpretation is that the sheep represent believers and the goats represent nonbelievers. The parable is found in Matthew 25:31–46.

STRAIGHT AND NARROW A popular expression sourced from

Jesus's statement, "Strait [narrow] is the gate, and narrow is the way, which leadeth unto life, and few there be that find it" (Matthew 7:14 KJV). To "stay on the straight and narrow" is to try to do what is right, particularly in the face of temptation to sin. See also *Wide is the gate and broad is the way that leads to destruction.*

STRAIN OUT A GNAT AND SWALLOW A CAMEL Jesus said this of the scribes and Pharisees as a metaphor for their hypocrisy: "Blind guides, who strain out a gnat and swallow a camel!" (Matthew 23:24). They followed some of the tiny details of the Mosaic law (for example, they strained their water to avoid swallowing a gnat, which was a ritually unclean animal), but they neglected far weightier aspects of the law (such as caring for widows and orphans). See also *blind leading the blind.*

SUFFER THE LITTLE CHILDREN TO COME UNTO ME One day some parents brought their children to Jesus so he could bless them, but the disciples told them Jesus was too busy. When Jesus saw that the disciples had rebuked the parents, he was indignant. The King James Version quotes Jesus as saying, "Suffer the little children to come unto me, and forbid them not: for of such is the kingdom of God" (Mark 10:14–15). The saying is confusing because the word *suffer* no longer means "allow." The New International Version reads, "Let the little children come to me, and do not hinder them, for the kingdom of God belongs to such as these. Truly I tell you, anyone who will not receive the kingdom of God like a little child will never enter it." Jesus then took the children in his arms and blessed them.

THE FIRST SHALL BE LAST One of the teachings of Jesus (Matthew 19:30). He meant that those who are not powerful or wealthy in this life will be greatest in the kingdom of heaven if they have followed him. Those who are wealthy and powerful will be the least in the kingdom of heaven (if they get there at all) if they have put worldly concerns first in this life. See also the entry for *eye of a needle*.

THE HEAVENS DECLARE THE GLORY OF GOD This beautiful passage from Psalm 19 is a reminder that all of creation shows God's creative splendor.

THE JUST SHALL LIVE BY FAITH This statement, found several times in the New Testament (for example, Romans 1:17), is a quotation from Habakkuk 2:4. It was one of the verses that helped the Reformer Martin Luther understand the concept of justification by grace, through faith.

THE LETTER KILLS, BUT THE SPIRIT GIVES LIFE A phrase from 2 Corinthians 3:6, in which Paul was contrasting the old covenant of the law and the new covenant of grace. He meant that trying to follow the Mosaic law "to the letter" will only result in death, but to follow the Holy Spirit will result in eternal life.

THE LORD BLESS YOU AND KEEP YOU The Lord told Moses that Aaron was to bless the people of Israel with this blessing: "The LORD bless you and keep you; the LORD make his face to shine upon you and be gracious to you; the LORD lift up his countenance upon you and give you peace" (Numbers 6:24–26 ESV). This blessing is frequently used as a benediction in Protestant churches today. It has also been featured as a popular praise and worship song.

"The heavens declare the glory of God." (Psalm 19:1)

THE LORD IS MY SHEPHERD The opening line of the Twenty-Third Psalm, the best-known of all the Psalms. For the complete text, see *Twenty-Third Psalm*.

THE LOVE OF MONEY IS THE ROOT OF ALL EVIL In 1 Timothy 6:10, the apostle Paul warns Timothy that a person who wants to be wealthy will be tempted to commit sin in order to gain wealth: "The love of money is a root of all kinds of evil, for which some have strayed from the faith in their greediness, and pierced themselves through with many sorrows." This expression is commonly misquoted as "Money is the root of all evil."

THE SPIRIT IS WILLING, BUT THE FLESH IS WEAK Shortly before Jesus was betrayed in the garden of Gethsemane, he asked his disciples Peter, James, and John to pray with him. They had fallen asleep while they were praying, and Jesus said, "Watch and pray so that you will not fall into temptation. The spirit is willing, but the flesh is weak" (Matthew 26:41 NIV). He meant that it is sometimes hard to follow through even when we have the best of intentions.

THE WAGES OF SIN IS DEATH This is the first phrase of a well-known verse from Paul's epistle to the Romans: "For the wages of sin is death, but the gift of God is eternal life in Christ Jesus our Lord" (Romans 6:23). It means that all people deserve to die because of their sin, but God has provided eternal life in heaven for anyone who believes in Jesus Christ.

THE WOLF SHALL DWELL WITH THE LAMB This phrase is from a prophetic passage in Isaiah 11:6: "The wolf shall dwell with the lamb, and the leopard shall lie down with the young goat, and the calf and the lion and the fattened calf together; and a little child shall lead them" (ESV). It is an example of the peace that will prevail at the coming of the Messiah.

THIS IS MY BELOVED SON, IN WHOM I AM WELL PLEASED A voice from heaven made this proclamation on two different occasions—when Jesus was baptized by John the Baptist (Matthew 3:17) and at the Transfiguration (Matthew 17:5). God the Father was identifying Jesus as his Son.

THIS IS MY BODY, WHICH IS BROKEN FOR YOU Jesus said this at the Last Supper as he broke the bread and shared it with his disciples (1 Corinthians 11:24). He meant that he would soon die, and that his death was for their benefit (as an atonement for the sins of mankind). This phrase is usually repeated as part of the Communion service. ➷ It has long been suggested that the pretend incantation *hocus-pocus* was originally a parody of the Latin phrase *hoc est corpus meum* ("this is my body") used in the Roman Catholic Mass.

THIS IS THE DAY THE LORD HAS MADE A popular verse from Psalm 118:24: "This is the day the LORD has made; we will rejoice and be glad in it."

THROUGH A GLASS, DARKLY In 1 Corinthians 13 (the love chapter), Paul used the metaphor of looking into a clouded glass (a mirror) to show that believers cannot presently fully understand God. But eventually they will see God face-to-face, and then they will know him more fully: "Now we see through a glass, darkly; but then face to face: now I know in part; but then shall I know even as also I am known" (1 Corinthians 13:12 KJV). See also *faith, hope, and love.*

TO EVERYTHING THERE IS A SEASON In Ecclesiastes 3:1, Solomon wrote, "To everything there is a season, a time for every purpose under heaven." Then follows a long and poetic list of opposites, including "a time to be born, and a time to die ... a time to mourn, and a time to dance ... a time of war, and a time of peace."

TRAIN UP A CHILD IN THE WAY HE SHOULD GO The entire quotation from Proverbs 22:6 is: "Train up a child in the way he should go, and when he is old he will not depart from it." It is a reminder that a child's early training affects the rest of his or her life.

TURN THE OTHER CHEEK In the Sermon on the Mount, Jesus taught his followers not to resist violence. He said, "Do not resist an evil person! If someone slaps you on the right cheek, offer the other cheek also" (Matthew 5:39 NLT). The expression can be used in any situation in which a person whose rights are violated refuses to retaliate. See also *Go the second mile*; *Heap coals of fire on his head*. This teaching of Jesus was one of the bases for the nonviolent resistance advocated by Mahatma Gandhi and Martin Luther King Jr.

TWENTY-THIRD PSALM The best-known and best-loved of all the psalms of the Old Testament. The complete text follows:

The LORD is my shepherd;
I shall not want.
He makes me to lie down in
green pastures;
He leads me beside the
still waters.
He restores my soul;
He leads me in the paths of
righteousness
For His name's sake.
Yea, though I walk through the
valley of the shadow of death,
I will fear no evil;
For You are with me;
Your rod and Your staff, they
comfort me.
You prepare a table before me in
the presence of my enemies;
You anoint my head with oil;
My cup runs over.
Surely goodness and mercy shall
follow me
All the days of my life;
And I will dwell in the house of
the LORD
Forever.

TWO SHALL BE ONE FLESH In the Genesis account of creation, God created Eve from Adam's rib, and Adam said, "This is now bone of my bones and flesh of my flesh." The text goes on to say, "Therefore a man shall leave his father and mother and be joined to his wife, and they shall become one flesh" (Genesis 2:23–24). In answer to a question about divorce, Jesus quoted this passage of Scripture and went on to say, "Therefore what God has joined together, let not man separate" (Matthew 19:6). See also *What God hath joined together, let not man put asunder.*

UNTO US A CHILD IS BORN Isaiah 9:6 contains this beautiful and familiar description of the coming Messiah: "For unto us a child is born, unto us a son is given: and the government shall be upon his shoulder: and his name shall be called Wonderful, Counsellor, The mighty God, The everlasting Father, The Prince of Peace" (KJV).

VALLEY OF THE SHADOW OF DEATH A phrase from the Twenty-Third Psalm. David, the psalmist, used this as a metaphor alluding to situations in which he had been near death. For the complete text, see *Twenty-Third Psalm.* ✎ This phrase has come to mean any situation in which one encounters the perils of life, especially a close brush with death.

VANITY OF VANITIES, ALL IS VANITY The book of Ecclesiastes begins with this gloomy statement (1:2). Solomon meant that everything is futile. He goes on to describe the futility of work, wisdom, pleasure, wealth, and knowledge, but in the end he concludes, "Fear God and keep his commands, for this is everyone's duty" (12:13 NLT).

VOICE OF ONE CRYING IN THE WILDERNESS When the Jewish leaders asked John the Baptist if he was the long-awaited Messiah, he said he was not. He went on to say, "I am 'the voice of one crying in the wilderness: "Make straight the way of the LORD"'" (John 1:23). He was quoting from the prophecy of Isaiah (40:3), and he meant that he was the spokesman whose role was to announce the coming of the Messiah. ✎ The expression is sometimes used today if a person has an important message but can't get anyone to listen.

WHAT GOD HATH JOINED TOGETHER, LET NOT MAN PUT ASUNDER When Jesus was asked a question about divorce, he quoted the passage from the account of the creation in Genesis that says, "Therefore a man shall leave his father and mother and be joined to his wife, and they shall become one flesh" (Genesis 2:24). Jesus went on to say, "What therefore God hath joined together, let not man put asunder" (Matthew 19:6 KJV). This quotation is part of the traditional wedding ceremony.

WHEN I WAS A CHILD, I SPOKE AS A CHILD A phrase from 1 Corinthians 13. Paul goes on to say that when he became a man, he put away childish things. In the same way, believers can only partially know God now, but eventually they will know him more fully. See also *through a glass, darkly*.

WHEREVER YOU GO, I WILL GO In the story of Ruth and Naomi, Naomi begins a journey back to her native Israel after living in the land of Moab. Her two widowed daughters-in-law start to accompany her, but Naomi urges them to return to their own people in Moab. Ruth responds, "Wherever you go, I will go ... Your people shall be my people, and your God, my God" (Ruth 1:16). This expression of commitment is sometimes quoted today in weddings.

WIDE IS THE GATE AND BROAD IS THE WAY THAT LEADS TO DESTRUCTION Jesus said this in the Sermon on the Mount (Matthew 7:13–14). He meant that it is easy to live a life that will result in destruction—eternal separation from God. In contrast, he said, "Strait [narrow] is the gate, and narrow is the way, which leadeth unto life, and few there be that find it" (KJV). Today this teaching is popularly alluded to by the expression, "staying on the straight and narrow."

WOLF IN SHEEP'S CLOTHING A saying taken from Jesus's warning about false prophets. He said, "Beware of false prophets, who come to you in sheep's clothing, but inwardly they are ravenous wolves" (Matthew 7:15). See also *By their fruits you will know them.* ✦ A wolf in sheep's clothing is anyone who appears harmless or innocent but has wicked or harmful motives.

YOU ARE THE CHRIST, THE SON OF THE LIVING GOD One day Jesus asked his disciples, "Who do people say I am?" They answered, "John the Baptist, Elijah, or Jeremiah." Jesus then asked, "Who do you say I am?" Peter answered, "You are the Christ, the Son of the living God" (Matthew 16:16). Jesus then warned them not to tell anyone that he was the Christ (the Messiah).

YOU ARE THE LIGHT OF THE WORLD A saying of Jesus in the Sermon on the Mount (Matthew 5:14). He used light as a metaphor for all that is good in the world. He was telling his followers that they were to bring goodness and the Good News of his salvation to people around them—indeed, to the whole world. See also *I am the light of the world.*

YOU SHALL HAVE NO OTHER GODS BEFORE ME This is the first of the Ten Commandments (Exodus 20:3). The people of Israel regularly broke this commandment by worshiping Baal, Ashtoreth, Molech, and other false gods of the neighboring nations.

YOU SHALL LOVE THE LORD YOUR GOD WITH ALL YOUR HEART, WITH ALL YOUR SOUL, AND WITH ALL YOUR MIND This was Jesus's response when someone asked him which of the commandments in the Mosaic law was the greatest. Jesus went on to say, "This is the first and great commandment. And the second is like it: You shall love your neighbor as yourself. On these two commandments hang all the Law and the Prophets" (Matthew 22:37–40). Jesus was not quoting directly from the Ten Commandments; rather, he was quoting from Deuteronomy 6:5 and Leviticus 19:18.

YOU SHALL NOT BEAR FALSE WITNESS AGAINST YOUR NEIGHBOR One of the Ten Commandments (Exodus 20:16). This commandment relates both to formal judicial proceedings (lying on the witness stand) and to everyday life (for example, lying to or about another person).

YOU SHALL NOT COMMIT ADULTERY One of the Ten Commandments (Exodus 20:14). Jesus expanded on the meaning of this commandment when he taught, as part of the Sermon on the Mount, "Anyone who even looks at a woman with lust has already committed adultery with her in his heart" (Matthew 5:28 NLT).

YOU SHALL NOT COVET The last of the Ten Commandments; it reads, "You shall not covet your neighbor's house; you shall not covet your neighbor's wife … nor anything that is your neighbor's" (Exodus 20:17). In the Roman Catholic and Lutheran traditions, this verse constitutes two separate commandments.

YOU SHALL NOT MAKE FOR YOURSELF A CARVED IMAGE The second of the Ten Commandments (Exodus 20:4). In the Roman Catholic and Lutheran traditions, the first two commandments (see also *You shall have no other gods before me*) are treated together as the first commandment. Whether it is one or two commandments, it is clear that the people of Israel were to have no carved images that they might be tempted to worship.

YOU SHALL NOT MURDER One of the Ten Commandments (Exodus 20:13). Jesus expanded on the meaning of this commandment when he taught, as part of the Sermon on the Mount, "Whoever is angry with his brother without a cause shall be in danger of the judgment" (Matthew 5:22).

YOU SHALL NOT STEAL One of the Ten Commandments (Exodus 20:15).

YOU SHALL NOT TAKE THE NAME OF THE LORD YOUR GOD IN VAIN One of the Ten Commandments (Exodus 20:7). This commandment relates both to taking an oath (for example, don't lie when you take an oath in court) and to cursing (don't do it).

YOUR WILL BE DONE Jesus used this expression in two different contexts. First, it is a phrase from the prayer he taught his disciples, traditionally known as the Lord's Prayer: "Your will be done on earth as it is in heaven" (Matthew 6:10). Second, at the end of his ministry, when he was praying in the garden of Gethsemane, Jesus was in deep anguish. He prayed, "Father, if you are willing, take this cup from me; yet not my will, but yours be done" (Luke 22:42 NIV). The "cup" is a metaphor for the terrible agony of his crucifixion that lay ahead, but in spite of it all, Jesus wanted to fulfill the will of God the Father.

YOUR WORD IS A LAMP TO MY FEET Psalm 119 is the longest chapter in the Bible. The entire psalm is about the wonderful attributes of the Word of God. Verse 105 reads, "Your word is a lamp to my feet and a light to my path."

"Your word is a lamp to my feet and a light to my path." (Psalm 119:105)

Quote, Unquote

A Quiz on Sayings from the Bible

Select one answer for each question.
Answers appear immediately after the quiz.

1 Who said, "Am I my brother's keeper?"

a. Jacob

b. James

c. Cain

d. Miriam

2 To whom did God say, "Be fruitful and multiply"?

a. Abraham

b. Noah

c. Jacob

d. Solomon

3 Jesus said, "Blessed are the meek ..."

a. "for they shall be called sons of God"

b. "for theirs is the kingdom of heaven"

c. "for they shall inherit the earth"

d. "for they shall be comforted"

4 When did Jesus say, "Do this in remembrance of me"?

a. While he was suffering on the cross

b. When he fed 5,000 people with a few loaves and fishes

c. Just before he ascended to heaven

d. At the Last Supper

5 Which one of the following statements is not one of the Ten Commandments?

a. "You shall love the LORD your God with all your heart, with all your soul, and with all your mind."

b. "Remember the Sabbath day, to keep it holy."

c. "You shall not commit adultery."

d. "Honor your father and your mother."

6 Who said, "Come to me, all you who are weary"?

a. Moses
b. Isaiah
c. Jesus
d. Mary Magdalene

7 Which of these quotations is found in the book of Psalms?

a. "Bless the LORD, O my soul"
b. "Make a joyful noise unto the LORD"
c. "The LORD is my shepherd"
d. All of the above

8 From what part of the Scripture was Jesus quoting when he said, "You have heard that it was said, 'Eye for eye, and tooth for a tooth'"?

a. Books of Moses
b. Books of History
c. Books of Poetry
d. Books of Prophecy

9 "Give us this day our daily bread" is a phrase from:

a. The Lord's Prayer
b. The Apostles' Creed
c. The Magnificat
d. The Beatitudes

10 The saying "salt of the earth" originated in a teaching from whom?

a. Paul
b. Peter
c. Solomon
d. None of the above

11 What is the first phrase of John 3:16?

a. "Blessed are the peacemakers"
b. "For God so loved the world"
c. "Our Father which art in heaven"
d. "You shall love your neighbor as yourself"

12 When Jesus said, "You cannot serve both God and money," he meant:

a. Only members of monastic orders can truly serve God.
b. A person cannot worship money and also pursue a right relationship with God.
c. Tax collectors could not hope to enter the kingdom of heaven.
d. None of the above

13 **To whom did Jesus say, "Get behind me, Satan!"?**

a. The demon-possessed Gadarene
b. Judas Iscariot
c. Peter
d. Pontius Pilate

14 **Who said, "If I perish, I perish!"?**

a. Cain
b. Jonathan
c. Esther
d. Jesus

15 **When Isaiah and Micah said, "They will beat their swords into plowshares," they meant:**

a. Their listeners needed farm implements more than they needed swords.
b. The Babylonians would come to Judah to help farm the land.
c. There will be no more war during the peaceful reign of the Messiah.
d. The people would use swords to dig up the ground.

16 **In which book of the Bible does the phrase "Let there be light" occur?**

a. Genesis
b. Psalms
c. Matthew
d. John

17 **What is the opening phrase of the Twenty-Third Psalm?**

a. "Make a joyful noise unto the LORD"
b. "Bless the LORD, O my soul"
c. "The LORD is my shepherd"
d. "Your word is a lamp to my feet"

18 **Which of these is incorrectly quoted from the Bible?**

a. "All have sinned, and fall short of the glory of God."
b. "Blessed are the meek, for they shall inherit the earth."
c. "Many are called, but few are chosen."
d. "Money is the root of all evil."

19 **Which of the following sayings is not found in the Bible?**

a. "There is nothing new under the sun."

b. "Vanity of vanities, all is vanity."

c. "Eat, drink, and be merry."

d. "We have left undone those things which we ought to have done."

20 **Who said, "A prophet is not without honor except in his own country"?**

a. Moses

b. Elijah

c. Daniel

d. Jesus

Answers

1. c
2. b
3. c
4. d
5. a
6. c
7. d
8. a
9. a
10. d
11. b
12. b
13. c
14. c
15. c
16. a
17. c
18. d
19. d
20. d

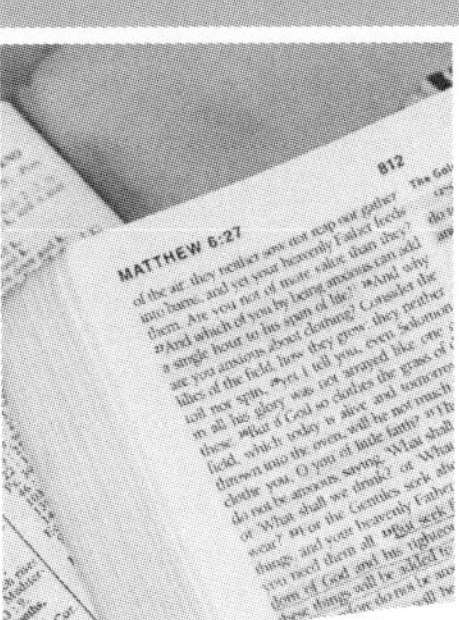

Appendix

Test Your Bible Knowledge

A Quiz on All Aspects of the Bible and the Church

Part 1

Select one answer for each question.
Answers appear immediately after this section.

1 Advent is:

a. A period of preparation before Christmas

b. A Christian celebration derived from the celebration of Passover

c. The angel Gabriel's announcement to the Virgin Mary that she would have a son

d. A period of preparation before Easter

2 A psalter is:

a. A musical instrument

b. A book of Psalms used for public or private worship

c. The podium where the minister stands

d. The round window above the door in a Gothic church

3 **What is a gentile?**

a. A Christian

b. A descendant of Jacob

c. A Jew

d. A person who is not a Jew

4 ***Grace* means:**

a. Everlasting life

b. Unmerited favor

c. Peace

d. Justice

5 **Palm Sunday:**

a. Commemorates Jesus's entry into Jerusalem

b. Is celebrated primarily in the tropics

c. Is the beginning of the church year

d. Celebrates the creation

6 ***Monotheism* means:**

a. Belief in one God

b. Belief in many gods

c. Belief that there is no God

d. Uncertainty about one's belief in God

7 **What is a covenant?**

a. A sacrifice

b. Another name for the Tabernacle

c. A residence for nuns

d. A solemn agreement between two parties

8 ***Anglican* refers to:**

a. Angels

b. The Eucharist

c. The Church of England

d. The African Methodist Episcopal Church

9 **What is an epistle?**

a. A theological discourse

b. The wife of an apostle

c. A letter

d. A Greek manuscript

10 A fitting description for the Jordan River is that it:

a. Flows into the Dead Sea

b. Was held back so the Israelites could cross over into Canaan on dry land

c. Is used as a metaphor for crossing over into heaven

d. All of the above

11 What land was described in the Old Testament as a land flowing with milk and honey?

a. Egypt

b. Canaan

c. Greece

d. Babylon

12 Where was this land located?

a. At the mouth of the Nile River

b. Between the Tigris and Euphrates Rivers

c. At the eastern end of the Mediterranean Sea

d. At the western end of the Mediterranean Sea

13 The land at the mouth of the Nile River is called:

a. Israel

b. Egypt

c. Babylon

d. Greece

14 Which empire controlled Israel at the time of Jesus?

a. Assyria

b. Babylonia

c. Greece

d. Rome

15 The gold-plated chest that was kept in the Holy of Holies was called:

a. The Holy Grail

b. The Sanhedrin

c. The ark of the covenant

d. The Torah

16 Who was one of the spies who said God would help the Israelites overcome the Canaanites?

a. Caleb

b. Jonathan

c. David

d. Balaam

17 **Which of the following is not another name for the Israelites?**

a. Canaanites
b. The Chosen People
c. Hebrews
d. Children of Israel

18 **Who was the first king of Israel?**

a. Herod
b. Moses
c. David
d. Saul

19 **What was the capital of Israel during King Solomon's reign?**

a. Jericho
b. Samaria
c. Bethlehem
d. Jerusalem

20 **The term *Northern Kingdom* refers to:**

a. The Roman Empire
b. The Kingdom of Israel
c. The Kingdom of Judah
d. Greece

21 **The Mount of Olives:**

a. Was the site of the Last Supper
b. Is where the Lord gave Moses the Ten Commandments
c. Is just east of Jerusalem
d. Is next to the Sea of Galilee

22 **Which event occurred first?**

a. The building of the Tower of Babel
b. The Flood
c. The Exodus
d. The Exile

23 **Which event occurred last?**

a. Samson's captivity by the Philistines
b. The exile of the people of Judah to Babylon
c. The coronation of David as king of Israel
d. The exile of the people of Israel to Assyria

24 **Who defeated the prophets of Baal on Mount Carmel?**

a. Elijah

b. Elisha

c. King Ahab

d. Nebuchadnezzar

25 **Which of the following was not an Old Testament prophet?**

a. Samuel

b. Solomon

c. Isaiah

d. Jonah

26 **Who tried to seduce Joseph?**

a. Potiphar's wife

b. Lot's wife

c. Jezebel

d. Bathsheba

27 **Who led the people in reconstructing the walls of Jerusalem after the Exile?**

a. Ezra

b. Nehemiah

c. Zechariah

d. Daniel

28 **Which of these bodies of water is essentially north of Jerusalem?**

a. Jordan River

b. Dead Sea

c. Sea of Galilee

d. Nile River

29 **Which one of the following was never part of the Israelite community living in exile?**

a. Ezra

b. Nehemiah

c. Esther

d. Job

30 **The Day of Atonement:**

a. Is also called Passover

b. Was the only day the high priest could enter the Holy of Holies

c. Is still celebrated by Jews as Hanukkah

d. Was the festival of the harvest

31 **Which of the following were tribes of Israel?**

a. Asher, Dan, Gad

b. Issachar, Moses, Naphtali

c. Abraham, Judah, Benjamin

d. All of the above

32 **The province of Galilee was located:**

a. North of Samaria and Judea

b. East of Judea

c. South of Samaria

d. West of Judea

33 **Which of these men did not become a follower of Jesus?**

a. Caiaphas

b. Nicodemus

c. Joseph of Arimathea

d. Peter

34 **Who first said, "All we like sheep have gone astray"?**

a. Jesus

b. Isaiah

c. George Frideric Handel

d. John the Baptist

35 **Who were the Pharisees?**

a. A religious party within Judaism

b. The nations driven out of Canaan by Joshua

c. The followers of Jesus

d. The descendants of Pharaoh

36 **When did Jesus say, "Father, forgive them; for they know not what they do"?**

a. When he threw the money changers out of the temple

b. In the garden of Gethsemane

c. In the Sermon on the Mount

d. While he was suffering on the cross

37 **According to orthodox Christian theology, God the Son:**

a. Has always existed with God the Father

b. Was created at the time Mary conceived the Christ child

c. Appeared to be human, but was not fully human

d. None of the above

38 **Who denied three times that he knew Jesus?**

a. Matthew

b. Judas Iscariot

c. John

d. Peter

39 **Who traveled with Paul on one of his missionary journeys?**

a. Barnabas

b. Dorcas

c. Peter

d. Andrew

40 **Who wrote the book of Philemon?**

a. Philemon

b. Onesimus

c. Paul

d. Peter

41 **Which of the following constitutes one of the three major branches of Christianity?**

a. Roman Catholic Church

b. Protestantism

c. Eastern Orthodox Church

d. All of the above

42 **What prisoner did Pontius Pilate release?**

a. Barnabas

b. Barabbas

c. Peter

d. Silas

43 **Which book contains stories of David?**

a. 2 Samuel

b. Judges

c. 2 Kings

d. 2 Chronicles

44 **Who wrote many of the Psalms?**

a. Isaiah

b. Paul

c. David

d. Moses

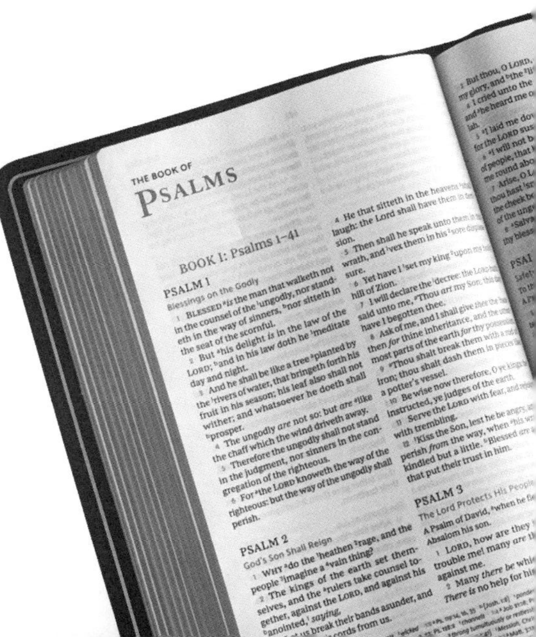

45 **Which one of the following was not a Bible translator?**

a. William Tyndale

b. Martin Luther

c. Johannes Gutenberg

d. Jerome

46 **Which translation of the Bible was first published in 1611?**

a. New International Version

b. Septuagint

c. Vulgate

d. King James Version

47 **Which of the following was an evangelist?**

a. Roger Williams

b. Karl Barth

c. William Wilberforce

d. Dwight L. Moody

48 **Which one of these was an influential black church leader?**

a. Martin Luther

b. Richard Allen

c. Jackie Robinson

d. Harriet Beecher Stowe

49 **What is the official approval by the Roman Catholic Church that a book may be printed?**

a. Gloria Patri

b. Anno Domini

c. *Imprimatur*

d. *Koiné*

50 **According to Roman Catholic tradition, who was the first pope?**

a. Jesus

b. Peter

c. John

d. Athanasius

51 **Where is the Vatican?**

a. Paris

b. Constantinople

c. Athens

d. Rome

52 **Which pope convened Vatican II?**

a. Pius XII

b. John XXIII

c. Paul VI

d. John Paul II

53 The Book of Common Prayer contains:

a. Prayers of confession

b. The liturgy of the Anglican Church

c. The traditional marriage ceremony

d. All of the above

54 Jesuits, Dominicans, and Franciscans are all:

a. Nuns

b. Members of religious orders

c. Teachers

d. Monks

55 Who wrote *Mere Christianity*?

a. John Bunyan

b. John Calvin

c. C. S. Lewis

d. Martin Luther King Jr.

56 Which of the following was a missionary in Africa?

a. Mother Teresa

b. John Wesley

c. Justin Martyr

d. David Livingstone

57 Papal infallibility means:

a. The pope is without original sin

b. The pope cannot be married

c. The pope must live a sinless life

d. The pope is without error when he speaks *ex cathedra*

58 On what mountain did Noah's ark come to rest after the Flood?

a. Mount Sinai

b. Mount Ararat

c. Mount of Olives

d. Mount Zion

59 What is the Gloria Patri?

a. A cathedral in Rome

b. The song of the angels who announced Jesus's birth to the shepherds

c. The Latin name of a hymn still frequently sung in churches today

d. The Latin translation of the Bible

60 What is a state church?

a. The principal church in the capital city

b. A cathedral

c. A church established by civil authorities

d. A small denomination located in only one state

61 What term has been defined as an outward and visible sign of an inward and spiritual grace?

a. Sacrament

b. Baptism

c. Confirmation

d. Last rites

62 Which of the following is primarily a Black denomination?

a. Assemblies of God

b. National Baptist Convention

c. Southern Baptist Convention

d. Presbyterian Church (USA)

63 Which of these is not a book in the Bible?

a. Isaiah

b. Hezekiah

c. Jude

d. Zephaniah

64 Who was Abraham's eldest son?

a. Isaac

b. Jacob

c. Ishmael

d. Cain

65 The Assemblies of God is a denomination in which tradition?

a. Baptist

b. Pentecostal

c. Episcopal

d. Presbyterian

66 Which term represents a public affirmation that an individual is a part of Christ's church?

a. Eucharist

b. Matrimony

c. Holy orders

d. Baptism

67 What is another name for the Eucharist?

a. Transubstantiation

b. The Lord's Supper

c. The Last Supper

d. All of the above

68 All Saints' Day is celebrated on:

a. January 6

b. Easter

c. October 31

d. November 1

69 As a religious group, the Amish are related to:

a. Southern Baptists

b. Mormons

c. Presbyterians

d. Mennonites

70 When does the church year begin?

a. The first Sunday of Advent

b. New Year's Day

c. Ash Wednesday

d. Easter

71 Members of the Church of Jesus Christ of Latter-day Saints are called:

a. Episcopalians

b. Pentecostals

c. Mormons

d. Seventh-day Adventists

72 Which of these churches does not have bishops?

a. Methodist

b. Episcopal

c. Congregational

d. Roman Catholic

73 When would you most likely hear the expression, "Dearly beloved, we are gathered together"?

a. At a christening

b. At a confirmation

c. At a wedding

d. At a funeral

74 **Which of the following is most likely to come at the end of a worship service?**

a. Benediction
b. Invocation
c. Collect
d. Confession

75 **The Mosaic law is found in which part of the Bible?**

a. The Pentateuch
b. The Gospels
c. The Psalms
d. The Epistles

Answers

Part 1

1. a	16. a	31. a	46. d	61. a
2. b	17. a	32. a	47. d	62. b
3. d	18. d	33. a	48. b	63. b
4. b	19. d	34. b	49. c	64. c
5. a	20. b	35. a	50. b	65. b
6. a	21. c	36. d	51. d	66. d
7. d	22. b	37. a	52. b	67. b
8. c	23. b	38. d	53. d	68. d
9. c	24. a	39. a	54. b	69. d
10. d	25. b	40. c	55. c	70. a
11. b	26. a	41. d	56. d	71. c
12. c	27. b	42. b	57. d	72. c
13. b	28. c	43. a	58. b	73. c
14. d	29. d	44. c	59. c	74. a
15. c	30. b	45. c	60. c	75. a

Part 2

Answers appear immediately after this section.

1 Match each of the following books of the Bible to its content:

____ Genesis
____ Exodus
____ Leviticus
____ Numbers
____ Deuteronomy
____ Joshua
____ Judges
____ Ruth
____ 1 Samuel
____ 2 Samuel
____ 1 Kings
____ 2 Kings

a. Moses's speech to the people of Israel before they entered the Promised Land
b. The story of Naomi and her daughter-in-law
c. Histories of the patriarchs of Israel
d. History of King Saul's reign
e. History of King Solomon's reign and the early years of the Divided Kingdom
f. Details of the Mosaic law
g. The years of wandering in the wilderness
h. Stories of Deborah, Gideon, and Samson
i. History of King David's reign
j. The latter years of the Divided Kingdom
k. Moses leads the Israelites out of Egypt
l. The Israelites' conquest of the Promised Land

2 Which book of the Bible records the history of the first years of the early church?

3 Who said, "Let there be light"?

4 **Identify each of these books as being from the Old Testament (OT) or the New Testament (NT):**

____ a. Revelation

____ b. Deuteronomy

____ c. Malachi

____ d. Hebrews

5 **List the five Books of Moses:**

6 **In what language was the New Testament first written?**

7 **List the four Gospels in the order in which they are traditionally found in the New Testament:**

8 **Who wrote, "Children, obey your parents"?**

9 **List three of the Ten Commandments:**

10 **Which two books of the Bible begin with the phrase, "In the beginning"?**

11 **List four of the nine fruits of the Spirit, as they are listed in Galatians 5:**

12 **About whom did John the Baptist say, "Behold! The Lamb of God ..."?**

13 **What is the first phrase of John 3:16?**

14 **Which psalm begins with the phrase, "The LORD is my shepherd"?**

15 **According to the apostle Paul, what is the root of all evil?**

16 **How does the Lord's Prayer begin?**

17 **Name three of the twelve tribes of Israel:**

18 **What annual celebration was established to commemorate the Exodus of Israel from Egypt?**

19 **What city was the capital of the Kingdom of Israel during most of King David's reign?**

20 **After the death of Solomon, the Kingdom of Israel divided into two kingdoms. What were they called?**

21 **What is the name of the region between Judea and Galilee?**

22 **Who was Abraham's wife?**

23 **Who was Aaron's younger brother?**

24 **Who was the third king of Israel?**

25 **Which of Solomon's sons succeeded him as king?**

26 **What were the names of Daniel's friends who were thrown into the fiery furnace?**

27 **List six of Jesus's twelve disciples:**

28 **Indicate the sequence (1, 2, 3, 4) in which these events took place:**

____ a. The Exile

____ b. The period of the judges

____ c. The Divided Kingdom

____ d. The Exodus

29 **List the correct order (1, 2, 3, 4) in which these people lived:**

____ a. Joash

____ b. Rehoboam

____ c. Ezra

____ d. Aaron

30 **In what village was Jesus born?**

31 **Who was converted on the Damascus Road?**

32 **This person was later known by another name. What was it?**

33 **Match each of the following books of the Bible to its content:**

____ 1 Chronicles

____ 2 Chronicles

____ Ezra

____ Nehemiah

____ Esther

____ Job

____ Matthew

____ Mark

____ Acts

____ Romans

a. The story of Jesus as told by an eyewitness who was not one of the disciples

b. The story of a queen who risked her life to save her people

c. History of the reign of King David

d. An epistle from the apostle Paul

e. The first return of the Jews after the Exile

f. History of Judah from the reign of Solomon to the Exile

g. History of the first years of the early church

h. The rebuilding of the walls of Jerusalem

i. The story of Jesus written especially for a Jewish audience

j. The tribulations of a just man

34 **What primary issue was resolved at the Council at Jerusalem in about AD 50?**

35 **Who wrote 1 Corinthians and 2 Corinthians?**

36 **In what language was most of the Old Testament first written?**

37 **Match each of the following books of the Bible to its content:**

____ Psalms	a. Shows the futility of life apart from God
____ Proverbs	b. A collection of Hebrew poems and songs
____ Ecclesiastes	c. The story of Jesus as told by a Gentile physician
____ Song of Solomon	d. The story of Jesus as told by one of Jesus's disciples
____ Isaiah	e. Prophecies to the Kingdom of Judah
____ Daniel	f. An epistle from the apostle Paul
____ Luke	g. A collection of pithy sayings
____ John	h. A celebration of romantic love
____ 1 Corinthians	i. A vision about future events, including the New Jerusalem
____ Revelation	j. Stories from the Exile in Babylon

38 **Indicate the sequence (1, 2, 3, 4) in which these events took place:**

____ a. The Virgin Birth

____ b. Pentecost

____ c. Missionary journeys of Paul

____ d. The handwriting on the wall

39 **On what special day was a scapegoat taken out into the wilderness each year?**

40 **Who was the first Christian martyr?**

41 **Who led the first group of Jews that returned to Jerusalem after the Exile in Babylon?**

42 **Why did Joseph and Mary take the infant Jesus to Egypt?**

43 **What was the relationship between the Herod who killed the infants in Bethlehem and the Herod who killed John the Baptist?**

44 **Complete this saying of Jesus: "Follow me, and I will make you ...":**

45 **What Roman centurion was converted after he was told in a vision to send for Peter?**

46 **Who was the "father of the Protestant Reformation"?**

47 **What mission organization was founded by J. Hudson Taylor in 1865 for the evangelization of China?**

48 **What is the name for the first day of Lent?**

49 **On what Sunday do Christians celebrate the resurrection of Jesus?**

50 **Two of the following are included in the seven deadly sins. Which ones are they?**

a. Adultery
b. Divorce
c. Gluttony
d. Covetousness

51 **What is the term for a religious awakening that sweeps through a congregation or even an entire nation?**

52 **According to the Westminster Shorter Catechism, what is the chief end of man?**

53 **List the correct sequence (1, 2, 3, 4) in which these events took place:**

____ a. Vatican II

____ b. Luther's posting of the Ninety-Five Theses

____ c. Council of Chalcedon

____ d. Council of Trent

54 **Who are the three Persons of the Trinity?**

55 **What term means that God is present everywhere?**

Answers

Part 2

1. Genesis, c; Exodus, k; Leviticus, f; Numbers, g; Deuteronomy, a; Joshua, l; Judges, h; Ruth, b; 1 Samuel, d; 2 Samuel, i; 1 Kings, e; 2 Kings, j
2. Acts
3. God (Genesis 1:3)
4. a, NT (Revelation); b, OT (Deuteronomy); c, OT (Malachi); d, NT (Hebrews)
5. Genesis, Exodus, Leviticus, Numbers, Deuteronomy
6. Greek
7. Matthew, Mark, Luke, John
8. Paul (Ephesians 6:1; Colossians 3:20)
9. Any three of the following (this wording is from the NIV):
    1. You shall have no other gods before me.
    2. You shall not make for yourself an image in the form of anything in heaven above or on the earth beneath or in the waters below.
    3. You shall not misuse the name of the LORD your God, for the LORD will not hold anyone guiltless who misuses his name.
    4. Remember the Sabbath day by keeping it holy.
    5. Honor your father and your mother, so that you may live long in the land the LORD your God is giving you.
    6. You shall not murder.
    7. You shall not commit adultery.
    8. You shall not steal.
    9. You shall not give false testimony against your neighbor.
    10. You shall not covet your neighbor's house. You shall not covet your neighbor's wife, or his male or female servant, his ox or donkey, or anything that belongs to your neighbor.
10. Genesis and the Gospel of John
11. Any four of the following (Galatians 5:22–23 KJV; terms from the NIV, if different, are in parentheses):
    - love, joy, peace, longsuffering (forbearance), gentleness (kindness), goodness, faith (faithfulness), meekness (gentleness), temperance (self-control)
12. Jesus
13. "For God so loved the world ..."
14. Psalm 23
15. The love of money (not simply money)
16. Any variations of the following: "Our Father in heaven ..."; "Our Father which art in heaven ..."
17. Any three of the following:
    - Asher, Benjamin, Dan, Ephraim (half-tribe), Gad, Issachar, Judah, Levi, Manasseh (half-tribe), Naphtali, Reuben, Simeon, Zebulun
18. Passover
19. Jerusalem
20. Israel (or Northern Kingdom) and Judah (or Southern Kingdom)
21. Samaria
22. Sarah (or Sarai)
23. Moses
24. Solomon
25. Rehoboam
26. Shadrach (or Hananiah), Meshach (or Mishael), and Abednego (or Azariah)
27. Any six of the following:
    - Andrew, Bartholomew (also called Nathanael), James (son of Alphaeus), James (son of Zebedee), John, Judas Iscariot, Matthew, Peter (also called Simon Peter), Philip, Simon the Zealot, Thaddaeus (also called Judas, son of James), Thomas

28. a. 4 (the Exile); b. 2 (the period of the judges); c. 3 (the Divided Kingdom); d. 1 (the Exodus)

29. a. 3 (Joash); b. 2 (Rehoboam); c. 4 (Ezra); d. 1 (Aaron)

30. Bethlehem

31. Saul of Tarsus (or Paul)

32. Paul

33. 1 Chronicles, c; 2 Chronicles, f; Ezra, e; Nehemiah, h; Esther, b; Job, j; Matthew, i; Mark, a; Acts, g; Romans, d

34. Whether Gentile believers had to be circumcised and obey every law of Moses that the Jewish people did. (Acts 15)

35. Paul

36. Hebrew

37. Psalms, b; Proverbs, g; Ecclesiastes, a; Song of Solomon, h; Isaiah, e; Daniel, j; Luke, c; John, d; 1 Corinthians, f; Revelation, i

38. a. 2 (the Virgin Birth); b. 3 (Pentecost); c. 4 (missionary journeys of Paul); d. 1 (handwriting on the wall)

39. Day of Atonement (or Yom Kippur)

40. Stephen

41. Zerubbabel

42. To escape Herod the Great's massacre of the infants in Bethlehem

43. Herod the Great killed the infants in Bethlehem; his son Herod Antipas killed John the Baptist.

44. fishers of men

45. Cornelius

46. Martin Luther

47. China Inland Mission (now known as Overseas Missionary Fellowship, or OMF International)

48. Ash Wednesday

49. Easter

50. c. gluttony; d. covetousness

51. Revival

52. "The chief end of man is to glorify God and enjoy him forever."

53. a. 4 (Vatican II); b. 2 (Ninety-Five Theses); c. 1 (Council of Chalcedon); d. 3 (Council of Trent)

54. God the Father, God the Son, and God the Holy Spirit (or Holy Ghost)

55. Omnipresence of God

Index

B

C

D

E

H

I

O

P

T

Image Credits

Unless otherwise indicated, cover and interior images are used under license from Shutterstock.com.

Maps copyright © Michael Schmeling, Arid Ocean Maps, aridocean.com.

Images used under license from Unsplash: pp. 8, 353 (open Bible, Sincerely Media); 288 (emmanuelphaeton); 359 (timwildsmith).

Images used from Wikimedia Commons (freely licensed): pp. 9, 22 (Papyrus 46); 62 (© Chris Yunker); 47, 68 (photo by Daderot of *Esther and Ahasuerus*); 74 (Chadner); 47, 100 (*Pharaoh's Daughter Finding Baby Moses*); 114; 47, 119 (model of Solomon's temple, photo by SalemOptix); 126 (Karmakolle); 142, 377 (*Christ on the Cross*); 152; 153, 353 (mosaic of Jesus, photo © Edal Anton Lefterov); 159 (© Avram Graicer); 167 (© Chris 73); 168 (photo © Jastrow); 169; 170 (BRBurton); 179 (© Alexey Goral); 3, 190 (photo of Jesus icon © JoeyEspo984); 196 (Daniel A. Payne); 198 (© Tamar Hayardeni [Tamarah]); 200 (The National Library of Wales); 201 (© Peter Nguyen); 203 (The National Library of Wales); 206 (photo © Anthony M.); 212 (Maull & Fox); 215 (The National Library of Wales); 219 (Warren K. Leffler); 220 (MC BSU); 223; 195, 225 (photo of Martin Luther King Jr. by Hugo van Gelderen/Anefo, Dutch National Archives); 226 (Wellcome Images); 230; 232 (Joconde); 195, 233 (Saint Patrick, Internet Archive); 234 (Quodvultdeus, retouched photo of mosaic); 235; 3, 236 (Martin Luther); 238 (Smithsonian Institution); 239 (Library of Congress); 195, 241 (page from *Summa Theologica*); 195, 242 (photo of Mother Teresa, © Manfredo Ferrari); 243 (from *Foxe's Book of Martyrs*); 245 (Wellcome Images); 246 (Yale Center for British Art); 247; 257 (US Navy, Brian May); 260 (© Auckland Museum Collections); 266 (© Giladtop); 285; 291 (Internet Archive); 309.

Images used from Artvee (public domain): pp. 61; 112; 229.

Images used from the Brooklyn Museum (paintings purchased by public subscription): pp. 96; 133, 134 (The Calling of John and Andrew); 150; 164; 181; 183; 186.

Image on p. 118 copyright © Rkckwwjd, Dreamstime.com.

Image on p. 184 used from GetArchive (Felix Bonfils, Hallwylska Museet; public domain).

Image on p. 275 used from flickr (photo by wl.glazewski of painting by Vasnetsov Viktor; public domain).

Image on p. 362 copyright © 1989 by Joseph Miralles.